LAW AND THE POLITICS OF RECONCILIATION

Law and the Politics of Reconciliation

Edited by
SCOTT VEITCH
University of Glasgow, UK

ASHGATE

Published by
Ashgate Publishing Limited
Gower House
Croft Road
Aldershot
Hampshire GU11 3HR
England

Ashgate Publishing Company
Suite 420
101 Cherry Street
Burlington, VT 05401-4405
USA

Ashgate website: http://www.ashgate.com

British Library Cataloguing in Publication Data

Law and the politics of reconciliation. - (The Edinburgh
    Centre for Law and Society)
    1. Reconciliation (Law) 2. Reconciliation - Political
    aspects 3. Law - Political aspects
    I. Veitch, Scott II. University of Edinburgh. Centre for
    Law and Society
    340.1'15

Library of Congress Cataloging-in-Publication Data
Law and the Politics of Reconciliation / edited by Scott Veitch.
        p. cm. -- (Edinburgh Centre for Law and Society series)
    Includes index.
    ISBN-13: 978-0-7546-4924-3
    ISBN-10: 0-7546-4924-5
    1. Reconciliation (Law) -- Political aspects. I. Veitch, Scott.

    K487.P65L393 2006
    340'.11--dc22

2006021147

ISBN-13: 978-0-7546-4924-3
ISBN-10: 0-7546-4924-5

Printed and bound in Great Britain by MPG Books Ltd, Bodmin, Cornwall.

Contents

List of Contributors

Fernando Atria – Professor of Law, University Adolfo Ibanez, Santiago, Chile

Zenon Bankowski – Professor of Legal Theory, University of Edinburgh

Brenna Bhandar – Lecturer in Law, University of Reading

Emilios Christodoulidis – Professor of Law, University of Glasgow

Carrol Clarkson – Senior Lecturer in English, University of Cape Town

Adam Czarnota – Associate Professor of Law, University of New South Wales, Sydney, Australia

H. Louise du Toit – Lecturer in Philosophy, University of Johannesburg

Lorna McGregor – Lawyer and researcher, Human Rights Institute, International Bar Association, London

Claire Moon – Lecturer in Sociology, London School of Economics and Political Science

Stewart Motha – Lecturer in Law, University of Kent

Andrew Schaap – Research Fellow in Politics, University of Melbourne

Karin van Marle – Professor of Law, University of Pretoria

Scott Veitch – Reader in Law, University of Glasgow

Peer Zumbansen – Canada Research Professor, Osgoode Hall Law School, Toronto

Introduction

Emilios Christodoulidis and Scott Veitch

The title reference to a 'politics' of reconciliation is an invitation to put to question what increasingly – more and more alarmingly too – is taken for granted in uncritical calls for reconciliation. In this fin de siècle 'fever of atonement', as one Nigerian scholar put it (Soyinka, 1999, p. 90), reconciliation has too often come to signify in the political discourse of our time the call not just to put the traumas of the past behind us but also, in a sense, to put behind us the very politics of the past. Against this, our main concern has been to emphasise that 'reparation of historical injustices' requires that we face up to these injustices. That is what it means to do justice to them and reconciliation can only, properly, be the contingent response, not the unconditional outcome, of how societies face up to precisely that task.

It is for that reason that we return, and must return again, to the *politics* of reconciliation. The term introduces a reflexivity and implants a doubt. And this double introjection aspires to balance out what must be seen as the risk of reconciliation: that it over-determines outcomes. One *must* reconcile, one is told, because reconciliation is an ethical demand *tout court*. In this mode 'reconciliation' marks the end of politics in the double meaning of telos and closure, the final chapter in the dialectic of a history of conflict. But none of this must be taken for granted. The politics of reconciliation alerts us to the fact that 'coming to terms with the past' invites a wealth of responses, where surrender, the burying of anger and the abandonment of hope for equal participation in the new society, or the submission to the exigencies of capital, are not, yet again, the conditions for any possible 'common' future.

It is these questions and these doubts that are at the root of the contributions here and the thoughts that informed the undertaking. The contributions to this volume are in fact reflections on these concerns, developed over a period of time during which we ran workshops and seminars on the theme of 'reconciliation'. We took it as the organising concept that serves to collect the understandings and self-understandings of people called to reconcile, apologise, face up to memories and obligations, compensate for injustices, recall collective memories and formative myths. The material is vast, and although the focus on *politics* serves to sharpen the attentiveness to what is taken for granted, and *law* served to focus on what is being achieved (and what not) institutionally, it also became necessary to organise thematic groupings that would allow us to cut routes through the complexity of the debates. For the purpose of giving some internal coherence to the debates, there are three themes that may be singled out as being reflected and pursued in depth and in different ways in the following essays: politics, theology, and temporality. We shall say something briefly about each in turn, beginning with the last.

Reconciliation is all about time, and yet the varied and important ways in which temporality underpins it too often go un-theorised. Reconciliation calls forth both a future that is uncontroversially common, but significantly also a certain past. This 'past' is one of conflict but, crucially, one where the conflict is seen as resolvable. If conflict requires the staking out of common boundaries, reconciliation calls forth a past where these 'common' boundaries are always-already. They may appear in many forms depending on how easy it is to overcome the differences of the past. They are collectable memories that will form the inventory of collective memory; they may appear as a 'communicative history'; as a latent historical consciousness; as a (common) past of differences. For legal purposes they can even be conceived as a 'common fund' of normative understandings , or proto-understandings, that inform the normative discussions of the present. In all these formulations reconciliation 'overdetermines' the past. It projects into it the origin of a common future. But this is a future that will only be had if, and this is the *if* that reconciliation misses, the past lends itself to the overcoming of the conflict that divided it.

This is not to pre-empt the possibility of reconciliation and it is certainly not the only question that can be asked in this context. It is merely to flag up the importance of addressing directly questions of temporality, teleology and 'protology', that is, questions of ultimate ends and origins, modes in which we selectively organise access to the past and envisage the future. And within this framework, of course, questions of a more concrete nature can be asked: how do we understand the ways in which time is deployed in law? How do we make sense of the terms in which the law operates temporal modalities and organises our modes of dealing with the past (through amnesties, indemnities, cut-off dates, statutes of limitations etc)? Is time shared across social institutions? What of historical injustices that remain present and dominate historical consciousness, like Joyce's hero Dedalus's 'nightmare from which we are trying to awake' as Ignatieff recalls it so eloquently in *A Warrior's Honour* (Ignatieff, 1998, pp. 164–168)?

A second organising theme is theological and a number of the chapters engage directly with this. It is significant in two respects; first, the concept of reconciliation has its deepest roots in the work and inspiration of theologians. This religious lineage has been a crucial component in establishing the terms of engagement in situations where some form of social reconciliation is called for. That this has been taken up and carried forward in a practical way has no better exemplar than in the person of Archbishop Desmond Tutu. In the context of helping establish and then chairing the Truth and Reconciliation Commission in South Africa, Tutu's energy marks the coming together of religious and secular motivations, the outcomes of which have in turn been enormously influential in the course of their transplantation beyond South Africa's borders. Given this, and this is the second aspect to the importance of addressing the theological dimension, it is surprising that this lineage has often been downplayed when it comes to an assessment of its bearing on institutional – and for present purposes, especially legal – involvement in reconciliatory politics.

A number of questions suggest themselves: to what extent, and in what ways, can institutions – and again specifically legal institutions – actually carry out the work that reconciliation as an ideal requires? To what extent, conversely, do legal institutions *undermine* that possibility, working, as they do, according to the logic of rights and obligations that may seem alien terrain to the more spiritual – in its broadest sense – aspirations of a reconciliatory discourse? There are no straightforward answers to these questions. In fact, the chapters in this book which engage with them, and others like them, seem to suggest a range of often divergent answers, answers that depend in large degree on a number of variables: conceptual, historical, and political.

But there is another sense, perhaps more in the background (more spectral, one is tempted to say), in which the theological aspect of reconciliation is significant. In this view – admittedly a more distant, and as yet probably still obscured one – it is feasible to suggest that the rise to prominence of reconciliation in political and legal discourse serves, firstly, as a reminder that our key social institutions are *themselves* deeply rooted in religious lineages; and secondly, as Durkheim and others have argued, that despite a decline in organised religious belief these same institutions retain, in their (and our) inspirations and deepest needs, responses that are in many ways functional equivalents to those once provided by theology. Thus after years of neglect, certainly in legal studies, the *sociological* role of these religious lineages, both at the level of grand constitutional design as well as in the mundane day-to-day workings of the law, need to be revisited as a matter of contemporary urgency. Because it is precisely here, to the extent that theological discourses have *in fact* returned to public and political consciousness in the West, that it ought necessarily to return us to our *critical* engagements with theology; that is, to the *politics* of theology, and to the theologies of the political that may underlie or inform what is ordinarily taken as merely mundane and regulatory. It is perhaps then the current and notable rise of reconciliation in political discourse which best signals the persistence of these – always more or less hidden – foundations from which our institutional and secular imaginations and practices have not, for good or ill, entirely moved away.

For the third theme let us return to where we began, with the direct engagement with the *politics* of reconciliation. This politics has two central aspects. First, it constitutes an acknowledgement that reconciliation has now become a component part of our political vocabulary in a way that simply was not the case even twenty years ago. Having its origin in transitional scenarios where attempts had to be made to come to terms with nations' traumatic pasts, and having then been conceptualised and implemented through a wide range of *institutional* forms, the language of reconciliation has now become a persistent and pervasive feature of contemporary politics. It has become, one might say, a regulative ideal in political discourse.

Any number of examples might be cited in this regard, but one contemporary one will suffice. After the capture of Saddam Hussein in December 2003, the British Prime Minister Tony Blair had this to say: 'The shadow of Saddam has finally lifted from the Iraqi people. We give thanks for that, but let this be more than a case simply for rejoicing. Let it be a moment to reach out and reconcile. … Where his rule meant terror and division and brutality, let his capture bring about reconciliation and peace between all the people in Iraq.'[1] Statements like this encapsulate the desire to promote reconciliatory politics at the centre of public policy agendas, and suggest their relevance not only in domestic affairs, but in the international arena as well. (In passing we might only comment – much more might justly be said on this – that any sense we might have of the premature nature of Blair's statement and its misguided optimism in light of prior warnings and the subsequent bloody turn of events, is itself underpinned by the fact that his view clearly displayed a superficial understanding of the social and political conditions in which reconciliation may be, or become, appropriate.)

And this links to the second aspect that we discussed earlier: there tends to be – even in the case of Iraq – a taken for granted assumption that the political goal of reconciliation is highly desirable. Why not, we might plausible ask. Why would it be rejected as a desirable outcome in situations of conflict? Yet reconciliation's coming to prominence entails that, as with all other core political ideals – rights, justice, the rule of law, and so on – it is necessarily a subject for political *contestation*, as a matter both of theoretical reflection and practical engagement. But it is this second aspect that has arguably been underdeveloped, and the essays here, in their critical investigations, seek explicitly to redress this. Thus they analyse and frequently challenge the political (and other) assumptions underlying discourses of reconciliation, and by drawing on a broad spectrum of disciplinary and interdisciplinary insights deepen our understanding of what is at stake *politically* in pursuing processes of reconciliation.

As reconciliation is called upon as a guiding light in times of social upheaval, these political aspects in turn directly engage concerns with law and legal concepts in the most profound ways. On the one hand, the use of legislation to establish and guide processes of reconciliation has now become familiar, and so questions about exactly which legal concepts – rights, amnesties, criminal laws, sanctions etc – are deemed to be appropriate play a prominent role in discussions directly tailored to the pursuit of reconciliatory ends. In this respect, one of the key issues concerns assessing the ability of law and legal mechanisms to perform a truly transformative social function. On the other hand, however, such issues quickly shade into more profound questions concerning basic assumptions about social and political relations, and the ways in which legal concepts, for their part, may reflect or distort them. In fact, we might go so far as to say that questions raised about the politics of reconciliation closely parallel – in fact themselves engage with – questions of social and political *constitution* at its most elementary levels. And where they do so they thereby require, in turn, attention to be paid to understandings of constitutional *law*. For it is here that legal concepts play a fundamental role in mediating or giving foundation to social relations, and it is in the arena of constitutional law where this role is at its most vivid. What is included in and what excluded from, 'normal' political contestation is commonly referred back to constitutional law, and since it is largely in this register

---

1   Downing Street Statement, 14 December 2003 reported at http://www.guardian.co.uk/ Iraq/Story/0,2763,1106963,00.html. (Accessed 7/4/06).

that reconciliatory politics might be thought to operate, it is vital to give exposure to the often hidden assumptions that might foreshorten or skew the terms of political debate carried out in the name of reconciliation.

The following chapters do not readily fall into clear cut categories, but rather lay emphasis on different aspects of the themes identified. Accordingly, we have not divided them into discrete sections. But it is worth saying something by way of introduction that explains the order in which they are presented.

Andrew Schaap's chapter locates the politics of reconciliation within the context of questions about the very constitution of community. It begins with the claim that reconciliation in communities torn apart by violence is best understood, politically, as revolution rather than renewal. Drawing on the work of Hannah Arendt, it explores the role of law in founding and mediating community conflict and consensus, and assesses how different aspects of temporality contribute to the varied potentialities of ethical, legal and political community.

The chapters by Fernando Atria and Zenon Bankowski urge us to deepen our understanding of some of the theological bases of reconciliation, and in so doing open out questions about the plurality of meanings of reconciliation, and the intellectual and social spaces within which it be appropriate or not. Atria, starting from the religious concept, argues for a specifically political notion of reconciliation, one that turns out to be unrelated to notions like punishment and forgiveness. In ways related to Schaap's analysis, reconciliation for Atria is conceived as a process that leads to the reconstitution of the *polis*, in that by reconciling ourselves we realise that it is only because of the artificiality of the political that we can lead human lives. The problematic nature of the status of victim and perpetrator – also taken up by Bankowski – is considered in light of the case of those with whom no reconciliation is deemed possible. Both chapters make insightful use of the work of Simone Weil and Rene Girard in developing an understanding of the relation of religious aspects to social reconciliation and politics.

The following three chapters focus more explicitly on a critique of the role of law in processes of reconciliation. The chapters by Stewart Motha and Brenna Bhandar explore a shared theme through an analysis of approaches to reconciliation in different jurisdictions. Situated at the supposedly transitional point between a colonial past and a post-colonial democratic present and future, their analyses show how reconciliatory goals, as instituted in Australia and Canada respectively, also operate in fact to hinder any genuine transformation to a post-colonial polity. In particular through legal interpretations of sovereignty and the jurisdictional limits of the courts, along with the construction of the 'proper subject' of aboriginality, they argue that contemporary legal mechanisms legitimate an ongoing dispossession and subjugation which is ironically carried out in the name of a reconciliatory politics. Here, the putative unity offered by discourses of reconciliation as a regulatory ideal – both in politics and law – operates in fact to undermine a move beyond colonialism, and provides evidence for the claim, as Motha puts it at its most forceful, that reconciliation is best understood as another form of *domination*.

McGregor's chapter offers a challenging interpretation of the relationship between reconciliation discourses and legal institutions, arguing that there is a pronounced tendency in transitional periods for law to be subordinated to reconciliatory goals. This results in the exclusion of law and legal institutions from the kind of critique – internal and external – that would be necessary to expose and challenge its complicit role in the injustices of the past, thus perpetuating their continuation into the future. Using examples from Northern Ireland and Sri Lanka, McGregor analyses the limitations to the scrutiny of legal institutions – especially of courts, as well as prosecution and police services – despite, and sometimes because of, the supposedly extant democratic processes available. Moreover, even specialist enquires and tribunals may operate as much to augment rather than lessen this problematic. Drawing on alternative lineages of critical legal thought she concludes that there are modes of thinking about and through law which harbour the potential to move beyond a simplistic 'functionalisation' or subordination of law, in order to renew its potential for emancipatory social practice.

The chapters by Peer Zumbansen and Adam Czarnota then broaden the framework of analysis in different ways. Zumbansen shows how specifically legal problems associated with dealing with the past must now be set within a framework of *transnational* law. That is, in order to do justice to the complexity and plurality of today's legal orders, and with which any reconciliatory politics must engage, the default position for analysis and action is one that transcends the state boundaries of modernity's law. Czarnota in turn considers the ways in which processes of globalisation impact upon problems of time and reconciliation, and in doing so returns us to the theological theme. Emphasising how competing traditions of temporality relate to theological underpinnings, and how these traditions in turn impact upon possible understandings of social conflict, he argues that problems of reconciliation necessitate, in essence, a temporal sensitivity whose key requisite is the development of an ethics of *synchronization*.

The final four chapters focus specifically on South Africa. By way of contrasting two versions of reconciliation – as therapy and as compensation – Claire Moon then uses an example of transnational litigation to show how compensatory legal mechanisms may be able to grapple with legacies of material injustice left untouched by therapeutic processes of truth and reconciliation. At stake here are a number of crucial issues concerning identity, responsibility and injustice and her analysis engages with, and puts to question at least implicitly, what Michael Ignatieff called the 'vital function of justice in the dialogue between truth and reconciliation': namely, 'to disaggregate individual and nation, to disassemble the fiction that nations are accountable like individuals for the crimes committed in their names' (Ignatieff, 1998, p. 178).

Louise du Toit offers a critical analysis of the reconciliation process in South Africa from a feminist perspective. The Truth and Reconciliation Commission's understanding and treatment of women, specifically with regard to rape and rape victims, reflected, she argues, a more general problematic found in western conceptual and material lineages that reproduce the marginalisation of women.

To the extent that reconciliation and forgiveness are seen as 'feminine', then their presence in what is often portrayed as the normally instrumentalist, individualistic and conflict-based public sphere might be thought to be some kind of advance. Yet, du Toit argues, that view remains limited and partial since it replicates rather than operates to unsettle conventional patriarchal social and political relations and their categories. Moreover, she concludes, where this occurs it facilitates and legitimates a *continuity* in the repression of women – from the apartheid era to the post-transitional democratic era – which still remains largely unaddressed. Thus, in the underlying assumptions of both reconciliatory and democratic politics where this failure to recognise the *politics* of sexual violence continues, the unprecedented levels of rape of women and girls that occurs daily in South Africa devastatingly undermine the claims of the new democratic dispensation to equality for all.

Karin Van Marle's chapter might be seen as an alternative reading of related concerns, but this time through a comparison of the different forms of memory that may be exemplified in the archive and in the Constitution. A sensitivity to the conditions of actualising and suppressing memory is necessary, she argues, in order that the various stresses on constitutional transformation are kept open to political risk and resistance and not ossified in the consummation of a national unity that would cement an essentially conservative outcome of 'business as usual'.

The collection closes with a contribution by Carrol Clarkson. Bringing together insights from philosophy and linguistics, Clarkson analyses the significance of two addresses made by Nelson Mandela, one from the Rivonia Trial in 1962, and the other on his release from prison in 1990. What is so powerful about these addresses, she argues, is the way in which Mandela was acutely sensitive not only to their express content, but to the ways in which the mode of their saying was able to shape and *re-configure the responsive range* of his words. Given the significance of ascertaining the sites of responsibility – whose responsibility, and responsibility for what? – in situations where reconciliation is called for, this highly suggestive analysis alerts us to the ways in which institutional boundaries normally thought of as fixed may be breached or transcended by a politics of speech according to which political potential – through unsettling the relationships of addressor and addressee and their projection through time – may be harnessed and deployed for progressive ends.

It will be clear, we hope, from this brief overview of the chapters that the range of perspectives taken on the subject matter of law and the politics of reconciliation is diverse, as diverse as the issues they themselves engage with. We believe this is no bad thing; as they explore the possibilities and drawbacks of law's role in processes of reconciliation through the themes we identified – of politics, theology, and time – and do so in divergent ways, we hope they open out insights for discussion and debate on some of the most significant and pressing aspects of contemporary social institutions and relations.

We would like to acknowledge thanks to a number of people and institutions. It was mentioned earlier that the book had its genesis in a project that was jointly conceived and run by the two present authors. Through a series of seminars in

Scotland, Holland and South Africa, participants were able to listen to and engage with a wide range of often conflicting approaches to understanding the relations between law and processes of reconciliation. These interdisciplinary exchanges were enormously productive, and we would both therefore like to thank all those who participated in these meetings, as well as the sponsoring institutions who made them financially possible. The Leverhulme Trust granted us an 'Interchange Grant' that allowed us to set up the collaboration. The British Academy and the Law Schools of the Universities of Edinburgh, Glasgow, Tilburg, Johannesburg and Cape Town provided funding for individual workshops. In all cases we thank them for their generous support. We would also like to thank Gavin Baillie for his assistance in the preparation of the final manuscript. Finally, our heartfelt thanks go to the authors, for their enthusiasm, commitment and patience in contributing to this collection.

Bibliography

Ignatieff, M. (1998), *The Warrior's Honor*, London, Chatto & Windus.
Soyinka, W. (1999), *The Burden of Memory*, New York, Oxford University Press.

Chapter 1

The Time of Reconciliation and the Space of Politics

Andrew Schaap

Reconciliation is often discussed in terms of restoring moral community. On this account, wrongdoing alienates the perpetrator both from the victims he has injured (by failing to show respect for them as his moral equals) and from the moral community he has disturbed (by violating its publicly shared norms). Reconciliation is initiated by the perpetrator's acknowledgement of the wrongfulness of his act, followed by remorse and reparation, which opens the way for forgiveness and, eventually, the restoration of community. I will proceed on the assumption that it is a political mistake to construe reconciliation in these terms, given the starkly opposed narratives in terms of which members of a divided society typically make sense of the violence of the past. Political reconciliation will not get off the ground if it is conditional on first establishing a shared moral account of the nature of past wrongs. In divided societies, neither community nor communal norms can be presupposed because the politics of reconciliation turn precisely on the question of belonging and the terms of political association.[1]

While moral judgement necessarily presupposes a universal *moral* community, the politics of reconciliation are always enacted in relation to an anticipated *political* community that is a contingent possibility of a particular historical context. To understand reconciliation politically, therefore, we should think of it in terms of revolution rather than restoration. As such, reconciliation would not begin with the *recollection* of a prior state of harmony in terms of which our present alienation might be understood and redressed. Rather, it would be initiated by the *invocation* of a 'we' as the basis of a new political order. In this contribution, then, I take seriously Bert van Roermund's (2001, p. 179) suggestion that in certain circumstances 'reconciliation is what makes the revelation of truth possible' and explore what I take

---

1 An earlier version of this chapter is published as Chapter 6 of my *Political Reconciliation* (Schaap, 2005, pp. 87–101). Thanks to Routledge for permission to reprint this material. In writing and re-writing this chapter I have particularly benefited from conversations with Bert van Roermund, Emilios Christodoulidis, Johan van der Walt, Scott Veitch, Keith Breen, Kimberly Hutchings and Hans Lindahl. I develop a critique of the restorative model of reconciliation more fully in Schaap (2005, pp. 13–23).

to be the first step in what he calls the 'anthropological' sequence of reconciliation, namely, the act of constitution.[2]

Following Hannah Arendt, constitution entails both beginning and promising. On the one hand, it requires that we conceive the present as a point of origin, which might appear in retrospect as the moment in which a 'people' first appeared on the political scene. On the other hand, it requires that former enemies promise 'never again' in order to condition the possibility of community in the future. By constitution, then, I do not refer only to issues of jurisdiction and state organisation. More fundamentally, I am concerned with the performative constitution of a 'we' through collective action and the constitution of a space for a reconciliatory politics in which the appearance of this 'we' is an ever-present possibility. As Hannah Pitkin (1987, pp. 167–168) discusses, constitution in this sense refers both to something 'we' are ('the distinctive way of life of a polis, its mode of social and political articulation as a community') and something 'we' do (the activity of 'founding, framing, shaping something anew').

I will explore the relation between the time of reconciliation and the space of politics by juxtaposing Arendt's early *Love and Saint Augustine* with her mature work *On Revolution*. In doing so, I suggest that the temporal modality in terms of which we conceive reconciliation might work to delimit a space for politics in a way that either opens or forecloses political opportunity. When reconciliation is conceived in terms of restoration, moral community tends to be represented as a regulative ideal that over-determines and thereby depoliticises the terms on which a reconciliatory politics might be enacted in the present. In contrast, representing political community as a contingent, historical possibility that depends upon our common action in the present reveals the contestability of the terms of reconciliation and so keeps the politics of reconciliation in view.

Of course, any delimitation of political space involves, by definition, both opening and enclosing. What is at stake in the relation between the time of reconciliation and the space of politics is the inter-relation between a normative order and the political action foundational to this order. In this sense, the relation between the time of reconciliation and the space of politics correlates approximately with that between *polity* (or 'the political') and *politics*. Following Ricouer (1965) and Lefort (1988), *polity* refers to the unity in terms of which *politics* or social conflict is staged (represented) and political evil is recognised. In this context, to understand

---

2   Roermund (forthcoming) describes the anthropological sequence of reconciliation, which he contrasts with the 'practical sequence' (i.e. restoration), in this way: 'forgiveness would come first as an offer made by the former victims of oppression. The offer would be a proposal to bury the past by honouring it as a history of 'right suffering' (orthopathema, as Robert J. Schreiter, following Samuel Solivan, calls it). According to this sequence, the readiness to forgive would create the space in which perpetrators can feel repentance so that they can come forward and reveal their wrongdoings.' See also Roermund (2001). Adapting Roermund's description slightly, I take the act of constitution to create a space for politics between enemies, which wanting to forgive helps to sustain. A willingness to forgive cannot, in itself, create this space.

reconciliation in terms of the second (political) temporal modality advocated here would entail, as Bert van Roermund (1996, p. 42 – emphasis in original) puts it (in a different context), '*postponing* every definitive legitimation of the *limits* a society has set itself in order to become "one"'.

Between past and future

The Christian faith in reconciliation is inseparable from the moral ideal, articulated by Jesus in his sermon on the mount, that we should love our enemies (Luke 6: 31–37). Yet, as Arendt shows in her intriguing dissertation on St Augustine, there is a paradox inherent in the ideal of loving one's neighbour as one's self, given the self-denying nature of Christian love. Since right love of God (*caritas*) involves relinquishing one's wrong love of the world (*cupiditas*), Arendt wonders how the individual who is 'isolated from all things mundane' in God's presence can be 'at all interested in his neighbour' (Arendt, 1996, p. 7). For to love one's neighbour as one ought to love oneself (in *caritas*) is to love him not in his singularity but by virtue of the universal quality of his createdness. The other's will toward me as friend or enemy is relevant only in the situation of worldly interdependence. In the presence of God his particular relation to me becomes irrelevant. To love one's neighbour in *caritas* is therefore to love the source of his being rather than the particular person who appears before me. Yet this seems an inhumane love that contradicts our mundane experience of love as both partial toward and dependent on its object.

As Arendt shows, this paradox of neighbourly love has a temporal dimension that arises from the alienation of *mortal* creature from its *eternal* creator, which reconciliation would overcome. To exist in the world is to be subject to time, to be always *no more* and *not yet*. In contrast, God always *is* and, as such, stands outside time. For Augustine, the human experience of alienation arises from the human awareness of being subject to time, which comes about through the imagination of the non-time of eternity. The desire to be reconciled with God, in this context, reflects the human aspiration to overcome the alienation of temporal existence by 'returning' to eternity. It is this anticipation of an absolute future – the re-presentation of an absolute past (before the Fall) as a radical future possibility (through Grace) – that gives rise to the paradox of neighbourly love.

Following Augustine, Arendt argues that time itself is unthinkable without a creature through whom time passes, a creature who is 'inserted' in time in such a way that it is broken up into the tenses of past, present and future (Arendt, 1996, p. 55). As the only animal that knows it was born and that it will die, the human agent experiences time as a stretching out between its first inexplicable appearance in the world and its ultimate disappearance from it. In other words, we actualise temporality through remembrance and anticipation.[3] This is the meaning of Faulkner's famous

---

3   As such, time is not reducible to the intervals by which we measure it. Rather, it is because we reckon with time through remembrance and anticipation that we are driven to measure it. Our preoccupation with the world leads us to reckon with time in such a way

claim that 'the past is never dead, it is not even past' (cited in Arendt, 1977, p. 10). For the achievement of memory is to re-present the past, to make present for our thinking attention what is no longer. Similarly, the future is actualised by our hopes and fears as the 'threatening or fulfilling "not yet" of the present' (Arendt, 1996, p. 13). We exist, then, in the broken middle of time – the 'gap between past and future' – since the present is only experienced as a particular now in relation to our representations of past and future. In our present situation we anticipate the future with fear or hope based on remembrance of what was and the knowledge that what has been could be again. Conversely, we remember the past with regret or nostalgia in terms of our imaginative anticipation of the possibilities that the future holds (Arendt, 1996, p. 48).[4]

Time, as it is humanly experienced, is therefore distinct both from the non-time of eternity (the absolute of temporality) and the time of nature (the everlasting cycles of life). Expectation of death and remembrance of birth make humans aware of their finitude in contrast to the infinity of a God who has no beginning or end but stands outside time (Arendt, 1965, p. 206). Against the dispersion of human existence into past, present and future, eternity is conceived as a standing still of time in which the presence of the whole of time is manifest in an enduring Now (Arendt, 1996, p. 53). We experience alienation from God because we are able to imagine eternity when we retreat from the world to think. Yet we remain aware of our own finitude due to our acting and suffering in the world.[5]

On the other hand, the human experience of time is in contrast to the time of nature because it follows a linear rather than a cyclical course. In contrast to the endless cycles of nature, which proceed along their course indifferent to human affairs, the stretching out of time through remembrance and anticipation means that events, actions, biographies, epochs are thought of as having a beginning, middle and an end. That every life can eventually be told as a story that begins with birth and ends in death is the 'pre-political and pre-historical condition of history, the great story without beginning or end' (Arendt, 1998, p. 184). As animals we are subject to the cycles of nature and to those necessities required to sustain life. Yet, we also transcend nature in our historical existence as world-building beings who seek to

---

that we can waste time or have the time, there can be a time to do this, a right time and a wrong time. Thus, human existence becomes meaningful, in temporal terms, through public interaction by which time is 'woven in common' with others (Ricoeur, 1981, pp. 169–171).

4   At least, this is what I make of Arendt's interpretation of Kafka's parable of 'He' who struggles with two antagonists. One 'presses him from behind, from the origin. The second blocks the road ahead. He gives battle to both' while each assists him in his struggle against the other (Kafka cited in Arendt, 1977, p. 7). It is only because He seeks to stand his ground that the flow of indifferent time becomes broken in the middle.

5   As Ricoeur (1983, p. 62) writes: 'The question of time is raised, or rather time is raised as a question, because man is the only being which knows that it is "mortal," because man alone thinks and thinks what is eternal.' Hannah Arendt never departed from this basic worldview – which is both pre-Socratic and Hebraic – that eternity is what we think, but that it is as 'mortals' that we think it.'

establish a sense of permanence in our affairs through work and remembrance. We experience alienation from Nature because, although we are subject to the never-ending cycles of biological life, we have a sense of the irrevocable succession of events – of time 'marching on.'

This ordering of experience in terms of a rectilinear time concept has the potential to redeem human existence from the futility of the endless repetition of nature. Yet it also threatens to empty experience of meaning by explaining our doing and suffering in relation to an ultimate end. Hope for reconciliation with God underpins a teleological conception of time as building towards a unique and shattering climax, a final judgement at the end of history, which will restore believers to their place in the eternal kingdom of God. Sheldon Wolin (1961, p. 124f.) argues that this Christian conception of time, which displaced the classical conception of cyclical time, had enormous political implications. Christianity transformed human beings' relation to the future with the promise of redemption. This enabled men to anticipate the unfolding of time with hope rather than the dread that had been characteristic of the classical mind.[6] But this new time-dimension was anti-political, according to Wolin (1961, p. 124), because 'political society was implicated in a series of historical events heading towards a final consummation which would mark the end of politics.' Consequently, politics was no longer looked on as an opportunity for glory but as a weary necessity of worldly existence. Moreover, the quest for the ideal polity was condemned as irreverent and proud ambition animated by the desire to establish Man's independence from God.

The manner in which we reckon with time therefore conditions how we *invest* the world with meaning or *divest* it of meaning. To some extent, Arendt concurs with Wolin's conclusions about the anti-political nature of the Christian conception of time (Arendt, 1998, pp. 21, 54–55, 120).[7] The ideal of an absolute future by which we make sense of the present leads us to take an instrumental attitude to the world, according to which events and actions are explained as means toward this ultimate end. An anticipated future of eternal life in God in this way serves as a point of reference that lies outside the world and regulates 'all things inside the world as well as … the relationships by which they are interconnected' (Arendt, 1996, p. 37). Since the world is used as a means toward realising this highest good rather than

---

6   The Greeks tended to understand time in terms of cycles which closely resembled nature's seasons of growth and decay. Consequently, heroic action (being able to answer the demands of the moment with excellence, with the hope of being immortalised by the poets) and founding a polis (which could withstand the destructive impact of time) were fundamental political aspirations. However, for the Christian, 'the classical notion of an eternally recurrent cycle governing human affairs, a rhythm which began in hope and ended in despair, seemed a mockery to both God and man' (Wolin, 1961, p. 124).

7   However, it is to Augustine that she frequently attributes the fundamental political insight that human freedom is inherent in our capacity to begin (e.g. Arendt, 1998, p. 177). Moreover, she observes that 'only under the condition of a rectilinear time concept are such phenomena as novelty, uniqueness of events, and the like conceivable at all' (Arendt, 1965, p. 27).

enjoyed for its own sake, it 'loses its independent meaningfulness and thus ceases to tempt man' (Arendt, 1996, p. 33).

The Christian eschatology thereby produces a tension between the vertical reconciliation hoped for between individual and God and the horizontal reconciliation sought among neighbours in the world.[8] Reconciliation between neighbours is predicated on a universal love that would render all distinctions between persons (including that between friend and enemy) irrelevant. But this seems to require ordering human affairs from a timeless standpoint such that community with the other is countenanced in terms too abstract to realise any meaningful 'we' in the world. Human affairs are divested of any intrinsic worth so that 'this world is for the faithful ... what the desert was for the people of Israel – they live not in houses but in tents' (Augustine cited in Arendt, 1996, p. 19). This leads Arendt to wonder, 'Would it not be better to love the world in *cupiditas* and be at home? Why should we make a desert out of the world?' (Arendt, 1996, p. 19).

Indeed, it is precisely such love of the world (*amor mundi* or 'worldliness') that Arendt advocates in her later work when she turns to politics to redeem human existence from the meaninglessness generated by a (secular) instrumental mentality in public life. In this context, Arendt affirms the striving for worldly immortality against the yearning for eternity. Philosophy begins from wonder at the eternal, which can only be experienced outside the company of others in the solitude of thought. Political life, in contrast, is animated by the desire of actors to win recognition from their peers and to establish a lasting remembrance of their words and deeds (Arendt, 1998, pp. 17–21). The achievement of a polity is that it makes possible an 'organised remembrance' to save political action and speech from being futile.[9] As Paul Ricoeur (1983, p. 62) observes, immortality is 'what we attempt to confer upon ourselves in order to endure our mortal condition'. The political enterprise of distinguishing ourselves through action and of founding and preserving a world in common is, in this respect, the 'highest attempt to "immortalise" ourselves. From this attempt springs both the greatness and the illusion of the whole human enterprise' (Ricoeur, 1983, p. 62).

Against the temptation to conceive the time of reconciliation in relation to a sacred origin or end of history in which our alienation is overcome once and for all, this suggests that a mundane (i.e. 'worldly' or political) reconciliation depends on constituting a space for politics in the present within which conflicting memories and expectations can be brought to bear on each other. Politics is concerned with men in

---

8   For a fascinating discussion of the sacrificial symbolism in terms of which reconciliation is construed in Christianity and its political implications see Fernando Atria's contribution in this volume.

9   Putting the same point in a different way, Bert van Roermund (forthcoming) writes that 'the historicity of human experience, pervasive as it may be, is so all-embracing that it cannot take on form on the level of individual existence without the mediation of socio-political institutions. Rather than trimming authentic self-expression to manageable proportions of 'normality', these institutions provide the very possibility of being expressive in the first place'.

their temporal existence and in their relation to each other as friends and enemies. As Arendt observes, morality may require us to imagine the 'earth as the homeland of all mankind' and to presuppose 'one unwritten law, eternal and valid for all' (Arendt, 1968, p. 81). Politics, however, does not deal with 'Man' in the abstract (as autonomous, rational being, subject to the laws he gives to himself) but with 'men' in their plurality (as earthbound creatures who belong to different communities and are 'heirs to many pasts') (Arendt, 1968, p. 81). Following from this, if reconciliation is to be political, it depends on citizens discovering good grounds to want to share a polity at all with their historical enemy or oppressor. This requires not that we transcend our relation to our neighbour as enemy but that we transform it into one of civic friendship.

Insofar as it is a political enterprise, therefore, reconciliation would not hypostatise moral community as an ultimate end in terms of which our present relations should be regulated. Rather, political reconciliation would be animated by the will that the present be remembered by a community to come as the moment in which it originated. This is why political reconciliation is initiated not by the acknowledgement of wrongdoing in terms of an already established set of shared norms but by the act of constitution: the constitution of a space for politics makes possible a future collective remembrance. Or, as Bert van Roermund (forthcoming) writes, it makes available 'a past to look forward to'. Reconciliation necessarily anticipates community. However, insofar as it is political, this anticipation is conditioned by an awareness of the contingency (and therefore the contestability) of the 'we' that it *invokes*.

Beginning

Political reconciliation presupposes a revolutionary moment. As Bruce Ackerman observes, revolutionaries divide history into a Before and a Now: 'Before, there was something deeply wrong with the way people thought and acted. Now, we have a chance to make a 'new beginning' by freeing ourselves from these blinders' (1992, p. 5). As such, political reconciliation is predicated on a 'recasting of the present as a point of *origin*' (Christodoulidis, 2000, p. 199 – emphasis in original). It is frequently observed that political reconciliation is both retrospective (in coming to terms with the past) and prospective (in bringing about social harmony) and, therefore, requires striking a balance between the competing demands of past and future. Past-oriented concerns with punishing human rights violators, for instance, must be considered in the light of future-oriented concerns with establishing stable democratic institutions (see, for example, Ackerman, 1992, p. 70f.; Teitel, 2000, pp. 191–211).

Yet, understanding the present as a point of origin entails a reckoning with time that is more subtle and complex than is immediately suggested by the metaphor of 'looking back' while 'reaching forward'. This is because political reconciliation refers to a future anterior, an imagined 'not yet' that is 'brought into the present to become constitutive of the experience of the present' (Christodoulidis, 2000,

p. 198). From the perspective of this imagined common future, the experience of the present is interpreted as a possible new beginning, as the moment in which reconciliation 'will have been' initiated. To perceive the present from the perspective of this future anterior is to recognise the contingency of the beginning that we seek to enact since what 'has been' could always 'have been otherwise'. Following Christodoulidis (2000, p. 198), this 'temporal modality' of political reconciliation is 'to be celebrated' because it 'imports an awareness that keeps community both attuned to the aspiration of being-in-common and aware of its vulnerability.' This awareness politicises reconciliation since it interprets the present in relation to a contingent historical possibility rather than a predetermined end.

But this temporal modality also requires that we reckon with an absolute that is neither anticipated nor remembered but, rather, confronts us in the present in the act of beginning. The act of constituting of a new polity is, for Arendt, as it was for the Romans, the political act *par excellence*. This is because it exemplifies the human potentiality to do the unprecedented. Beginning is exhilarating because it is the actualisation of freedom in action. Yet the act of constitution is also perplexing because it confronts us with the arbitrariness inherent in every beginning. In the case of the beginning we are confronted with 'an unconnected, new event breaking into the sequence of historical time' (Arendt, 1965, p. 205).[10] It is this arbitrary aspect of every beginning that makes it so difficult to be pleased with human freedom. Consequently, when confronted with the new we are driven to justify it in terms of what came before. The riddle, for those who wish to constitute a new political order, is therefore 'how to restart time within an inexorable time continuum' (Arendt, 1977, p. 214).

In its political sense, constitution refers to the founding act by which a space for politics is established. According to Arendt, this space 'comes into being wherever men are together in the manner of speech and action' and so 'precedes all formal constitution of the public realm' (Arendt, 1998, p. 199). Yet, because its existence ultimately depends on its actualisation through performative action it quickly disappears when citizens withdraw from public life (Arendt, 1998, p. 200). In its legal sense, constitution refers to the fundamental law of the polity that is laid down in the founding act. The formal organisation of the public realm according to legal principles provides a measure of continuity and stability that the space of appearances would otherwise lack (Arendt, 1958, p. 463). In its third, ethical sense, constitution refers to the emergence of a 'we' as an 'identifiable entity' in the act of foundation (Arendt, 1977, p. 201). As Arendt observes, a 'we' arises wherever people come together to act and speak in public and it may take many different forms. Because this identity is a potentiality of collective action, it never simply *is* but is always in the

---

10   Because it is unprecedented, it is as though the revolutionary act came out of nowhere and, as such, it seems to have 'nothing … to hold onto' (Arendt, 1977, p. 208). In the revolutionary moment, it is 'as though the beginner had abolished the sequence of temporality itself, or as though the actors were thrown out of the temporal order and its continuity' (Arendt, 1965, p. 206).

mode of becoming. Nevertheless, 'no matter how this "We" is first experienced and articulated, it seems that it always needs a beginning, and nothing seems so shrouded in darkness and mystery as that "In the beginning"' (Arendt, 1977, p. 202).

Constitution thus refers to the complex inter-relation between politics (democratic will), law (constitutional reason) and ethics (the identity of the people), according to which the constitution of a 'we' emerges from the articulation of law and politics (Christodoulidis, 2001, p. 115). Fundamentally, the act of constitution requires holding together the apparently 'irreconcilable and even contradictory' logics of performing and legislating: on the one hand an 'exhilarating awareness of the human capacity of beginning'; on the other hand, a 'grave concern' with establishing an enduring regime (Arendt, 1965, p. 223). For revolutionaries, the legitimacy of the founding act does not derive from tradition but the will of the demos in the present. Yet, it is in the name of the present revolutionary will that they would bind the will of future actors according to the rational principles laid down in a legal constitution. The founding principles become the higher source of law from which the authority of future positive law should be derived (Arendt, 1965, p. 160). The act of foundation, in which the revolutionaries actualise their freedom to begin, thus, paradoxically, seems to deny this same freedom to future generations for the sake of the stability of the political association (Arendt, 1965, p. 232f.).

In temporal terms, this paradoxical articulation of performance and legislation emerges in the fact 'those who would get together to constitute a new government are themselves unconstitutional, that is, they have no authority to do what they set out to achieve' (Arendt, 1965, pp. 183–184). As Jacques Derrida (1986, p. 10) makes clear, it is only in retrospect that they might be understood as founders of law; in the act of foundation they are outlaws since the democratic will they purport to represent is not yet legally constituted.[11] In the revolutionary moment, the will of the people lacks an institutional framework in terms of which it may be represented as such. We are here confronted by the paradox of sovereignty: 'the people' who are supposed to be sovereign in a democratic polity are both inside and outside the legal order that is constituted; political power both institutes a new legal order while the newly instituted legal order is supposed to enable and restrain that very political power (Roermund, 2003a, p. 38).

This is not to say that 'the people' in whose name a polity is constituted *participate directly* in the moment of foundation whereas they can only be *represented* within the constituted order, as Arendt (1965, p. 273) often seems to argue. Rather, those who seek to enact a new beginning must also act as representatives of 'the people'

---

11   In his commentary on the American Declaration of Independence, Derrida (1986, p. 10) writes: 'The "we" of the declaration speaks "in the name of the people." But this people does not yet exist. They do *not* exist as an entity, it does *not* exist, *before* this declaration, not *as such*. If it gives birth to itself, as free and independent subject, as possible signer, this can hold only in the act of the signature. The signature invents the signer. The signer can only authorise him- or herself to sign once he or she has come to the end, if one can say this, of his or her own signature, in a sort of fabulous retroactivity'.

in whose name they speak. The fundamental arbitrariness that is inherent in the act of foundation here reveals itself in terms of the problem of constituency, that is, 'of who belongs to the "we" that decide to band together and grant themselves mutual rights, beginning with those accruing to citizenship' (Lindahl, forthcoming). The problem of determining the relevant constituency of a polity cannot be settled by democratic means but rather is *precondition* for democracy and deliberation despite the fact that boundary-drawing is the most political of all decisions (see Roermund, 1996, 2003b; Wheelan 1983). As Hans Lindahl (forthcoming) discusses, Arendt is aware of this problem, although for the most part she ignores it.[12] But Arendt does offer one clue as to how we might understand this decisive moment in the act of constitution when she writes that 'every action, accomplished by a plurality of men, can be divided into two stages: the beginning which is initiated by a "leader," and the accomplishment, in which many join to see through what then becomes a common enterprise' (Arendt, 1964, p. 205).[13] As Lindahl (forthcoming) notes, 'this passage effectively deconstructs the sharp opposition Arendt elsewhere sets up between "representation" and "action and participation"… For, to initiate a community, a "leader" must claim to act on behalf of group'.

When the act of constitution is understood in these terms it becomes clear why political reconciliation is initiated by the *invocation* of a 'we'. To invoke is 'to call upon, to call to (a person) to come or to do something' (OED). In another, closely connected sense, it means 'to appeal to, cite or posit in support of a course of action, explanation, etc' (OED). Those who would initiate political reconciliation must invoke the people in both senses of 'calling upon' and 'positing' a *united* people. First, the act of constitution *calls upon* 'a people' that remains to come, which does not exist prior to the foundational act and which is not even present (except as re-presented) in the moment in which it is supposed to be constituted. The people will come, if it comes at all, only in retrospect. Only if the founders succeed in establishing a new beginning will the present in which they now act come to be collectively remembered as the moment in which the people first appeared on the political scene. To the extent that the act of constitution succeeds therefore a future 'we' will come to commemorate a (communal) past that was never present.[14]

In the second sense, the invocation of a 'we' *posits* a unity that is the enabling condition for the reflexive self-determination of the people. It establishes the possibility, as Roermund (2003a, p. 45) puts it, of 'a people relating … to the political self they claim to belong to as a whole. Only if there is this relationship can politics be situated in a public realm; only then can politicians and citizens use and

---

12   For an excellent discussion of Arendt's ambivalent account of the role of decision in politics see Andreas Kalyvas' s (2004) 'From the Act to the Decision'.

13   Kalyvas (2004, p. 336) similarly draws attention to two passages in the 'Life of the Mind' where Arendt admits that willing/deciding is a precondition for action: 'Action in the sense of how men want to appear needs a deliberate planning ahead … choice becomes the starting point of the actions themselves' (Arendt 1977, pp. 5, 60).

14   I am indebted to Hans Lindahl who put the point to me in this way (personal communication, January 2005).

understand notions like 'the public interest', the 'common good', 'national security', etc.' Following from this, it is by appealing to this posited unity that those agents who would initiate political reconciliation hope to authorise their deed. Political reconciliation might be initiated, for instance, with the declaration 'We the peoples of Australia, of many origins as we are, make a commitment to go on together in a spirit of national reconciliation'.[15] It is important to differentiate here between the 'we' that *enacts* or performs this speech act and the 'we' that is imputed to be its author (and which therefore *authorises* it). Since the 'we' that is called upon to authorise the act of constitution cannot itself say 'we', those who would initiate the constitutive act must 'pose as representatives in the double sense of the term "representatives": authorised substitutes and actual co-executives of this authority' (Roermund, 2003b, p. 241). The 'we' to whom the intention of this speech-act is imputed is not same as the 'we' that performs the speech act and its success therefore depends upon those members of the 'we' to whom the speech act is addressed (at least implicitly) endorsing the intention that is imputed to them. The success of an initial act of constitution therefore depends on ongoing invocations of the 'we' that is presupposed in the founding moment: 'because the subject of the novel legal order must be both presupposed and created in one fell swoop, this initial act is ever dependent on iterations which lend credence to the claim of collective self-determination' (Lindahl, 2003, p. 473).[16] It is in this context, that the importance of promising in sustaining a reconciliatory politics, becomes apparent.

Promising 'never again'

Political reconciliation is predicated on the promise *nunca más* or 'never again'. This, for instance, was the title of the report of the truth commission established in Argentina to investigate the 'disappearance' of 10,000–30,000 people by successive military juntas between 1976 and 1983.[17] The promise 'never again' locates the possibility of community between former enemies in their present intention to prevent the recurrence of wrongdoing. In this context, the ethical constitution of a

---

15 Council for Aboriginal Reconciliation, *Declaration Towards Reconciliation* cited in Patton (2001, p. 26, note 2). This is an example of a failed speech act since the declaration recommended by the (now defunct) Australian Council for Aboriginal Reconciliation in 2000 remains unendorsed.

16 As Paul Connerton (1989, p. 59) writes: 'Through the utterance of the 'we' a basic disposition is given definitive form, is constituted among the members of the liturgical community. The community is initiated when pronouns of solidarity are repeatedly pronounced. In pronouncing the 'we' the participants meet not only in an externally definable space but in a kind of ideal space determined by their speech acts. Their speech does not describe what such a community might look like, nor does it express a community constituted before and apart from it; performative utterances are as it were the place in which the community is constituted and recalls to itself the fact of constitution.'

17 Since its publication, a digest of the report has become one of the bestselling books in Argentina's history (Hayner, 2001, pp. 33–34).

'we' depends, as van Roermund (forthcoming) suggests, on prolonging the present moment in which this intention is expressed in order to avoid either a preoccupation with the past (that unduly limits future opportunity) or a preoccupation with the future (that too easily forgets the past).[18]

Thus, beginning depends on the invocation of a 'we' that remains to come for its authorisation, promising the conditions by which the possibility that this 'we' will remain authoritative in the future by lending it institutional representation. There is 'an element of the world-building capacity of man in the human faculty of making and keeping promises', Arendt insists, because it is animated not so much by a concern with ourselves and our own time but with that of those who will succeed us (Arendt, 1965, p. 175). The achievement of promising is that it establishes a 'limited independence' of our present actions 'from the incalculability of the future' (Arendt, 1998, p. 245). By establishing shared expectations, promising reduces the radical contingency of the future so that we are able to make plans and form projects. It provides a partial remedy against the predicament of unpredictability by establishing certain 'guideposts of reliability' or 'isolated islands of certainty in an ocean of uncertainty' (Arendt, 1998, pp. 224; 244). Yet, it can only provide a partial remedy against the risk of action because, as Alan Keenan (1994, p. 317) puts it, 'a promise, like any agreement, is at best a point of conjecture, a site at which conflicting goals, intentions, forces, and projects find a common expression or formulation but never an identity of meaning.'[19]

As social contract theory attests, the capacity to make and keep promises is fundamental for securing the individual rights of those who would enter into political society together. Arendt understands this role of a constitution in securing the private freedom of citizens not as the fundamental principle of limited government but as an enabling condition for the exercise of political freedom (Arendt, 1965, p. 218). Far from being a natural attribute of individuals, equality is an artificial achievement of the political association, which establishes an 'equality of unequals' for the limited purpose of enabling politics between them (Arendt, 1998, p. 215). 'We are not born equal' but become so 'as members of a group on the strength of our decision to guarantee ourselves mutually equal rights' (Arendt, 1958, p. 301). As the plight of stateless people demonstrates, human rights acquire a concrete reality only to the extent that they are institutionalised and guaranteed by the political association (Arendt, 1958, p. 297; Arendt, 1965, p. 149). The constitutional guarantee of rights establishes civility by assigning public roles to private individuals. It provides 'channels of communication' between citizens by attributing to them a legal 'persona' (Arendt, 1958, p. 465; Arendt, 1965, pp. 106–109).

---

18   Similarly, as Mario Di Paolantonio (1997, p. 456) observes, to promise 'never again' is to make a promise about a future that can never arrive. As such, it is a promise that can never be fulfilled.

19   The context of this sentence in Keenan's critique suggests that he is making this point against Arendt, whereas this seems to me a fundamentally Arendtian insight.

As such, promising helps to constitute and preserve a 'space where freedom as virtuosity can appear' (Arendt, 1965, p. 175). Due to its frailties, action alone is insufficient to sustain a space for politics through time. Rather, it is the force of promise that establishes a measure of stability in human affairs and so makes possible an organised remembrance, which conditions the possibility of community in the future. In order to be actualised as a tangible reality, freedom must be 'spatially limited' (Arendt, 1965, p. 275; Arendt, 1958, p. 465).[20] Politics is always transacted within a complicated framework of laws and institutions that are constituted through promising (Arendt, 1977, p. 164). Without the common reference points that such limits provide, public action and speech would be incoherent. In this sense, the 'boundaries of positive laws are for the political existence of man what memory is for his historical existence: they guarantee the pre-existence of a common world' (Arendt, 1958, p. 465). Laws and covenants establish a continuity that transcends the life span of each generation. They provide a context within which action can appear meaningful by providing a stable structure to house the movement of action. In reducing the contingency of the future, a legal constitution thus not only forecloses certain options it 'makes available possibilities which would otherwise lie beyond reach' (Holmes, 1988, p. 226).[21]

Yet, despite her celebration of promising as a faculty inherent to action that mitigates the risk of unpredictability without reducing its performative quality, Arendt suggests (in her reflections on revolution) that promising may be insufficient to assure the perpetuity of a political association. If the legal constitution is to become the 'higher law' of the polity, 'authoritative and valid for all' both now and in the future, it seems it must derive its authority from a source that transcends politics (Arendt, 1965, p. 182). The fundamental law of the polity seems to require a more stable ground than the promises of men can provide. In order to arrest the potentially destructive aspect of democratic will, it seems that revolutionaries must appeal to a higher source of authority – an Absolute – to authorise the fundamental law they seek to establish.

Such an appeal to an Absolute is articulated, for instance, in the Preamble of the Declaration of Independence, which states 'we hold these truths to be self-evident' (Arendt, 1965, p. 192). As Arendt discusses, Jefferson's famous words paradoxically combine a relative agreement with an Absolute. To the extent that the truths of the Declaration are 'held' by those who articulate them they are a matter of opinion. They are relative because they relate to those who acknowledge their authoritative

---

20 'The laws hedge in each new beginning and at the same time assure its freedom of movement, the potentiality of something entirely new and unpredictable' (Arendt, 1958, p. 465). Again, for an insightful elaboration of the implications of this claim, see Lindahl (forthcoming).

21 Stephen Holmes illustrates this power generating potential of promising by comparing constitutions to the rules of a game. Whereas regulative rules govern pre-existent activities (for example, 'no smoking'), constitutive rules 'make a practice possible for the first time' (for example, 'bishops move diagonally'). Constitutive rules, in this way, are not primarily disabling but enabling. They do not merely restrain power but assign and channel power.

status for the life of the polity. Yet, if they are self-evident they stand in no need of agreement because they compel with the force of reason. Their self-evidence 'puts them beyond disclosure and argument' so that 'they are not held by us but we are held by them' (Arendt, 1965, pp. 192, 193). Their validity is independent of the democratic will. With this appeal to self-evidence, Arendt argues, Jefferson promotes reason to a transcendent source from which the legitimacy of the legal constitution is derived. Yet, she suggests, he must have been aware that the claim 'all men are created equal' is not self-evident to all or he would not have felt it necessary to include the performative 'we hold', according to which moral truth becomes politically relevant.

Although the need for an Absolute was revealed in the moment of foundation, Arendt suggests that this dilemma was, in part, based on a misunderstanding of the nature of law. Only if law is conceived in terms of a commandment to which men owe their obedience irrespective of their consent and agreement does it require an absolute foundation (Arendt, 1965, p. 189). For the Romans, the law needed no such basis but was the outcome of conflict. Law was predicated on an alliance, which not only established peace but constituted a new unity between two different entities that had been thrown together by war. Thus, a war was concluded to the satisfaction of the Romans not merely with the defeat of an enemy but 'only when the former enemies became 'friends' and allies (*socii*) of Rome' (Arendt, 1965, p. 188). The Romans thus recognised in alliances and covenants a powerful institution for the 'creation of politics at the point where it was reaching its limits' (Arendt cited in Tamineaux, 2000, p. 176).[22] On this account, as Jacques Tamineaux (2000, p. 176) puts it, law is the 'institution of a relationship between conflictual sides of a pluralistic interaction.' Law expresses a relation or *rapport* (Montesquieu) rather than an imperative and so has no need of absolute validity (Arendt, 1965, pp. 188–189).

Arendt proposes to solve the problem of the Absolute, which seems to be required in order to break the vicious cycle of constitution, by looking not to a source of authority that transcends politics but to the foundational act itself (Arendt, 1965, p. 213). By proposing a conception of authority as *augmentation*, which involves a binding back to the beginning, Arendt believes she has resolved the paradox of sovereignty. Rather than looking to an Absolute that transcends the realm of politics (such as a mythical origin or end) to legitimate the founding law of the polity we should look to the founding act itself. For, she suggests, it is 'futile to search for

---

22   Alliances allowed the extension of politics beyond 'relationships between citizens of one and the same City' (as the Greek conception of politics was limited) to include relations 'between foreign and dissimilar nations' (Arendt cited in Tamineaux, 2000, p. 177). Indeed, the *res publica* was itself the outcome of war between the patricians and plebeians, 'whose internal strife was concluded through the famous laws of the Twelve Tables' (Arendt, 1965, p. 188). Moreover, the foundation myth of Rome was based on Virgil's reversal of the Homeric epic of the sacking of Troy according to which the 'end of the war is not victory and departure for one side, extermination and slavery and utter destruction for the others, but "both nations, unconquered, join treaty forever under equal laws" [Virgil] and settle down together' (Arendt, 1965, p. 209).

an absolute to break the vicious cycle in which all beginning is inevitably caught, because this "absolute" lies in the very act of beginning itself' (Arendt, 1965, p. 204).

In this context, she suggests that the 'political genius' of the American people derived from their 'extraordinary capacity ... to look on yesterday with the eyes of tomorrow' (Arendt, 1965, p. 198). The stability of the polity derived from their willingness to bind themselves back to a contingent historical beginning. The authority of the legal constitution depended on its being taken as a common reference point for action. Consequently, Arendt suggests, rather than denying future generations the freedom to act it bestowed a 'communicative legacy' that might inspire future action (see Buckler, 2001, p. 296), for the legitimacy of political action depended on the extent to which it would increase and enlarge the principle of public freedom as enacted in the foundation of the polity (Arendt, 1977, p. 122; Arendt, 1965, pp. 201–202).

The founding act, in which the freedom to begin is dramatically enacted, becomes exemplary for all future action. The authority of the constitution thus depends on its illumination by the memory of the founding itself. This is because the beginning carries its own principle in itself, which inspires the subsequent acts of citizens (Arendt, 1958, p. 467; Arendt, 1965, p. 212). In this context, Arendt suggests that 'the authority of the republic will be safe and intact as long as the act itself, the beginning as such, is remembered whenever constitutional questions in the narrower [legal] sense of the word come into play' (Arendt, 1965, p. 204). By conceiving authority in terms of augmentation of the founding act, Arendt claims to have established the basis on which change and permanence are tied together such that 'change could only mean increase and enlargement of the old' (Arendt, 1965, p. 201).

Yet, intriguing as Arendt's attempt to reconcile the contradictory constitutional moments of performance and legislation is, this is a reconciliation that ultimately fails. For, in emphasising the relational aspect of law – its capacity to create politics at the point at which it reaches its limits – she tends to neglect the extent to which this achievement rests on a reduction that simultaneously forecloses politics. If the achievement of law is that it establishes certainty and stability in human affairs, its failing is that it tends to over-determine the terms in which we make sense of the world. Law reduces the vast complexity of the world by filtering information as either fulfilment or disappointment of the expectations it institutionalises. Consequently, much that happens in the world does not register at all or registers only on the law's own terms (Christodoulidis, 2000, p. 198).

While politics is enabled by the invocation of a 'we' as an indeterminate potentiality, law tends to over-determine this 'we' since it must represent community as already existing in order to establish its legitimacy (see Christodoulidis, 2001). Thus, as Christodoulidis (2001, p. 124 – emphasis in original) explains, a legal constitution at once 'frustrates and facilitates the political': *facilitates*, as Arendt recognises, by staking out 'joint boundaries' in terms of which it is possible for adversaries to engage in a rational dispute that lends itself to resolution; yet *frustrates*, as she sometimes forgets, because in order to discipline conflict the law must represent it selectively 'by setting the thresholds of valid dissensus, the *when* and *how* of possible conflict.'[23] In allowing political conflict to be 'played out and resolved as *internal* to the constituency' in this way, law 'removes any potential threat *to* the constituency, i.e. to the unity of the polity' (Christodoulidis, 2001, pp. 127–128 – emphasis in original). Since conflict can be concluded *satisfactorily* only with the establishment of society between former enemies, the law must re-present political conflict as always-already communal.

Against Arendt, then, we must recognise the paradox of constitution as real and unavoidable, since it involves the articulation of the irreconcilable logics of law and politics. Constitutional democracy is, as Christodoulidis (2001, p. 122) puts it, 'a hybrid, harbouring and enabling the co-existence of two radically incommensurable orders: one that is driven by disruption, and openness and is thus radically contingent; and one that is driven by the need to reach a state of order through normative closure and the curtailment of contingency.' Whereas law looks to the past in order to bring the future under control (i.e. by reducing contingency through securing expectations), politics freely inclines into the openness of future, imports the risk of what is not yet as its enabling condition in the present (Christodoulidis, 2000, pp. 196–199). If reconciliation relies on the indeterminacy of community to constitute a space for politics in the first instance, a legal constitution tends to undercut political reconciliation by making community a regulative ideal and, hence, over-determining the terms within which a reconciliatory politics can be enacted. A legal constitution thus seems to be predicated on a *necessary forgetting* of the founding act that brings it into being, the moment of beginning which imports an awareness of the frailty and contingency of community.

Yet, with Arendt, we might resist this tendency to forget by invoking politics as indispensable in prolonging the present moment in which the intention 'never again' is expressed. What I want to take from Arendt, then, is the idea that political reconciliation is impelled by an anticipated remembrance by the 'we' that is invoked in the constitutive moments of beginning and promising. As such, political reconciliation is impelled, on the one hand, by recasting the present as a point of origin and, on the other hand, by the attempt to memorialise this beginning by promising 'never again'. It is from the effort to hold together these two moments that a 'we' might be constituted, in terms of which a collective reckoning with the past becomes possible. Yet, against the tendency of a legal constitution to over-determine the terms within which this 'we' is constituted, political reconciliation must be conditioned by a sense of the risk of this venture: that the beginning 'we' seek to enact in the present might not come to be remembered as such.

---

23 I say *sometimes* forgets because Arendt shows an awareness of this reductive tendency of institutions when she writes that the 'moment promises lose their character as isolated islands of certainty in an ocean of uncertainty, that is, when this faculty is misused to cover the whole ground of the future and to map out a path secure in all directions, they lose their binding power and the whole enterprise becomes self-defeating' (1998, p. 244).

'We the people'

Bruce Ackerman (1992, pp. 5–6) defines revolution as a 'successful attempt to transform the governing principles and practices of a basic aspect of social life through an act of collective and self-conscious mobilisation'. In this context, constitution should be understood not just in terms of the procedures and rules that discipline conflict but as the performative act in which 'a people constitutes itself into a body politic' (Arendt, 1965, p. 203). This aspect of constitution is vivid in the transitional moment of political reconciliation when 'citizens are most alive to their problem in political construction: How, given fundamental disagreements, are they to elaborate principles of justice that will give all a fair and equal opportunity to pursue their different lives?' (Ackerman, 1992, p. 26). It is because the identity of the people cannot be taken for granted at such times that citizens are aware of the fragility of community. In these circumstances, constitutional politics inevitably turn around the question: who are 'we'? It is by invoking community in the twofold sense of *calling upon* a 'we' that remains to come and *positing* a unity in terms of which citizens might appear 'divided' that the act of constitution initiates political reconciliation.

Of course, given the role a *legal* constitution is supposed to play in preventing state wrongs, there are other, common-sense reasons why so much attention is paid to constitutional issues during a transition to democracy. The legitimacy of modern government depends upon its limitation by the rule of law whereas tyranny comes about when the will of the sovereign is presumed to be above the law. Constitution-making during a political transition, therefore, is typically associated with 'restoring' the rule of law, the reinstatement of a publicly known set of procedures by which to arbitrate political conflict and secure the rights of citizens. The turn to constitutionalism thus underscores both the legitimacy of the new regime (as *Rechtstaat*) and the illegitimacy of the old (*Unrechtstaat*). Whereas the legitimacy of the *Rechtstaat* depends on its 'self-binding', its commitment to abide by publicly agreed decision-making procedures, the illegitimacy of the *Unrechtstaat* was due to its failure to be bound by such predetermined procedural limitations to power. These kinds of concerns were clearly fore-grounded, for instance, during the transitions to democracy in Eastern Europe following the collapse of the Soviet Union. Important as the rule of law is as a legitimating principle of the *Rechtstaat*, however, it is politically relevant only to the extent that it is related to an agent that executes, applies and enforces it. 'The pursuit of justice requires some form of *agency* setting the norm for what justice is here and now' (Roermund, 2003a, p. 37).

In this context, as Ackerman emphasises, the creative aspect of constitution-making is equally important as concerns with procedural justice. Negotiation over a new constitution provides a 'crucial mechanism' through which former enemies 'try to work out the terms of their new beginning together' (Ackerman, 1992, p. 116). Indeed, Ackerman insists that this unifying project of constitutional creation should take precedence over the divisive concern with corrective justice, which tends to emerge from a rights-centred approach, for while an emphasis on corrective justice tends to divide a citizenry into 'evil doers and innocent victims', the framing of a constitution 'invites citizens to put the past behind them and to think about how they all might contribute to a definition of the new order' (Ackerman, 1992, pp. 70–71). Leaving aside doubts about what 'putting the past behind' means here, I agree with Ackerman that, given its orientation to the future, the constitution of a space for politics may initiate political reconciliation. However, I share Christodoulidis's (2000, pp. 192–194; 2001, pp. 116–122) suspicion that Ackerman (like other republican legal theorists) is unduly optimistic in entrusting to a *legal* constitution the task of sustaining a reconciliatory politics.

As we have seen, law frustrates political reconciliation by representing community as the given end of politics rather than a contingent historical possibility that conditions the possibility of politics in the present. The tendency of a legal constitution to undercut the ethical constitution of a 'we' in this way was demonstrated, for instance, in the constitutional politics of South Africa. The temporal modality of political reconciliation is clearly revealed in the much cited postscript to the Interim Constitution of South Africa (1993), in which it is declared: 'With this constitution and these commitments, *we the people* of South Africa open a new chapter in the history of our country' (emphasis added). The constitution is supposed to provide 'a historic bridge between the past of a deeply divided society, characterised by strife, conflict, untold suffering and injustice, and a future founded on the recognition of human rights, democracy, peaceful coexistence and development for all South Africans.' Moreover, it should establish the 'foundation for the people of South Africa to transcend the divisions and strife of the past', which left a 'legacy of hatred, fear, guilt and revenge' (cited in de Lange, 2000, p. 21).

The present of the interim constitution is taken as a point of origin, a transitional moment between the 'no more' of civil strife and the 'not yet' of peaceful coexistence. In this context, the twofold aspect of constitution as beginning ('opening a new chapter') and promising ('these commitments') is explicit. But, as Christodoulidis (2000, pp. 190–194) discusses, this renders the 'we' that is invoked in the constitution problematic. For just as there could be no collective identity (no unified 'people' of South Africa) in the past characterised by strife and gross violations of human rights, so the legacy of hatred, fear and guilt precludes community in the present. The 'we' that is invoked in the interim constitution can belong, then, only to the democratic future. And yet, since the legitimacy of the constitution is founded on the restoration of community, it must presuppose the continuity of this community (albeit a community that was previously divided) over time. Yet, in this the constitution makes an unwarranted presumption of a 'we' since it elides the risk of politics by re-presenting the conflict of the past as communal. In doing so, the law takes as a given what political reconciliation is supposed to achieve: the constitution of a 'we'. In legal terms, the conflict of the past can only be 'resolved' and community thereby 'restored' by a reductive representation that silences political objections that question how such a 'we' is possible in the first place. Yet it is precisely the possibility of such questioning that is the enabling condition of a reconciliatory politics.

If reconciliation is to be conceived politically, it must accommodate the risk that the beginning on which it is predicated may not eventuate. Although less dramatic than the transitions to democracy in South Africa and elsewhere, demands for constitutional recognition by indigenous groups in settled democracies may be similarly understood as attempts to establish such a new beginning, what Ackerman would call a constitutional moment. It was no coincidence, for instance, that Aboriginal demands for a treaty coincided with the debate over whether Australia should become a republic in the late 1990s. For what was at stake in both issues was the question of identity of the Australian 'people', their relationship to their government(s) and the terms of association between settler and indigenous societies. Constitutional politics in Australia in the 1990s turned around competing interpretations of the founding moments of the state. While the settler society celebrated its bicentennial in 1988, many indigenous Australians and their supporters mourned what they understood to be invasion day. Similarly, during the republican conventions leading up to the celebration of the centenary of federation in 2001, Aboriginal leaders called attention to the fact that indigenous Australians were omitted from the original contract on which the foundation of the Commonwealth of Australia was based (Rowse, 2002, p. 30; Patton, 2001).

State commemorative activities in this way provided focal points that were understood by some to present a political opportunity to establish a new beginning by calling into question the legitimacy of the 'we' represented in the constitution, while for others they were supposed to consolidate state sovereignty. While for one side the possibility of reconciliation depended on inaugurating a new friendship between settler and indigenous societies, for the other side it depended upon leaving the past behind by assimilating indigenous Australians into the broader society. For instance, in his Redfern Park speech, Prime Minister Keating (2000, p. 62) declared that the High Court's *Mabo* decision provided 'an historic turning point, the basis of a new relationship between indigenous and non-Aboriginal Australians'. Yet, this was a beginning that never eventuated. For under the Howard government, recognition of native title provided a legislative framework in terms of which the legitimation crisis of the settler society could be 'resolved' only by allowing for the historical extinguishment of an entitlement recognised belatedly 'in law' after it had been extinguished 'in fact' (see Schaap, 2005, p. 52f.).

Despite the well-attended celebratory marches for reconciliation in the 1990s, many indigenous Australians continue to insist that there is unfinished business between settler and indigenous societies. Indeed, a central recommendation of the final report by the Council for Aboriginal Reconciliation in 2000 was that the state 'put in place a process that will unite all Australians by way of an agreement or treaty, through which unresolved issues of reconciliation can be resolved' (cited in Patton, 2001, p. 26).[24] In calling for a treaty, indigenous Australians have sought to establish

---

24 As Paul Patton (2001, p. 26) notes, 'The re-emergence of demands for a treaty at the end of the reconciliation process is not without irony since the establishment of a Council for Aboriginal Reconciliation was a political response to the failure of treaty proposals put

a framework within which the new beginning that reconciliation was supposed to establish might become more meaningful. A treaty would provide a measure of historical justice by recognising that indigenous peoples did have a political claim over the territories that were appropriated from them by the settlers and that treaties ought to have been sought with them at the time of settlement.

In this context, the failure to provide for constitutional recognition of indigenous Australians perpetuates the original injustice. In the absence of a treaty, argued former Aboriginal and Torres Strait Islander Commission (ATSIC) chairman, Geoff Clark (2000, p. 229), reconciliation is like 'a football game without goal posts or accepted referees'. The value of a treaty for Clark is the measure of continuity and certainty it would bring to relations between indigenous people and the settler society. For the history of indigenous peoples' dealings with the state 'leaves us suspicious. Decisions and agreements reached during one term are too easily revoked during the next.' What is required, rather, is 'an explicit commitment about our place in the community that will endure changes in political fortunes' (Clark, 2000, p. 233). Without the common reference point that such a promise would establish there is only a directionless and futile talking-past-each-other. The opportunity for a meaningful political dialogue between indigenous and non-indigenous Australians – one which might transform their historical relation to each other – is undermined.

These examples reveal how a legal constitution both reduces and makes available political opportunity. By establishing a common reference point, it provides an opportunity for an overlapping dissensus. In this context, law institutes a relationship between conflicting sides of a pluralistic interaction. Consequently, the absence of a treaty in Australia *undermines* the prospect of reconciliation between indigenous and settler societies, since politics lacks a stable ground that the institution of common expectations establishes. However, a legal constitution renders conflict resolvable by reducing contingency, which is the enabling condition of politics. As such, a legal constitution forecloses the opportunity to contest the terms within which such a relationship is determined. Thus, because the legal constitution of South Africa presupposes that the conflict of the past will turn out to be communal, it cannot represent an objection that might call into question the legitimacy of this community in the first place (see Schaap, 2006).

Following Arendt, there can be no collective subject that pre-exists the act of constitution. Rather, this 'we' emerges from political interaction. Since the possibility of this 'we' depends on its ongoing actualisation through public action and speech, a legal constitution cannot guarantee community. As a foundational act, the constitution invites the risk and promise of politics by establishing reconciliation

---

forward in the period leading up to and after the 1988 Bicentenary of European settlement/ invasion ... In effect, the formal reconciliation process was the best that Australian political parties could agree to in response to the assertion of unrelinquished sovereignty on the part of Australian indigenous people. The re-emergence of the demand for a treaty at the end of this process shows that many indigenous people will reject any attempt at reconciliation which does not recognise their claim to sovereignty.'

as a 'joint enterprise in time' (Bankowski, in this volume). As foundational law, however, it elides both by institutionalising the terms within which reconciliation is to be enacted such that any conflict which might call into question the legitimacy of community fails to register as meaningful. The ethical constitution of a 'we', then, cannot be entrusted solely to the 'rule of law', but ultimately depends on the willingness 'to live together with others in the mode of acting and speaking' (Arendt, 1998, p. 246).

The possibility of reconciliation thus depends on forsaking the certainty of law for the risk of politics. As such, the attempt to enact a new beginning in the present and to memorialise this beginning by promising 'never again' always involves a leap of faith. It politicises reconciliation by inculcating an awareness that there is no inevitability to community; that the conflict of the past might turn out to drive communities further apart than bring them closer together. Yet, invoking community as a contingent future possibility also enables a reconciliatory politics in the present by projecting a horizon in terms of which former enemies *might* eventually arrive at a shared understanding of the significance of past wrongs for their political association.

Bibliography

Ackerman, Bruce (1992), *The Future of the Liberal Revolution*, New Haven: Yale University Press.

Arendt, Hannah (1958), *The Origins of Totalitarianism*, 2nd edn, London: Allen & Unwin.

Arendt, Hannah (1964), 'Personal responsibility under dictatorship', *The Listener,* 6 August, 185–187, 205. Recently republished in *Responsibility and Judgment*, Jerome Kohn (ed.), New York: Schocken Books, 2003.

Arendt, Hannah (1965), *On Revolution*, London: Penguin.

Arendt, Hannah (1968), *Men in Dark Times*, New York and London: Harcourt Brace and Company.

Arendt, Hannah (1977), *Between Past and Future: Eight Exercises in Political Thought*, Harmondsworth: Penguin.

Arendt, Hannah (1977), *The Life of the Mind II: Willing*, in one volume edition, Mary McCarthy (ed.), New York and London: Harcourt Brace and Co.

Arendt, Hannah (1996), *Love and Saint Augustine*, in J V Scott and J C Stark (eds), Chicago and London: University of Chicago Press.

Arendt, Hannah (1998), *The Human Condition*, 2nd edn. Chicago: University of Chicago Press.

Atria, Fernando (in this volume), 'Reconciliation and Reconstitution'.

Bankowski, Zenon (in this volume), 'The Risk of Reconciliation'.

Bhandar, Brenna (in this volume), '"Spatializing History" and Opening Time: Resisting the Reproduction of the Proper Subject'.

Buckler, Steve (2001), 'The curtailment of memory: Hannah Arendt and post-Holocaust culture', *The European Legacy*, **6** (3), 287–303.

Burns, Robert (1987), 'Hannah Arendt's Constitutional Thought', in J Bernauer (ed.) *Amor Mundi: Explorations in the Faith and Thought of Hannah Arendt*, Dordrecht: Martinus Nijhoff.

Christodoulidis, Emilios (2000), '"Truth and reconciliation" as risks', *Social and Legal Studies*, **9** (2), 179–204.

Christodoulidis, Emilios (2001), 'The aporia of sovereignty: on the representation of the people in constitutional discourse', *King's College Law Journal*, **12**, 111–133.

Christodoulidis, Emilios (2003), 'Constitutional irresolution: law and the framing of civil society', *European Law Journal*, **9** (4), 401–432.

Clark, Geoff (2000), 'Not Much Progress', in M. Grattan (ed.), *Reconciliation: Essays on Australian Reconciliation*, Melbourne: Black Inc.

Connerton, Paul (1989), *How Societies Remember*, Cambridge: Cambridge University Press.

de Lange, Johnny (2000), 'The Historical Context, Legal Origins and Philosophical Foundations of the South African Truth and Reconciliation Commission', in C. Villa-Vicencio and W. Verwoerd (eds), *Looking Back Reaching Forward: Reflections on the Truth and Reconciliation Commission of South Africa*, London: Zed Books.

Di Paolantonio, Mario (1997), 'Argentina after the "Dirty War": reading the limits of national reconciliation', *Alternatives*, **22**(4), 433–465.

Derrida, Jacques (1986), 'Declarations of independence', *New Political Science*, **15**, 7–15.

Hayner, Priscilla B (2002), *Unspeakable Truths: Confronting State Terror and Atrocity*, New York and London: Routledge.

Holmes, Stephen (1988), 'Precommitment and the Paradox of Democracy', in J Elster and R Slagstad (eds), *Constitutionalism and Democracy*, Cambridge: Cambridge University Press.

Honig, Bonnie (1991), 'Declarations of independence: Arendt and Derrida on the problem of founding a republic', *American Political Science Review*, **85** (1), 97–114.

Keating, Paul (2000), 'The Redfern Park Speech', in M. Grattan (ed.) *Reconciliation: Essays on Australian Reconciliation*, Melbourne: Black Inc.

Keenan, Alan (1994), 'Promises, promises: the abyss of freedom and the loss of the political in the work of Hannah Arendt', *Political Theory*, **22** (2), 297–322.

Kalyvas, Andreas (2004), 'From the act to the decision: Hannah Arendt and the question of decisionism', *Political Theory*, **32** (3), 320–346.

Lefort, Claude (1988), 'The Permanence of the Theologico-Political?' in *Democracy and Political Theory*, Cambridge: Polity Press, pp. 213–255.

Lindahl, Hans (2003), 'Acquiring a community: the acquis and the institution of European legal order', *European Law Journal*, **9** (4), 464–481.

Lindahl, Hans (forthcoming), 'Give and take: Arendt and the nomos of political community', *Philosophy and Social Criticism*.

Patton, Paul (2001), 'Reconciliation, Aboriginal rights and constitutional paradox in Australia', *Australian Feminist Law Journal*, **15** (1), 25–40.

Pitkin, Hannah Fenichel (1987), 'The idea of a constitution', *Journal of Legal Education*, **37**, 167–169.

Ricouer, Paul (1965), 'The Political Paradox', in *History and Truth*, Evanston: North Western University Press, pp. 247–270.

Ricoeur, Paul (1983), 'Action, story and history: on re-reading *The Human Condition*', *Salmagundi*, **60**, 60–72.

Roermund, Bert van (1996), 'The concept of representation in parliamentary democracy', *Current Legal Theory*, **14** (1), 31–52.

Roermund, Bert van (2001), 'Rubbing Off and Rubbing On: The Grammar of Reconciliation', in E Christodoulidis and S Veitch (eds), *Lethe's Law: Justice, Law and Ethics in Reconciliation*, Oxford and Portland: Hart Publishing.

Roermund, Bert van (2003a), 'Sovereignty: Popular and Unpopular', in Neil Walker (ed.), *Sovereignty in Transition*, Oxford and Portland: Hart Publishing.

Roermund, Bert van (2003b), 'First-person plural legislature: political reflexivity and representation', *Philosophical Explorations*, **6** (3), 235–250.

Roermund, Bert van (forthcoming), 'Never again: time frames in anamnesis and reconciliation', paper presented at the colloquium on *Law, Time and Reconciliation*, Rand Afrikaans University, Johannesburg, December, 2004.

Rowse, Tim (2002), 'Treaty talk 2002: notes on three conferences', *Arena Magazine* **62** (Dec), 30–37.

Schaap, Andrew (2005), *Political Reconciliation*, London and New York: Routledge.

Schaap, Andrew (2006), 'Agonism in divided societies', *Philosophy and Social Criticism* 32 (2) 255–277.

Tamineaux, Jacques (2000), 'Athens and Rome', in D. Villa (ed.), *The Cambridge Companion to Hannah Arendt*, Cambridge: Cambridge University Press.

Teitel, Ruti (2000), *Transitional Justice*, Oxford and New York: Oxford University Press.

Whelan, Frederick G. (1983), 'Prologue: Democratic Theory and the Boundary Problem', in J. Roland Pennock and John W. Chapman (eds), *Liberal Democracy*, New York and London: New York University Press.

Wolin, Sheldon (1961), *Politics and Vision: Continuity and Change in Western Political Thought*, London: George Allen & Unwin.

Chapter 2

Reconciliation and Reconstitution

Fernando Atria[1]

Only he who has measured the dominion of force, and knows
not to respect it, is capable of love and justice
Simone Weil, *The Iliad, or The Poem of Force* (1940)

In many of the countries that have undergone processes of what is called 'transitional justice' the fundamental aim has been to achieve *reconciliation*. It is not a coincidence that most of the bodies created to 'come to terms' with a past of terror have 'reconciliation' in their titles. But what exactly is reconciliation? What is its relation to concepts like forgiveness, forgetting and punishment? In this essay I would like to consider some of the issues involved in answering these questions.

Why worry?

We begin by noticing that reconciliation is a concept that has been taken from non-political domains: theology and personal relationships are the most obvious. 'God reconciled the world to himself in Christ' says Paul in the Second Epistle to the Corinthians (2 Corinthians 5:19). Reconciliation here is the restoration of God's relationship with humankind that had been broken by sinful humanity. But what exactly is the connection between Jesus' death on the Cross and the restoration of God's relationship with humankind? Why was it necessary for him to die so that the relationship could be restored? Why couldn't God simply forgive humankind? We shall see that there are different answers to these questions, and that they differ in the way in which they understand the idea of reconciliation. These different religious understandings of reconciliation are mirrored by different understandings of reconciliation in politics, and in particular the role that punishment and forgiveness play in it. Understanding the religious notion of reconciliation will turn out to be highly relevant for the formulation of a political conception of it.

---

1   This paper has been funded by the Chilean council for scientific development (FONDECyT, proyecto 1010461).

Since the early 1990s, reconciliation was the concept used to express the hope that societies could emerge after a period of terror and somehow 'come to terms' with that particular piece of their past. The concept of reconciliation rose to political relevance in the midst of what were probably the most dangerous, passionate and consequential conflicts of the time. But, of course, there is little time or use in theoretical reflection in the midst of a passionate and dangerous conflict, and this is the reason why the concept of reconciliation was usually alluded to as a sort of wild card, with every party claiming that whatever was in their interest (usually, oblivion in the case of perpetrators, punishment in the case of the victims) was what reconciliation 'really' demanded.

This is why an examination of the political notion of reconciliation is necessary. The reason for this necessity is not the now rather discredited idea of early analytical philosophy who claimed that clarifying the meaning of words was the way to solve all philosophical controversies. Political conflicts over terms like reconciliation are not disputes over the meaning of words. Hence the analytical philosopher's recipe to solve all disputes is of no avail in the political realm. The reason why the use of the idea of reconciliation as a sort of political wild card is a problem is that we need to have some idea as to what reconciliation is if we are going to pass judgement on whether all the effort invested on achieving reconciliation was successful. This in turn is important because in politics, for something to be the case, it is usually necessary and sometimes even sufficient that citizens of a particular *polis* think it to be the case: a *polis* is reconciled when its members believe it to be reconciled, and reconciliation has failed if citizens believe it to have failed.

Therefore, when post-transitional societies look back at the transitional times, and try to ascertain what was done and how that affects what is to be done in the future, the question of what reconciliation is will turn out to be crucial, insofar as in most transitional societies one of the most important goals of transitional politics was indeed to achieve reconciliation. This is why a political notion of reconciliation is important, and this chapter endeavours to provide some criteria from where we can look back, this time not to terror, but to our efforts to get reconciled to each other, and ascertain what has been done and what is to be done in this regard. But let us begin by outlining three objections.

Objection 1   A mystic delusion

Tomás Moulian, one of the most respected Chilean intellectuals, has defended the view that reconciliation is not a decent political goal, that there is no reason for victims to reconcile with their perpetrators, and that all the 'reconciliation-talk' is a pernicious 'mystic delusion':

> There won't be any reconciliation. In the first place, reconciliation is a bad word. Reconciliation is brotherhood. That is to say, it is for two brothers that were separated by some conflict, but recognise the fact that they share the same history and the same blood. Pinochetists and anti-Pinochetists, however, don't share the same blood. Reconciliation is

a fake subject. Granted, we have to learn to tolerate each other, but I have no reason why I should love the torturer. No. It is simply a mystic delusion. It is a concept from theological discourse that has been displaced to political discourse. We can say that we need to be able to live in peace, for ethical and practical reasons, so that there won't be any more killing. I am not the son of a disappeared, but I am not reconciling with those who killed or tortured them. No, I am not reconciling.[2]

Moulian touches upon many of the themes I would like to discuss in this chapter. He is right in saying that reconciliation was originally a religious rather than a political concept. But he assumes that the content of the religious concept was retained as it moved to the political domain. If the argument to be deployed in this chapter is correct, it is this assumption, rather than the very idea of reconciliation, that ought to be rejected.

As is common in the comparative literature, Moulian understands political reconciliation in terms of something other than itself: reconciliation in politics is like reconciliation in personal relations (among lovers, spouses, friends or relatives) or in religion (with God), and to be *politically* reconciled victims need to learn to establish a new relationship with the perpetrators. The question is: why would victims accept this new relationship? When we speak of reconciliation in terms of personal relationships, we can assume (as Moulian assumes) that the parties to be reconciled have something in common both of them care about: typically they love each other and because of this they will be willing to forgive the other or forget his or her offence. Moulian talks about brothers, others about spouses or friends (see, for example, Govier, 2002, pp. 141–142; Van Zyl, 2000, p. 70). The same can be said about reconciliation in a religious sense between God and mankind: God loves mankind, indeed He loves them so much that He is willing to sacrifice His son to make reconciliation possible. (Or is He? We shall return to this issue shortly.) When we look at reconciliation from this viewpoint Moulian's argument seems overwhelming: we can very well expect victims not to take justice into their own hands, hence we can expect them to respect the physical integrity of perpetrators, but can we expect them to *love* them? Why would it be good for victims to love them? Moulian's conclusion seems obvious: reconciliation is a fake term, it is simply a mystical delusion.

And yet the issue is not so obvious. I will try to explain why I believe Moulian's thesis to be mistaken, precisely because he thinks that the content of the idea of reconciliation is invariable across the different domains he identified. There is something in virtue of which religious and personal and political reconciliation are all related notions, but they mean different things, and these differences make all the difference.

---

2   In an interview to www.elperiodista.cl.

Objection 2   Indecent symmetry

The second criticism of the very idea of reconciliation as a political *desideratum* has been neatly formulated by the Argentinian political philosopher Ernesto Garzón Valdés. Rather than being concerned by the religious nature of the idea of reconciliation, as Moulian was, Garzón (2000, p. 312) believes that reconciliation 'presupposes by definition the guilt of the parties that are reconciled, the existence of reciprocal offences'.[3] For Garzón, reconciliation is the coming together of two parties that have wronged each other, each one forgiving the other's offence and agreeing to re-establish a 'symmetrical relationship' (p. 312) for the future.

After explaining his understanding of the idea of reconciliation, Garzón quite legitimately rejects it: 'after the overthrow of a terrorist government, no collective reconciliation can be proposed' (p. 312). Garzón is scandalised by statements like that of General Bignone, the last of the Generals to rule Argentina, who reacted to the criticism of the role of the military in the terror by retorting, 'Let him who is without blame cast the first stone.' Garzón's sympathies here are with former Argentinean President Arturo Illia, who replied from his home town of Cordoba, 'my hands are full of stones' (p. 312). In Garzón's view, any talk of reconciliation after terror is straightforwardly immoral, because it equates the moral standing of those who committed atrocious and barbaric acts and those who suffered them, victims and perpetrators (1996, p. 313):

> I have always believed that the appeal to the idea of reconciliation is deceitful and frustrating; it opens up the way of impunity for the guilty, and places the innocent under a shadow of blame.

Given his understanding of the concept of reconciliation, Garzón's rejection of it seems guaranteed. Indeed, if reconciliation is what Garzón believes it to be, it seems to be not only *not* a political *desideratum*, but an abominable idea. I will argue that Garzón is mistaken in his understanding of reconciliation, that reconciliation is indeed a symmetrical process but not one in which we accept that in a way we are all perpetrators, but victims.

Objection 3   Forgiveness

The final objection to the idea of reconciliation I want to consider is based on the identification (partial or otherwise) of the idea of reconciliation with that of forgiveness. If for victim and perpetrator to reconcile with each other victims need to *forgive* perpetrators, then a host of questions present themselves: *can* acts of torture or political killing (etc) be forgiven? Can the rest of us, those who were not directly involved as victims or perpetrators, demand or even *expect* victims to forgive? If the

---

3   The idea that reconciliation is symmetrical in this sense is shared by Margalit, 'Is truth the road to reconciliation?', p. 63.

evil performed by the perpetrators is not a private evil, are victims *entitled* to forgive? Eventually, this last question seems to lead to another: who is to forgive? That is to say, who has been wronged? Can any person living in a society that underwent terror say that they have not been wronged?

Additionally, is there a political notion of forgiveness? Forgiveness seems to be a moral, personal act. One forgives for the sake of someone, the victim forgives the wrongdoer for the wrongdoer's sake. Hannah Arendt (1958) argued that because forgiving is always something done for the sake of the forgiven, some sort of relationship between the forgiving and the forgiven must exist. For Arendt, it had to be either love or respect (pp. 242–243). But why would a person who has suffered at the hands of another some act of unspeakable cruelty be moved to respect, let alone love, the other? Arendt herself accepted that to ground forgiveness upon respect was becoming increasingly difficult in the modern world, where respect 'is due only when we admire or esteem' (p. 243); maybe this was the reason why Arendt concluded that what she called 'radical evil' (p. 241) could not be forgiven (I will return to this later). If this was becoming increasingly difficult, it seems that we must reject not the *possibility* of forgiveness for the cases we are considering, but the claim that forgiveness, as reconciliation, is a reasonable goal to aim for.

Perhaps, however, we can draw a line between the personal and the political before reaching the conclusion that reconciliation is an impossible political goal. Perhaps Arendt's argument only means that, *insofar as reconciliation is the consequence of forgiveness*, there is no possibility of reconciliation in a society that has experienced radical evil. Thus to discuss reconciliation in politics it ought to be disentangled from the idea of forgiveness. And indeed, there is no reason to understand reconciliation in politics as it is understood in personal relations, between lovers or friends; reconciliation as forgiveness is a particular case of reconciliation, it is reconciliation among those who love each other. I will claim that in fact there is no connection between the political notion of reconciliation and the personal notion of forgiveness; or indeed, that there is nothing to forgive in the doer, that the doer, like the victim but in a different sense, must be pitied. The process of realising that the doer must be pitied rather than punished or forgiven is the process of reconciliation. Reconciliation not only does not presuppose forgiveness; it actually shows that there is no space for forgiveness.

How can the killing of the Son reconcile us to the Father?

Jesus' coming, and particularly his death on the Cross, was a reconciling event; before that, we were enemies of God, as Paul says in his letter to the Romans, and we were reconciled to Him through the death of his son (Paul 5:10). But what is the meaning of this 'through'? Why did Jesus' death contribute to our reconciliation with God? I would like to consider two possible answers to this question, and then relate them to two different conceptions of reconciliation.

The first understands the passion through the eyes of criminal law: someone had to pay for humankind's sins, and out of love Jesus offered himself as a substitute: Jesus as the sacrificial victim offered to God in substitution of mankind. We can call this reading of the passion the 'sacrificial' reading, insofar as it understand Christ's suffering on the cross as a vicarious form of punishment to mankind.

What is difficult to understand in this reading is the reason why the Father would insist on his son's vicarious punishment: why was it the case that Jesus *had* to die on the Cross so that God could be reconciled to mankind? The sacrificial reading seems caught up in notions of revenge and retribution, notions that in this case seem to be at odds with what a loving father would expect or demand from his son.

In the sacrificial reading, reconciliation is reached through expiation. There is no possibility of reconciliation without some form of suffering, in the form of some victim, compensating for the evil already done. Indeed this reading is incompatible with the gratuitous nature of God's love for humanity. It presents God as a kind of sadist, who is willing to insist on His right to get *something* in return for the forgiveness He is conditionally willing to grant.

An alternative, non-sacrificial reading understands the passion as something necessary for mankind *learning something about itself* that would allow it to get reconciled with God. In this case Jesus' death on the Cross would be necessary not because the father demanded it as a right (the right of the aggrieved to see the perpetrator punished, or – as in this case, and more implausibly – to see *someone* punished for the perpetrator's crime), not because of the existence of some metaphysical imbalance between the evil done and the punishments received, but because of what it actually *is* to be reconciled.

One possible non-sacrificial reading is that defended by Rene Girard. According to Girard, no communal life among intelligent beings, such as human beings, is possible without some mechanism for reducing and preventing self-destructive violence. Self-destructive violence, in the form of *mimetic conflict*, is bound to arise in all forms of communal life among humans, and thus only those communities that have found a way to deal with, prevent, channel and control it, can hope to survive. The process by which conflict arises starts with what Girard calls *acquisitive mimesis*: A desires an object X, and because A desires it B also desires it. This conflict is contagious (Girard, 1987, p. 26):

> ... and if the number of individuals polarised around a single object increases, other members of the community, as yet not implicated, will tend to follow the example of those who are.

Acquisitive mimesis leads to *conflictual mimesis*, in which 'the rivalry is purified of any external stake and becomes a matter of pure rivalry and prestige' (p. 26). Since there is no more acquisitive mimesis, conflict between the parties will not be about getting the object (all reference to external stakes has been removed), but simply about the antagonists themselves. Now this is a form of conflict which has the potential to destroy communal life. Therefore all forms of communal life we are familiar with have found a way to overcome it. The 'normal' way is the substitution of the antagonists: by substituting the antagonists, conflictual mimesis can tend to unity rather than division (p. 26):

> If *acquisitive mimesis* divides by leading two or more individuals to converge on one and the same object with a view to appropriating it, *conflictual mimesis* will inevitably unify by leading two or more individuals to converge on one and the same adversary that all wish to strike down.

All the conflictual mimesis of the antagonists, therefore, focuses upon one particular individual, one that is arbitrarily (and unconsciously) chosen by the warring parties. This convergence of everybody against the innocent victim unifies them. The height of conflict is reached when the arbitrary victim is killed. In contemplation of the dead body of the victim former antagonists realise that they are at peace now. But the working of the scapegoat mechanism is hidden to them: they do not realise what has happened, they just notice that by killing the victim the community regained peace. Girard sees in this the origin of myth, prohibitions and eventually all religions (p. 27):

> The observation of religious systems forces us to conclude (1) that mimetic crisis always occurs, (2) that the banding together of all against a single victim is the normal resolution at the level of culture, and (3) that it is furthermore the normative solution, because all the rules of culture stem from it.[4]

Myths, prohibitions, rituals and religion are, therefore, the group's attempt to perpetuate the pacifying effect of the original murder: 'human beings do not understand the mechanism responsible for their reconciliation; the secret of its effectiveness eludes them, which is why they attempt to reproduce the entire event as exactly as possible' (p. 28).

In this context, Girard notices a significant difference between biblical and non-biblical myths: 'biblical writers have an undeniable tendency to take the side of the victim on moral grounds, and to spring to the victim's defence' (p. 147).[5] In Rome's founding myth, for example, Remus is the victim, but he is not presented as fully innocent: he did transgress the rules of the city, by failing to respect the city's ideal limits as traced by Romulus. In the biblical stories, the founding victim is always innocent: Abel, Joseph, and so on. For Girard the theme that is being developed

---

4   Girard explains the point: to keep this newly regained state of peace, 'two principal imperatives must come to play. (1) Not to repeat any action associated with the crisis, to abstain from all mimicry, from all contact with the former antagonists, from any acquisitive gesture towards objects that have stood as causes or pretexts for rivalry. This is the imperative of the *prohibition*. (2) To reproduce, on the contrary, the miraculous event that put an end to the crisis, to immolate new victims substituted for the original victim in circumstances as close as possible to the original experience. This is the imperative of ritual' (Girard, *Things Hidden Since the Foundation of the World*, p. 28).

5   Girard refers to Weber's *Ancient Judaism*.

through the whole of the Old Testament is precisely the unearthing of the victimage mechanism, a process that will reach completion in the passion of Jesus. The reason why the passion is the completion of this progressive exposure of the mechanism is that in it the victim is presented as fully and radically innocent, as being the scapegoat through which communal conflict is resolved.[6] The story of the passion replays all myths, but with one crucial difference: when in myths the murdered is presented as guilty, as the one who is threatening the survival of the group and whose elimination causes the pacification of the group by eliminating the cause of discord, in the Gospels the victim is presented as fully innocent. The Gospel story is the story of all founding murders, told, for the first time, from the point of view of the victim. Jesus' passion is God's disclosure to mankind of the nature and working of the scapegoat mechanism, of the fact that all forms of human communal life, all forms of religions, are founded upon violence, upon murder of the innocent.

If we accept (something like) Girard's non-sacrificial reading of the passion, we shall see that the sacrificial reading is the reading of the Gospels as if it were simply another myth, another sacrificial murder: God and mankind reconciling themselves, 'coming together' on the strength of the murder of the innocent. But in Girard's non-sacrificial reading, reconciliation is made possible not by the sacrifice of the innocent victim, but by God's disclosing to mankind *something about mankind* that stands in the way of reconciliation, both of one another (of members of the group and the utterly innocent victim) and with God. The fundamental point about Jesus' life, including his death on the Cross, is that it brings into the open this human mechanism to deal with violence by blaming the innocent, thus robbing it of any virtuality, for the scapegoat mechanism works only insofar as it is hidden: 'awareness of these mechanisms is what decomposes them' (Girard, 1987, p. 128). The coming of the Lord, according to Girard, must be understood as God's attempt to reveal to humanity something about humanity, to reveal to us the fact that we live indeed under original sin (there is no Jewish doctrine of original sin): only *after* the passion we learn of the original sin (see, Alison, 1999), the sin of violence against the innocent that infects all our communal forms of life, i.e. all forms of human life. According to the non-sacrificial reading, what is important about the murder of Jesus is that it allows humanity to realise the original sin embedded in our forms of community: we learn something about ourselves by the passion, and once we learn it, *by* learning it, we are ready to reconcile both to our brothers (to the countless victims of human history) and also, consequentially, to God.

But reconciliation is contingent: there is no guarantee that the reconciling event will eventually reconcile the parties, and thus in the Gospels there are two parallel lines of preaching of Jesus: one announcing the coming of the Kingdom, if humans

---

6   Thus the conflict between Pilate and Herod disappears as they unite against Jesus the victim: 'That day Herod and Pilate became friends – before this they had been enemies' (Luke 23:12).

learn to lead communal lives without the scapegoat mechanism,[7] rendered useless by its disclosure in the passion of Jesus; and the other apocalyptic, announcing the end of the world, if humanity shows itself incapable of controlling violence once the scapegoat mechanism is unavailable (Girard, 1987, pp. 202–205).

The point I want to make is that in Christian religion there is a reconciliatory event, the radical meaning of which can be understood only when reconciliation is conceived as having to do not with punishment and expiation but with trying to understand the event as it discloses something about the reconciling parties. This is the idea that provides the key to understanding the political notion of reconciliation. We shall therefore be looking for an idea of reconciliation that is unashamedly Christian in origin, but which is conceived in specifically political terms, i.e. distinct both from the legal concept of punishment, the moral concept of forgiveness and the personal idea of love.

The symmetry of reconciliation

Hannah Arendt famously said that what she called 'radical evil' (1958, p. 241) could neither be forgiven nor punished. One of the reasons why it cannot be forgiven (I will come to punishment shortly) is that we cannot understand it (Arendt, 1994, p. 307).[8] Thus it seems that reconciliation in the aftermath of radical evil is impossible, or at least something extraordinarily pretentious: it amounts to the claim that we can not only understand but also forgive acts of radical evil, of inhuman treatment of fellow human beings.

Furthermore, casting the situation as one in which the crucial notion is forgiveness makes reconciliation impossible, for reconciliation is the re-discovery of the common humanity of victims and perpetrators, while forgiveness is necessarily a non-symmetrical relationship (this is Garzón's point, and is well taken). Forgiveness occurs when the moral standing of one party is superior to the other: victims and perpetrators are not on the same moral level. To emphasise the need for forgiveness can in this way be an obstacle rather than a goal for the restoration of the bonds of community between victims and perpetrators, because in this sense reconciliation is possible only among equals. As opposed to forgiveness, reconciliation is a symmetrical process, but the symmetry is not one that implies that victims are to blame for the acts of perpetrators.

Rights

I have avoided using the common label, 'human rights violations' to refer to terror. I do so because the very idea of *rights* distorts our problem, lending it a private

---

7   That is to say, by renouncing all violence: see Matthew 5:3–11 (the Sermon on the Mount).

8   I have discussed this issue in some detail in Atria, (2005).

nature that is at odds with the public notion of reconciliation I want to defend. The Chilean debate on reconciliation and reparation is a good example of the privatising effects of rights-talk (Atria, 2005). In general, the most pressing aspect of the issue of 'human rights violations' is addressing the situation of those who were affected by terror: people who were brutally harmed in the past whose predicament moves us (those who did not suffer such harm) to action. As in the case of victims of natural disasters, such as floods and earthquakes, their suffering interpellates us and moves us to action. This outburst of sympathy (Smith, 1984, p. 10) for those who have been badly harmed is explained because we feel their pain, but it is *their* pain. Once we have done what we can to ameliorate their suffering, we will not owe them anything for the remainder. Crucially, their suffering does not make us reflect about the basis of our communal bonds.

The rhetoric of rights also imposes its corresponding notion of reconciliation. Whatever *else* it is, a right is a protected individual interest. Therefore when a right is violated the relationship between the victim and the perpetrator can only be restored after the victim's harm is duly restored and the perpetrator has been either punished or forgiven by the victim. The private idea of rights thus imposes a private conception of reconciliation: it amounts to restoring the balance between victim and perpetrator, a balance that was broken by the latter's infringement of the former's rights. The balance is restored if the victim forgets the act, just as it is restored if the perpetrator is duly punished for his or her offence.

Politics

The political meaning of the idea of reconciliation is different. Politically speaking, reconciliation amounts to the re-discovery of the common humanity of victims and perpetrators. It implies understanding that in some non-obvious sense victim and perpetrator are victims (Weil, 1993, p. 11):

> Force is as pitiless to the man who possesses it, or thinks he does, as it is to its victims; the second it crushes, the first it intoxicates. The truth is, nobody really possesses it. The human race is not divided up, in *The Iliad*, into conquered persons, slaves, suppliants, on the one hand, and conquerors and chiefs on the other. In this poem there is not a single man who does not at one time or another have to bow his neck to force.

Nobody can read or hear about, say, torture sessions (or watch the merry faces of US soldiers in Iraq as they posed for those infamous pictures with naked bodies piled up in front of them) without asking him or herself: 'How was this possible?' It is a misunderstanding to read this question as asking for a sociological or psychological or historical answer (Gaita, 1998, p. 39). The question does not ask about the processes that led to terror, but about *agency*: 'How could a human being behave in this way towards another?' Now *this* question is 'a question without answer, and someone who offered … an answer would fail to understand' (p. 39) the nature of the question.

It is in this sense that Arendt was right in saying that we cannot understand these acts. But even if we cannot understand them we can ask what made them possible. And there is indeed an answer to this question, something that the twentieth century taught us in the hardest and clearest possible way: it was a situation governed by force, which intoxicates those who believe they control it, and crushes those who suffer it. Possession of force intoxicates the former into losing the capacity to that 'halt, that interval of hesitation, wherein lies all our considerations for our brothers in humanity' (Weil, 1993, p. 14). In *War and Peace* it is precisely this interval of hesitation that saved Pierre as he was going to be executed as a Russian spy under the orders of Davout:

> Davout looked up and gazed intently at him. For some seconds they looked at one another, and that look saved Pierre. Apart from conditions of war and law that look established human relations between the two men. At that moment an immense number of things passed dimly through both their minds, and they realised they were both children of humanity and were brothers.[9]

Davout was precisely not intoxicated by force, he hadn't lost the capacity for that 'interval of hesitation'. The intoxication to which Weil (1993) refers makes those who believe they control force lose the capacity to pause and recognise the humanity of the victim who lies at their feet, tied up and naked, and therefore, in a less obvious but real sense, robs them of their humanity: 'To the same degree, though in different fashions, those who use [force] and those who endure it are turned to stone' (p. 25).

To lose the ability to show that interval of hesitation is to lose the ability to recognise the other as human, which is (in a different fashion) to lose the ability to *be* human. A clear testimony of this dehumanisation is the statement made by Army Major Carlos Herrera during the trial which led to his conviction as author of the murder of union leader Tucapel Jiménez:

> As to the reasons he was given [to justify the order to murder the victim], he said that it was indispensable for the mission, because "Tucapel Jiménez was a traitor" and "given the circumstances of those years, that was enough; I did not need any further explanation".[10]

Reconciliation then is the possibility of seeing the perpetrators as victims in some sense, i.e. in the sense that they were turned into stone, de-humanised to the same degree, though in different fashions by their illusory belief that they controlled force. In this sense, then, they were victims of force.

The question then is: what can control force? How can we avoid being either crushed or intoxicated by force? I believe the answer here is in the notion of *power* (Arendt, 1969, p. 56):

---

9   Tolstoy, *War and Peace*, Book XII chapter 10. This passage is discussed, though in another context, by Detmold (1989, p. 457).

10   In *El Mercurio de Valparaíso*, 13 April 2002.

Politically speaking, it is insufficient to say that power and violence are not the same. Power and violence are opposite; where the one rules absolutely, the other is absent. Violence appears where power is in jeopardy, but left to its own course it ends in power's disappearance. This implies that it is not correct to think of the opposite of violence as non-violence; to speak of non-violent is actually redundant. Violence can destroy power; it is utterly incapable of creating it.

In brief: what stands in the way of force taking over, of human beings being either crushed or intoxicated into stone is the existence of power, i.e. the political. Only because we live under political conditions can we display that 'interval of hesitation' that makes us human.

> If we step aside for a passer-by on the road, it is not the same thing as stepping aside to avoid a billboard; alone in our rooms, we get up, walk about, sit down again quite differently from the way we do when we have a visitor. But this indefinable influence that the presence of another human being has on us is not exercised by men whom a moment of impatience can deprive of life, who can die before even thought has a chance to pass sentence of them (Weil, 1993, p. 7).

What this means – the lesson of the twentieth century mentioned earlier – is that fully human forms of life are highly artificial: 'perhaps all men, by the very act of being born, are destined to suffer violence' (p. 13); it is artificial for men and women to 'see their relations with other human beings as a kind of balance between unequal amounts of force' (p. 14). This is something we learn by living with others that do the same; hence when some realise others do not, they 'conclude that destiny has given complete license to them, and none at all to their inferiors' (p. 14). This explains why we cannot explain terror on the basis of the evil nature of the agents of terror, but on the fact that they lost the ability to see their victims as human, *because* they possess force (p. 14):

> The man who is the possessor of force seems to walk through a non-resistant element; in the human substance that surrounds him nothing has the power to interpose, between the impulse and the act, the tiny interval that is reflection. Where there is no room for reflection, there is none either for justice or prudence. Hence we see men in arms behaving harshly and madly. We see their sword bury itself in the breast of a disarmed enemy who is in the very act of pleading at their knees. We see them triumph over a dying man by describing to him the outrages his corpse will endure. We see Achilles cut the throats of twelve Trojan boys on the funeral pyre of Patroclus as naturally as we cut flowers for a grave.

Hence the only and obvious (though difficult) way in which we can live like human beings is to live in such a way that inter-individual relations will express a 'kind of balance between unequal amounts of force', and the only way in which this is possible is forming communities with others we recognise as equal. Thus, only under political conditions can we lead properly human lives. A process of reconciliation makes explicit this connection between human-ness and the political. Reconciliation thus is the re-discovery of the value of the political as *that* which we need in order to live human lives. But the political is contingent. There is no transcendental reassurance that it will not break down. All we can hope for is a *political* reassurance; and to provide this reassurance of the maintenance of the political is what reconciliation does.

Sacred things

Still, what does this understanding of reconciliation imply for our treatment of victims and perpetrators? There is no reason why we must give a blunt answer, covering all cases. The basic insight defended here is that perpetrators cannot be treated as if they had committed a similar crime under normal times. This is the reason why they cannot be punished, even if they are convicted. The notion of reconciliation I am trying to defend here implies that perpetrators are in a sense victims, and ought to be treated like that.

So we seem to be back to Garzón's objection, because it seems that reconciliation is indeed premised on some sort of symmetry between victims and wrongdoers. And again, Moulián, however willy-nilly, gives us the clue to the answer. Under a non-sacrificial reading of the passion of Christ, God reconciles with humanity not on the strength of Jesus' sacrifice (no violence, in any way, can be attributed to God in the Gospels: it always has a human origin), but by letting humanity see that in a sense all men and women are victims: victims of their own blindness to the fact that they live in communities constituted by murder. This does not imply symmetry between the sacrificed innocent victim and their unconscious sacrificers. It simply means that having witnessed the passion, we are now in a position to *understand* that we were blind and change our ways accordingly. So we must accept Garzón's objection but reject it by reversing it: we reconciled to each other not because we are all equally to blame, but because we are all, in varying degrees, victims (Weil, 1993, p. 19):

> Violence obliterates anybody who feels its touch. It comes to seem just as external to its employer as to its victim. And from this springs the idea of a destiny before which executioner and victim stand equally innocent, before which conquered and conqueror are brothers in the same distress.

The 'in varying degrees' is important because it points to the fact that reconciliation, as with all things political, is contingent. There is no transcendental reassurance that we will get reconciled (we have seen that in the Gospels the preaching of the Kingdom is paralleled by apocalyptic vision). When power is constituted again, and the political established or re-established, and thus normality regained, some perpetrators will come to realise the horror of what they did (as Major Herrera did), and their realisation of the significance of their deeds will make it possible for us to understand that they were victims and thus reconcile to them: they have been harmed by absence of power, by the situation in which they were deluded into believing that they controlled force. Some others will be unrepentant. Osvaldo Romo, one of

Chile's most notorious and merciless torturers, is still saying from his prison cell to the interviewing journalist: 'if I am told to cut your throat I'll do it right here, right now' (Guzmán, 2000, p. 40). How can we reconcile with them? If they believe *now* what they did to be right, it can only be because the intoxication they suffered was too severe, and thus it robbed them not only temporarily but permanently of their capacity for that interval of hesitation. What they were robbed of, in other words, is the capacity to be in the world as a human being, to *be* human: they have been turned into things (Arendt, 1994, p. 279):

> From [force's] first property (the ability to turn a human being into a thing by the simple method of killing him) flows another, quite prodigious too in its own way, the ability to turn a human being into a thing while he is still alive. He is alive; he has a soul; and yet – he is a thing. An extraordinary entity this – a thing that has a soul. And for the soul, what an extraordinary house it finds itself in!

There is a sense, therefore, in which the worst victims of terror are the Osvaldo Romos of this world, those who lost their human lives and yet did not die. They are most extraordinary entities, things with souls. How should we treat them? Hannah Arendt thought that, since 'no member of the human race can be expected to want to share the earth' with them, they must hang. But actually, we have a duty (to us, not to them, because one cannot have duties towards things) to treat them as sacred things. *Sacred*, because they have souls, but *things*, because they cannot be human anymore.

Bibliography

Alison, J. (1999), *The Joy of Being Wrong*, New York, NY: Crossroad Herder.

Arendt, H. (1958), *The Human Condition*, Chicago, IL: University of Chicago Press.

Arendt, H. (1969), *On Violence*, San Diego, CA: Harcourt Brace and Company.

Arendt, H. (1994), 'Understanding and Politics (the Difficulties of Understanding)', in J. Kohn (ed), *Arendt. Essays in Understanding*, New York: Hartcourt Brace & Co., pp. 307–327.

Arendt, H. (1994), *Eichmann in Jerusalem. A report on the banality of evil*, London: Penguin; original edn. 1963.

Atria, F. (2005), 'The time of law. Human rights between law and politics', *Law and Critique* **16**, 139–159.

Detmold, M. J. (1989), 'Law as practical reason', *Cambridge Law Journal* **48**, 436–471.

Gaita, R. (1998), *A Common Humanity*, London: Routledge.

Garzón Valdés, E. (2000), *El Velo de la Ilusión*, Buenos Aires: Sudamericana.

Girard, R. (1987), *Things Hidden Since the Foundation of the World*, London: The Athlone Press.

Govier, T. (2002), *Forgiveness and Revenge*, London: Routledge.

Guzmán, N. (2000), *Osvaldo Romo. Confesiones de un Torturador*, Santiago: Planeta.

Margalit, A. (2002), 'Is Truth the Road to Reconciliation?', in O. Enwezor, C. Basualdo, U. M. Bauer, S. Ghez, S. Maharaj, M. Nash Y. O. Zaya (eds), *Experiments with Truth*, The Hague: Hatje Cantz, pp. 61–64.

Smith, A. (1984), *The Theory of Moral Sentiments*, Indianapolis: Liberty Fund, original edn. 1759.

Van Zyl, F. (2000), 'Truth Without Reconciliation, Reconciliation Without Truth', in W. James Y. L. Van De Vijver (eds.): *After the TRC. Reflections on Truth and Reconciliation in South Africa*, Athens, OH: Ohio University Press.

Weil, S. (1940), *The Iliad, or the Poem of Force*, Wallingford, PA, London: Pendle Hill, original edn. 1940.

Chapter 3

The Risk of Reconciliation

Zenon Bankowski

Introduction

In this chapter I want to look at some of our responses to questions of reconciliation, of how we respond to wrongs that we or our society has committed, or is committing. In what manner do we take responsibility for them so that we can go forward in the difficult and risky business of building connectedness both in our individual and societal relationships? Though much of what I have to say emphasises the risky and vulnerable forward-looking nature of this enterprise, its reflexivity and refusal to decomplexify, this is not to say that it is incompatible with law. The enterprise of reconciliation and law are not, as Emilios Christodoulidis (2000) claims, different modalities that contaminate each other. In his article on reconciliation and the Truth and Reconciliation Committee (TRC) for example, he sees some of the problems of that institution as its close connection with law. For him, put very broadly, law looks to the past to create a story that will make the world simple while reconciliation looks to the future, something that will make the world risky. Since the TRC used the language of the law it disguises that risk and makes it impossible to deal with.

Part of what law does, he says, is to construct a mythical community, a mythical 'we' which it then tries to save and restore. But how can you talk about a 'we' when there was no common past but different narratives? How can two mutually exclusive narratives provide the common 'we' from which we can go forward? Most importantly this gets the whole project of reconciliation off on the wrong foot – since it assumes that that perfected past can perform reintegration when all it does is hide conflict, and perhaps create new exclusions.[1] An example of this might be seen also in the way some lawyers in Post-Apartheid South Africa have seen the Roman-Dutch Law – as part of a common heritage that can now, again purified, help create and reintegrate the 'we' of a purified community.[2]

---

1   Thus, for example, we might create another narrative of excluded white segregationists. This is dangerous since apartheid Afrikaner identity, it could be argued, was constructed from such a narrative (see the second section).

2   See van der Merwe (1998) and van der Walt (1998). Such a view is shared by other small jurisdictions which recreate a joint myth of the Roman-Dutch Family. See Zimmerman and Visser (1996).

What this does is try to produce a legal accounting of the past which hides the possibility of disintegration and turns activity away from the risky task of building community. Thus, as Christodoulidis claims, a law-infected institution like the TRC fails to produce a collective memory to sustain the reconciled community because it inserts an *a priori* community when there was none and thus turns collected memories into collective memories.

I agree with much of what Christodoulidis says when he carefully describes what can go wrong. But to say this does not mean that one has to accept his conclusions about the distinct modalities of law and reconciliation and the appropriateness of each. In what follows much of what I say will emphasise the future orientation and the risk of the process, but I will not thereby exclude it from the law.

Remorse, the self and history

I begin with a point Rowan Williams (2000) makes about remorse, which illustrates some of these problems. Remorse is a 'joint enterprise' because one needs to recognise what one did and wherever we might have been in the past, in this time we are together. This is necessary because otherwise one has a self which has no sense of how it has been unavoidably formed by its various actions and actions of others that have impinged on it in the world – the consequences of which are not always in its control. I have to see myself enmeshed in history and being made in this process. My identity is in part not in my control since it rests in the sometimes difficult ways that others see and deal with me. Remorse does not bring time to a standstill – we do not start again for we are a product of these choices. This implies that though forgiveness is important it is not the most important part of reconciliation – the need for the other is not to forgive so much as to join in the risky business of constructing the self and society; of refusing to put the self beyond challenge.

Remorse then is not a matter of just repairing my timeless ahistorical self. But, Williams goes on, we live in time and we have to realise that we are implicated in all sorts of choices. We cannot stop history and start again – it is about living through the consequences of what has happened in the present. This can be risky and dangerous and we might be killed in opening up the dialogue but that is what we have to do. He illustrates this in a short story by George Steiner. In this the protagonist, a German soldier, returns to Normandy where he was stationed during the war and goes to where he was billeted and where he was responsible for the execution of the son of the family. He wants to marry the daughter of the family. To soften the tension he talks of the time during the fire bombing of Hamburg where he had to shoot a woman dying of phosphorus burns (he believes this was his sister). He also says that in Normandy he was able to escape from this horror. No reparation is possible for the killing of the brother but there must be something that will not just start off the cycle of violence. He says (cited in Williams, 2000, pp. 107–108):

… On the contrary. It's much simpler to stiffen in silence or hate. Hate keeps warm. That's child's play. It would have been much simpler for me to die in Hamburg near the canal …

Do you think it's easy to come back here? In Germany we don't talk about the past. We all have amnesia or perhaps someone put an iron collar around our necks so that we can't look back. That's one way of doing it. Then there's the other, the unrelenting way. Steep yourself in the remembered horrors. Build them round you like a high safe wall. Is that any less easy or dishonest?

She lashed out 'God knows I wish the past didn't exist! I didn't ask for these memories did I? You forced them down our throats ... and now you come and tell us we should forget and live for the future. You're spitting on graves.[3]

They agree to a marriage and the night after the ceremony he is set upon by some local youths, including his new brother-in-law, and kicked to death.

The impartiality of the world

The sacred victim

Apart from the risky and hard nature of remorse, Steiner's nuanced, ambiguous and troubling story offers no certainties. We see that 'joint enterprise' means just that, and no-one can or should escape the consequences of putting their own identity in question. This applies as much to the victim as the oppressor – both can put the self and community beyond question and construct it *a priori* and mythically and help to restart the cycle of violence.

The self, Williams (2000, ch. 3) goes on, lives in time and we make a self by telling a story. But every time we tell a story about ourselves that self changes because that is another story in time. That process requires both sides because, if we are not to be oppressors again, then we must not see the other selves as competitors but rather as partners in the often fractious struggle of producing an identity. What this implies is that we cannot concentrate too much on rights for then we become competitors and not collaborators. This concentration on rights, seen as part of a concentration solely on reparations, makes it appear that we can assuage everything within a timeless historical frame; the timeless subject that is owed something. The self and identity become invulnerable again. In that sense the oppressed become similar to the oppressor who refuses remorse for they retire behind the protection of their identity and are not willing to risk it in the tricky and risky business of negotiating and thus creating and recreating a modified identity. Victimhood cannot be something that is pure and making of the victim holy. Resting secure in your victimhood defines your identity as timeless and unwilling to engage. The political consequences of that can be disastrous. The Afrikaner view of things (in itself quite justified) was constructed through their view of their victim status at the hands of the British. This also applies to the Middle East. Placing the Holocaust out of time and making Israel always the eternal victim means we cannot live in the politics of time

---

3   Quoted in Williams pp. 107–108.

and place in the Middle East. Williams quotes Gillian Rose. For her the appropriate response to the Holocaust is: 'How easily could I have let this happen?' rather than identification with the pain of the victims and anguish as to my responsibility. For it is only then that we can have a language to deal with the complexity of the issues at the level of public policy. To see some of this natural evil as a manifestation of a plan, divine or otherwise is a form of idolatry, to give it a significance it does not possess. But it also then gives us a significance that we do not possess; for giving the event a meaning singles us out as the recipients of that meaning as something special because we have been singled out that way. This gives us a sense of superiority as ones singled out, our victimhood gives us special status. And, as we saw above, politically this makes us something special, impervious to criticisms since we are marked out as sacred victims. Our selves become invulnerable. Williams puts it like this (p. 126):

> If the Holocaust somehow takes us beyond language and politics, the actions of the remnant community are outside law and negotiation and the recognition of self in the other, and it is no use trying to discuss collective regional security, presupposition about historical rights of residence on the part of non-Jewish people, politically defensible frontiers or any kindred matters.

Metaphysical guilt

The above is not to say that we should not think of responsibility and identification for that might help us move towards committing ourselves, or 'staking ourselves' as Williams puts it. This is illuminated in the way Karl Jaspers (1971) characterises German guilt and responsibility in the aftermath of the Third Reich. Jaspers differentiates political liability, the political consequences of the actions which we have now to live with and are liable for; criminal guilt, which can affect those who in defined circumstances can be found guilty of acts of atrocity, war crimes and so on; and moral guilt. He shows the different ways in which people might have been complicit. Finally, after exhausting all that, there is the idea of metaphysical guilt (Jaspers, 1971, p. 46):

> But there is within us a guilt consciousness which springs from another source. Metaphysical guilt is the lack of absolute solidarity with the human being as such – an indelible claim beyond moral meaningful duty. This solidarity is violated by my presence at a wrong or crime. It is not enough that I cautiously risk my life to prevent it; if it happens, and if I was there, and if I survive where the other is killed, I know from a voice within myself: I am guilty of still being alive.

This might, as Jaspers himself says, appear like the obscure metaphysical ravings of a German professor, which, if we and the oppressed take seriously, will drag us into the pit painted by Rose and Williams. What Jaspers is getting at however is that the one appropriate reaction to this evil or disaster is to die with everyone else and we did not. The fact of survival makes one's ethical status problematic. Think of the attitudes of survivors from the camps – one of the common reactions was guilt in that they survived and others did not. But we can move this away from the liminal cases that we have been discussing and on to matters that affect us now. This is one way that one can make sense of what sort of responsibility we might bear, for example, for Third World hunger. We might distinguish political liability, and criminal guilt and also moral responsibility, as Jaspers did in the German case. But beyond that is something that is akin to the notion of metaphysical guilt which does not bear responsibility in those ways but is still there as the ethical surplus. What I mean by that is the fact that we are well fed and alive and others are not, that we survive and they do not; the quotation from Jaspers is entirely appropriate. We should not thereby be consumed by a narcissistic guilt that is politically unproductive and morally problematic as we saw above. But again it should not be the case that we should treat our situation as completely unproblematic. Indeed one might say there is something ethically worrying about someone who does not see their situation as problematic in this way.

Force and affliction

How does this observation link up to our discussion above? Firstly, it means that we have to recognise that there is nothing special about us that allows us to survive, it is not our merit that marks us out, rather it is our luck that the juggernaut did not hit us this time. We can make sense of this if we consider Simone Weil (1986) in her essay *The Iliad: A Poem of Force*.[4] The true hero of the Iliad according to her is not Achilles or any of the heroes but the concept of force. She sees all in thrall to the relentless juggernaut of force – at times some benefit from it and at times they suffer. Thus Greeks and Trojans alike are both victims and oppressors riding and being ridden by force (Weil, 1986, p. 171):

> Force is as pitiless to the man who possesses it, or thinks he does, as it is to its victims; the second it crushes, the first it intoxicates. The truth is, nobody really possesses it. The human race is not divided up, in the *Iliad*, into conquered persons, slaves, suppliants, on the one hand, and conquerors and chiefs on the other. In this poem there is not a single man who does not at one time or another have to bow his neck to force.

What is important here is to see how this is something that for Weil has no favourites – it operates on us impartially and at any stage we could become victim or oppressor. Force is that power that turns 'anyone subject to it into a thing'.

---

4   I wish here to acknowledge my debt to Fernando Atria. During his doctoral studies in Edinburgh, we both discovered Simone Weil and Rene Girard and together read and discussed the texts and continue to do so. What understanding I have has been immeasurably deepened by these discussions and our engagement with them. It has led me to areas where I would not have ventured otherwise. See his careful discussion, in this volume, of Weil and Girard in relation to these issues.

Secondly, it is germane to our discussion because there is more here than a relentless and clear exposition of the horror of war and what it does to everyone. It tells us something about our response. For Weil, force is one of the mechanisms at work in human relations and it operates with the same rigidity as mechanical force. It is about power and the need for control. Those crushed by it are described by her as 'afflicted' (Weil, 1990, p. 284):

> Affliction is a device for pulverising the soul; the man who falls into it is like a workman who gets caught up in a machine. He is no longer a man but a torn and bloody rag on the teeth of a cog-wheel. ... To acknowledge the reality of affliction means saying to oneself: I may lose at any moment, through the play of circumstances over which I have no control, anything whatsoever that I possess, including those things which are so intimately mine that I consider them as being myself. There is nothing that I might not lose.

I feel your pain

The response to the cry of the afflicted one's pain, 'I am hurt' is the urge to do something. We recognise another's affliction when we 'pay attention' to them (Weil, 1951). We realise that we are in the same position as they are in the sense that where we are is to do with luck and power, and will not be stable. At any time we might be in the position they are in. We pay attention to a human when we see them as an obstacle to a project we have which we cannot ignore. If we did not 'attend' to them in this way we would pursue our project ignoring and crushing them as though they were some inanimate being. We would not stop our movement to avoid them and would just drive over them.

Matter is an obstacle which we push aside or move around but when we meet a person we do injustice if we just do that. In the *Iliad* Weil pictures someone 'walking through a non-resistant force'. We must instead search for their consent and that is the supreme virtue of justice. In the 'interval of hesitation' when we see our common humanity, we pay attention to the person and are able to allow them to consent.[5] That can only be done in conditions of equilibrium where we can live in truth and not be forced to live a lie.

Attention then is about compassion, caring, justice and equality. We see that we are all in the same pitiless void. When we see that and act in that way we will be seen as mad. It is that 'the madness of love' which acts against the necessity of power and denies that power its victory. Only when we see that will we struggle for justice. Well-fed people, she says, do not stand pressed against the windows of restaurants looking at the food inside. Only the hungry stand there desperate. So also will we only work for justice if we hunger and thirst for it. We who are well-fed and not in pain will only hunger and thirst if we have the grace to allow the injustice in the cry of pain, wherever it comes from, to lacerate our soul because of its existence. It is that pain that is affliction. It is then that we pay attention to the afflicted – those who

---

5   For a full account of this see Atria in this volume.

cry 'I am hurt', 'I suffer an injustice', 'I have been wronged' and pay attention to them (Dietz, 1988, p. 129):

> Attention towards others is not an act of impartial disengagement at all, but rather an act through which the unafflicted "project their being" into the afflicted. Relatedly, she [Weil] insists that attention to the afflicted is not rooted in our recognition of any one attribute, like the rational dignity of man, but instead is consumed by the whole person, the "neighbour" in his or her completeness.

This is not just the empathy and impartial spectator of Adam Smith. Rather it is something real. Thus it is not like the modern psychobabble of 'I feel your pain' but rather I have pain because you have pain. The pain that I have though is *my* pain and not your pain.

The point for Weil is that affliction is contagious and we will do everything to avoid it. We do not want the pain but it is only when we recognise it that we can do anything. But much of our routines are aimed at avoiding that pain (Weil, 1990, p. 285):

> To put oneself in the place of someone whose soul is corroded by affliction, or in near danger of it is to annihilate oneself. It is more difficult than suicide would be for a happy child. Therefore the afflicted are not listened to. They are like someone whose tongue has been cut out and who occasionally forgets the fact. When they move their lips no ear perceives any sound. And they certainly soon sink into impotence in the use of language, because of the certainty of not being heard.

Weil illustrates this by picturing a judge who tries to shield himself from the pain of the defendant, to shield himself from letting his affliction take him over by maintaining an 'elegant flow of queries and witticisms while [the defendant] is unable to stammer a word'.

The vulnerability of self and the risk of action

What I have tried to show so far is that Christodoulidis is right in that there is no mythical 'we'. But equally reconciliation cannot just concentrate on the mythical future reconciled community. We are now locked together in a joint enterprise. Reconciliation has to start from the recognition of our common humanity and equality in pain and affliction. We have been formed by actions that went on before and we cannot, oppressor or victim, escape them by constructing purified selves, invulnerable to what went on before. What all this means is that we have to start from where we are together in our pain.

What we need now is to develop a politics.[6] Gillian Rose's (1992) notion of acting in the middle illuminates what I want to say here.[7] For Rose, the middle is the

---

6   Atria, in his chapter, develops a somewhat different position from the one I take though we use many common starting points.

7   I am deeply indebted to Claire Henderson Davis for many insights and fruitful collaboration. See also Bankowski and Davis (2000).

space where politics occurs; where we stake ourselves in the business of creating our lives within society. For her this is a way of holding apart the polarities of the universalism of law and the particularity of love, or in the example of the TRC, the polarities of law and mercy. If these are not held apart they slide into an unreflective mass. It is in this space that there is a place for politics. This place is ambiguous and tension ridden because it is there we stake ourselves and our vulnerability is exposed. Thus it is the beginning of anxiety for there we confront the possibilities of failure even though law defines the powers we possess. We might say that the collapse of the middle into one or the other of the polarities, into the soulless application of the law or the nihilist passion of love, is part of the desire to escape that tension, to be able to find some calculable answer.

For her, acting in the middle produces what she calls the singular. This is the product of the meeting of the opposites and helps to keep them apart. It is an anxious place in two senses. First of all it is risky and unsettled for it is there we place the vulnerability of ourselves. Secondly it is anxious precisely because it is the *middle.* There is no end – it is there that we always act and there is no safe haven which, risky though the journey is, we can aim for. Again we have to guard against the reverse move and construct a beginning which makes our journey easier – to defuse the anxiety of beginning by constructing some mythical starting place so as to underpin the jump into the unknown that we would otherwise have to make. For Rose this refusal is to 'suspend the ethical' which in this context means refraining from seeing something as an incarnation of universal law.

Take the following example. If we are in a position where we have to decide whether we should break the law, we might approach the question generally and universally in terms of a social contract argument which will give us the conditions and parameters we should use in making the decision. But that is trying to do away with the anxiety and risk of acting in the middle because we first construct some mythical past (the social contract) from which we can calculate our present duty and so keep our security and certainty. Working in the 'middle' would mean asking whether I should break *this* law at *this* time. My decision will be the product of an encounter with all pertinent reasons including the universal ones of social contract theory – but I will never be certain I am right and I will make myself vulnerable.

The leap of faith

The point about that beginning is that ultimately we have no beginning or end to guide us in safety and certainty. We have to commit and stake ourselves to a decision which, *ex hypothesi*, we will not know is correct until we see what happens. But it is not a consequentialist decision and nor is it one guaranteed by the certainty of, for example, the Kantian categorical imperative. It is not, however, a nihilist way of looking at things, with each judgment guaranteed by nothing at all. A version of the prisoner's dilemma can be used as an example. The dilemma itself is a way of seeing how the logic of individual action and therefore rationality gets in the way of collective and common good; how what it is right for you to do is not right for everyone collectively and therefore wrong for you. Consider the problem of traffic. It is irrational for me to give up my car since my giving it up in the context of all the traffic, in (say) Edinburgh, will not make any difference. It is only rational for me to give it up if everyone else will do so and that is not rational, since *a fortiori* I do not know how everyone will act. So the logic of individual rationality pulls me to act in a collectively irrational way as it does everyone else.

This is not about selfishness or selflessness. Giving up the car can be characterised as selfish also – for it is for the collective good and that includes you. If I go ahead and give up my car then that action will be right if everyone goes ahead and does it as well. If no-one else does then I will not be right regardless (the Kantian position) – I will just appear foolish and irrelevant (and traffic will still snarl up Edinburgh). Rather, what is special about the act of giving up the car is that I am not using it as the end of a rational calculation (Kantian or consequentialist) in that way. I am using it as a model for others to follow. This is a leap of faith into the dark – I accept defeat in the hope of victory but that victory is not dependent on me but on everyone else recognising that it is the right thing to do and then doing it. At the liminal case this is terrifyingly hard, but much of our political action can be seen in this way – the willingness to go forward in hope, to be unafraid to be seen as mad and learn from the inevitable mistakes.

Institutions of reconciliation

What sort of institutions for reconciliation might this 'middle' politics imply? As we saw in our discussion of Williams, we must not concentrate too much on the language of reparation and rights. The notion of rights is, as Simone Weil says (Weil, 1990, p. 279):

> … linked with notion of sharing out, of exchange, of measured quantity. It has a commercial flavour, especially evocative of legal claims and arguments. Rights are always asserted in a tone of contention; and when this tone is adopted, it must rely on force in its background, or else it will be laughed at.

But that does not imply a rejection of law *tout court* – if it did we would not be acting in the middle. Weil goes on to say (p. 286):

> Justice consists in seeing that no hurt is done to men. Whenever a man cries inwardly: 'Why am I being hurt?' harm is being done to him. He is often mistaken when he tries to define that harm, and why and by whom it is being inflicted on him. But the cry itself is infallible.

> The other cry, which we hear so often: 'Why has someone else got more than I have?' refers to rights. We must learn to distinguish between the two cries and do all that is possible, as gently as possible, to hush the second one with the help of a code of justice, regular tribunals, and the police. Minds capable of solving problems of this kind can be formed in a law school.

It might be said that institutions like the TRC bridge the gap between those two cries. They can be seen as what I have called elsewhere 'bridging institutions' (Bankowski, 2001) which help to manage the encounter between the two polarities I have talked of above and keep a space open for the 'middle'. That is what the coming together of people in institutions like the TRC might allow to happen. One can get glimpses of it in Christodoulidis's (2000) article when he looks at the reactions of various people, torturers and tortured, in the TRC. It appears to incorporate mercy and reconciliation. Thus, it seems to be something of a third way between blanket prosecution and blanket amnesty.

Looking at it from the point of view of both those who want justice at all costs and those who want to go forward with reconciliation in truth can show us the problems of using and designing such institutions. The TRC has been attacked both for not being legal enough and for being taken over by the law. Yet, what it tries to do is to bring these things together, to marry the two in the one institution. Christodoulidis (2000) details what he calls the impossible tension between 'law's reductive moment and the confessional's reflexive one'. He gives many examples as to how the TRC was pushed towards the legal mode of doing things. He is not against reconciliation, he says, but does not believe it can come about by legal means. What he says is important and well evidenced but the fact remains that the experiment was tried and did have some partial success. The problem, it seems to me, is that if you have theoretically argued that linking the two, reconciliation and law, is impossible, that it is an 'impossible tension', your interpretation of the empirical evidence will be more pessimistic. You will be pessimistic because your theory precludes optimism. What I have argued is not that Christodoulidis is empirically wrong, but that one can at least theorise the possibility of such institutions, however much they fail in the concrete world. For Christodoulidis, all such failure will not be the inevitable by-product of living in the middle and from which we might learn, but something defined by the nature of its being infected by law – for law is just that sort of institution; one which is exclusionary and non-reflexive. So he argues, very subtly, how reconciliation or mercy is the absence in, or the horizon of, law and it is only in there that it has its place. But what he is ultimately saying is that law is closed to the outside, to the reflexivity of such areas as reconciliation and can only bring them in on its own terms. So a view like the one presented here is ruled out *ab initio* because it sees the tension of the middle as theoretically impossible.

The Good Samaritan

I agree with many of the *caveats* and problems concerning the TRC that Christodoulidis and others bring up and of course law has a tendency to exclude. But what is important is that the way I have outlined here, and elsewhere, gives us a way of seeing transitional justice not as that to be replaced by proper legality but perhaps the true form of legality (see Bankowski, 2000). But the risk is still there. Here we have a risky journey of negotiating identity, of reconstructing a 'we', a recognition that both sides are equally vulnerable and it is only in that mutual vulnerability that we can go forward. That is why, for Weil, the parable of the Good Samaritan was so important, for it emphasises the creativity of 'attention' to the cry of pain, of 'affliction'. It takes us on a journey where we are all potential victims, as oppressors and oppressed, and that these positions can change at any time. That is why one has to temper the language of rights for that lays stress on victory, on a completion where one will be the winner and one will be the loser.

For Weil then, the parable of the Good Samaritan is not merely a matter of grasping what a neighbour is. It was also a constitutive act making the other a neighbour by the act of helping. This is an invitation to enter a risky voyage with the other and thus transform your world – the outcome of which is risky and unpredictable. What that does for Weil is literally to breathe life into someone that was as stone, non-human in their affliction. It is an act of 'creative attention' (Weil, 1951; cited in Grote, 1990, pp. 146–7):

> Christ taught us that the supernatural love of our neighbour is the exchange of compassion and gratitude which happens in a flash between two beings, one possessing and the other deprived of human personality. One of the two is only a little piece of flesh, naked, inert, and bleeding beside a ditch; he is nameless; no one knows anything about him. Those who pass by this thing scarcely notice it, and a few minutes afterwards do not even know that they saw it. Only one stops and turns his attention towards it. ... The attention is creative.

But there is more to 'Love thy Neighbour'.[8] The neighbour in the parable is the Samaritan, the one in the privileged position, and the Samaritans were outside the Law and the bitter enemies of the Jews. Jesus inverts the common understandings. He is telling the lawyer to whom the story is addressed that it is not just a matter of someone in a privileged position extending help to someone outside. It is asking that privileged person to imagine themselves in radical need and accept the community of those whom they hate. And more than that, not to think that the possession of the Law gives you power. For the law itself is vulnerable and needs the love from outside to sustain it. But the gift of that love means it receives the law's weakness (the man lying injured could have been part of a ruse to rob the unwary traveller). So we are united in our mutual vulnerability and affliction.

Creative attention

But as I said above, we need to build institutions that will stabilize that flash of compassion upon which law depends and thus make that connectedness actual and enduring over time. Let us look at two images from Gaita (2000). He tells the story of when he was working in a mental hospital as a young man in the 1960s. The patients there were treated by many of the staff as worse than animals. There were some (he included) who tried to treat the patients as human. But there was also a nun whose humane demeanour and attitude with the patients put them all to shame.

---

8   See White (1989) for a discussion of parables and, in particular, The Good Samaritan and The Prodigal Son.

He asks what it was about her that was so different. Here we can see the 'creative attention' of Weil. But how, one might ask, can you base a society and a legal system on that? The answer is that we cannot begin to think about how to organise such a system unless we can recognise and respond to the deep cry of hurt. The move to set up law and stability will only come if we respond with love to the pain we hear.

But we do need the stability and institutionality of a legal system otherwise the flash of compassion will be just that – an ephemeral flash. Gaita talks of a film by Costa Gavras, *The Confession*. This is a film of the Soviet Show trials of 1952. In one scene a prisoner is being brutally harangued by the presiding judge. He lifts his hands and, since his belt has been confiscated, his trousers slip down. He is frightened and looks at the judge. There is silence and then the judge laughs, at first mocking and then sympathetic. All the other prisoners join in. Here we see the 'interval of hesitation' and then the recognition of the humanity of our equality in affliction. The judge knows that he is on the podium but might the next day be in the dock. No one is secure because of their merit (innocence) and at any moment the juggernaut might hit them. The moment is real but it goes and it is the task of law to nurture and institutionalize these moments.

Power and the moral economy

The construction of these institutions is not something that we do once and for all. It must be a continuing process otherwise we will sit in comfort and not hear that cry but drown it out. The law will atrophy and we will be blind and deaf to the poor and hurt. This construction is not easy because it means accepting a world where we cannot be determined wholly by our own choices; where we are where we are because of all sorts of contingent circumstances; where we have to start from there and not hide by constructing a mythical past or future; where we have to accept the world as it is and move on from there.

That is the risk we have to take if we are to live together in the 'middle' and outside of the moral economy of exchange and power. Living there means problematising victory. It means not just basing our decisions on a narrative of victim and oppressor, winner and loser, where now it is the oppressor's turn to be the oppressed. 'Who's Sorry Now?' – where I rejoice because though I have been sorry, now it is your turn – is precisely what we must eschew. Breaking out of that cycle means recognising the 'metaphysical guilt' of us all. We have to start from where we are and not construct a theoretical beginning.

I have thus tried in this chapter to look at reconciliation as something that is a journey where we join in the risky business of creating a self and society. In that, forgiveness and remorse will play a large part and hard decisions will have to be taken. But it is also important to note that on both sides it means acknowledging that identities will change, that our cherished notions of ourselves and our societies will die and resurge as something different, sometimes frightening.

The cycle of violence

Let us now further explore that moral economy of power. Here I take up the work of Girard (1996).[9] Though much of his work is theological and is concerned with setting up an alternative reading of the Passion of Christ, it has resonances for our theme here (see also Atria, this volume). There are two points from Girard that are relevant for this chapter. Firstly he has a theory of the violence behind all societies and secondly a way out of that through the recognition of that violence and the setting up of alternative models. Girard sees violence at the base of society. This comes about through mimetic rivalry. I am constituted by desire and imitation. We desire according to the desire of another. I desire something because you desire it and it is there. Therefore you and I become rivals for that desire. I do not realise that I am imitating you and I think that you are taking something from me, wanting something that is mine. I do not want to accept that I am imitating you. This, according to Girard, is known as acquisitive or conflictual mimesis in the sense that I am a rival for the desiring object. The point is that though we want to be ourselves that involves taking on the other's identity and that means a destroying of ourselves – we lose, as Fraser (2001) says, our ontological security. But violence is difficult to stop and we keep imitating it – we cannot break the cycle of violence. The way that rivalry is dealt with is to find someone quite arbitrarily who is to be the scapegoat and who, though innocent, is to be seen as the cause of all of this violence.

For Girard this applies at a societal level to all societies. So at the base of society is this founding violence. Religion is the means by which this initial scapegoating violence is institutionalized. The sacrifice of the innocent victim destroys the guilt of our violence and gives us peace. Religion is the organising of a cult around this sacrifice and victim – sacred since by the scapegoat's sacrifice peace comes from violence. Religion becomes then sacrificial and retributive, the scapegoat dies for our sins and redeems them. So for Girard, the violence of mimetic desire and scapegoating, which produces peace, are the basis of human culture. But this only works if the culture denies its complicity in violence, denies the innocence of the scapegoat. Once this starts it is almost impossible to break out of the cycle of violence and resolution by sacrifice (Girard, 1997):

> The mechanism of reciprocal violence can be described as a vicious circle. Once a community enters the circle, it is unable to extricate itself. We can define this circle in terms of vengeance and reprisal, and we can offer diverse psychological descriptions of these reactions. As long as a working capital of accumulated hatred and suspicion exists at the centre of a community, it will continue to increase no matter what men do. Each person prepares himself for the probable aggression of his neighbours and interprets his neighbours' preparations as confirmation of the latter's aggressiveness. In more general terms the mimetic character of violence is so intense that once installed in a community, it cannot burn itself out.

---

9   For a short Introduction see Kirwan (2004). See also Fraser (2001) which deals with Girard in relation to some of the themes discussed here.

To escape from the circle it is first necessary to remove from the scene all those forms of violence that tend to be self-propagating and to spawn new, imitative forms.

The practice of peace

For Girard, Christianity is unique in that it seeks to expose religion, as defined above, and the cult of the sacred, as being complicit in this founding violence. It can thus be seen as an attack on religion. He therefore reads the Passion of Christ in a non-sacrificial way, not as the necessary atonement for our sins. So for Girard the message of the Cross is not some form of retributive atonement, for that would only perpetuate the violence upon which all societies are based in the form of a self-destructive mimesis. Christ is the victim who goes to his death to expose the scapegoating mechanism and show the truth of the violence at the base of our societies. The mechanism, once exposed, can never be so effective.

The holy anarchist

Nietzsche,[10] in his attack on Christianity, says something similar. For Nietzsche, Christianity is essentially a practice (Kaufman, 1974, p. 341):

> [Jesus] This "bringer of glad tidings" died as he lived, as he had *taught – not* to "redeem men" but to show how one must live. This *practice* is his legacy to mankind: his behaviour before the judges, before the catchpoles, before the accusers and all kinds of slander and scorn – his behaviour on the *cross*. He does not resist, he does not defend his right, he does not take steps to ward off the worst; on the contrary, *he provokes it*. And he begs, he suffers, he loves *with* those, in those who do him evil. *Not* to resist, *not* to be angry, *not* to hold responsible, but to resist not even the evil one – to *love* him.[11]

He dies not for the guilt of others (a sacrificial redemption) but for his own guilt – a 'holy anarchist' whose attack was not against corruption but against a whole hierarchical order, against 'caste, privilege, order and formula'. Nietzsche calls Christ 'an idiot' but this is from the image of the holy fool found most typically in Dostoyevsky. Richard Holloway remarks that there is something even more to it than that. It is not just a sort of holy naiveté but a genuine subversiveness by these seemingly outlandish actions. But this is turned into a barbarous doctrine of sacrificial redemption. Revenge and retribution come to the fore. 'The Kingdom of Heaven' is part of the judgement which rewards the 'just' against one's enemies (the sinners) and is all the more pleasurable for the suffering of those below in Hell. In that hate-fuelled *ressentiment* of a slave religion, the fact that for Jesus the Kingdom of God was living as he lived is forgotten.

---

10   I thank Richard Holloway who brought these themes to my attention in a stimulating weekend led by him at Scottish Churches House, 'Losing Power: An Encounter with Simone Weil, Nietzsche and Jesus'.

11   See generally Kaufmann (1974) chapter 12.

Jesus then offers a different model. Conflictual mimesis is not the only mimesis there can be. There is also non-rivalistic mimesis. Though fragile, and always prone to degeneration, it can be seen in the relations between disciple and a teacher and parents and children. Jesus chooses to live beyond the normal forms of organised power. His message is not so much that the downtrodden will now have their turn, for that just perpetuates the cycle of violence and power – rather, He shows how we can live in a world where violence is not the determinant (see the Beatitudes). 'My Kingdom is not of this Earth' does not mean that it is in some nebulous Heaven but rather a place where the normal polarities of power will not hold sway, where the exclusion of the founding violence will be replaced by a narrative of inclusion. And He exposes the shallowness of those conventional notions and the violence they are based on by being supremely indifferent to them even unto death. Peace cannot be bought by the violence of exclusion and we are offered a model to imitate which is non-rivalistic and inclusionary where we conquer and do not fear, as Jesus did not, death.

What does it mean to 'conquer death' in our present context? Much of the narrative of reconciliation that I have presented is about the way selves go forward together and reconstruct themselves, moving in new and uncharted directions. The narrative of inclusion means we open out ourselves to others and learn from them and are changed by them. The self always seeks to be at one with itself. But the very act of thinking that shows how I am formed by a multiplicity of things and experiences that can never be stable. So my desire to be at peace is frustrated because I define myself in the act of thinking what I am. But that is always something that slips away as I think it – if we think that we have grasped the knowledge of what we are we have lost it. This is a sort of death, since the self and selves that we are will be different and will not be fixed in a timeless and ahistorical way. And that means that there is a part of us over which we have no control and that we can change in new and terrifying ways. Our selves will always be 'dying' and recreating. This also applies to communities and states. For example part of the fear of immigration is that our national identity will die with the influx of 'alien' cultures, part of the fear of the EU opening out toward Turkey is the fear of Islam swamping our 'Judeo-Christian Heritage'.[12]

Models for peace

If we no longer fear this ontological destruction, then we no longer have to be complicit in the violence that keeps our identity secure – we recognise that together and in varying degrees we are victims and to blame for that violence, and the urgent task is together to eradicate that cycle of violence and produce, as Girard says, new forms to imitate that will help so to do. Then death will no longer have dominion and we can reconstruct by being brave enough to do seemingly mad and unexpected things.

---

12 See, for example the pronouncements of Pope Benedict XVI.

We can see the TRC as one of these new forms, as such attempting to break that mimetic cycle of violence (Desmond Tutu, Foreword to TRC Report):

> We have been concerned that many consider only one aspect of justice. Certainly, amnesty cannot be viewed as justice if we think of justice as only retributive or punitive in nature. We believe however, that there is another kind of justice – restorative justice which is concerned not so much with punishment as with correcting imbalances, restoring broken relationships – with healing harmony and reconciliation.

What is important in the attempt to act 'in the middle' is that it does not attempt to create a pure beginning from which to start. So the aim is not to start from the 'ideal blame and guilt position' and take decisions based upon that but rather start from where we are, all complicit and compromised by the choices that have been made – some that we had no control over. This does not mean that responsibility is to be ignored or that one should, as some say, forget about blame and concentrate on building the good society.[13] For all the choices in the past will have an effect and cannot be ignored. We should not however, use that as the Archimedean starting point. Decisions here will, as we saw in the third section, use all criteria but will be concerned with what to do in *this* case at *this* time. The fact one was an apartheid judge, for example, will have an effect, but what effect will depend upon a concatenation of other criteria.

Conclusion

I finish with two parables, one from the New Testament and one from Dostoyevsky; not merely to illustrate the point I have been making but also to begin to explore further. For parables are, as White (1989) shows, an invitation to undertake a risky journey paying attention to the sometimes startling twists and turns of the stories – unsure of where they will lead us.

The Prodigal Son

A particular reading of the parable of the Prodigal Son is apposite in looking at the TRC and reconciliation in general. Is the parable really a message of repentance and forgiveness? It is not obvious that the son is really repenting. He is making some sort of utilitarian calculation. His portion of his father's inheritance has run out, he is reduced to abject poverty. As White says, one can imagine him rehearsing what he is going to tell his father but the confessions of having 'sinned against Heaven and against thee' reflect not conviction of wrongdoing but the situation that he is in. But as the story goes on, it becomes unnecessary since the father simply welcomes him. His wrongdoing and his sin do not seem to enter into the calculation. Jesus is being challenged for associating with 'sinners' (feasting with prostitutes, tax gatherers).

---

13   As was argued in the debate about apology in Australia.

But what is important, says White, is not that fact, but that he does so – in the same way as the Father in the Parable – without waiting for them formally to repent. That might come in the risky future but it is not demanded *ab initio*.

But one can go further. The eldest son is, not unnaturally, upset. But one does not just have to characterise his behaviour as mean-spirited and grasping. In many ways it is perfectly reasonable. He has followed the law and obeyed his Father. But is that all there is to family or community life? Part of the parable is to say that you cannot begin to understand law without love to underpin it.

We might say that what I am doing here is making the mistake that Christodoulidis cautions against, creating a mythical 'we' when there was none before. Here there is a family but elsewhere there is not. But, as we saw above, if we view the parable in a performative way then the point is that community is created by one's actions. After all what sort of family was it before the Prodigal went away? Could we really call it a community?

Finally, White invites us to think, following Donald MacKinnon, of the Father as a 'silly old fool'. We might automatically think, in a pious way, of the love of God and approve of the father. But why? Has he really behaved ethically? Has he treated his eldest son fairly? Has he not been overtaken with emotion and acted in a completely undignified way? Will anyone, even the younger son, be able to respect him for the way he has acted (White, 1989, p. 69)?

> The parable … ends most significantly on a question – a question in the end addressed to us. The future life within the family is entirely open. Will the elder brother persist in his hostility and rejection of his father? Will the younger brother regard his father as a soft touch and continue to abuse his love? Nothing in what we are told begins to settle such questions.

And they cannot for they are part of the risk and journey that we have to take. The resonances with South Africa are clear.

The kiss glows in the dark

> Words of the middle region, such as *right, democracy, person* are valid in their own region which is that of ordinary institutions. But for the sustaining inspiration of which all the institutions are, as it were, the projection, a different language is needed. (Weil, 1990, p. 228)

I want to finish by adapting an image that Williams (2000) uses from *The Brothers Karamazov*. In the Grand Inquisitor scene, Ivan tells his brother Aloysha a parable. Jesus comes back to Spain and continues his work. He is arrested at the Grand Inquisitor's command and put on trial. In his cell he is approached by the Grand Inquisitor and accused of causing human misery by his insistence on the free response of love. People cannot, the Inquisitor says, live like that. In our work, he goes on, by supplying authority and power we enable people to live in peace. The accused remains silent and all he does in response is to kiss the Grand Inquisitor who tells him to go. Aloysha to whom this story is being told by his brother in the context of a comprehensive attack on his beliefs does the same, replying only with a kiss. The point says Williams is, even if what the Inquisitor says is true and the world is like that, that kiss expresses the possibility of a break from that moral economy. The kiss is an act inspired by what Weil calls 'the madness of love' – it engages, but not on the level of that moral economy. The Inquisitor sticks to his idea but 'the kiss glows in the dark'. He is sad because something of the Kiss, that needs nothing and is another way of looking at the world, remains in him.

Bibliography

Bankowski, Z. (2001), *Living Lawfully*, Dordrecht: Kluwer.

Bankowski, Z. and Davis, C. (2000), 'Living In and Out of the Law', in Oliver Douglas-Scott and Tadros (eds), *Faith in Law*, Oxford: Hart Publishing.

Christodoulidis, E. (2000), 'Truth and reconciliation as risks', *Social and Legal Studies*, **9** (2), pp. 179–204.

Dietz, M. (1988), *Between the Human and Divine*, New Jersey: Rowan and Littlefield.

Fraser, G. (2001), *Christianity and Violence*, London: Darton, Longman and Todd.

Gaita, R. (2000), *A Common Humanity*, London: Routledge.

Girard, R. (1977), *Violence and the Sacred*, Baltimore: Johns Hopkins Press.

Girard, R. (1996), *The Girard Reader*, New York: Crossroad.

Grote, J. (1990), 'Prestige: Simone Weil's theory of social force' in *Spirituality Today* **42**, pp. 217–232.

Jaspers, K. (1971), 'Differentiation of German Guilt' in H. Morris (ed.), *Guilt and Shame*, Belmont, CA: Wadworth Publishing Company.

Kaufmann, W. (1974), *Nietzsche* 4th ed., Princeton: Princeton University Press.

Kirwan, M. (2004), *Discovering Girard*, London: Darton, Longman and Todd.

Rose, G. (1992), *The Broken Middle*, Oxford: Blackwell.

Steiner, G. (1996), 'Return no More' in *The Depths of the Sea and Other Fiction*, London: Faber and Faber.

Tutu, D. (1996), 'Foreword', *South African Truth and Reconciliation Commission*, Final Report, Volume 1.

van der Merwe, D (1998), 'Roman Dutch Law: from virtual reality to constitutional resource', *Acta Jurida*, pp. 117–137.

van der Walt, J. (1998), 'Un-doing things with words: the colonization of the public sphere by private-property discourse', *Acta Juridica*, pp. 235–281.

Weil, S. (1951), 'Reflections on the Right Use of School Studies with a View to the Love of God' in *Waiting for God*, New York: Harper.

Weil, S. (1986), 'The Iliad: A Poem of Force' in *Simone Weil, An Anthology*, Sîan Miles (ed.), London: Virago Press.

Weil, S. (1990), 'On Human Personality' reproduced in McLellan D. *Utopian Pessimist: The Life and Thought of Simone Weil*, Poseidon Press: New York.

Williams, R. (2000), *Lost Icons: Essays on Cultural Bereavement*, Edinburgh: T & T Clark.

White, R. (1989), 'MacKinnon and the Parables' in K Surin (ed.) *Christ, Ethics and Tragedy: Essays in Honour of Donald MacKinnon*, Cambridge: Cambridge University Press.

Williams, R. (2000), *Christ on Trial*, London: Fount.

Zimmerman, R. and Visser, D. (1996), *Southern Cross*, Oxford: Clarendon Press.

Chapter 4

Reconciliation as Domination

Stewart Motha[1]

Introduction

In settler-colonies such as Australia and South Africa, the illegitimacy of the colonial foundation of law and society, and the legacy of racially discriminatory laws have generated a demand for the renewal of juridical and political institutions. In such 'postcolonial' contexts, the juridical and the social (predominantly in the form of the nation-state) have been undergoing processes of transformation.[2] The concern of this chapter is to set out how 'postcolonial' reconciliation presents itself as the problem of the 'political'. The discussion will be centred on reconciliation in Australia. It will be argued that the renewal of the juridical and the political harbours the contradiction of at once preserving and disavowing colonial sovereignty, law, and political community. Importantly, it is through a notion of 'political community' and the insistent 'commonality' of a nation with 'one-law' that this 'postcolonial' contradiction is sustained. The 'time' of reconciliation is marked and delineated by the possibility of producing a renewed polity or 'political community'. This process of re-inscribing the 'political' under 'one-law' subordinates indigenous laws and customs, once again, in the name of 'civilisation', and its new effigies, democracy and human rights. Reconciliation, I will demonstrate, returns a form of domination through the subordination of 'backward' indigenous cultures that are to be overwhelmed by 'modernity'. I elaborate this argument through a discussion of recent debates in Australia on whether the causes of high levels of violence and

1   Earlier versions of this paper were presented at the Law and Anthropology Workshop Birkbeck, London, 2004; and the 'Law in a Time of Reconciliation' workshop at Glasgow University, 2004. Participants at those gatherings offered crucial encouragement, and helpful comments. I am very grateful for the invaluable research assistance provided by Toni Johnson. Regular interventions from Brenna Bhandar, Peter Fitzpatrick, Colin Perrin and Karin van Marle have sustained me through the process of writing. A productive engagement with Scott Veitch and Emilios Christodoulidis about an earlier version helped to shape this Chapter. Irene Watson not only read and commented on several drafts, she generously gave her time in Hamburg and Berlin for long discussions. All opinions and errors are mine.

2   I deploy the term 'postcolonial' to indicate the politically and juridically acknowledged imperative to depart from the colonial ordering of law and society. But this 'postcolonial' demand harbours a contradiction. 'Postcolonial' law and society demands the preservation and disavowal of colonial laws and social formations – a contradiction I elaborate below.

poverty in indigenous communities is inherent to forms of 'traditional' indigenous 'culture'. How does reconciliation and 'postcolonial' renewal of law and society lead to the re-emergence of the notion of a backward native who must be dragged into modernity through 'modern' law? What is it about the 'postcolonial' response to the demand for responsibility that results in the return of a patronising cultural and juridical supremacy? Reconciliation has all too readily manifested itself through the verb 'to be reconciled' – for indigenous people to be reconciled to their domination (Fitzpatrick, 2004, 282ff).

Reconciliation has its enthusiasts. The possibility of rewriting the historical narrative of the nation can sustain the hopes of a 'postcolonial' polity (see generally, Behrendt, 2001a; Dodson and Strelein, 2001; Muldoon, 2003; Schaap 2004; Short 2003). These accounts demonstrate how a polity demands the 'truth' about past crimes and massacres, and that the state, community or individuals that committed such acts be made to bear responsibility. Truth Commissions and Inquiries – such as the Truth and Reconciliation Commission in South Africa or the Australian Human Rights Commission's Report on the 'stolen generation' – have sought to 'restore' and inaugurate a polity that acknowledges the abhorrent actions or omissions of the past (see generally, Krog, 1999; and Human Rights and Equal Opportunities Commission of Australia, 1997). Such endeavours are supposed to serve as a 'bridge' to a more harmonious future. However, the possibility of 'responsibility' has tended to run aground on the impossibility of a just response. How is an individual or polity going to remember ungraspable imperial excesses? And in the absence of 'memory' there can be no memorials or monuments – and without these, it seems, there can be no departure from an unjust 'past' towards a just future.[3] In the face of this impasse, juridico-political renewal has often been subordinated to pragmatic negotiations and judicial decisions which belatedly allocate 'rights' to the dispossessed and disenfranchised.

The recognition of 'indigenous land rights', for instance, is one response to the complex demands of re-grounding a 'postcolonial' polity, taking responsibility for past injustices, and redistributing ill-gotten gains. In Australia, the 'past' is being selectively memorialised in landmark court decisions such as *Mabo v Queensland* (1992), and in Declarations 'toward' reconciliation (see Appendix to this chapter, and discussion below). And yet there is a persistent colonial imposition that cannot be shaken off. Indeed, the return of explicitly assimilationist policies are predicated on the need to 'rescue' the native from 'traditional' stasis and move her towards the light of modernity.[4] In Australia, the process of reconciliation has rapidly run

---

3   I will not pursue the issue of memory and memorialising the past, a central issue in relation to reconciliation that is developed by van Marle (2004).

4   Peter Sutton (2001), one of Australia's influential anthropologists, argues for a return to assimilation in order to eradicate violence he claims is inherent to indigenous 'culture'. I critically examine his arguments, and the Australian Government's policy of 'Mutual Obligation Agreements' (MUAs) between indigenous 'communities' and the state as a condition for the provision of general services provided by the state.

aground on the insistence of a unitary political community governed by one 'law of the land'. I suggest that it is the failure to grapple with the problem of the 'political' that is one major flaw in how reconciliation has been conceived and deployed. I also argue that discursive notions of 'responsibility' and 'moral community' do not remedy the foundational problems of the juridical and the political.

The 'postcolonial' as a problem of political community

Let's begin with a preliminary account of what I mean by the 'political' when I use the phrase 'political community'. The question of the 'political', as with sovereignty, is a problem of the 'limit'. Indeed, as Lacoue-Labarthe and Nancy explain it, the 'political' is a problematic constituted by the concepts of 'people' and 'sovereignty' (Lacoue-Labarthe and Nancy, 1997, pp. 115–6).[5] The 'people' and 'sovereignty' are questions of the 'limit' to the extent that they are staged as a 'closure' (*ibid.*). There is a 'measure' for membership of the 'people' as 'race', 'ethnos', or civilised 'humanity'. Similarly, sovereignty is partly a spatial notion that is asserted over a specific territory, symbolising a politically united 'people', and often co-appears with a legal order that is specific to that 'people' or territory (this last quality of sovereignty is often elaborated through judicial decisions on 'jurisdiction').[6] Who are the 'people', who is 'proper' to a 'people', which collective's law has the status of normativity, and when should self-determination be entitled to a 'sovereign' expression – are usually questions determined with reference to some 'essence'.[7] The essence is regularly racialised – it is a matter of 'blood and soil'. The problem of the 'political', then, is one of determining who is 'inside' or 'outside' the community or nation, and the basis for this decision. How does this problem of the political arise in the 'postcolonial' context? Permit me to offer a concrete example drawn from the

---

5   Lacoue-Labarthe and Nancy insist that a re-treatment of the 'political' must take place through an examination of the "co-belonging" of the philosophical and the political (1997, p. 109). This is a questioning of the relationship between *logos* (as a relation shared in-common) and the 'social bond'. Both are presented in the city, *polis*, civilisation, political community etc. That is, they wish to call into question *logos* as the philosophical ground of the *polis*. It is the presentation of an 'essence', as *logos* for instance, as the ground of community that they wish to discredit.

6   For further elaboration of the co-relation between sovereignty, law and political community manifested in the notion of jurisdiction, see Motha (2005, and 2006).

7   Aristotle's opening teleological assumption that 'every state is an association and that every association is formed with a view to some good purpose' leads him to proclaim the state, the 'most sovereign of associations', as the entity that pursues the 'most sovereign of all goods', 'the political', see Aristotle (1981, para. 1252aI). The 'political' immediately raises the question of what determines membership. What cohering force or essence will form the 'we' of a particular political community? Carl Schmitt's opening assertion in the *Concept of the Political* is: 'The concept of the state presupposes the concept of the political', Schmitt (1996), p. 19.

Australian 'postcolonial' context. This will enable a discussion of how the 'time' of reconciliation takes place as a 'political' event.[8]

A stable nation and proper native

In Australia the attempt to inaugurate a 'postcolonial' political community in *Mabo v Queensland* was subject to two regulative devices: the stability of the 'nation', and the insistence on an authentic 'native' determined by the continuity of Aboriginal 'tradition and custom'.[9] These devices manifest the insistence on the 'unity' and

---

8   The political is also deployed in the common-place 'everything is political' – a 'blindingly obvious' notion from which Lacoue-Labarthe and Nancy would wish to 'withdraw' the notion of the 'political' (Lacoue-Labarthe and Nancy, 1997, p. 112). The 'political' is also a question of 'space' and the 'spacing' of being (Nancy, 1993, p. 75). In Nancy's critique of the finitude of being we can observe the impossibility of being One – a singular being cannot 'be alone being alone'. The 'relation' this implies has no ground, no foundation. Existence as relation is the 'co-appearance' of being. In his thought on freedom, Nancy stresses that "existence as the sharing of being" takes place in a "political space" which is not a space for guaranteeing freedom – for instance through a community of natural right, 'humanity' or 'equality' – but in a space of the 'political' which is a 'spaciocity' that cannot be determined by any 'measure' (*ibid.,* pp. 71–5). Rather than being determined by a 'measure' (humanity, equality etc), freedom and the political (as the sharing of being) must measure itself against "nothing" (*ibid.*, p. 71). This nothing is an 'excess', a *démesure* (*ibid.*). The 'political' as the 'space' of the 'sharing' of the plurality of being should have no absolute 'measure', no determination by 'essence'. I will now contextualise these claims about the 'political' through the notion of the stable 'nation' and 'traditional Aboriginal community' that were deployed in *Mabo* as the elements that conditioned or delimited the law's attempt to inaugurate a 'postcolonial' law and society in Australia.

9   *Mabo v Queensland* (No 2) (1992) 175 CLR 1. (Note: the following in-text references are to *Mabo*.) In *Mabo* the High Court of Australia was asked to determine whether the annexation of the Murray Islands to the Colony of Queensland in 1879 or 1895 vested absolute ownership of the land in the Crown (Brennan J's decision is commonly regarded as the leading judgment, (*Mabo*, pp. 16–76)). The plaintiffs, representatives of the Meriam people, claimed that the Crown acquired 'radical title' (title to the territory or *imperium*) but not 'beneficial title' to the land (possession or *dominium*) (ibid., p. 30). The respondent, the State of Queensland, argued that the Crown acquired absolute beneficial ownership of the land on the assertion of sovereignty (*ibid.*, p. 26). By accepting the distinction between radical title and beneficial ownership of the land, the Court confirmed the acquisition of sovereignty over the Murray Islands but recognised that a *sui generis* form of title called 'native title' was capable of recognition by the common law and was thus a burden on the radical title of the Crown. The incidence of native title would be determined by the traditional laws and customs of the indigenous community making the land claim (*ibid.*, pp. 58–9). Importantly, if an indigenous community lost its physical connection with the land or ceased to practice their traditional laws and customs, both questions of fact determined by the courts, native title could not be recognised: 'when the tide of history has washed away any real acknowledgement of traditional law and any real observance of traditional customs, the foundation of native title has

'essence' of a political community as a means of re-positioning a now abhorrent form of 'colonial' sovereignty. How does 'political community' facilitate the positioning and re-positioning of sovereignty in relation to law? The Australian High Court's response to indigenous claims for justice was regulated by the imperative of maintaining the stability of 'one' political community, the Australian 'nation', and 'one' law, 'Australian law', as the 'law of the land'. The recognition of indigenous law and custom and the existence or absence of indigenous community were subordinated to preserving past 'sovereign' decisions that usurped sovereignty, appropriated land, and established a legal order and political community.

An exemplary instance of the significance of 'political community' for understanding the relationship between sovereignty and law may be gleaned through the two elements that regulated the recognition of native title in *Mabo*. The first is the significance of the stability or 'peace and order of Australian society' as the factor that regulates (sets limits on) the extent of law's responsiveness to indigenous claims for justice. As Brennan J put it:

> The peace and order of Australian society is built on the legal system. It can be modified to bring it into conformity with contemporary notions of justice and human rights, but it cannot be destroyed. (*Mabo*, p. 30)

The limits of justice (and thus of law's responsiveness to the 'previously' marginalised) is determined by the need to maintain the stability of 'Australian society' and its 'legal system'. It is not surprising, however, that 'Australian society' is not given any content as such. Indeed, it is clear from previous decisions of the High Court, including in cases such as the *Seas and Submerged Lands Case* which greatly informed the treatment of sovereignty in *Mabo*, that the Court cannot clearly assert what the 'nation' is or when it came into existence.[10] The practical consequences of

---

disappeared' (*ibid.*, p. 60). Such a determination would effectively declare the 'non-existence' of a particular indigenous community with traditional law sufficient to sustain a land claim. The High Court also stated that native title was capable of being extinguished by the grant of inconsistent tenures or the Crown's appropriation of land for its own purposes. Brennan J attributed acts of alienation and appropriation solely to the Crown exercising its 'sovereign authority over land', thus attempting to absolve the common law from any responsibility for extinguishment of native title (*ibid.*, pp. 68–9). The power that dispossessed indigenous people is thus an 'exceptional' power whose actions cannot be reviewed by a 'postcolonial' legal system.

10   See *New South Wales v The Commonwealth (Seas and Submerged Lands Case)* (1975) 135 CLR 337. In this case Stephen and Gibbs JJ dissented, but their decisions on the nature of sovereignty and 'act of state' influenced Brennan J's reasoning in *Mabo*, p. 31. A nation state, it seems, can be a power unto itself even before it achieves the status of 'nation' in international law. The Commonwealth is 'by the Constitution, endowed with the capacity to take its place as a nation state' (per Stephen J, *Seas and Submerged Lands Case, ibid.*, p. 444). But this is initially 'an *inchoate* capacity to act and be recognised as an international person' (*ibid.*). While it is the case for both Stephen and Gibbs JJ that 'for the purposes of international law, Australia is now a sovereign state' (Stephen J, 444; Gibbs J, 385), the ascent to this status

these assertions are that land tenures issued by the Crown following the usurpation of indigenous land cannot be disturbed. Nor will indigenous people be granted a form of self-determination that contests or disturbs the monistic sovereignty of one nation, or 'Australian society'.

The second element that regulates justice in *Mabo* is the determination of the continuity or not of 'traditional indigenous community' (*Mabo*, pp. 59–60). Indigenous communities must be sufficiently 'traditional' though without elements that would be 'repugnant' to the common law in order to benefit from the recognition of land rights (*ibid.*, p. 61). By deploying 'Australian society' or 'acceptable tradition' as the factors that limit legal responsiveness, the overarching political power of 'one sovereignty', 'one law' and the homogenising drive of a 'civilised society' is reiterated in the name of justice and human rights. It is through this assertion and regulation of political community, I want to argue, that a monistic sense of sovereignty and the limits of law are instantiated. These assertions about the significance of 'political community' for re-positioning sovereignty call for further elaboration.

In *Mabo* the problem of the 'political' is converted into a question of indigenous proprietary rights in land and water ('native title'). The political is inscribed and regulated by the Court's characterisation of the 'event' of sovereignty and its relationship to past and present law. According to the Court the colonial sovereign acquired title to the territory but not absolute property in the land. This difference is wrought (with no sign of irony given the task at hand was to inaugurate a 'postcolonial' law and society) by reinvigorating the English feudal system of land tenure in which a distinction is drawn between 'title' to territory held by the sovereign, and 'possession' of land either by the sovereign or anyone else (pp. 43–52).[11] The attempt to graft a 'postcolonial' law and polity out of Australia's brutal colonial history is purportedly accomplished by recasting the indigenous inhabitants as proper(tied) subjects. The proprietary interests in land of the native inhabitants (native title) are now recognised as a species of title that is a burden on the radical title of the Crown. The incidence of native title, though determined by Aboriginal 'traditional law and custom', is subject to the continuity of such 'tradition and custom' being recognised

---

of a state with international personality is a gradual, and indeterminate phenomenon. Indeed, none of the judges is clear about when, what they are now certain of, that Australia is a state in international law, took place:

> At the time of federation the Commonwealth was not an independent nation – not a person recognised by international law. That remained the situation until after the First World War – probably until after the Imperial Conference of 1926. At federation, and until the Statute of Westminster, the Commonwealth had no more power to enact legislation having extra-territorial operation than did any State (Gibbs J, *ibid.*, p. 408).

He is referring here to the States of the Commonwealth of Australia. See also, Stephen J at 444.

    11   Fitzpatrick provides a more nuanced account of the 'feudal' notion deployed in *Mabo*, see Fitzpatrick, (2002), p. 241.

by the common law.[12] Native title is thus subject to the recognition of the common law, providing it has not already been destroyed by sovereign appropriation and alienation (the grant of freehold tenures for instance). Granting property rights to the natives, rights which were apparently always already theirs, is the means by which a 'postcolonial law' based on a colonial foundation attempts to redeem itself. But this renewal is regulated by yet another imposition, this time by 'postcolonial' law. The principles for recognition set out in *Mabo* insist that the 'tradition and custom' which determines the incidence of native title be sufficiently continuous with 'tradition and custom' at the time sovereignty is asserted. Recognition by the common law depends on the natives being sufficiently native. A 'traditional community' must exist in order to sustain 'traditional law and custom'.[13] This is another sense (in addition to the 'peace and order' of the Australian 'nation') in which 'political community' sits between colonial sovereignty and 'postcolonial' law and society. Let me explain this further.

Despite the High Court's attempt to turn the question of sovereignty into a question of title to land, the 'postcolonial' moment cannot be confined to the recognition of the natives' antecedent property rights. Both colonial and 'postcolonial' law insist on a community whose essence is announced and regulated by law. Colonial law viewed the native as 'barbarous and without a settled law' (pp. 37–38). 'Postcolonial' law seeks the 'native' in order to include her. As noted above, 'postcolonial' law calls on the two modes of regulating and regularising political community. There can be no change to the consequences of the colonial assertion of sovereignty (the recognition, now, of native title) unless this renewal of law and society is 'delimited' or regulated in some way. The delimitation of the 'postcolonial' moment is contingent on what is deemed favourable to maintaining the 'peace and order of Australian society'. 'Postcolonial' inclusion and recognition is also contingent on the natives being members of a sufficiently 'traditional' community.

The *position* of a colonial sovereign and its law was refashioned in *Mabo*. Australian law, Brennan J insistently declares, 'is free of Imperial control' (*ibid.*). The following assertion is deployed to sustain this: 'The law that governs Australia is Australian law' (*ibid.*). Thus there is a re-positioning of Australian law in relation to the enterprise of the imperial sovereign and its courts. The reason given for this re-positioning is the emergence now of a post-racist political community that seeks justice and respects human rights. Brennan J announces a post-racist nation whose 'people' (p. 42) now respect the 'values of justice and human rights' (p. 30). The sovereignty of this renewed nation is itself positioned in a wider legal and political frame, for the courts must respond in accordance with the 'expectations of the international community' (p. 42). The response to indigenous claims for justice thus renews and purportedly re-inaugurates a 'nation' and its 'people'. The concomitant of this repositioning of sovereignty and law is the common law's recognition of

---

12 More detailed examination of cases which illustrate this point follow below.

13 For a treatment of the more recent native title cases which have applied this regulation of indigenous community, see Motha (2005).

'traditional' Aboriginal interests. However, only the factual incidence of native title is to be determined by indigenous traditional laws and customs (pp. 58–63).[14]

The difference between a colonial sovereign operating on racist assumptions and a 'postcolonial' law is cast explicitly through the sovereign/legal acts of dispossession. There is a 'difference', a separation, asserted between colonial sovereignty and the 'postcolonial' law that now recognises 'native title'. The conception of sovereignty deployed in *Mabo* must be both finite and infinite. A finite sovereignty is attributed to the establishment of the colony and an infinite quality is attributed to its ever 'present' effects – the dispossession of indigenous people by 'acts of state'. The 'difference' between colonial sovereignty and 'postcolonial' law is recognised by Brennan J as manifesting itself in relation to community: the dispossession of indigenous peoples 'underwrote the development of the nation' (p. 69). What's more, this is not a matter for which 'law' is responsible or accountable. Dispossession is the (now) disavowed practice that enables the separation between colonial sovereignty and 'postcolonial' law:

> As the *Governments of the Australian colonies* and, latterly, the *Governments of the Commonwealth, States and Territories* have alienated or appropriated to their own purposes most of the land in this country during the last two hundred years, the Australian Aboriginal peoples have been substantially dispossessed of their traditional lands. They were dispossessed by the *Crown's exercise of its sovereign powers* to grant land to whom it chose … . *Aboriginal rights and interests were not stripped away by operation of the common law* on first settlement by British colonists, but by the exercise of sovereign authority over land exercised recurrently by Governments. (p. 68, emphasis added)

According to this formulation, the injustice of the appropriation of land cannot be addressed by the common law. The common law, it is asserted, cannot call these sovereign, governmental decisions into question.

The impossibility of a clear separation between colonial sovereignty and postcolonial law is precisely what haunts attempts at reconciliation. This impossibility is sustained through a notion of political community that is a modern instantiation of the 'nation', but one that must also accommodate the traditional 'native' as bearer of property rights. The apparently reconciled polity is one that is backward looking in two senses – it has its foundation in a colonial assertion of sovereignty that cannot be disturbed, and the native must conform to the characteristics of one that would have been found in pre-colonial time. Reconciliation is then between a coloniser, and a native that cannot be found (though of course the colonial state continues to impose itself as a continuous entity). Let me turn, now, to address more explicitly the problem of reconciliation – a reconciliation that is caught between the time of colonial sovereignty and a backlash that resists moves to inaugurate a 'postcolonial' law and society.

---

14 A 'primitive', 'sacred' , law will determine the nature and incidence of native title. But the common law will determine the continuity and acceptability (repugnance) of the sacred in the modern (*Mabo*), p. 61.

Being-with natives: The neo-imperial gestures of reconciliation

There are multiple gestures of reconciliation in Australia. A formal national reconciliation process was set in motion in 1991 through the *Council for Aboriginal Reconciliation Act* 1991 (Cth) which established the Council for Aboriginal Reconciliation (CAR). Over the following decade CAR consulted widely and drew up two documents of reconciliation: the *Australian Declaration Towards Reconciliation* and the *Roadmap for Reconciliation* (Council for Aboriginal Reconciliation, 2000, see Appendix (below) for the former). As we observed above, the Australian common law also attempted to reconcile the colonial assertion of sovereignty with the recognition that indigenous people have antecedent proprietary interests in land and water (*Mabo*). However, Australian courts have been steadfast in their refusal of indigenous sovereignty and self-determination (see *Coe v The Commonwealth* (1979) and *Coe v The Commonwealth* (1993)).[15] The foundation of the Australian colony and its law on the theory that the natives were 'barbarians without a settled law' has been retained (*Mabo*, pp. 37–8). This colonial 'past' has had to be reconciled with a 'postcolonial' law and society that now respects 'human rights and the equality of all citizens' (*Mabo*, pp. 41–2). At the heart of this 'postcolonial' gesture are the contradictory lineaments of retaining the 'past' as the foundation of the present and disavowing this now abhorrent 'past' at the same time. Colonial sovereignty must be rendered finite in time, confined as an 'event' that took place 'back then', but also have an infinite reach (transcending the colonial era) as the foundation of present and future law and society. This conditions the failure of attempts at reconciliation – it is manifested in the impossibility of *retaining* and *disavowing* the excesses of the 'past' *at the same time*.

'We, the peoples of Australia, of many origins as we are, make a commitment to go on together in a spirit of reconciliation'. This is the opening sentence of the *Australian Declaration Towards Reconciliation* (Council for Aboriginal Reconciliation, 2000).[16] The *Declaration* is premised on a presumed and insistent 'commonality'. Reconciliation is supposed to be the basis for a 'postcolonial' future – a work of remembering, forgiving and forgetting, a promise 'towards' which the

---

15   For a thorough overview of the case law on sovereignty in the Australian context, see Brennan, *et al* (2004). For a critical account of the sovereign event in 'postcolonial' Australia, see Motha (2002 and 2005).

16   The *Declaration* was the end-product of a process commenced by the *Council for Aboriginal Reconciliation Act* 1991 (Cth). The Council for Aboriginal Reconciliation sought to consult widely among 'all' Australians and set out a strategy for promoting reconciliation. The Council spent a decade in community consultation. In this same period, the production of a postcolonial society and juridical order through the recognition of native title, for the most part, failed to deliver land, self-determination or wider recognition to indigenous communities. By the end of the 1990s, and with the evident failure of native title as a vehicle for restorative justice, reconciliation gained momentum as one of the strategies for producing a 'postcolonial' society. The *Declaration*, as we will see, provides a succinct encapsulation of the problem of colonial sovereignty and its relationship to 'political community'.

former 'colonies' will journey. But a singular 'We' is the first word, the ground, of this future. It is followed, in the text, by the recognition of a plurality of 'peoples' with 'many origins' but then returned, subordinated, to a 'being together', a 'spirit' no less, of reconciliation. What holds this plurality of peoples with their 'many origins' together? It is, unsurprisingly, a concept of sovereignty in its original imperial terms: 'We recognise this land and its waters were settled as colonies without treaty or consent' (*ibid.*). This is an admission, a confession, but importantly a preservation of a sovereign assertion which is at once finite (an event that took place 'back then'), and infinite (it can never be parted from or addressed). The *Declaration* repeats the colonial assertion of sovereignty in the 'original terms' of a 'settlement' of land and waters 'without treaty or consent' (*ibid.*). Thus the colonial appropriation of land is recognised but elevated beyond question (infinite sovereignty). The lack of treaty or consent must not get in the way of redeeming the past for the sake of a future, and thus inaugurating a new law and society. The colonial sovereign event is lightly marked as an abomination, but one that ultimately cannot be wholly left behind. The imperial assertion of sovereignty cannot be exceeded, after all, what could exceed this, what could overwhelm it?

The solution turns out to be yet another imposition of a juridical order with a superior law. The basis for recognising the previously excluded is a new inscription of an absolute, unavowable Law: 'Reaffirming the human rights of all Australians, we respect and recognise continuing customary laws, beliefs and traditions' (*ibid.*). The colonial assertion of sovereignty is crystallised in the unity of a 'nation' of 'peoples' with 'many origins' (*ibid.*). But plural 'cultures' are only recognised providing they conform to the overarching law of the "human rights of all Australians" (*ibid.*). This is where reconciliation must be assessed in the context of the 'extinguishment machinery' of native title. Any 'traditional or 'customary' norm that conflicts with 'Australian law' must give way to the latter (I will shortly consider the more extreme manifestations of the superiority of Australian law, 'culture' and civilisation). Where there is no Aboriginal law, there can be no native title. In *Yorta Yorta* the High Court of Australia insisted that 'traditional law and custom' cannot be treated as a parallel law making system. To do so would be to 'deny the acquisition of sovereignty'.[17]

As the *Declaration* reiterates, Aboriginals and Torres Strait Islanders may have 'self determination', but it has to be 'within the life of the nation' (*ibid.*). The 'postcolonial' nation vows to go on into a future as a movement 'towards' reconciliation. But this must be One 'nation' which abides by One law. There are, then, at least three moments of the 'postcolonial' condition where a 'monistic' and accomplished commonality is asserted in the *Declaration*. The first is the event of the colonial assertion of sovereignty. The second is the terms of its alteration which re-inscribes One law, Australian law, which is based on the common law of England brought by the colonisers. The third is the insistence of One community in the form of the 'nation'. One nation, one law, has evolved more recently into a demand to complete the conquest of a native 'culture' by a modern legal order.

---

17   *Yorta Yorta v Victoria* [2002] HCA 58 at para. 44.

Reconciling with natives

The question of what amounts to 'reconciliation' or 'postcolonial' recognition of indigenous rights to land and self-government has been a subject of considerable debate over the last decade. In more recent years there has been a debate about the practical successes and failures of 'Aboriginal Affairs policy' in Australia. Attention has been directed at whether the last thirty years of what is loosely termed 'self-determination' and 'liberation politics' has delivered indigenous Australians from the vast disparities of mortality, poverty, intra-group violence, youth suicide, incarceration, and drug addiction when compared with non-indigenous Australians. It is irrefutable that these disparities exist and that neither government agencies nor indigenous organisations have developed effective strategies to reduce the scale of the tragedy. Who has a right to speak about this tragedy has itself been a controversial question. But this dilemma about a 'subaltern' voice, identity and political intervention often misses the point. Taking responsibility for the causes of the plight of the colonised subject is not only about deciding on perpetrators and 'true' victims. Responsibility and its limits must also be examined by the 'beneficiaries' of the colonial enterprise. Few would escape that ambit of responsibility. But this debate is also peripheral, since in Australia the discourse on 'postcolonial' justice continues to view indigenous 'culture' as part of the problem and 'assimilation' as part of the solution. Many commentators now argue for a return to policies of 'assimilation'. The causes of the social and economic devastation in indigenous communities are being laid at the door of indigenous 'culture'. It has been suggested that indigenous people, if they conform to their old 'cultural' ways, will not escape the high levels of violence, mortality, suicide, and poverty that plague their communities.

The incompatibility between 'modernity' and the 'ancient' traditions and 'culture' of indigenous people is at the heart of a lengthy essay by one of Australia's most prominent anthropologists, Peter Sutton.[18] According to this view, Aborigines, caught in the stasis of their 'culture', are not coping with modernity. What is this 'modernisation' that indigenous people find so difficult to cope with? It is 'self-government', the introduction of local and corporate models of governance. Sutton argues that these policies seem to be built on 'a willingness to ignore publicly the profound incompatibility between modernisation and cultural traditionalism in a situation where tradition was, originally at least, as far from modernism as it was possible to be' (p. 132). Never mind the fact that indigenous people in Australia have not been granted anything that remotely resembles 'self-determination'. There is little or no reflexive interrogation of the opposition asserted between 'traditional' and 'modern' – but I will reserve commentary on the persistently 'mythical' dimensions of modernity for another discussion (see generally, Fitzpatrick, 1992 and 2001). Though Sutton acknowledges that the impetus for cultural change may come from indigenous people themselves, there is a strong suggestion that indigenous 'culture' must be rethought (p. 156). This return of assimilationist views to the Australian

---

18   Sutton (2001, pp. 125–173). Note: future *in-text* references are to this work.

'postcolonial' context harbours the contradiction – the one I identified at the outset as a central aspect of the 'postcolonial' condition – of expecting indigenous people to alter their 'problematic culture' *and* make 'culture and tradition' the condition-precedent to the recognition of 'native title' rights (the principal mode of recognising the antecedent rights of Australia's indigenous people).

Lawlessness among the 'natives' was one of the justifications for the heinous practices of the colonial 'frontier'. Their 'culture' is now the currency of the new missions to the frontier between what is being called 'tradition' and modernity. The notion of 'culture' is deployed with little reflexivity about the 'culture', political-economy, and ideology of the 'modern' managers and civilisers. Peter Sutton leaves no ambiguity about the position he is taking with regard to indigenous 'culture'. It is his 'unqualified position' that a number of the serious problems faced by Indigenous Australians arise from a 'joining together of recent, that is post-conquest, historical factors of external impact, with a substantial number of ancient, pre-existent social and cultural factors' (p. 127). His account of the 'historical context' of the 'downward spiral' in Aboriginal communities includes the following:

> The period after about 1970 was not only one of passive welfare but also, very crucially, the era in which systems of control and repression imposed on Indigenous people by church, state and private enterprises were generally displaced by the freedoms of liberal democratic policy, with its emphasis on community self management and Indigenous self-determination. (p. 128)

To free the 'native' from the bonds of Church and state in response to democratic demands is here turned into a reason to indict democratic gestures. Sutton is asserting the need to roll back some of the humanitarian, democratic gestures. Aboriginal people now need to be protected – it seems they need to be *immunised* from democracy. Sutton's argument *itself*, far from being a lament about the inability of indigenous communities to cope with 'liberal democratic policy', is instead symptomatic of the 'auto-immunity' or auto-destruction of liberal democracy (Derrida, 2005, p. 35). That is to say, the negation of the 'postcolonial' gestures which recalibrated Australia's juridical institutions and social policies is a disavowal of the multicultural democratic polity and its key features (plurality, multiple ways of being, and self-government). What we are observing in Sutton's analysis is the auto-immunity of liberal democracy – undermining the culture of a (native) subject who has just been admitted to the polity on the basis of her 'nativeness'.[19] One must recall that 'nativeness' was a condition-precedent to the belated recognition which sought to create a 'postcolonial', liberal multicultural political community. This is not to say, however, that the terms of 'postcolonial', multicultural recognition should

---

19   Of course this is not to say that we should accept Sutton's characterisation of various practices as 'cultural' or 'traditional'. Hypostatising 'culture' or 'tradition' is, more acutely, a problem to which lawyers and anthropologists contribute. There is not the space to take this issue up here.

not be vigorously called into question. My challenge is to the manner in which this is undertaken by Sutton.

According to Sutton, the release of external control, indeed repression, was misguided because it apparently assumed that 'pre-colonial' 'ideological and coercive systems of social discipline would revive' (p. 128). The faulty logic here is the failure to question why it is assumed that the removal of coercive and repressive structures – the Church and state control of indigenous peoples' lives through the various *Aborigines Acts* etc – should necessarily involve the return to pre-colonial social and cultural formations. Why did the 'future' for indigenous people have to be a return to the 'past'? Is this a problem inherent to the discourses and practices of 'reconciliation'? At the heart of the 'postcolonial' enterprise of 'reconciliation' in Australia is the idea that rights and benefits granted to indigenous people must flow to the authentic 'native'. As we observed earlier, this was the mode of regulating recognition and a device for limiting the social, economic and political benefits that would have to be returned to the indigenous population. 'Freedoms of liberal democratic policy, self management and self-determination' are also blamed for the downward spiral – even though Sutton himself calls these apparent processes into question as they often amounted to external control in any case, now by 'imported community advisers' (p. 128). If this is so, then Sutton himself would deny that there really was 'self-determination'. But this paucity of evidence of 'self-determination' is not permitted to get in the way of his larger claim that indigenous 'culture', and its revival, is partly the cause of the degradation faced by indigenous people – a result of traditional natives who cannot govern themselves.

Let us consider some of the other policies, practices and liberal humanitarian gestures which, according to Sutton, have apparently led to the degradation of indigenous communities (pp. 128–133). The introduction of equal wages to Aboriginal stockworkers led to unemployment and further displacement from traditional lands. But it was not only mechanisation that displaced indigenous labour. It was also the unwillingness of those who owned the means of production to pay equal (leaving aside fair) wages to indigenous people (pp. 129–30). The secularisation of indigenous community administrators is indicted because it led to the loss of the moral and political authority of the Church (p. 130). The natives, left to their own devices, practice sexual violence against women and children of both sexes. This is apparently 'significantly attributable to the withdrawal of older, coercive and culturally prescribed regimes, both Indigenous and imposed, without provision for something resilient that would fill the resulting vacuums' (p. 129). There is in Sutton's analysis an unexplained faith in structures of authority over the economic and social conditions in which people live. The move from focusing on the emancipation of the individual to that of the community is described as 'a major policy failure' (p. 132) – though the successors of the former policy are not listed. What the hapless natives received was a shift from a focus on the individual – the goal of assimilation – to 'a "communalising and corporatising" approach based on a doctrine of self-determination, combined with an emphasis on non-interference with Indigenous custom' – that is, the promotion of 'culturally appropriate values' (p. 132). The priority given to custom and tradition was inappropriate because it was incompatible with modernisation and modernism (p. 132).

Although Sutton is sure that the return of 'culture' was a ruinous road, he cannot give a consistent account of this thing called 'culture'. The problem with 'culture' was that on the one hand 'custom and culture' involve social forms that are 'recently developed and consciously contrived' (p. 132). On the other hand 'culture' 'consists of the interplay between "unreflexive daily practices" ... and our partial awareness of what we are doing and thinking' (p. 135). When 'culture' is mixed with the ambitions of 'reconciliation', 'culture' includes the broader support for a 'freedom to retain a way of life', in this case "'retaining Indigenous cultures"' (p. 137). So it is not culture *per se* that is problematic. It can vary between 'consciously contrived daily practices' and 'high culture' (p. 137). The problematic variant of 'culture' is that version which is mixed with the drive for reconciliation which introduced a respect for 'Aboriginal culture' as a set of practices that ceased to be controlled by the Church and state. It is also a version of culture that was set loose from those other authorities that apparently held 'indigenous culture' in check, including for instance the discipline of anthropology. The lost ground of Aboriginality results from the removal of 'indigenous culture' from the authoritative declarations of anthropologists. This is how Sutton puts it: there are contradictions in Australian indigenous affairs policy which supports 'culture' in the selective sense of 'high culture' and retains support for the broader freedom to choose a way of life (p. 137). The real complaint, however, is closer to the ground of his own profession. The problem turns out to be that 'culture' has been 'hijacked' and 'anthropology has lost control of it' (p. 137). There is an acknowledgement that indigenous people are involved in the 're-creation of non-modern identities' (pp. 160–161, fn. 27) – but given the previous complaints about the lack of authority, these are presumably not ones that are sufficiently authoritarian to replace the Church. The only attempt to historicise or contextualise these practices is to lodge them in the paradigm that Sutton finds most problematic, the movement from assimilation to self-determination (pp. 160–161, footnote 27, and accompanying text, and pp. 137–38). The fact that indigenous identity (traditional law and custom) is central to 'postcolonial' recognition – that is, the hypostatisation of 'culture' and 'tradition' through what is juridically regarded as properly indigenous – is not considered. Neo-traditionalism is partly driven by the coloniser's processes of recognition.

For Sutton, with the 'return' of indigenous culture comes an abhorrent violence that is inherent to it. Evidence for the inherent violence in indigenous culture is drawn from archaeological examination of 'prehistoric' human remains – evidence which is supposed to settle "decisively" any doubt that serious assaults took place on women and men, and on women at higher levels when compared to men (pp. 152–153). The examination of human remains by palaeopathology expert Stephen Webb discloses a high incidence of 'deliberate aggression' towards women (*ibid.*). Sutton then asserts the primacy of anthropology over the attempt to explain social behaviour from bones. Understanding violence cannot be reduced to examining 'criminality' or the 'pathology' of individuals (pp. 154–155). Violence must be examined over time (*ibid.*). It is the 'in-depth methodology of anthropology and its encompassing theoretical base, not mere assemblages of medical or criminal facts alone, that can assist official policies and practices to move beyond their present, tragically ineffectual standing to a point where communities have a chance of a better life' (p. 155). Sutton acknowledges that anthropology will not have the same influence as in previous eras, now that the context is so 'politicised' (pp. 154–155). But more anthropology is what is recommended.

The solution, according to Sutton, is more ethnography to show how violence is learned by the growing child (p. 155). Violence is apparently introduced early by the practice of 'cruelling': children even in their first months are physically punished and then encouraged to seek retribution by punishing the punisher (*ibid.*). Ethnography could show up the contradictions – the punished child may also be comforted by the mother offering the child her breast (*ibid.*). Another example is aggressive behaviour, temper tantrums by boys when they want food. These are examples, according to Sutton, where '"rethinking culture" might prove beneficial' (p. 156). Kinship also prevents indigenous people from joining the 'post-industrial world' (p. 156). To complete the neo-liberal panacea to the problems faced by indigenous people, Sutton argues that 'success will only come by individual and not collective empowerment' (p. 157). The anthropologist, on this account, can observe the native and instruct the state on how she should be acculturated into modernity and liberal society. According to Sutton there is thus a need to shift the focus from racism to the violence inherent in indigenous culture. Racism is apparently in serious decline in Australia, and though people need to be vigilant against its return, it is 'no longer the main issue' – the 'political situation has moved on' (p. 140). Racism as a persistent feature of Australian society is hardly a matter that I need go on to elaborate.

Does criticising Sutton amount to the 'racial cringe' (to 'political correctness') which he claims to be boldly challenging – that is, the refusal or reticence of non-indigenous activists and scholars to discuss serious abuses and other problems in indigenous communities, particularly sexual violence by Aboriginal men against Aboriginal women and children (p. 142 and accompanying notes)? In my view a robust debate on these issues is needed. Sutton draws on accounts of violence in indigenous communities as an urgent and pressing situation which he as a non-indigenous person should not be prevented from raising. I agree that there should not be such 'no go' areas. But for this reader, the place in his text of this emotive and sensitive material is telling. The material about sexual violence is deployed in order to establish his own ground – his authority as an anthropologist to comment on indigenous 'culture'. He grounds his authority, indeed the imperative to speak, like many anthropologists before him, with reference to the sex practices of the natives. This is no novel gesture to secure the ground of anthropology. In *The Cunning of Recognition* (2002) Elizabeth Povinelli describes how throughout the twentieth century anthropologists have been setting themselves up as the mediators, controllers, and managers of the integration of indigenous culture with liberal democratic society.[20] Povinelli argues that the question is not one of a 'true/false' moment of alterity that needs to be overcome before the writer/academic can speak on a particular issue. It is about how the 'metaethics' of

---

20 See the detailed discussion in Povinelli (2002, Ch. 3).

Australian multiculturalism is deployed (Povinelli, p. 114). 'Multiculturalism' and liberal democracy used 'culture' as the currency for negotiating the renewal of the settler-colony, and its juridical and social institutions. Unsurprisingly, recognition of 'culture' failed to transform the economic and social conditions of indigenous lives. The failure of recognition and reconciliation, and the limited terms by which that settlement was sought, are not matters for which indigenous culture should be inducted. The failure of state-policy has now been laid at the door of people being depicted as pre-modern natives. This backlash is being completed by a radical reversal of state policy in indigenous affairs.

What amounted to indigenous self-government in the form of the Aboriginal and Torres Straight Islander Commission (ATSIC), an indigenous peak body with representatives elected by indigenous peoples, has been abolished. The backlash against recognition has moved state policy away from pluralism and multiculturalism towards an insistence that indigenous communities re-enter the nation's social and economic agenda by entering into 'mutual obligation agreements' ('MOAs'). These MOAs may scrap some forms of welfare to remote communities, and impose a regime whereby the Government will only provide services in exchange for what it deems to be desirable transformations in indigenous behaviour. The policy of MOAs resonates with the agenda of calling for transformations in Aboriginal culture.

Irene Watson, who offers a timely critical appraisal of MOAs, describes them as follows:

> Aboriginal children living in remote communities could expect assistance in learning English, technology, and understanding the western world, but their parents should take responsibility for teaching their own language, culture and traditions. (Watson, 2005, p. 19)

This is the outcome of a process which Watson compares to the '*nigger hunts*' of the colonial frontier, when white men would go on hunting expeditions to exterminate indigenous people (original emphasis, *ibid.*, pp. 26–8). The potency of her criticism is drawn from what she perceives to be the likely outcome of MOAs. Without essential services there may be an exodus to cities – another means of driving indigenous people from their lands. Is this anything less than yet another instance of ethnic cleansing?

The new mode of disciplining indigenous people through the sham social contract is yet another civilising gesture backed by a sanction. The Federal Government Minister charged with the process, Amanda Vanstone, has put it like this:

> For too long we have let ideological positions like self-determination prevent governments from engaging with their indigenous citizens. … Unconditional welfare will become a thing of the past. Our agreements for funding will need to include incentives and in some cases sanctions targeted at changing behaviour. (*ibid.*, p. 20)[21]

---

21   Watson citing Amanda Vanstone, *Opening Address*, Benelong Society Conference: Pathways and Policies for Indigenous Futures, Sydney, 3–4 September, 2004.

As Irene Watson pertinently asks, who is taking responsibility here for colonial legacies and the conditions in indigenous communities? What does it mean to take responsibility in a time of reconciliation? And if self-determination is abandoned, is this not another drive to hunt the native out of their traditional lands, to crush indigenous communities and their modes of social organisation (*ibid.*, pp. 18–20)? Let us turn now to this question of responsibility in a time of reconciliation and consider its links to the problem of political community.

Reconciliation, responsibility and political community

I have just identified how a juridical, rights-based approach to reconciliation in Australia has run aground on the demand for a modern liberal subject – a subject who is made to wash her face a requisite number of times in order to benefit from the reciprocal obligations of the state such as providing infrastructure and health checks.[22] Assimilation has returned with a vengeance to the barely multicultural polity. Why this swift reversal? For Paul Muldoon the emergence of the 'culture' wars, and the complaint about the 'black armband' version of history, is a backlash created by the 'academic register' of truth telling in processes of reconciliation (Muldoon, 2003, 188–189). Where the attempt to renew the polity takes place through a revision of history through 'historical/juridical' modes of truth telling, the 'public cannot readily follow' (*ibid.*, pp. 189). He contrasts modes of reconciliation in Australia with South Africa's TRC. With the latter, the public were involved in very public confessions, testimony, and all too religious absolutions (*ibid.*, 191–2). The key point, for my purposes, is the link between modes of reconciliation and political community. Muldoon eschews the historical/juridical and confessional modes of reconciliation because they fail to treat the political community as an entity that traverses time. He states (quoting Schaap, who I will shortly consider):

> Because the political community is extended in time, a thread that connects the past, present and future, it provides a "space of remembrance that outlasts the natural lives of its particular members". (*ibid.*, p. 193)[23]

Hence responsibility for the past is possible without personal blame – all in the name of being 'citizens' of a 'just political order' (*ibid.*, p. 194). And what will usher in this new era? That turns out to be Habermasian dialogical practices of intersubjective

---

22   Under the Howard Government's scheme of Mutual Obligation Agreements, the Mulan Aboriginal community 'signed up' to wash the faces of their children 'twice daily' in return for petrol bowsers and 'regular testing for the eye disease trachoma, skin infections and worm infestations'. It is reported that the scheme was condemned as 'sanctimonious' by the only indigenous Federal parliamentarian, Senator Aden Ridgeway, and as paternalistic and reminiscent of Mission societies by academic Larissa Behrendt, see Shaw (2004); and for an alternative range of views, Dodson and Pearson (2004). For critical treatment of this agreement, see McCausland (2005).

23   Muldoon cites Schaap (2001) at 753.

argument. These will apparently enable conversation, telling and listening, and trying to see through the eyes of the others (*ibid.*, pp. 194–6). With this there could be 'legitimate changes to the moral order through publicly validated truth claims' (*ibid.*, p. 196). At the heart of this communicative ideal is the notion that the impossible, ideal speech and understanding, can produce what should never arrive. The dialogic approach enables an openness, a community that is still to come – for to truly grasp the position through the eyes of the excluded would annihilate her. But leaving the dialogue open and incomplete will not usher in a just polity which has to deal with colonial sovereignty, the usurpation of lands and other resources, and the ongoing suffering of indigenous people. Here procedural rules about moral conversations seem no less 'academic'.

For Andrew Schaap reconciliation is 'an agonistic struggle to realise commonality within the historical circumstances that continue to divide citizens who share the same political institutions' (Schaap, 2004, para. 13). He is quite right to see reconciliation as a problem of realising 'commonality' and founding political community. But his attempt to treat this question of the 'political' as the possibility of a 'moral community' which can be examined through an analytical distinction between the 'juridical' and 'ethical' leads him to embrace the impossibility of reconciliation while urging an agonistic struggle to 'understand the significance of past wrongs' (*ibid.*, at para. 39, and see paras 12, 13, 38). Indeed, responsibility for the past and the measure for a reconciled community are linked political and juridical problems arising out of attempts at reconciliation. But is this not a formulation of a mode of reconciliation that all too readily embraces the limits of the judicial/institutional decision as the condition of commonality?

According to Schaap, juridical responsibility involves the calculability of harm, cause, responsibility, reparations – ultimately the delimitation of 'response' while still taking responsibility. In this juridical mode, responsibility becomes a possibility – the incalculable becomes manageable. On the other hand, responsibility as an ethical response is infinite – it is 'unassumable' (*ibid.*, para, 20, 21). For Schaap, after Ricoeur and contra Agamben, a juridical notion of responsibility may be necessary:

> but it is a mistake to make it the cornerstone of a moral theory, for the only genuine ethical response to the kind of responsibility that arises in relation to the grave wrongs perpetrated [for instance] in the death camps is to acknowledge its unassumability. (para. 21)

Contrite apologies are cheap because they avoid juridical accountability. The moral 'we' should have good intentions because 'we' may be judged harshly and condemned by future generations (*ibid.*, para. 37). There are strong parallels here with Muldoon's 'community over time' thesis. The answer for Schaap lies in the Arendtian notion of 'action' and 'speech' – a mode of *being* in the world which sees acting *with* others as the mode of re-creating commonality, albeit a 'fragile' polity (Schaap 2004, 29–33). But the 'calculations' of the moral accountant appear unavoidable, if unacknowledged by Schaap. Following Gillian Rose, political responsibility in the 'broken middle' (between love and law) involves finding the 'just measure' between taking responsibility for actions of which 'we' are not the authors, and the paralysis of infinite responsibility (*ibid.*, para. 35). A balance will have to be struck; and hence I wonder whether this does not mark the return of the moral accountant. A legal decision will have to be taken, even, for instance one about the 'lawfulness' of genocide (the 'measure' of responsibility in Australia has elicited decisions about whether the removal of Aboriginal children from their families is authorised by law). While this is not where Schaap would strike the balance, in cases such as *Kruger* and *Yorta Yorta*, responsibility and recognition, respectively, have been (legally) delimited in order to validate the past acts of the colonists.[24] This is certainly not the stance of 'unassumable responsibility', but one that conditions the terrain of *being-with*. For what political/juridical response is appropriate in the face of an irresponsible measure for responsibility?

Schaap, like Muldoon, has to rely on the productive impossibility of reconciliation:

> For although the aspiration to reconcile enables a reconciliatory politics in the present, its realisation would undermine those conditions that constitute its possibility in the first place. The ideal of reconciliation is self-negating to the extent that it would overcome the plurality that enables a potentially world-disclosing interaction in the first place. Reconciliation necessarily presupposes a community that is not yet. However, if reconciliation is to be conceived politically, this end must be recognised as a good that exists as good only as long as it cannot be reached. (para. 40)

The openness and 'fragility' of a not-yet-reconciled polity is thus the condition of a political community actively (and dialogically) engaged in processes of reconciliation. For Schaap, after Arendt, it is acting and speaking with political adversaries, rather than juridical institutions that enable community. On this formulation plurality is possible on the basis of an ever unrealised unity. I can see the appeal of this approach as it sustains openness, keeps the violent grounds of community at bay, and suggests that what is in 'common' is always to be invented. The 'common' will then not operate as a debilitating closure of community. There is something potentially liberating about this stance.

However, reconciliation as a dialogic process which accepts the impossibility of grasping the trauma and violence of the past also appears to be an ideological device by which the processes that constitute a 'postcolonial' juridical order and political community are concealed and obfuscated. The problem of authors, perpetrators and beneficiaries, each without an absolute measure by which responsibility can be calculated with certainty, is one intractable problem. But this should not be allowed to define the contours of the debate on how the juridical and political are grounded, on how commonality and unity are re-produced. As we observed in the discussion of the return of assimilationist policies, in the indictment of Aboriginal 'culture' as essentially violent and inconsistent with modernity, and in the re-inscription

---

24 *Kruger v The Commonwealth* [1997] HCA 27; and *Yorta Yorta v Victoria* [2002] HCA 58.

of a social contract based on neo-liberal conditions of individual empowerment, reconciliation and responsibility constitute a double move: both emancipatory demand and device by which an enforced commonality can be re-inscribed. In the latter move reconciliation is nothing less than domination. Plurality as an ever-open, always impossible ideal must grapple with the reality of this double move.

Conclusion

In this discussion I have sought to explain how reconciliation presents itself as the problem of the political. In Australia, reconciliation has taken the multiple forms of juridical recognition of antecedent property right of indigenous people, and aspirations to create a reconciled polity. The limits of reconciliatory gestures have been determined by a unitary 'political community' as the regulative device ('stable' nation, 'proper' native and so on). But the liberal, multicultural gestures of inclusion are being reversed in a backlash that re-inscribes a subordinate, backward status to indigenous culture. Selectively deployed perceptions about the pre-modern practices of 'natives' are once again being invoked to drive a civilising mission that is at once neo-liberal and destructive of liberal democratic gestures. The 'native' is at once recognised and negated for being a 'native'. How can a nation-state be at once 'multicultural' and pluralistic, but also insist on a crude distinction between traditional and modern, native and citizen? The answer to this question lies, at least in part, in the auto-immunity of the liberal democratic polity. Responsibility, plurality and democratic equality harbour the suicidal destruction of the other as the condition for becoming a reconciled polity. Approaches to reconciliation in Australia have not overcome these auto-immune tendencies of liberal democracy. How democracy will overcome its suicidal tendency is what remains to be thought.

Appendix

This is the full text of the Australian Declaration Towards Reconciliation.

Australian Declaration Towards Reconciliation

We, the peoples of Australia, of many origins as we are, make a commitment to go on together in a spirit of reconciliation.

We value the unique status of Aboriginal and Torres Strait Islander peoples as the original owners and custodians of lands and waters.

We recognise this land and its waters were settled as colonies without treaty or consent.

Reaffirming the human rights of all Australians, we respect and recognise continuing customary laws, beliefs and traditions.

Through understanding the spiritual relationship between the land and its first peoples, we share our future and live in harmony.

Our nation must have the courage to own the truth, to heal the wounds of its past so that we can move on together at peace with ourselves.

Reconciliation must live in the hearts and minds of all Australians. Many steps have been taken, many steps remain as we learn our shared histories.

As we walk the journey of healing, one part of the nation apologises and expresses its sorrow and sincere regret for the injustices of the past, so the other part accepts the apologies and forgives.

We desire a future where all Australians enjoy their rights, accept their responsibilities, and have the opportunity to achieve their full potential.

And so, we pledge ourselves to stop injustice, overcome disadvantage, and respect that Aboriginal and Torres Strait Islander peoples have the right to self-determination within the life of the nation.

Our hope is for a united Australia that respects this land of ours; values the Aboriginal and Torres Strait Islander heritage; and provides justice and equity for all.

Council for Aboriginal Reconciliation (2000), Final Report of the Council for Aboriginal Reconciliation to the Prime Minister and the Commonwealth Parliament, December, 2000.

Bibliography

Aristotle (1981) *The Politics*. Trans. T.J. Saunders, Middlesex: Penguin Books.

Behrendt, Larrisa (2001a) 'Mind, Body and Spirit: Pathways Forward for Reconciliation' Vol: 5/1 *Newcastle Law Review* 38–52.

Behrendt, Larissa (2001b) 'Indigenous Self-Determination: Rethinking the Relationship Between Rights and Economic Development' Vol 24/3 *University of New South Wales Law Journal* 850–861.

Brennan, Shaun, Gunn, Brenda, Williams, George (2004) '"Sovereignty" and its Relevance to Treaty-Making Between Indigenous Peoples and Australian Governments' 26 *Sydney Law Review* 307–52.

Derrida, Jacques (1995) *Archive Fever: A Freudian Impression.* Trans. Eric Prenowitz, Chicago: University of Chicago Press.

Derrida, Jacques (2005) *Rogues: Two Essays on Reason.* Trans. Pascale-Anne Brault and Michael Nass, Stanford: Stanford University Press.

Dodson, Michael and Strelein, Lisa, (2001) 'Australia's Nation-Building: Renegotiating the Relationship Between Indigenous Peoples and the State' Vol: 24/3 University of New South Wales Law Journal 826–839.

Dodson, Pat and Pearson, Noel (2004) 'The Dangers of Mutual Obligation' *The Age* (December 15, 2004).

Fitzpatrick, Peter (1992) *The Mythology of Modern Law*, London: Routledge.

Fitzpatrick, Peter (2001) *Modernism and the Grounds of Law*, Cambridge: Cambridge University Press.

Fitzpatrick, Peter (2002) '"No Higher duty": Mabo and the Failure of Legal Foundation' Vol: 13 *Law and Critique* 233.

Fitzpatrick, Peter (2004) '"We know what it is when you do not ask us": The Unchallengeable Nation" Vol: 8 *Law:Text:Culture* 263–286.

Human Rights and Equal Opportunities Commission of Australia, (1997) *Bringing Them Home: Report of the National Inquiry into the Separation of Aboriginal and Torres Strait Islander Children from Their Families*, Sydney: Australian Government Printer.

Krog, Antjie (1999) *Country of My Skull: Guilt, Sorrow and the Limits of Forgiveness in the New South Africa*, New York, Three Rivers Press.

Lacoue-Labarthe, Philippe and Nancy, Jean-Luc (1997), *Retreating the Political*, London: Routledge.

McCausland, Ruth (2005) 'So Just Who is Sharing the Responsibility in Indigenous Affairs Policy?' Issue 28 *Matilda* (March, 9, 2005).

Motha, Stewart (2002) 'The Sovereign Event in a Nation's Law' 13 *Law and Critique* 311 – 336.

Motha, Stewart (2005) 'The Failure of "Postcolonial" Sovereignty in Australia' Vol: 22 *Australian Feminist Law Journal* 107–125.

Motha, Stewart (2006) 'Guantanamo Bay, "Abandoned Being" and the Constitution of Jurisdiction' in S. Mcveigh (ed.) *The Jurisprudence of Jurisdiction* (London: UCL Press).

Muldoon, Paul (2003) 'Reconciliation and Political Legitimacy: The Old Australia and the New South Africa' 49/2 *Australian Journal of Politics and History* 182–196.

Nancy, Jean-Luc (1993), *The Experience of Freedom.* Trans. B McDonald, Stanford, California: Stanford University Press.

Pearson, Noel (1993), 'Reconciliation: To Be Or Not To Be – Nationhood, Self-Determination or Self Government' 61 *Aboriginal Law Bulletin* 14–17.

Pearson, Noel (1997) 'The Concept of Native Title at Common Law' in Galarrwuy Yunupingu (ed.) *Our Land is Our Life: Land Rights – Past, Present and Future*, Brisbane: University of Queensland Press.

Pearson, Noel (2000) 'The Light on the Hill', *Ben Chifley Memorial Lecture*, Bathurst Panthers Leagues Club, August 12th, 2000 – www.capeyork-partnerships.com/noelperson/pdf/light-hill-12-8-00.pdf – last accessed 23 July, 2005.

Povinelli, Elizabeth (2002) *The Cunning of Recognition: Indigenous Alterities and the Making of Australian Multiculturalism*, Durham: Duke University Press.

Pritchard, Stephen (2000) 'Sacred-secrets, Justice and Reconciliation' Vol: 3/3 *International Journal of Cultural Studies* 389–406.

Schaap, Andrew (2001) 'Guilty Subjects and Political Responsibility: Arendt, Jaspers and the Resonance of the "German Question" in Politics of Reconciliation', 49/4 *Political Studies* 749–766.

Schaap, Andrew (2004) 'Assuming Responsibility in the Hope of Reconciliation' 3 *borderlands: e-journal* http://www.borderlandsejournal.adelaide.edu.au/vol3no1_2004/schaap_hope.htm – last visited, 12 July, 2005.

Schmitt, Carl ([1922] 1985), *Political Theology: Four Chapters on the Concept of Sovereignty*. Trans. George Schwab, Cambridge, Massachusetts: MIT Press.

Schmitt, Carl ([1932] 1996), *The Concept of the Political*. Trans. George Schwab, Chicago: University of Chicago Press.

Shaw, Meaghan (2004) 'Hygiene Pact in Deal for Blacks' in *The Age* (December 9, 2004).

Short, Damien (2003) 'Reconciliation, Assimilation, and the Indigenous Peoples of Australia' Vol: 24/4 *International Political Science Review* 491–513.

Sutton, Peter (2001) 'The Politics of Suffering: Indigenous Policy in Australia since the 1970s' Vol: 11/2 *Anthropological Forum* 125–173.

Toohey, Paul (2000) 'The Fruits of Political Correctness: White Dreaming of a Black Future Rots into the Desert', *The Weekend Australian*, (July, 22–23, 2000).

van Marle, Karin (2004), 'Lives of action, thinking and revolt – A feminist call for politics and becoming in post-apartheid South Africa' 19 *SAPR/PL*.

Watson, Irene (2005) 'Illusionists and Hunters: Being Aboriginal in this Occupied Space' 22 *Australian Feminist Law Journal* 15.

Williams, George (2000) 'Race and the Australian Constitution: From Federation to Reconciliation' Vol 38/4 *Osgoode Hall Law Journal* 643–665.

Chapter 5

'Spatialising History' and Opening Time: Resisting the Reproduction of the Proper Subject

Brenna Bhandar

> We have to decide to- and decide how to- be in common, to allow our existence to exist. This is not only at each moment a political decision; it is a decision about politics, about if and how we allow our otherness to exist, to inscribe itself as community and history. We have to decide to make – to write – history, which is to expose ourselves to the nonpresence of our present, and to its coming (as a 'future' which does not succeed the present, but which is the coming of our present). (Nancy, 1993, p. 166)

Introduction: history as politics

How 'we' *do history* is a political act and a decision about politics. It is through doing history that 'we' constitute ourselves as subjects and as communities. For the purposes of the present discussion of how 'history' is related to the formation of the 'subject' and how this relationship is manifest in the particular context of processes of reconciliation, I employ the concept of 'history' with an understanding of it as a modality – with spatial and temporal dimensions – through which we constitute ourselves as subjects. The spatial and temporal dimensions of history both determine and reflect our self-understanding as subjects and communities of subjects. For instance, a linear, teleological spatial and temporal conception of history lends itself to, or supports, the idea of the subject as a work in progress that develops over time, eventually reaching its fully developed state as a civilized being. Thus, the political act involved in how we 'do history' is a decision about how we understand the relationship between what has happened in the past – and more specifically, the very *shape* that our understanding of the 'past' takes – and contemporary social and political realities. In other words, the decisions about how we come to make sense of things, or give meaning to events, is the means through which we accomplish an understanding of how we come to be who 'we' are, as individuals and as communities. History can thus be understood as one of the primary means through which the 'we' – of political community, or of nation – is produced.

In a colonial settler context, such as Canada, the attempt to deal with the denial of rights and entitlements of the indigenous population in the transition to a postcolonial, constitutional democracy requires the production of an understanding of the past of colonial settlement that will facilitate such a transition. Through the production of an understanding of the process of colonial settlement, the nation and its constituent parts enable themselves to construct and configure an image of a legitimately founded, multicultural, constitutional democracy. What is at stake is not only creating a settled version of the past, but also creating a 'background' that will support an image of the future that the nation aspires to. I argue that in the colonial context, the transition from colonial settler society to post-colonial democracy that is performed through processes of 'reconciliation' requires a bounded history that is teleological and linear. While the content of this narrative may shift with time, the essential form remains the same. This has implications for the subject that is recognized through legal and political processes that aim towards a reconciliation of the violence of colonial settlement with the nation as a postcolonial entity.

In this chapter, I will argue that a linear, teleological conception of history produces a subject that is (always already) the 'proper' subject. The much vaunted social and political objective of reconciliation, prevalent in colonial settler societies which attempt to grapple with the injustices that accrued during the course of violent settlement, demands a settled, unified notion of what transpired, which in turn compresses history into a seamless, progressive narrative of nation formation. The result is that the objective to recognize previously marginalized and oppressed 'others' in the post-colonial landscape is resolved through the recognition of a 'difference' that is always and only proper to the status quo of social, material and political inequality.

By elucidating the temporal and spatial dimensions of the historical narratives that have been employed by the courts in their efforts to effect the constitutionally driven objective of reconciliation, I hope to point in the direction of alternative conceptions of history that might hold open the political potential for a different outcome in the ongoing struggle for legal and political recognition by aboriginal communities in the Canadian context. The question that remains is whether the idea of reconciliation is compatible with this alternative political and ethical vision.

Constitutional openings and closures: reconciliation as the new legal fiction?

The concept and objective of 'reconciliation' reveals a desire for the movement towards unification. Reconciliation has become the much celebrated panacea for a wide range of injustices committed by states against their own citizens. A basic definition of the verb 'to reconcile' is to 'bring (a person) again into friendly relations *to* or *with* (oneself or another) after an estrangement'; and 'reconciliation' is defined as 'the action of reconciling persons, or the result of this; the fact of being reconciled'.[1]

---

1   *Oxford English Dictionary*, Second Edition, Vol XIII.

A broader and perhaps less literal understanding of the concept of reconciliation would suggest that it is a means of dealing with the injustices that accrued during periods of totalitarian rule, apartheid, or colonial settlement; a means of dealing with the past that is not (or not primarily) legalistic. Alternatively, as I will discuss in the Canadian context, it provides a means of dealing with historical injustices through legal rights claims. That is, it sees reconciliation as a *political* and social means of resolving claims for restitution and rights.

Both the literal and broader, contextual definition of the concept of reconciliation require a 'settling' of the past in the nation's attempt to move towards a post-conflict, post-colonial state of being. Reconciliation, as a means of bringing together, 'reuniting, mending, or resolving' two (or more) entities to one another, demands the creation of a common historical terrain, a 'single universe of comprehensibility' (Asmal, Asmal and Roberts, 1997, p. 9). The problems with such an endeavour have been widely and thoroughly discussed and I will not reiterate those arguments here (see, for example, Perrin and Veitch, 1998). The impossibility of creating such a 'single universe of comprehensibility' about injustices that have occurred, particularly when the creation of this understanding relies on the shadowy concept of memory, is a problem that inevitably remains at the heart of efforts 'to reconcile' communities in conflict. History is a compilation of different threads of memory, threads that are intertwined but also in conflict. Historical memory is fragmented, making the idea of one historical 'truth' or a unified narrative nothing more than a fiction. However, the demand of reconciliation that one version of history be constructed and agreed upon – at least temporarily – so that conclusions can be reached about what and how the past unfolded, in order that restitution may be delivered, persists.

This demand of reconciliation, that the past be settled in a unified narrative, requires history to take on a particular temporal and spatial structure. The complexities and contradictory forces of colonial settlement – including problems associated with plural sovereignties – are smoothed over in the attempt to produce a unified version of the nation's past, which in turn enables the nation to embrace its idealized self-image of a post-colonial, constitutional democracy.

Canadian aboriginal rights jurisprudence is rife with illustrations of this phenomenon. A British colonial settler society, Canada came into being as a confederation in 1867. Its Constitution, the *British North America Act*, was not patriated until 1982, under a Liberal government. Along with the patriation of the Constitution, the *Charter of Rights and Freedoms* was ushered into existence, along with section 35 of the *Constitution Act*, which dealt with aboriginal and treaty rights. Alongside the *Constitution Act, 1982*, sits the *Indian Act,* 1985. The *Indian Act* originally came into force in 1886 as a means of racially inscribing aboriginal peoples as 'Indian' by defining who qualified as a 'status Indian' through blood quantum rules, and also spatially containing the native population through the creation of the reserve system. Although it has gone through many changes since its first enactment, it still governs 'Indians' and lands reserved for Indians. Despite attempts in recent decades to rectify the injustices suffered by aboriginal peoples, aboriginal communities remain impoverished materially, politically disenfranchised, and on average have a lower life expectancy than their non-native counterparts.

As a liberal constitutional democracy Canada is forced to struggle with the legacy of colonial violence as it attempts to assert the legitimacy of its democratic, human rights respecting political and legal culture. The 'transition' from a colonial settler society to that of a post-colonial nation can be understood as two competing ideological and discursive modes of governance that exist in conflict within the same spatial boundaries: a smooth, seamless progression from an ugly colonial past to the bright new future of post-coloniality. While the patriation of the Constitution, the inauguration of the *Charter of Rights and Freedoms*, and section 35 were meant to engender a new era, a new time in the history of the nation, the legacies of colonial settlement continue to haunt the present.

Writing about the transition from the apartheid to a post-apartheid era in South Africa, Grant Farred notes that the idea of teleological progression from the apartheid system to a non-racist, post-apartheid state ushered in with the democratic elections of 1994 had great purchase for many people. However, the persistence of profound socio-economic and racial inequality (among other things) ensured that 'the marking of epochal progress, from apartheid to post-apartheid, quickly showed itself to be less a march toward an ideal political future – let alone present – than a new democracy living in a double temporality' (Farred, 2004, p. 593).[2]

This notion of a double temporality is one way of describing the disjunctures and ruptures that occur as the nation-state attempts to deal with the ongoing legacies of colonial settlement, while (discursively) constituting itself as a state that is already effectively post-colonial. This moment of play between past, present and future – the moment in which the new Constitution is enacted, and the first democratic election held – holds open the possibility for political transformation. This potential has, in my view, been closed off as a result of the political-economic prerogatives of 'post-

---

2   Louise du Toit points to the presupposition of many discourses on reconciliation: "Forgiveness and reconciliation seem to logically come (if they come) only after the injustice has ended and the 'crime' or damage has been well defined and understood by both parties. These terms seem to only make sense *after a lapse of some non-violent time and a redefinition of power relations*" (du Toit, this volume – emphasis added). In a context where there has not been a redefinition of power relations or a lapse of non-violent time, the forms of violence and exclusion that give rise to the need for reconciliation and forgiveness pass into the time of the 'new' post-colonial order. The exclusion of aboriginal communities from the mainstream economy of private property relations (and the material impoverishment which this exclusion exacerbates) – in the context of aboriginal *rights* claims – has not changed in a significant way despite the stated objective of reconciliation because the aboriginal subject of rights is defined in reference to 'traditional' or 'pre-contact' *cultural* practices and pre-contact *cultural* distinctiveness. In other words, despite the newly stated objectives of reconciliation, there has not been a shift in power relations insofar as the subject of aboriginal rights remains defined and circumscribed through a colonial temporality (the point in time when the colonial power asserted sovereignty).

colonial' nations such as Canada.[3] While there appears to have been the political (and ethical) will necessary on the part of the government of Canada, for instance, to remedy the injustices suffered by aboriginal peoples throughout centuries of colonization through the recognition of their aboriginal and treaty rights in section 35 of the Constitution, the desire to maintain the political and economic structures created on the foundation of colonial settlement appears to be ever stronger. As I will explore below, this is made clear by the reluctance of the Supreme Court of Canada to recognize commercial or economic dimensions of aboriginal rights: the materialist dimensions of aboriginal rights that would actually begin to remedy colonial dispossession through the redistribution of resources seems to be left outside of the section 35 rights jurisprudence.

Reconciliation has become a key mechanism for effecting the transition from a colonial settler past to a democratic present (and future). However, as I will argue below, the concept of reconciliation has become a means of justifying the assertion of colonial sovereignty, and more recently, has been used as something akin to a *quid pro quo* for the assertion of colonial sovereignty. Reconciliation has resulted in an overcoming of one entity by another: aboriginal interests have been subsumed by and within those of the mainstream, non-Aboriginal nation, all under the rubric of ostensibly desirable objectives such as 'accommodation' and the recognition of rights.

In the Canadian context, reconciliation is identified as an objective of section 35 of the Constitution, which recognizes and affirms existing aboriginal and treaty rights. Although aboriginal rights had been recognized at common law, section 35(1) elevated those rights, affording them constitutional status and protection. Section 35(1) of the *Constitution Act* provides that:

> The existing aboriginal and treaty rights of the aboriginal peoples of Canada are hereby recognized and affirmed.

In 1997, the Supreme Court of Canada issued their judgment in *Delgamuuwk v. British Columbia*, which was the first case to deal with the definition and content of the right to aboriginal title under section 35(1) of the *Constitution Act*, 1982. In delineating the right, the Court stated that the purpose of section 35(1) is to reconcile the prior presence of aboriginal peoples on the land with the assertion of Crown sovereignty. The Supreme Court of Canada reiterated earlier judgments in positing 'reconciliation' as one of the main purposes behind the enactment of section 35(1). In *Gladstone v. R.* the Court reaffirmed *Van der Peet* with respect to the objects of this reconciliation (para. 72):

---

3   This argument has been made in the context of South Africa. Zine Magubane argues that the unproblematic adoption of neo-liberal economic policies by the ANC government has ensured the continual reproduction of socio-economic and racial inequality in the new South Africa (see, Magubane, 2004).

[F]irst, the means by which the Constitution recognizes the fact that prior to the arrival of the Europeans in North America the land was already occupied by distinctive aboriginal societies, and as, second, the means by which that prior occupation is reconciled with the assertion of Crown sovereignty over Canadian territory.[4]

The Court recognizes the fact of the prior existence of aboriginal communities on the land. There is recognition of a plurality of origins, indeed, a *prior* origin to the assertion of British sovereignty over the land. A rupture in the seamless story of Canadian nation-formation occurs. Given that the traditional rationales of international law for the colonization of other peoples' lands, such as the *terra nullius* doctrine, or the doctrine of recognition have been rejected as plausible justifications for the assertion of sovereignty over other peoples' territories, the Supreme Court of Canada had to find a way to acknowledge (and *reconcile*) the prior occupation of the land by aboriginal peoples with the assertion of Crown sovereignty (Mandell, 2003, p.166).

The Court reconciles the existence of plural sovereignties, indeed, a prior originary sovereignty over the land, by simply defining aboriginal title as an inferior legal interest: a burden upon underlying Crown title. The Court produces an astoundingly tautological rationale for the legitimacy of Crown title: Crown title is paramount because it would not make sense to speak of aboriginal title as a burden upon Crown title if it were not paramount. As the Court expressed it in *Delgamuukw v. British Columbia* (para. 45, emphasis added):

[F]rom a *theoretical standpoint*, aboriginal title arises out of prior occupation of the land by aboriginal peoples and out of the relationship between the common law and pre-existing systems of aboriginal law. Aboriginal title is a burden on the Crown's underlying title. However, the Crown did not gain this title until it asserted sovereignty over the land in question. *Because it does not make sense to speak of a burden on the underlying title before that title existed, aboriginal title crystallized at the time sovereignty was asserted.*

Although the Court recognizes aboriginal title as something that derives from the fact of prior occupation, the court makes a deft move from its 'theoretical' standpoint to a position that posits aboriginal title as a mere burden on Crown title, asserting a difference between the radical title of the Crown and the merely beneficial title granted to the aboriginal community. The Court ultimately, and imperiously finds that the legitimacy of the assertion of Crown sovereignty is 'beyond any doubt' simply because 'it would not make sense' to speak of aboriginal title as an inferior legal interest on any other basis. The assertion of Crown sovereignty becomes the temporal referent point for aboriginal title claims, thereby entrenching perhaps the greatest symbol of colonial occupation and settlement at the heart of the doctrine of aboriginal title.

---

4   The Court in *R. v. Gladstone* refers to *Van der Peet v. HMTQ* (para. 43). In *Van der Peet* the court also states that the 'intended focus' of s.35(1) is 'aboriginal people and their rights in relation to Canadian society as a whole' (para. 21).

The reconciliation performed by Canadian courts in the context of aboriginal land claims entails a continual reiteration of the legitimacy of the assertion of colonial sovereignty in Canada in order to capture the potentially disruptive force of the sovereign aboriginal subject. In *R v. Sparrow*, a case involving the aboriginal right to fish, the Supreme Court of Canada sets out a litany of injustices experienced by aboriginal communities at the hands of the colonizers, only to come to the following conclusion (p. 1103, emphasis added):

> It is worth recalling that while British policy towards the native population was based on respect for their right to occupy their traditional lands, a proposition to which the Royal Proclamation of 1763 bears witness, *there was from the outset never any doubt that sovereignty and legislative power*, and indeed the underlying title, to such lands vested in the Crown.

From the perspective of particular aboriginal communities, nations and individuals, the assertion that 'there was never any doubt' (Borrows, 1997, p. 155) about Crown sovereignty over land is more than problematic. The Court acknowledges the injustices of the colonial past and its history of racist discriminatory laws, only in order to close off and contain this past. The past is remembered only so that it may be forgotten in the push towards maintaining the foundation of the existing economic and social order.

The objective of reconciliation also forms the basis of the 2004 judgment in *Haida Nation v. British Columbia*. This case involved a claim by the Haida Nation that the provincial government has a legal duty to consult with the Haida, who have an unresolved title claim to all the lands of Haida Gwaii and the waters surrounding it, with respect to the granting of tree farm licences which affect the disputed land (para. 10). The Supreme Court of Canada found that the provincial government does have a duty to consult the Haida, pending the outcome of their title claim. The court found that there is a range of duties and obligations that arise from the duty to consult, which depend on the strength of the aboriginal rights being asserted (paras 43–44). The court noted that this process does not give rise to an aboriginal veto over plans for land use, but rather, in keeping with the spirit of accommodation, involves varying degrees of consultation (para. 45).

The outcome of this case was, without a doubt, desirable. The provincial government's ability to grant tree farm licences to logging companies on lands claimed by the Haida has been somewhat curtailed, resulting in the recognition of the Haida's claim and potential legal interest in the land. However, the Court reached its judgment on the basis that the objective of reconciliation, which flows from the assertion of Crown sovereignty over the land, is what gives rise to the Crown's duty (para. 32, emphasis added):

> The jurisprudence of this Court supports the view that the duty to consult and accommodate is part of a process of fair dealing and reconciliation that begins with the assertion of sovereignty and continues beyond formal claims resolution. Reconciliation is not a final legal remedy in the usual sense. Rather, it is a process flowing from rights guaranteed

by s.35(1) of the *Constitution Act, 1982. This process of reconciliation flows from the Crown's duty of honourable dealing toward Aboriginal peoples, which arises in turn from the Crown's assertion of sovereignty over an Aboriginal people and* de facto *control of land and resources that were formerly in the control of that people.*

In my view, this judgment signals an important shift. No longer is the Court coming up with alchemical, tautological rationales for the assertion of sovereignty. They have moved from having to *justify* the colonial assertion of sovereignty to finding that it puts into motion a *de facto* process of reconciliation. There is no choice, no process, no acknowledgment of indigenous resistance; instead there is the depiction of a kinder, gentler (honourable) sovereign power who asserts colonial sovereignty and then begins a process of negotiation. Yet the other sleight of hand that takes place through asserting reconciliation as a process that *began* with the assertion of colonial sovereignty, is the erasure of 19th and 20th century racist ideologies that underpinned much of the Crown's policies towards aboriginal peoples in Canada. The notion, for instance, that reserve lands were created to protect indigenous populations (Tobias, 1985, p. 39), or that residential schools were created to enhance and improve (or 'civilize') the lives of aboriginal peoples (Miller, 2000) were undoubtedly based on the alleged inferiority of aboriginal peoples. Rather than squarely dealing with the violence and injustice wrought by the assertion of colonial sovereignty, the Court imposes, retrospectively, a duty of reconciliation and accommodation that is said to flow from Crown control over native land.

In the judgments in *Sparrow* and *Haida*, the court attempts to create a new ground upon which present and future Crown-aboriginal relations will be based. It will be a foundation that will 'uphold the honour of the Crown' and will be in 'keeping with the unique contemporary relationship, grounded in history and policy' (*R. v. Sparrow*, para. 10). But the 'new' ground occupies the same time and space as the 'old' ground, and by re-establishing the power of the Sovereign, is ultimately subsumed by the latter. The Supreme Court of Canada will go so far as to undo the idea upon which *terra nullius* is based, but will not go so far as to question the raw assertion of sovereignty which is the basis upon which the legitimacy of a bounded territorial state, and bounded political community, rests. The double temporality of the colonial past and the aspiration of a post-colonial future produce a conflict that is resolved, in the name of reconciliation, by the suppression of any realities that would produce a permanent rupture in the dominant narrative of Canada as a tolerant, multicultural society.

In the post-1982 Constitutional rights discourse in Canada, the law attempts to re-found its origins as a tolerant, multicultural society in which the rights of aboriginal communities are respected even though there is 'no doubt' about the legitimacy of Crown sovereignty. The re-grounding is not only necessary to right the wrongs of the past, but is perceived as morally and ethically 'good'. This new ground respects difference and cultural plurality. The law, and the liberal capitalist order it supports, devises historical narratives that continually re-territorialise the past for their own legitimation, smoothing over any disjunctures that exist in fact between multiple and plural origins, and holding the appearance of a linear and teleological narrative of the nation state in place.

In this re-territorialisation of the past, and in order to found a post-colonial future that is premised on the colonial assertion of sovereignty, the Courts have recognised an aboriginal subject that is always already *proper* to the existing political, economic and legal structures of the nation-state. To recognise an aboriginal subject who is *sovereign* (rather than an aboriginal subject whose rights, while no longer dependent on the goodwill of the Sovereign, are still a burden upon Crown sovereignty), would conversely give rise to rights and entitlements to land, resources, and political sovereignty that were, if not paramount, at least equal to those of non-Aboriginal interests. The recognition of aboriginal sovereignty, would, in short, actually transform the political, legal and economic foundations of Canada.

The nature of the subject being produced through the recognition of aboriginal rights, premised on a seamless historical narrative of nation formation, becomes clear when the outcomes of a range of section 35 rights claims are examined. It is my contention that rights involving a commercial dimension have been deemed to be insufficiently 'aboriginal' according to the criteria established by the Court to prove the existence of an aboriginal right. In order for an aboriginal community or nation to make out a claim for an aboriginal right, the claimant must prove that the 'practice is a central and significant part of the society's distinctive culture', and must not have existed in the past 'simply as an incident to other cultural elements, or in response to European influences'(Mandell, 2003, p. 169). With regard to a claim for an aboriginal right to land, or to establish aboriginal title, the group must prove that they occupied the land prior to the assertion of sovereignty, that the occupancy was exclusive, and if present occupancy is relied upon as proof of occupation pre-sovereignty, there must be a continuity between present and pre-sovereignty occupation (*Delgamuukw v. British Columbia*, para. 143). There is recognition, but recognition of a right and entitlement that is inferior to the underlying right of the colonial sovereign. And this is only possible if indigenous peoples were *always already* others subsumed within the political and legal paradigm of the colonial power. Aboriginal communities were present on the land before the arrival of Europeans, and to prove the existence of an aboriginal right, an aboriginal claimant must show a connection with this primordial past. The aboriginal subject recognized through the law, however, is not one who has the capacity (or 'right') to develop, change, or transform over time, in relation to other, non-Aboriginal communities. The *proper* aboriginal subject recognized through section 35 rights claims is one who can demonstrate a viable relation to the pre-contact ways of life and cultural practices of his or her community, thus denying aboriginal communities 'the right of every Nation, to borrow ideas, change and evolve over time, and maintain their economic rights in the process' (Mandell, 2003, pp. 169–170).

The proper aboriginal subject who is continually reproduced in aboriginal rights jurisprudence is one who, because of his or her *difference* as an indigenous subject, but due to his or her contemporaneous lack of sovereignty, finds that claims which would result in a challenge to the economic, political or spatial hegemony of state sovereignty continually fail. One reason for these continual failures is that in *Delgamuukw v. British Columbia* the Court found that a wide range of activities and 'the settlement of foreign populations' in supporting 'the development of agriculture, forestry, mining, and the general economic development of the interior of British Columbia were consistent with the objectives [of reconciliation]' and hence could legitimately infringe aboriginal rights (*Delgamuukw v. British Columbia*, p. 1111). However, in addition to this extensive limitation on the scope of aboriginal rights, a number of cases further show how aboriginal interests, when they involve economic dimensions, are confounded by the position of the aboriginal litigant as an essentially *different* subject whose right claims derive from their prior occupation of the land, but one who is without sovereignty.

In *Mitchell v. M.N.R.*, the Mohawk of Akwesasne asserted the aboriginal right to cross-border trade with a community south of the Canada–US border. The Court concluded that there was insufficient evidence to establish the existence of a northerly trade prior to contact (para. 41, emphasis in original):

> There was ample evidence before McKeown J. to support his finding that trade was a central, distinguishing feature of the Iroquois in general and the Mohawks in particular. This evidence indicates the Mohawks were well situated for trade, and engaged in small-scale exchange with other First Nations. A critical question in this case, however, is whether these trading practices and northerly travel *coincided* prior to the arrival of Europeans; that is, does the evidence establish an ancestral Mohawk practice of transporting goods across the St. Lawrence River for the purposes of trade? Only if this ancestral practice is established does it become necessary to determine whether it is an integral feature of Mohawk culture with continuity to the present day.

The Court held that even if the evidentiary basis did exist to find that the community engaged in a northerly trade during pre-contact times, this would not fulfil the requirements of establishing an aboriginal right since trade was not integral to the *distinctive culture* of the band. The requirement that the right asserted be integral to the 'distinctive culture' of the aboriginal claimant operates, powerfully, in two different ways: one is to define the right in reference to *cultural* practices, which in turn serves to hamper or cap any rights that have a commercial component. The second is its melding with another requirement – that the claimant show a link with pre-contact practices – to produce a range of rights recognition that is circumscribed by *time* and the conditions which existed *at that time*; namely, the time before the arrival of Europeans. Although the court has explicitly warned against a 'frozen rights' approach, the outcome of the tests devised to establish an aboriginal right do not seem to escape this fate. Thus, the requirement that the right being asserted can be shown to have a link with pre-contact practices also serves to limit rights that would reflect the evolving needs and practices of aboriginal claimants. The aboriginal subject who is accommodated within the section 35 jurisprudence is one who has been in existence prior to contact with Europeans, but paradoxically, is presumed to have always existed within the political, economic and territorial boundaries of the nation state.

It is worth contrasting this with another case, this time involving aboriginal litigants and reserve lands, but absent an aboriginal rights claims, to show that the reproduction of the proper aboriginal subject goes beyond the particular parameters of aboriginal rights claims. This case is particularly interesting as the Musqueam were asserting the right to have the rents renegotiated in the same manner as any other land in fee simple. In *Musqueam Indian Band v. Glass*, the Court had to interpret the rent-review provisions of several individual leases of reserve lands granted to the appellant leaseholders. The reserve land had been surrendered to the Crown in 1960 for the purpose of leasing the land. In 1965, the Crown entered into an agreement with a company called 'Musqueam Development Company Limited', which enabled the company to subdivide and service the land, after which the Crown provided the Company with individual leases. In 1966, the Company assigned the leases to individuals, who built houses on each lot. Without going into further detail about the nature of the leases, suffice to say that the rent-review clause stipulated that the rent would be reviewed after the first 30 year period (and then for the three successive 20 year periods and final 9 year period of the 99 year leases). Thus, the first rent-review came up in 1995. The lease established that rent would be a 'fair rent for the land negotiated immediately before the commencement of each such period.' Further, the clause stipulated that:

In conducting such negotiations the parties shall assume that, at the time of such negotiations, the lands are

(a)   unimproved lands in the same state as they were on the date of this agreement;

(b)   lands to which there is public access;

(c)   lands in a subdivided area; and

(d)   land which is zoned for single-family residential use.

Fair rent was defined in the lease as 6 per cent of the current land value, calculated at the time of renegotiation (*Musqueam Indian Band v. Glass*, paras 3–5).

The issue before the Court was whether the fact that the leaseholds were located on reserve land ought to be taken into consideration when determining the current value of the land. The majority of the Court held that reserve lands cannot be lands to which a title in fee simple can be held, unless they are surrendered to the Crown for disposal, in which case they lose the character of reserve lands. In this case, the lands were never surrendered in this way, but were surrendered for the purposes of leasing and thus retained the character of reserve lands. From this, the majority of the Court found that Indian reserve lands were not as valuable as non-reserve lands because of 'reserve related factors' such as 'speculation about unrest, limitations on non-natives' standing to be elected to the governing body, and uncertainty about property taxation (para. 17). The result was that the land was valued at only 50 per cent of what it would have been valued if it had been deemed fee simple land not related to the Indian reserve.

In this case, the Musqueam Indian Band fell victim to a statutory regime that does not allow them to hold onto their reserve lands and also fully enter the mainstream economy of property relations. Their reserve lands are only alienable to the Crown; and as a result, they are caught within the archaic provisions of the *Indian Act*, which regulate the administration of reserve lands. Being unable to assert an interest in and maintain control over their (ancestral) lands as fee simple (without making a full fledged title claim), the Musqueam's interest in the land retains the character of *reserve* land, but on this very basis is devalued as Indian reserve land. The result is the denial of full entry into the mainstream economy with all of its benefits (the land in this case involved prime real estate in Vancouver, British Columbia) on the basis of a (racially or culturally based) *difference* that was historically inscribed. When we compare this judgment with *Mitchell v. M.N.R.*, it is arguable that the Supreme Court of Canada has also denied Aboriginal peoples the recognition of an independent Aboriginal economy based on their identity as aboriginal, and their status as the prior occupants of the land (Mandell, 2003, p. 168). The underlying logic of both of these judgments is the reproduction of the aboriginal subject who is caught within the asphyxiating confines of a (racially and culturally inscribed) *difference* without sovereignty.

Spatialising history and the 'time' of reconciliation

> History is the subject of a structure whose site is not homogenous, empty time but time filled by the presence of the now. (Benjamin, 1990, p. 253)

> [W]hat is 'now,' and what does it mean to be filled by 'the now'? 'Now' does not mean the present, nor does it represent the present. 'Now' presents the present, or makes it emerge ... A time full of 'now' is a time full of openness and heterogeneity. (Nancy, 1993, p. 166)

The objective of reconciliation as it has been articulated in the Canadian legal landscape demands a unified version of history, which, embedded within a legal paradigm that also requires the certainty and predictability of one sovereign authority, envelops any potentially transformative challenges to legal, political and economic structures built upon a foundation of colonization. The acknowledgement of the prior existence of aboriginal communities on the land is 'reconciled' with the assertion of colonial Crown sovereignty through the force of judicial pronouncement, which simply posits the 'doubtlessness' of the legitimacy of colonial occupation.

The linear, teleological temporality upon which a seamless historical narrative of nation formation is premised forecloses the decision about how we choose to constitute ourselves as subjects through our conception of history. And, as I have argued, choosing to construct our meaning of the past through a linear, teleological temporality produces a subject that is always already *proper* to the status quo. Yet what other temporalities – alternative spatialisations of time – can we conceive of? What other modes of history would enable the coming into being of a decolonized subjectivity?

Beyond asserting that we ought to understand the shape of time as non-linear and non-teleological, the question of how to spatialise time in a different way, that would allow a plurality of sovereignties to co-exist, can be explored through our relationship with the 'past'. How do we choose to understand the past, construct the past, and how does the past relate to the future? By way of beginning to address this in the current context, there are three points, drawn from Walter Benjamin's *Theses on the Philosophy of History*, that prompt us in the direction of a 'revolutionary' temporality: the critique of progress; recognizing the historical consciousness(es) that constitute our understanding of history; and attempting to divorce the concept of history from temporality all together.

The first point is that it is necessary to critique the notion of progress. If time is no longer to be conceived of as linear and teleological, the notion of 'progress' which relies upon this temporality must be taken apart (Benjamin, 1990, p. 252). We are not heading toward any final destination, just as there is no single, knowable point of origin behind us. The space or spacing of time is not contained along a single, forward looking pathway. If time is no longer understood as being progressive, and progress not necessarily linear or developmental, then history – as a means through which we constitute ourselves as subjects – would be, similarly, neither progressive nor developmental. In other words, if we accept this provocation from Benjamin, then we would not understand 'the past' as a time that had ended; nor would we understand 'the present' as a fixed or finite time that defines or reflects in a determinate way 'who we are'.

This leads to the second point about the *spatialisation* and *movement* of time. Benjamin's concept of 'revolutionary' time is particularly useful as a means of understanding the political choice involved in how we conceptualize temporality and our relationship to the past. Revolutionary time, unlike the time kept by clocks, is constituted by and through historical consciousness. There is a choice about whether or not to give in to a linear concept of time, enclosed within a progressive narrative where the past lies behind us and we look forward to the future. Benjamin's revolutionary figure refuses to give into this temptation and instead 'blasts open the continuum of history' so that past (revolutionary) moments fill the time of the 'now' (Benjamin, 1990 pp. 253–254).

The past is uncontainable; intergenerational experiences coalesce and mix. What is the shape of this revolutionary time, and the thought from which it arises? Benjamin asserts, thirdly, that thinking involves not only flows of thoughts but their arrest as well. Thought that flows and stops; and crystallises at different moments to form the structure of a monad. The monad is a space for thought freed from the strictures of representation, freed from the past as 'eternal' and completely knowable, and of the subject who is borne out of this history. It is within the space of the monad that

Benjamin's (imagined) historical materialist is able to interrupt the 'continuum of history' (Benjamin, 1990, p. 253) and constitute him or herself differently.

This third point resonates with some of Nancy's reflections on the time and space of the 'now', and the formation of the subject. Thinking the 'now' requires a radical shift in how we think of history, and how we *think* or 'do' history, for history is something to be *thought*. If we are at the end of history, Nancy (1993, p. 149) surmises, this also means the end of history as representation of a completed, presented essence of Humanity. Accepting the philosophical understanding of history as the 'ontological constitution of the subject' (Nancy, 1993, p. 148),[5] history is not representational of some point of arrival, some accomplished formation of the subject, but becomes the mode through which the 'we' comes into being, as community. History *is* community.

History, divorced from *any* notion of temporality, becomes a space, a space in time, in which the 'happening' or 'event' of community takes place. This space, or 'now' is not the 'present' in a temporal sense, it does not represent the 'present'. Rather, 'the 'now' is the 'present of happening' ... is a time full of openness and heterogeneity' (Nancy, 1993, p. 166). This 'openness' and 'heterogeneity' reflect the radically anti-essentialist nature of Nancy's ontological provocations. The community that takes place or 'shares' (in) this space is a plurality of singular beings who relate to each other as 'others'; that is, 'all the selves are related through their otherness, which means that they are not 'related'; in any case, not in any determinable sense of relationship. They are together, but together is otherness' (Nancy, 1993, p. 155).

The three points taken from Benjamin (and augmented by Nancy) illuminate the nexus between thought *as* history, thought (history) that arrests and flows; creating a space (the 'now') in which representation of the subject is suspended and subjects relate to each other in their otherness. This heterogeneity is what creates the conditions for the co-existence of a plurality of (singular) beings.[6]

This radically anti-essentialist theory of being does not easily, if at all, translate into the realm of indigenous rights, which are based on an identity that is *represented* – even if just temporarily – as a cognizable, definable entity with its own exclusions and inclusions. This is perhaps symptomatic of rights claims in general (Butler, 2004, pp. 24–25). However, accepting that the related problematics of representation and the self-present subject are inescapable in the realm of legal rights, I will nonetheless briefly explore how the 'revolutionary' concept of time and history set out above could ameliorate some of the difficulties that inhere in aboriginal rights jurisprudence.

---

5   Nancy (2003, p. 148) writes that: 'Philosophically understood, history is the ontological constitution of the subject itself. The proper mode of subjectivity – its essence and its structure – is for the subject to become itself by inscribing *in its "becoming"* the law of the self itself, and inscribing in the self the law and the impulse of the process of becoming'.

6   The concept of the 'singular' being that is always plural, or a plurality, is drawn from the work of Jean-Luc Nancy on the philosophy of existence of Being, a description of which is beyond the scope of this chapter (see Nancy, 1991; Nancy, 2000).

As I have argued, the proper aboriginal subject is produced as a result of the court's refusal to call into question the assertion of colonial sovereignty. This refusal relies on the erasure of aboriginal sovereignties, and the forgetting of the violence of colonization. The continual reassertion of colonial sovereignty assumes and presumes already the presence of aboriginal peoples within the territorial, political, and economic parameters of the nation state. To call into question the legitimacy of colonial sovereignty, to acknowledge a plurality of sovereignties, and to suspend determinative judgment on the putative point of origin of these sovereignties, would be one way of recognizing an aboriginal subject who is not assumed to be confined to the existing boundaries of the nation state.

To call into question the sovereign authority of the law might seem a fatuous suggestion given the inherent need for certainty and predictability in the law. However, as John Borrows has argued, the principles of justice, democracy, and the rule of law (among others) demand that the assertion of colonial Crown sovereignty be called into question. Drawing on a biblical analogy, Borrows (2002, p. 115), writes that 'a house built upon a foundation of sand is unstable, no matter how beautiful it may look or how many people may rely upon it'. Borrows makes a compelling and cogent argument for why and how the Supreme Court of Canada ought to call into question the legitimacy of the Crown's assertion of exclusive underlying title to all of Canada and recognize the Aboriginal sovereignty that exists contemporaneously with Crown interests. The failure to recognize this plurality of sovereign interests is to perpetuate the instability and chaotic disruptions of aboriginal communities and First Nations (Borrows, 2002).

Contrast Borrows' argument for the recognition of multiple and plural sovereignties with the minority judgment in the Supreme Court's discussion of the issue of sovereignty in *Mitchell v M.N.R.* (para. 114–115, per Binnie J):

> The common law concept of aboriginal rights is built around the doctrine of sovereign succession in British colonial law. The framers of the *Constitution Act, 1982* undoubtedly expected the courts to have regard in their interpretation of s. 35(1) to the common law concept. This point was made by McLachlin J. (*Van der Peet*, paras 227 and 262):

> The issue of what *constitutes* an aboriginal right must, in my view, be answered by looking at what the law has *historically* accepted as fundamental aboriginal rights. ... Given the complexity and sensitivity of the issue of defining hitherto undefined aboriginal rights, the pragmatic approach typically adopted by the common law – reasoning from the experience of decided cases and recognized rights – has much to recommend it. [Emphasis added in original.]

> I agree. The *Constitution Act, 1982* ushered in a new chapter but it did not start a new book. Within the framework of s. 35(1) regard is to be had to the common law ('what the law has historically accepted') to enable a court to determine what constitutes an aboriginal right.

Binnie J. finds that the scope of aboriginal rights is contained within the parameters of common law; the *Constitution Act* that enshrined aboriginal rights within the constitutional order of the country 'opened a new chapter' in the progressive narrative of the development of the post/colonial nation state and its legal order. Reconciliation, as one of the objectives of this 'new chapter' most certainly seems to have effected a closure of the meaning and content of aboriginal rights, which exist as a recognition of the fact that when the settlers arrived, aboriginal communities were already living on the land, with their own political systems and structures of governance.

Refusing to fall prey to the temptation to see the past as a closed chapter would dramatically change the landscape of aboriginal rights claims. The notion that the experience of past generations both weighs on us like a debt not easily repaid (Derrida, 1994) and is also a spur to action and resistance (Benjamin, 1990) prevents the cutting off of conditions, experiences, and events that continue to inform relations between subjects and communities even though they may have shifted form or shape, or transformed into other conditions, experiences and events. Here, Derrida's notion of spectrality is particularly useful. The notion of a fixed, stable distinction between the past, present and future is challenged by the spectre and its *revenant* – or its repeated coming back, coming back from the past – a coming back that also destabilizes a progressive notion of a future. The spectre comes back to haunt and exist in the present. The spectre comes and goes as she pleases, and thus there is little scope for predictability or order in time. The figure of the spectre also challenges fixed notions of corporeality. The spectre is 'a paradoxical incorporation, the becoming-body, a certain phenomenal and carnal form of the spirit. It becomes, rather, some "thing" that remains difficult to name: neither soul nor body, and both one and the other … . One does not know if it is living or it is dead' (Derrida, 1994, p. 6).[7]

This spectrality is what does not allow the past to be contained or shut off; it resists the closure of finite representations of the self. In the context of aboriginal rights claims, this *spectral* approach to understanding the time and space of history would mean that the past is not re-territorialised or retrospectively 'mapped' in such a way as to impose a uniform narrative structure that assumes and takes for granted the acquiescence of the aboriginal subject. The assertion of sovereignty would not 'naturally' give rise to a process of reconciliation and accommodation (see the discussion of *Haida,* above), which simply assumes aboriginal compliance. In turn, this would not facilitate the foreclosure of challenges to Canada's economic and political boundaries. Rather, the transformative potential that section 35 holds for aboriginal and non-aboriginal communities could be mobilised in a thoroughly expansive way.

By way of conclusion, I have argued that how we *think* history involves a political choice about how we constitute ourselves as subjects and communities. The objective of reconciliation, in post-colonial contexts such as Canada and South Africa, has demanded the creation of a unified, linear and teleological conception of the nation's

---

7   Derrida discusses the spectral nature of capital as Marx elaborated in his work, which is useful for challenging the political economic order engendered through a liberal capitalist teleology of development (Derrida, 1994, pp. 6; 147–148).

past and present. To argue for an alternative temporality and spatiality of history and to hold on to the objective of 'reconciliation' would, in my view, potentially strain the meaning of the concept of 'reconciliation'. It seems incongruent to aspire, on the one hand, to a type of existence characterized by an open and heterogeneous concept of the subject, but then to try to make this vision fit within the political objective of reconciliation which is about unification, restoration, accommodation and harmonization. Arguments for a suspended movement towards reconciliation certainly present one way to avoid the confining and violent implications of a fully achieved reconciliation (if one is possible) (see Van der Walt, forthcoming). However, I argue that in approaching one another – of in*clining* towards the other and remaining in tension with the differences that exist between each other – the *clinamen* that allows a plurality of beings to co-exist without the need for a progressive narrative of history does not need the language of 'reconciliation', and indeed, may even be at odds with it.

Bibliography

Asmal, K., Asmal, L. and Roberts, R. S. (1997), *Reconciliation through Truth: A Reckoning of Apartheid's Criminal Governance*, Cape Town: David Philip.

Benjamin, Walter (1990) 'Theses on the Philosophy of History', *Illuminations*, trans. H. Zorn, London: Pimlico.

Borrows, John (1997), 'Wampum at Niagara: The Royal Proclamation, Canadian Legal History, and Self-Government' in *Aboriginal and Treaty Rights in Canada: Essays on Law, Equality and Respect for Difference*, M. Asch (ed.), Vancouver: UBC Press.

Borrows, John (2002), *Recovering Canada: The Resurgence of Indigenous Law*, Toronto: University of Toronto Press.

Butler, Judith (2004), *Precarious Life*, London, Verso.

Derrida, Jacques (1994), *Specters of Marx*, trans. P Kamuf, London: Routledge.

Farred, Grant (2004), 'The not-yet counterpartisan: a new politics of oppositionality', *South Atlantic Quarterly*, **102** (4), Fall, 589–605.

Magubane, Zine (2004), 'The Revolution Betrayed?', *South Atlantic Quarterly* 102(4) Fall, pp. 657–671.

Mandell, Louise (2003), 'Offerings to an Emerging Future', in *Box of Treasures or Empty Box? Twenty Years of Section 35*, Ardith Walkem and Halie Bruce (eds.), Canada: Theytus Books Ltd, pp. 157–174.

Miller, J. R. (2000), *Skyscrapers Hide the Heavens: A History of Indian–White Relations in Canada*, Toronto: University of Toronto Press, pp. 125–128.

Nancy, Jean-Luc (1991), 'Inoperative Community' in *The Inoperative Community*, P. Connor (ed.), trans. P. Connor, L. Garbus, M. Holland, and· S. Sawhney, Minneapolis: University of Minnesota Press.

Nancy, Jean-Luc (1993), 'Finite History', in *The Birth To Presence*, Stanford: Stanford University Press.

Nancy, Jean-Luc (2000), 'Being Singular Plural' in *Being Singular Plural*, Werner Hamacher and David E. Willbery (eds), trans. Robert D. Richardson and Anne E. O'Byrne, Stanford: Stanford University Press, pp. 1–99.

Perrin, Colin and Veitch, Scott (1998), 'The Promise of Reconciliation', *Law, Text Culture*, **4** (1), 225–233.

Tobias, John (1985), 'Protection, Civilization, Assimilation: An Outline History of Canada's Indian Policy', in *As Long as the Sun Shines and Water Flows: A Reader in Canadian Native Studies*, Ian A.L. Getty and Antoine S. Lussier (eds), Vancouver: University of British Columbia Press, pp. 39–55.

Van der Walt, Johan (forthcoming), 'The Time of Reconciliation'.

Cases

Delgamuukw v. British Columbia [1997] 3 S.C.R. 1010.

Haida Nation v. British Columbia (Minister of Forests) [2004] S.C.C. 73.

Mitchell v. M.N.R., [2001] 1 S.C.R. 911.

Musqueam Indian Band v. Glass [2000] 2 S.C.R. 633.

R. v. Gladstone [1996] 2 S.C.R., 723.

R. v. Sparrow [1990] 1 S.C.R. 1075.

Van der Peet v. HMTQ [1996] 2 S.C.R., 507.

Chapter 6

Reconciliation: Where is the Law?

Lorna McGregor

> Here a silence is walled up in the violent structure of the founding act. (Derrida, 1989–1990, p. 943)

The current vogue towards reconciliatory politics has enabled the subversion and suppression of the role of the law as a key contributing factor to the transitional period. As reconciliation is the 'sine qua non for democracy' (Ratner, 1999, p. 734), law becomes relevant only in so far as it provides a mechanism through which to enable the realisation of reconciliation, rather than a substantive theme in need of redress and transformation itself. The defunct or biased state of the legal system, a lack of resources and the fragility and power-politics inherent in the transitional period all justify the avoidance of the law beyond securing amnesties or establishing quasi-judicial bodies, such as commissions of inquiry and truth commissions. Thus, a stronger or more comprehensive role must wait until the unidentifiable, reconciled future. Such avoidance would be acceptable had law played a non-divisive role in perpetuating conflict. Yet, the treatment of law as a mechanical tool of reconciliation misses the crucial role law itself plays in enabling or denying reconciliation, precisely because law routinely creates the structural conditions necessary to sustain conflict.

In his seminal article, 'Force of Law: The Mystical Foundations of Authority', Derrida depicts law as both originating in and perpetuated through violence. This chapter adopts as its point of departure an examination of the nature of law as a violent structure founding and operating within the context of colonial, international and post-colonial conflict. In considering the reductive force of reconciliation – in a sense to be developed – through its removal of law from the time and space of the transitional period, this chapter seeks to demonstrate reconciliation's endorsement and facilitation of the re-emergence of hegemonic laws in the post-reconciliation society. Rather than actively deal with the oppressive history of the law, reconciliation's avoidance merely freezes the hegemony rather than attacking its roots. In recognition of Baxi's question of whether the 'law, in its deepest structure, [is] "colonial"?' this chapter explores the potential to transform law away from its inherent violence towards a less coercive future. Using Northern Ireland, South Africa and Sri Lanka as case studies, this chapter challenges the assumptions underlying the current role of law outside and within the reconciliation rubric. Part I considers reconciliation's ironic assumption of the conventional reductive role of law through the limitation of law to functionality. While the portrayal of law as a coherent system generally presents one of the key challenges to the place of law in society, in the context of reconciliation the *denial* of the systemic nature of law actually enables the denial of the hegemonic and biased role of law in conflict, thus leaving unaddressed the potential for law to re-emerge as an oppressive force. Part II explores the historical and contemporary role of law as an inevitably hegemonic force in conflict, arguing that, as the point of transition presents the law in its most vulnerable state, it is here where the greatest potential for transformation exists. Part III attempts to prompt a discourse which seeks to identify potential spaces, capacity and limitations for the transformation of the law away from its colonial roots towards a less hegemonic future and assesses the limitations thereof.

Reconciliation's hostile takeover of the law: The emptiness of reconciliation

The popular aggregation of transitional objectives into the quest for reconciliation draws together and amalgamates a wide range of disciplines, encompassing philosophy, psychology, political science, religion and the law to provide the asserted metaphysical base for the amorphous concept of reconciliation (Teitel, 2003, p.83). On closer inspection, the essence of reconciliation stands at the pinnacle of a pyramid of uncertainty and intangibility. Reconciliation bears a shifting meaning dependent on the context of its usage. Each school of thought attempts to define its objectives and mandate, both inwardly and across disciplinary boundaries, but fails to provide a concrete meaning and purpose. For example, Huyse endeavours to bring tangibility to the term by temporal definition, yet his explanation remains vague and abstract (Huyse, 2003, p. 19):

> As a backward-looking operation, reconciliation brings about the personal healing of survivors, the reparations of past injustices, the building or rebuilding of non-violent relationships between individuals and communities, and the acceptance by the former parties to a conflict of a common vision and understanding of the past. In its forward-looking dimension, reconciliation means enabling victims and perpetrators to get on with life and, at the level of society, the establishment of a civilised political dialogue and an adequate sharing of power.

Despite the lack of definition, virtually every transitional state now cites reconciliation as the core objective of the transitional period. Indeed, Daly acknowledges that, '[w]hile the word itself is seen on every transitional government's "to do" list, its precise meaning is unclear' (Daly, 2002, p. 75). At its minimum, the term 'reconciliation' suggests the sense or spirit of a movement drawing society together into an improved, happier, more equitable whole. No benchmarks exist to indicate the manner by which to realise and identify the achievement of the vague reconciliatory objectives (Baxter, 2002). As a result, the spaces remain both open and closed, infinite and finite, for the potential of reconciliation, without a normative conception of how and where 'to do' reconciliation.

Legal patchworks within reconciliation

Multiple myths and denials operate within reconciliation discourses in their relationship to law. Law is not a participant in the reconciliation process but is rather a functional tool at the political disposal of reconciliation. In this manner, reconciliation follows the global trend of the functionalisation of the law according to which, as Santos (2002, p. 445) argues:

> the neo-liberal globalization under way is replacing the highly politicized tension between social regulation and social emancipation with a depoliticized conception of social change whose sole criterion is the rule of law and judicial adjudication by an honest, independent, predictable and efficient judiciary.

Functional arguments routinely support the subordination and reduction of the law. For example, in East Timor, access to the law was limited as the court houses and legal texts had been burnt; in Sierra Leone, the law was ten years out of date; in Rwanda, the majority of legal personnel had been killed or exiled during the genocide; in South Africa, the judges were marked as biased towards the former political regime. Legal incapacity and the fragile political climate provide for an assessment of the limitations of the law in justifying a 'pick 'n' mix' approach, rather than giving fuller consideration to the potential contributions of the law. Further, the law's biased aspects are identified as justifications against resort to the law in its previous form and substance entirely. Whereas in the post World War II period law played a central role in determining the transition, the identification of individual prosecutions as an inadequate, incomplete, partial and inconsistent form of victor's justice in response to mass atrocities, has diminished rather than developed the role of the law in the transitional period. Instead of looking behind the criticisms of the Nuremburg tribunals to assess the complex challenges facing law in the transitional period, the emergence of the reconciliatory dynamic subordinates law to a functional capacity in the provision of rules and institutions, rather than a substantive theme in need of redress. The identification of bias does not progress to an inward examination and acknowledgement of the structural role of the law in the conflict in order to provide new legal building blocks for a society distrustful of and disillusioned by the significance of the law. Rather, a strict demarcation between the law of the past and the present is imposed without a deeper understanding of the connection between the two.

The compression of the law into a functional form rather than a substantive theme as justified by the pragmatic and realistic needs of the transitional period would not prove problematic – and would perhaps even be persuasive given the demands placed upon the transitional state – if the law could be identified as a neutral bystander during conflict. (The emergence of an interdisciplinary approach partly emanates from the response to the inadequacies of the law.) Yet, the overemphasis on the need to address the blind-spots of law with interdisciplinary solutions only adds more ambiguity without solving the underlying problem of the law itself, which is denied the space for the necessary critical reflection to resolve its own crisis. This tends to leave the structural conditions untouched and unavailable for re-mobilisation.

In his discussion of the application of the specificity of colonial law, as opposed to the contextuality used by historiography, Guha provides scope to argue for the need to apply contextuality to the role of the law in conflict in order to achieve a connected narrative of the past, present, future role of the law, exposing its past and envisaging a new future. Guha argues that without contextuality, the 'insatiated urge for more and more linkages to work into the torn fabric of the past and restore it to an ideal called the full story', remains frustrated by the work of fragmentation (Guha, 1986, p. 138). Just as law traps 'crime in its specificity' (Guha, 1986, p. 140), reconciliation reductively traps law in the presence of functionality, thereby denying its oppressive history or the potential for a transformative future. Reconciliation not only excludes the law but also its subjects who suffered at the hands of the law. The denial of the complicity of the law locks those subjects in a marooned space, rather than locating the role of law in the narrative of history which would create 'an archive to dignify them as the textual site for a struggle to reclaim for history an experience buried in a forgotten crevice of the past'. Instead, reconciliation protects law as the 'state's emissary' and thus preserves the 'power balance' (Guha, 1986, p. 142).

On the surface, the failure to address the hegemonic role of law during conflict would appear to leave an element of the reconciliation project incomplete. However, a closer examination of the underlying reasons for the functionalisation of the law within reconciliation discourse may reveal why law is routinely subordinated. Yet without structural examination and renewal, the marginalisation of the law will only enable the law to reappear in a repeated, hegemonic form. In his examination of the rule of law within the structure of constitutional democracy, Rosenfeld presents the rule of law as requiring, 'fairly generalised rule through law; a substantial amount of legal predictability (through generally applicable, published, and largely prospective laws); a significant separation between the legislative and the adjudicative function; and widespread adherence to the principle that no one is above the law' (Rosenfeld, 2001, p. 1313). Rosenfeld depicts a functioning legal system through the picture of a holistic map connecting and encompassing international, regional, national and local laws to his minimal rule of law criteria, which maintains the possibility of expansion but not contraction. However imagined the holistic system may be in reality, law as a coherent system proves threatening to the amorphous nature of reconciliation. The assumption that reconciliation presents a good worthy of pursuit without any principled basis to guide its manifestation results in a deficit of deontological content. Without a clear picture of how reconciliation should look normatively, no clear obligations present themselves. Law attaches concrete reductive meaning to clearly identifiable spaces, whereas reconciliation inhabits a temporally detached universe appearing both everywhere and nowhere. Thus, the transition period might be viewed as a power-based struggle between the metaphysical structures of reconciliation and the law, in which reconciliation ultimately defeats the law.

Discourses of reconciliation therefore attempt to depoliticise the law thereby simplifying their own task by holding law captive as an applicable tool, rather than attempting simultaneously to understand, revise and reformulate the legal system as a participant of the previous regime. Reconciliation monopolises the space to define the conflict, inevitably producing its own biases on truth and memory. Law thus presents an obvious and polar challenger as a result of its history and its tendency towards strict categorisation and the production of singular, linear truths. The net effect of the power struggle results in the imposition of distorted reconciliatory politics onto the fermenting past politics *of the law*, without an outlet through which to rid law of its past or conceive a vision of how law should look normatively in the future in light of its history. The assumption that law can magically reinvent itself denies the opportunity to deal with law in a monumentalising manner: if law is actively brought into the process it becomes an issue for contestation itself, in the same way as attitudes towards the role and significance of monuments to particular sides of a conflict change as the state moves further from conflict (McEvoy and Conway, 2004),[1] creating a synergy of moving discourses exploring the meaning of the past and its place in the future between and within communities.

By reducing law in the time and space of the transition, reconciliation presumes that law can act in a servile capacity. Yet Derrida's (1989–1990, p. 941) depiction of the violent core of the law demonstrates the fallacy of this assumption:

> The very emergence of justice and law, the founding and justifying moment that institutes law implies a performative force, which is always an interpretative force: this time not in the sense of law in the service of force, its docile instrument, servile and thus exterior to the dominant power but rather in the sense of law that would maintain a more internal, more complex relation with what one calls force, power or violence.

Through the enunciation of violence as the essence of law, the use of Derrida's characterisation shows the impossibility of the reduction of law without challenge to its central roots or body. Thus, as the next section explores, violent law cyclically re-emerges, despite organisational, social or political revolutions or upheavals.

The rise, freeze and rise of the centrality of law in society

The central concern of this section relates to the pivotal role of the transition period as a temporal space in which to allow transformation of the law away from its hegemonic past. As commonly understood, the transitional space results in a pause, a prolonged intake of breath, in the oppressive function of the law which is temporally cast to the sidelines of society. Thus, the waves in the movement of law currently rise, freeze and rise again before, during and after the conflict. This section first explores

---

1   In the context of Northern Ireland, McEvoy and Conway (2004) discuss the evolution of Republican attitudes to their own monuments which are now dealt with under equality legislation rather than controlled by the Republican community.

the centrality of law in society as an oppressive force to demonstrate the stakes of not addressing the law, looking both at the way in which the legacy of colonialism remains prevalent in post-colonial societies and international law. It then considers the linear connection between the law of the past, present and future through the case studies of two societies embroiled in reconciliation discourse, Northern Ireland and Sri Lanka. The section concludes with a discussion on the importance of disrupting the time and space commanded by hegemonic legal structures within the vulnerable space of the transition.

The centrality of law in society: the law as an oppressor

Baxi analyses the conception of law as a statist hegemonic discourse – one that denies parallel or competing legal structures – by contrasting it to the longer history of westernised law (Baxi, 1988, p. 252).[2] Through an investigation into the statist assumptions for the recognition of law, Baxi argues that alternative or parallel legal discourses become excluded (Baxi, 1988, p. 250). The sovereign appropriates legal terminology such as the 'court', 'justice' and especially 'law', to mean that non-state legal structures become alternatives couched in references to 'community', 'unofficial' or 'customary' enterprises mimicking, but not reaching the status and recognition of, the law of the state (Baxi, 1988, p. 251). By preferring and elevating state law as the exclusive form of legal discourse, Baxi asserts that law 'creates a discursive field, that of conspiratorial collectivity' (Baxi, 1988, p. 259) which imposes 'repression by formal rationality' (Baxi, 1988, p. 257). He argues that the absence of formal colonialism fails to undo its legacy; rather 'the puzzling thing is that this colonial law still persists' (Baxi, 1988, p. 262). In a similar manner, the simple action of ignoring and excluding the law in the reconciliation period, contributes to a failure to address the legacy that will inevitably re-emerge.

In his thorough examination of the hegemonic history of international law, Anghie argues that, despite widespread acknowledgement of the oppressive, exclusionary character of the emergence and development of international law, the denunciation of the roots of international law has failed to translate into any form of institutional change (Anghie, 1999). Anghie traces the emergence and development of international law during the nineteenth century as a positivist and ostensibly scientific discipline that attached the mutually reinforcing conceptions of sovereignty and society to exclude and oppress non-European states through the requirement of 'civilisation' to reach the threshold of the recognition theory, a threshold which colonised states failed to achieve. In explaining this 'recognition doctrine', Anghie asserts that it 'is implicitly based on the assumption that a properly constituted sovereign exists. Only those principles created and accepted by sovereigns constitute law, and only those

---

2   Upendra Baxi (1988) argues that the western legal tradition emerged as a pluralistic system which only became narrowly concentrated on the appropriation of law to the state through the development of positivist jurisprudence, which he characterizes as 'genesis amnesia'.

entities granted legal personality by the sovereign exist within the legal universe. Once established, the sovereign can reconstitute the legal universe' (Anghie, 1999, pp. 64–65).

The hegemonic approach to international law served to ensure the exclusion of the non-European states at two critical junctures. First, the exclusion not only precluded the non-European states from participating in the development of the international legal system but also prevented them from addressing the 'sovereign behaviour' of the colonizers, meaning that the European states controlled the application of the law to evade their own accountability (Anghie, 1999, p. 51). Second, the law controlled their later entry to the system through the requirement of assimilation to the pre-existing inequality. Anghie asserts that although the interaction between European and non-European states was couched in equality terms, the non-European states continued to be denied *de facto* sovereignty through the requirement to 'comply with European standards as the price of membership into the family of nations' (Anghie, 1999, p. 67). Thus, even once the non-European states were technically located 'within' the system, they remained substantively 'outside' through the use of law as an ostensibly neutral discourse (Anghie, 1999, p. 68). Anghie asserts, therefore, that for the non-European world, 'sovereignty was the complete negation of independent power, authority, and authenticity' (Anghie, 1999, p. 70).

While acknowledging the number of developments in international law since the nineteenth century, Anghie argues that the core structure remains fundamentally unchanged. He recounts the optimism of scholars from developing nations in the 1960s who advocated the (re)acquisition of sovereignty by developing nations and the consequent equal participation in the international legal arena as the means through which to overcome the oppressive history of international law (Anghie, 1999, p. 75). However, Anghie cites the economic and political legacy of colonialism and token gestures such as the International Court of Justice's superficial removal of the civilised/non-civilised distinction from the language of the court without substantive change, such as the integration of non-European legal traditions into its jurisprudence and the adherence to treaties (agreement to which was often extracted by force), as demonstration that the ostensible changes in the international legal system failed to remove the structural premise (Anghie, 1999, p. 76). He locates the struggle of jurists and courts attempting to overcome the legacy of the nineteenth century within 'established frameworks' of a system predicated on the hegemony of the nineteenth century, thus illustrating the limited space afforded to effect change (Anghie, 1999, p. 77). Furthermore, he identifies the barriers of silence and denial of the history of international law as compounding the challenge to overcome its legacy (Anghie, 1999, p. 77):

> The question is not so much whether the nineteenth century has been transcended but how its continuing effects within the contemporary legal system may be obscured. Any tendency to treat the nineteenth century as being only of historical interest must be treated cautiously … there appears to be an inherent reflex within international law to conceal the colonial past on which its entire structure is based … The process of distancing and

suppressing the past is a common feature of the discipline, and a ritual enacted whenever it attempts to renew and revive itself.

In the conflict setting, law often retains the structure of formal legality, the organisation of which Rosenfeld argues 'may well contribute to the legitimacy of contemporary legal regimes to the extent that it equally endows all legal actors with rational means to coordinate their pursuit of self-interest' (Rosenfeld, 2001, p. 1327). In line with the position of the Critical Legal Studies movement in relation to silencing and paralysing impact of the application of positivism to formally conceal underlying but mobilised political goals (see Unger, 1983), the emphasis on predictability both evinces the appearance of fairness and legitimacy but subjects large portions of society to the knowledge that the law will predictably be used against their interests as a powerful, yet apparently neutral tool of the state, a point which Rosenfeld (2001, p. 1347) later concedes may result in a 'badly fragmented society'.

In light of these observations, in the context of reconciliation the further a society moves into the 'formalities of peace', the harder any initiative becomes to attack to the underlying historical structure of the law as an oppressive tool due to the apparent a-politicised nature of law, confirmed by the treatment of law as a functional tool during the transitional period.

Manifestations of the perpetuation of colonised law: the impact of the rise, freeze and rise again of the oppressive law

(i) Failure to connect past complicity to the present transition: Northern Ireland   The transitional justice experience in Northern Ireland acutely pronounces the detrimental effect of failing to adopt a comprehensive and reflective approach connecting the complicity of the past to the role of legal system as a whole during the transitional period. Far from a neutral arbiter in the conflict, the law, particularly the judicial organs, reflected a partial and complicit institution in the perpetuation of the conflict. Set against the substantial prosecutions of paramilitaries and political activists, the lack of prosecutions against state agents (even in light of the European Court of Human Rights judgment in *Ireland v United Kingdom* which found the United Kingdom in violation of its obligations under the Convention), engendered a strong perception of bias on the part of the legal system. Such an understanding was compounded, as Rolston exemplifies, by the general impunity of state agents in 'incidents' like Bloody Sunday, in which the military forces killed 13 civil rights protesters, and through 'policies', like that of 'shoot to kill' (Rolston, 2000, p. 32), as well as the majority composition of the judiciary as Unionists (Hillyard, 1983, p. 35).

Despite the Good Friday Agreement and the consequent move towards a political transition, the law has failed to demonstrate an internal change in relation to incidents occurring during the conflict by virtue of the failure to inform and connect the complicity of the past to the transitional processes. Hegarty argues that the push for truth processes and accountability in Northern Ireland in large part reflects a response to the abrogation of the rule of law as a 'public, unconscious but articulated need to reinstate those fundamental democratic values' (Hegarty, 2003a). At the same time, she maintains that the commissions of inquiry employed to address specific incidents during the conflict operate antithetically to the truth and accountability objectives of victims' groups. Rather, as processes instituted by the state itself, she argues that the motivating force of such processes is 'to give legal cover to governments and justify or minimise their actions, while constructing an official version or "memory" that denies the original abuse' (Hegarty, 2003b, p. 1151). Indeed, the most high-profile public inquiry, the Bloody Sunday Tribunal, represents an excessively legalistic process more reflective of an adversarial than a truth process. Yet, the state has been able to control the proceedings, and consequently the truth, through the disappearance and destruction of evidence and the delays and challenges in producing witnesses and soldiers.

Hegarty further asserts that in the particular use of legal processes as focused on individual prosecutions and investigations, 'the law tends to obscure the pattern created by abuses and its part in an overall programme of political repression employed by governments' (Hegarty, 2003b, p. 1170). The dual omission to address the impact of law as a holistic system connected temporally and institutionally, and the use of law by the State to assert its neutrality through official denial, serves to continue to perpetuate the conflict through a process of officially sealing the past but claiming to engage in reconciliatory politics (Hegarty, 2003b, pp. 1169–1170). Thus, the law continues in the politicised vein of the past and as such cannot transform into the embodiment of a human rights and equality framework which is key to undoing the harm of the past. If Hegarty (2003a) is correct in her assertion that 'only the law can undo the harm done by the law', by 'repair[ing] the rule of law and establish[ing] public confidence in the legal process' (Hegarty, 2003b, p. 1188) then the denial and complicity of the role of the law both during the conflict and at the point of transition, entrenches the perception of powerlessness and disenfranchisement, thus obstructing the potential for reconciliation. As a result, a dual process of external and internal examination of the law presents a crucial lever in the success of any efforts towards reconciliation, however defined, in shaping the acceptance of state institutions by the Republican and Unionist communities. For example, as observed by the Pat Finucane Centre (O'Connor, 2003):

> that the police completely failed in their domestic and international duty to investigate, especially when the state was involved. That the Director of Prosecutions completely failed in his duty to prosecute when the necessary evidence was available. And how the judiciary ensured that on those few occasions when soldiers ever landed in front of them that they were treated with the utmost leniency. It's almost the institutions being on trial as opposed to the individuals.

The impact of the partiality of the law and the refusal to expose and transform its role in perpetuating the conflict and sustaining a mode of denial which inhibits a full political transition is of particular concern given the location of the conflict in a purported democracy. The claim of democratic functioning denies the need for transformation of the law given the pre-existence of the same democratic institutions. Without a clear investigation into and exposure of the manner in which these purportedly democratic organs conceded to the political ideology of the particular government in power during the conflict, the law cannot transform itself under the same democratic hat. Societal perception need only look to the official denial prevalent in the Bloody Sunday Tribunal to confirm law's complicity in covering up the past in the transitional period.

(ii) The impact of the disconnection between present and future: Sri Lanka   In common with Northern Ireland, Sri Lanka experienced a complicit legal system during the conflict. Beyond a failure to use the past complicity to inform the transitional model, both demonstrate the danger to law and reconciliation of omitting to connect the transitional model to the future vision of law in the post-conflict society.

In Sri Lanka, the current discussions surrounding reconciliation barely even consider the role of the law. Rather, the idea of reconciliation excludes the law or defines it narrowly in relation to legal or quasi-legal institutions (see Ferdinands *et al.*, 2004). The current apathy towards the utility of the law with regard to transitional justice or reconciliatory politics derives from three sources. First, the huge backlog of cases situates the law as an inaccessible, expensive and often futile recourse. Second, the impunity prevalent throughout the conflict deters victims from identifying the law as a neutral arbiter of their complaints, in particular given reports of further abuse when attempting to approach law enforcers, such as the police. Finally, the failure of the four commissions of inquiry – which were initially met with significant enthusiasm, expectation and participation – to implement the recommendations set forth in the respective reports, disillusions victims as to the role law plays in raising hopes and expectations without any follow-through.

One of the most revealing examples of the apathy and distrust in the law lies in the common resort to religion, spirit mediums, ghost stories and other traditional rituals as a means of dealing with and remembering the past. In his study of the use of narratives of spirit possessions and ghost stories by victims of violence in Southern Sri Lanka, Perera (2002, p. 181) exemplifies the rationale for seeking alternate means to redress the past:

> In fact, the police and the military, which are integral components of that law and order system, have been directly responsible for many of the violent deaths, disappearances and experiences of torture. In such a context, many people have lost faith in the secular legal system and do not expect justice to be served in the legal sense. Many also do not have the physical, mental, or financial means to seek such justice through the secular legal system. A lone fight, as some have attempted, could lead to their own elimination. Thus, many people in such situations seem to believe in divine or demonic intervention as the only hope for justice or revenge available to them.

Without denouncing the role of traditional coping mechanisms, which clearly assist in the healing process, the dependency on such methods does not replace or equate to the possibility of legal justice. There is a clear difference between the desire for and the expectation of justice. Yet, in a context in which access to justice is unavailable, the risk of overplaying the reach of the traditional coping mechanisms builds a justification for the failure to provide strong legal processes, thus denying victims the ability to avail themselves, should they so wish, of official options.

The potential for the emergence of cycles of revenge in the face of a lack of secular justice also presents a strong counterargument to the claim that the law potentially threatens reconciliation. Indeed, Perera concludes that the desire to remember or the inability to forget persisted and was heightened by the subversion of justice in the 'secular and legal sense' (Perera, 2002, p. 160). He couples this with the assertion that while victims generally claim closure in terms of their loss, the use of particular deities related to revenge within the narratives suggests otherwise (Perera, 2002, p. 182). Without the availability of justice as a rational converter of revenge (Minow, 1998, p. 12), the risk to reconciliation becomes significantly pronounced (Minow, 1998, p. 11). Indeed, Minow warns that '[f]inding some alternative to vengeance – such as government-managed prosecutions – is a matter, then, not only of moral and emotional significance. It is urgent for human survival' (Minow, 1998, p. 14). In the situation where victims frequently live alongside their perpetrators in the same village, the lack of justice denies the Orwellian removal of the 'monster' in the perpetrator (Minow, 1998, p. 188).[3]

In common with Northern Ireland, the legal system in Sri Lanka also needs to be held accountable for its role during the conflict. In consideration of Laqueur's location of the division in Sri Lanka as a 'chasm between their respective views of the state' – citing the need for 'the general acceptance not of a theory of rights but of a common view of power and its exercise' (Ignatieff, 2003, p. 137) – the law needs to be transformed from a tool of the powerful to an accessible and equitable organ relevant to the lives of Sri Lankan society. Connecting to the experience of Northern Ireland, transformation needs to be explained in a manner connected to, and in recognition of, the partial and defunct role of the law in the past. The law should also demonstrate, at the outset, that it can offer an alternative or addition to traditional coping mechanisms and revenge.

The transition period as the optimal point for change

Christodoulidis (2001, p. 208) asks, 'what future does not seek its point of departure in some origin in the past?'. Looking to the future time and space of the post-transitional society, the immediate response to Christodoulidis' question demands the identification of the origin of law's future: the hegemonic conflict period or the reconciliation period? The pattern of attachment of colonial, oppressive laws to societies that are emerging or have emerged from conflict persists in the determination of the future law's origin. Thus, reconciliation's reductive restriction of law to a technical capacity fails to offer an alternative or fresh point of departure but rather entrenches and endorses the colonial legacy through the superimposition

---

3   Perera is discussing George Orwell.

of reconciliatory politics. The failure of reconciliation to highlight and address the politicisation thus enables the denial of the responsibility and complicity of the law itself during conflict as an agent and participant of repressive regimes, layered with the masked complicity of the law in the present in functionally serving the reconciliatory agenda, despite the latter's ill-definition and uncertainty.

Although law will inevitably regain power and control as an organising system, reconciliation fails to consider the effect of the fermentation of legal politicisation on a revived legal system. Self-interestedly, the failure to respond to the politicisation of law as an agent of and participant in repressive regimes during conflict will eventually disable a reconciliation in whose name it is subverted through the denial of the opportunity for law to transform – from a complicit, partial and hierarchical order to an inclusive, rights and equality-based system – thus revealing the destructive impact of the law's subordination. The preservation of the law's status quo confirms Derrida's insight into the law's 'mystical foundation of authority', displacing ideas of the derivation of the law's legitimacy from some broad notion of consent,[4] rather the continuation of hegemonic legal structures demonstrates the inability to identify the source of the legitimacy of law emerging from conflict absent an attempt at institutional change. Thus, the emergent law confirms its coercive force as an entity indistinct from the institution which commanded oppression and hegemony against a substantial percentage of the population during conflict.

The characterisation of the rise, freeze and rise again of the centrality of the law demonstrates the way in which the current reductive treatment of the law by reconciliation preserves the time and space occupied by the law in society, a location which Santos characterises as '*the national state time-space* [which] configures not only the action of the state but also social practices in general' (Santos, 2002, pp. 449–450). It is in this vein that van Marle advocates 'the disruption of a chronological and linear conception of time that could contribute to an acceptance of the notion of multiple truths and fluidity of meanings and the other supporting the notion of slowness, where difference and particularity can be explored and recognised in contrast to law's speed, universalisation and generalisation' (van Marle, 2003, p. 2). Although she advocates the disruption of legal time frameworks in their relationship to the wider participants of the reconciliation process, the same logic may be assumed for the purposes of relocating the point of origin of the law's future through the disruption of the fluidity between the hegemonic structures of the law past, present and future. However, as the frozen space provided by the reconciliation period presents the law in its most vulnerable – and thus malleable – state, the slowness for which van Marle appeals cannot be applied to the law itself as the confines of the transition period paradoxically require an immediacy in response to the contextuality of law throughout the conflict. Whereas Christodoulidis depicts the 'stilling' and stabilising tendency of the law (Christodoulidis, 2000, p. 20), I suggest that law must endorse the risk that he locates in reconciliation in order to assume the challenge of

---

4   As promoted through the idea of social contract by Hobbes, Kant, Locke, Rawls and Rousseau and from the Habermasian requirement of consensus.

transformation, and, working antithetically to its constitutive base (Finley, 1989, p. 890), reach for more radical understandings rather than clinging to the status quo.

Conclusion: the potential to undo law's fate

The point of transition offers the space in which to re-examine the boundaries and legitimacy of the construct of law in its vulnerable, subordinated and fragmented form. Yet, the temporary hostile takeover by the metaphysics of reconciliation only subordinates and ostracises the law from such a transformative opportunity. Post-transition, however, law routinely returns to play a significant role in the ordering of society. Through the re-establishment of the rule of law, the law reappears in a technically packaged form, lending it ostensible legitimacy and thus denying the space for examination of what remains a hegemonic core. Equally however, the question arises as to whether a transformation through critical engagement rather than apathetic acceptance of the law within the uncertain social space of the transition actually presents a tangible possibility for change or whether the law remains destined and constrained by its 'fate'.

Addressing the realm of writing as a whole, Derrida asserts that, 'no knowledge can keep it from essential precipitation towards the meaning that it constitutes, and that is, primarily its future' (Derrida, 1978, p. 11). Baxi applies this principle of 'fate' to explain the hegemony of law, raising the central question of the capacity of the law to transform (Baxi, 1988, p. 255). Baxi asserts that 'law becomes fate for individuals when it combines within its manifold self the dominance of both the state and civil society' (Baxi, 1988, p. 255). Yet, in a similar vein to Hunt's depiction of Foucault's 'expulsion' of law – as a sovereign and centralised enterprise redundant in the modern era – as a failure to acknowledge the relationship between state-centric discourse and society (Hunt, 1992, p. 8), Baxi departs from a wide range of subaltern studies texts that disregard the law – termed by Baxi as the 'collapse of law from a whole range of associated practices in redoing and recreating history' – to bring the law back. Rather than reject the law as a result of its reductive, abstract capacity, illustrated by Guha in his metaphorical portrayal of law as the 'state's emissary', Baxi argues that the paradoxical concreteness of 'abstract legality' through the oppressive production of an official, exclusive truth necessitates the author of subaltern truth to 'combat the state's emissary, both in its phallic and epistemic roles' (Baxi, 1988, p. 250). Thus, the possibility to transcend the fate of the law does potentially exist. Indeed, Guha (1986, p. 161) concedes that 'the triumph of fate helped to enhance rather than diminish human dignity'. Viewed in this way, the realisation of fate through the complicity of law and the dominance of the state actually opens the space for transformation, rather than closing and constricting possibilities.

Derrida asserts that the 'State is afraid of fundamental, founding violence, that is, violence able to justify, to legitimate ... or to transform the relations of law ... and so to present itself as having a right to law' (Derrida, 1989–1990, p. 989). Thus, Derrida seeks a counter-violence to undo or transform the violence of the law. By way of contrast, through his exploration of the capacity of the law to act as an emancipator, Santos identifies a 'sociology of emergence which entails interpreting in an expansive way the initiatives, movements or organizations that resist neo-liberal globalization and social exclusion, and offer alternatives to them ... it acts upon both possibilities and capacities. It identifies signals, clues or traces of future possibilities in whatever exists' (Santos, 2002, p. 465). The sociology of emergence thus chips away at the hegemony of the law without attempting to exclude state law from the overall initiative. Rather than denounce state law, the movement extracts law from its 'hegemonic mould' (Santos, p. 466), recognising the potential to use 'hegemonic tools for non-hegemonic objectives [in fact] there are alternative, non-hegemonic conceptions of such tools' (Santos, p. 467). Thus, rather than reduce and ostracise the law, discourses of reconciliation should explore the means available to combat the hegemony produced by the law, either through violence or emancipation.

The characterisation of law as a coherent system based on objective rules (Trubek, 1990)[5] clearly raises questions as to the mythology created by the law to buttress its own reality and strength. In contrast, Finley's feminist critique of the law appropriates the image of a system to expose the totality of the patriarchical structure (see MacKinnon, 1989) of the law (Finley, 1989, p. 897):

> The language of individuality and neutrality keeps law from talking about values, structures, and institutions, and about how they construct knowledge, choice, and apparent possibilities for conducting the world. Also submerged is a critical awareness of systematic, systemic, or institutional power and domination.

Such alternative discourse opens the closed space of the perceived neutrality of the law '[t]o talk openly about the interaction between historical events, political change and legal change' (Finley, p. 897). Thus, reconciliation can appropriate the traditional tools of oppression used by the law through the conception of a system to counter the hegemony of the law. In the same way that Trubek asserts that 'the neutrality of law is more myth than reality, but that the existence of this myth sometimes makes a difference' (Trubek, 1990, p. 14), the mythology vitally assists in the employment of law's own traditional tools to construct an alternative reality through a connected narrative that demonstrates the collective sum of law's parts in its role as an oppressive collaborator rather than an a-political entity in the perpetuation of conflict. The appropriation of the use of narrative by the law as a tool of the powerful against the powerless reverses the emphasis on the use of narrative to reduce, control and abstract (Amin, 1986, p. 167). Thus, the act of narrating, as posited by Ricoeur, 'does not consist simply in adding episodic events one another; it also constructs meaningful totalities out of scattered events' (Amin, 1996, p. 186).[6] As a result, reconciliation can both denounce law as a coherent system but appropriate the image of a system to build a narrative of the past and present role of

---

5   See David M. Trubek (1990) discussing the original understanding of law by the Law and Society Movement.

6   Amin references Ricoeur, *The Narrative Function.*

the law as a destructive force in perpetuating conflict. An alternative understanding of a system thus may enable what Santos (2002, p. 446) identifies as the 'radical unthinking of law ... that is, reinventing law to fit the normative claims of subaltern social groups and their movements and organizations struggling for alternatives to neo-liberal globalization'.

However, the problem remains of the normative content of the transformation of the law. The historical experience of the hegemonic concentration of the law illustrates from where the law should move in the reconciliation period but the future location remains ill-defined. Equally, the need for exploration of a reconstructed vision of law should not halt the project before it begins. As law does not arise in a vacuum but operates in society through the direction of its colonial, oppressive history and in spite of the freezing effect of reconciliation, it will continue to present an active component within society, thus no choice exists but to initiate the investigation. As Rosenfeld inadvertently demonstrates, curbing the hegemony of state law presents nothing but a necessity: 'So long as [the state] retains a monopoly in lawmaking and law enforcement, nothing short of revolution would seem capable of prompting it to desist from a deliberative course of natural rights infringement' (Rosenfeld, 2001, p. 1335). Thus, transformation does not adopt as its point of departure the eager enthusiasm of the 'Law and Society Movement' which believed that law provided the necessary tools to effect 'progressive social change' (Trubek, 1990, p. 9). Rather, the idea of transformation arises in the acknowledgement of the inevitable presence of law and the need, at least, to attempt to prevent a recurrence of the oppressive role of the past by engaging the law itself (Finley, 1989, p. 907). Equally, the task does not emerge as a new or foreign concept for legal discourse, but simply joins a long list of movements addressing the evolution of the legal system and the place of law in society, traceable at every juncture back to the founding of the law itself. Indeed even Derrida, who agrees with Benjamin that there 'is something decayed or rotten in law', (Derrida, 1989–1990, p. 999) asserts:

> [t]hat justice exceeds law and calculation, that the unpresentable exceeds the determinable cannot and should not serve as an alibi for staying out of juridico-political battles, within an institution or a state or between one institution or state and others ... Not only must we calculate, negotiate the relation between the calculable and the incalculable ... we must take it as far as possible, beyond the place we find ourselves and beyond the already identifiable zones of morality, or politics or law ... each advance in politicization obliges one to reconsider, and so to reinterpret the very foundations of law such as they had previously been calculable or delimited.

In this way, for as long as justice and law remain somehow interrelated, the quest for transformation must continue. As Derrida later argues, '[o]nly the yet-to-come (*avenir*) will produce intelligibility or interpretability of this law' (Derrida, 1989–1990, p. 993). On this view, the fate of law can only be determined retrospectively, producing the interminable quest to overcome, challenge and defy its potential existence. Without knowing whether the fate of law does embody violence, the inevitability of its position in society requires continual counter-movements, attacking the violence of its essence.

Against this background, the need to define the expectations of the law in the future and locate the transformation inside and outside of the reconciliation dynamic presents a challenging task. The expectation of the law relates to a transformation in how law is used in memorial, constitutional and reconciliation processes in the transition from partial politics favouring the powerful and privileged towards a more transparent, inclusive law. This transformation should not be viewed as a pretension towards an ideal of a purified law but rather the depiction of law as an organic organising vehicle evolving to provide opportunities (Olsen, 1985, p. 863), access and options to subjects previously marginalised by the legal system. Rather than focus on law on its limitations, the transformative approach concentrates on what law can do in its limited but maximalist sense. In assessing how law can play a role in the transition, the issue moves from the defunct argument of whether law can ever embody a profile purged of politics, and looks instead at whether law can participate in social change and transformation. While law is not sufficient for social change, it does present a necessary facet where its future role continues to be presumed, accepted and present.

Equally, law as a hegemonic force may clash with reconciliatory politics, thus the hierarchical nature of the law needs reassessment – without eroding its authority completely – in forming a partnership with reconciliation which sets law in its social and historical context. Such transformation requires internal as well as external participation, necessitating law's intervention in its own history in order to resolve its own biases. Yet the assumption and usurpability (Markovits, 2001) of law for political purposes questions the capability of the law to reveal and resolve its own blind spots. Thus the more realist stance posits expectations and deontological content upon the law to undergo a process of internal change whilst, simultaneously, critical external forces exert pressure for further change and evolution. The transformation of the law necessitates processes pushing in and out of law's boundaries. Such a process should not seek to create one truth but rather a synergy of multiple truths through discussion and movement and the development of law within society.

To conclude then, if in the current transition reconciliation commands the entire space, a revised picture may portray overlapping circles of law and reconciliation, both sharing and maintaining independent spaces. In such a shared space both may work together, with law introducing some structure and security in expectations to the amorphous concept, and reconciliation softening the harshness of legalistic methodology in dealing with mass human rights violations and pushing for the development of a more participatory law placed in its social context. In their individual circles, reconciliation maintains its ethical component separate and distinct from the regulation of law. And in the legal circle, law endeavours to transform itself through the vision of its legal institutions as the living face of its normativity.

Bibliography

Amin, Sahid (1986), 'Approver's testimony, judicial discourse: the case of Chauri Chaura', *Subaltern Studies* **5**, Delhi, 166–202.

Anghie, Anthony (1999), 'Finding the peripheries: sovereignty and colonialism in nineteenth-century international law', **40** *Harvard International Law Journal* 1 – 80.

Baxi, Upendra (1988), '"The state's emissary": the place of law in subaltern studies', *Subaltern Studies* **7**, Delhi, 247–264.

Baxter, Victoria (2002), *Empirical Research Methodologies of Transitional Justice Mechanisms*, Conference Report, Stellenbosch, South Africa: AAA Science and Human Rights Program, 18–20 November.

Christodoulidis, Emilios A. (2001), 'Law's immemorial' in Emilios Christodoulidis and Scott Veitch (eds) *Lethe's Law: Justice, Law And Ethics In Reconciliation*, Oxford, Portland Oregon: Hart Publishing.

Christodoulidis, Emilios A (2000), '"Truth and Reconciliation" as Risks', *Social and Legal Studies*, **9** (2), 179–204.

Daly, Erin (2002), 'Transformative justice: charting a path to reconciliation', *International Legal Perspectives*, **12**, 75–183.

Derrida, Jaques (1989–1990), 'Force of law: the "mystical foundation of authority"', trans Mary Quaintance, *Cardozo Law Review*, **11**, 921–1045.

Derrida, Jacques, (1978), *Writing and Difference*, trans Alan Bass, Chicago: Chicago University Press.

Ferdinands, T. Rupesinghe, K. Saravanamuttu, P. Uyangoda, J. and Ropers, N. (2004), *Sri Lankan Peace Process at Crossroads, Lessons, Opportunities and Ideas for Principled Negotiations and Conflict Transformation*, Sri Lanka: Berghof Foundation of Conflict Studies, Colombo, January.

Finley, Lucinda M. (1989), 'Symposium: The moral lawyer: Article: Breaking women's silence in law: the dilemma of the gendered nature of legal reasoning', *Notre Dame Law Review*, **64**, 886–910.

Guha, Ranajit (1986), 'Chandra's Death', *Subaltern Studies* **5**, Delhi, 135–165.

Hegarty, Angela (2003a), Interview February 4.

Hegarty, Angela (2003b), 'Dealing with the past: the government of memory: public inquiries and the limits of justice in Northern Ireland', *Fordham International Law Journal*, **26**, 1148–1192.

Hillyard, Paddy (1983), 'Law and order', in John Darby (ed.) *Northern Ireland: the Background to the Conflict*, Belfast: Appletree Press Ltd.

Hunt, Alan (1992), 'Foucault's expulsion of law: towards a retrieval', *Law and Social Inquiry*, **17**, 1–38.

Huyse, Luc (2003), 'The Process of Reconciliation' in *Reconciliation After Violent Conflict: a Handbook*, Sweden: IDEA Handbook Series.

MacKinnon, Catherine (1989), *Toward a Feminist Theory of the State*, Cambridge: Harvard University Press.

Markovits, Inga (2001), 'Papers of general interest: selective memory: how the law remembers and forgets what we remember about the past – the case of East Germany', *Law & Society Review*, **35**, 513–563.

McEvoy, Kieran and Conway, Heather (2004), 'The dead, the law and the politics of the past', *Journal of Law and Society*, **31** (4), December, 539–562.

Minow, Martha (1998), *Between Vengeance and Forgiveness after Genocide and Massive Violence*, Boston, MA: Beacon Press.

O'Connor, Paul, Finucane, Pat (2003), Centre, Interview, 4 February.

Olsen, Frances E. (1985), 'The myth of state intervention in the family', *University of Michigan Journal of Law Reform*, 835–864.

Perera, Sasanka, (2002), 'Spirit Possessions and Avenging Ghosts. Stories of Supernatural Activity as Narratives of Terror and Mechanisms of Coping and Remembering', in Kleinman Das; Ramphele Lock and Reynolds, *Remaking A World: Violence, Social Suffering And Recovery*, New Delhi: Oxford University Press.

Ratner, Steven R. (1999), 'New democracies, old atrocities: an inquiry in international law', *Georgetown Law Journal*, **87**, 707–748.

Rolston, Bill (2000) *Turning the Page Without Closing the Book: The Right to Truth in the Irish Context*, Irish Reporter Publications.

Rosenfeld, Michel (2001), 'The rule of law and the legitimacy of constitutional democracy', *Southern California Law Review*, **74** 1307–1351.

Santos, Boaventura de Sousa (2002), *Towards a New Legal Common Sense: Law, Globalization and Emancipation*, Second Edition, UK: Butterworths, LexisNexis.

Teitel, Ruti G. (2003), 'Transitional justice geneology', *Harvard Human Rights Journal*, **16**, 69–94.

Trubek, David M. (1990), 'Symposium: back to the future: the short, happy life of the law and society movement', *Florida State University Law Review.* **18**, 4–55.

Unger, Roberto (1983), 'The critical legal studies movement', *Harvard Law Review*, **96**, 561–675.

van Marle, Karin (2003), 'Law's time, particularity and slowness', *South African Journal on Human Rights*, **19**(3), 245.

Cases

Ireland v. United Kingdom, Series A, Vol. 25, 1978.

Chapter 7

Transnational Law and Societal Memory

Peer Zumbansen[1]

…wherever men become absorbed in a medieval search for the magic formula of universal truth the creeds of government grow in importance and the practical activities of government are mismanaged. Holy wars are fought, orators and priests thrive, but technicians perish. Color and romance abound in such an era, as in all times of conflict, but practical distribution of available comfort and efficient organization is impossible. T.W. Arnold, *The Folklore of Capitalism* (1937) p. 21

Introduction

The 'big bang' of military or political revolution that accompanies the setting free of powerful dynamics of transition and transformation, of post-conflict, post-apartheid and post-war justice, has triggered a widespread and wide-ranging research agenda around the world that is concerned with the chances of a new 'beginning' and the need to account adequately for the legacies of past experiences in the process (Teitel, 2000). From post-apartheid South Africa (Gross, 2004), the East- and West-German narratives of the Nazi past (Herbert and Goehler, 1992) and Germany's Reunification (see Markovits, 2001), to post-genocide Rwanda (Mgbako, 2005; Agbakwa, 2005) and the 'transformative occupation' (Bhuta, 2005) of Iraq (Anderson, 2004; Frame 2005), the existing accounts of this process challenge our understanding of how to go about the future while minding the past. In a crucial way, such fragile and vulnerable societal projects also challenge the role of law as we learn to recognize its distinct role in ascertaining past deeds committed, plights suffered and answers found to the often unspeakable events of the past. Importantly, coupled with this reconstructive, dialogical dimension of the law's addressing of the (and its) past, we find its institutional dimension.[2] While the former encompasses accountability, reconstruction and 'truth', the latter relates to the re-creation or foundation of

---

1 A first sketch of this paper was presented in Glasgow in May 2004. I am grateful to Scott Veitch and Emilios Christodoulidis for their invitation and to the workshop's participants for their comments.

2 'One of the most important and difficult challenges confronting a post-conflict society is the re-establishment of faith in the institutions of the state. Respect for the rule of law in particular, implying subjugation to consistent and transparent principles under state institutions exercising a monopoly on the legitimate use of force, may face special obstacles' (Chesterman, 2004, p. 154).

democratic institutions, constitutions and the rule of law.[3] But it is this tension between the allegedly extraordinary status of the events on the one hand, and the regular and reliable workings of the legal order on the other that informs and structures our approach to bringing the law to bear upon these challenges. Is law silent in states of exceptions[4], during *les heures zero*, and at notorious 'new beginnings', suggesting something uniquely separate from the otherwise regular or violent workings of the law (Hay, 1992)? New beginnings offer themselves as opportunities for coinciding legality and legitimacy, yet the law of new beginnings is in fact tainted and burdened by the past experiences of law that question the acceptable meaning and substance of the very term itself (Radbruch, 1946, p.105).[5] As Ruti Teitel (2000, p. 6) puts it, 'What is deemed just is contingent and informed by prior injustice.'

This chapter seeks to bring to contemporary discussions of post-conflict justice and nation-building a uniquely focused perspective. Its basis lies in an understanding of the challenges faced by law in different post-conflict contexts where law is expected to provide the grounding and starting point for national and societal reconstruction. While the distinct experiences that we can observe are deeply embedded in particular histories and trajectories of countries and peoples, the law's response has, at least since the Nuremberg trials, taken on a wider perspective. Far from suggesting a one-size-fits-all answer to the legal void after periods of atrocities and human suffering, we can observe the emergence of a *transnational law of post-conflict justice*. It develops from the increasingly shared experiences in designing a legal answer in situations of post-conflict reconstruction. These situations illustrate the utmost challenge of legally addressing the downfall of law, of reliability, and legitimacy. Whether law can at all adequately address the absence of (a higher sense of) law *ex post*, remains a fundamental conundrum no different from the question of how to adequately speak of the unspeakable (Hunt, 2004).[6] Worldwide experiences with

---

3   For an excellent overview of the panoply, see Teitel (2000); see also Chesterman (2004).

4   This goes back to Cicero's *oratio pro annio milone*, where he states: *inter arma silent leges*. This has found a great renaissance in the widespread curtailment of civil rights in the international and domestic war on terror. See, for example, Morgan (2004, pp. 525–544); Scheppele (2004, pp. 1001–1083); Oliver Lepsius (2002, III 7). For its legacies, see Schmitt (1986); Koskenniemi (2002, pp. 159–175).

5   See the debate between Hart (1958, pp. 593–628), and Fuller (1958, pp. 630–672).

6   'Die formelhafte Zusammenfassung der Eltern für das Geschehen war der *Schicksalsschlag*, ein Schicksal, worauf man persönlich keinen Einfluss hatte nehmen können. *Den Jungen verloren und das Heim*, das war einer der Sätze, mit denen man sich dem Nachdenken über die Gründe entzog. Man glaubte mit diesem Leid seinen Teil an der allgemeinen Sühne geleistet zu haben. *Fürchterlich* war eben alles, schon weil man selbst *Opfer* geworden war, Opfer eines unerklärlichen kollektiven Schicksals. Es waren dämonische Kräfte, die entweder außerhalb der Geschichte walteten ode Teil der menschlichen Natur waren, auf jeden Fall waren sie katastrophisch und unabwendbar. Entscheidungen, in die man sich nur schicken konnte. Und man fühlte sich vom Schicksal ungerecht behandelt' (Uwe Timm, 2003, p. 91).

village courts, truth commissions and international and domestic criminal tribunals testify to a border-transcending inquiry into the intricacies of transitional justice. Such experiences are being portrayed, researched, communicated and compared, and they inform contemporary and future efforts. The boundaries between legal process and alternative or complementing forms of societal reconciliation have been shown to become increasingly porous in light of the overwhelming challenge to those engaged in transformative politics. It is against this background that the distinctive role of law warrants closer inspection.

The following section of this chapter will introduce the notion of transnational law [TL]. The subsequent parts will mobilize the concept and idea of transnational law to further explore the particular qualities of law's capacity to address past injustice. The transnational perspective illuminates the impasses and blind spots that straightforward legal approaches to righting past wrongs have in common. While a growing number of examples involving litigation for the compensation of historic crimes have become prominent over the past years (Baumgartner, 2002; Sarkin, 2004), truth commissions in post-apartheid South-Africa or the Gacaca Courts in post-genocide Rwanda have been taken as powerful examples for alternative, or not exclusively law-based, routes to societal reconciliation. The development of alternatives proved to mature quickly, and contemporary assessments reveal an increasingly refined focus of inquiry into the structure of mass crimes (see Eltringham, 2004). This refinement brings into play again the intricate relationship between legal process and other societal communications in post-conflict situations. The transnational law of post-conflict justice, then, unfolds less as a firmly established or contained body of law, than as an approach to structuring, with the help of legal norms and legal theory, processes of establishing accountability and legal responsibility. While contemporary acts of public remembrance might be accompanied with solemn declarations of 'historical', 'moral', or 'political' responsibility,[7] *legal responsibility* seems much harder to attain. The definitive nature of legal responsibility seems to stand in stark contrast to the truth-finding efforts that are illustrated by the examples of South Africa or Rwanda. With victims or their heirs ardently seeking their 'day in court', often many decades after the deed (see Neuborne, 2002), we are confronted with the challenge of designing legal processes in a manner that makes the practice of the law as it was known *then* (that is, in the immediate past) visible and comprehensive while opening all possible ways for reconciliation today. The obstacles we face in the struggle for truth, for a better understanding of the past and, ultimately, for forgiveness and forgetting,[8] may seem insurmountable in light of the arbitrary ways

---

7   See, for example, the preamble to the Law establishing the compensation fund 'Remembrance, Responsibility and the Future' available at http://www.compensation-for-forced-labour.org/pdf/Foundation_law_consolidated_E.pdf.

8   See on the eminent role of forgetting Margalit (2002), Chapter 6: 'Forgiving and Forgetting'.

in which the rulers are separated from the ruled, the oppressors from the oppressed:[9] as Christodoulidis (2001, p. 221) notes, 'Why should one assume that the end result of our accounting of the past will move us any closer to a shared community rather than a break-down of community?'

It is here, however, where the eminent role of the law shines through, both with regard to its contribution to the preceding, unjust legal state as well as to its current role in shaping the communicative processes that unfold between the perpetrators and the victims during transition.[10] In these highly contested moments of human conflict, the role of the law is itself questionable. Against this challenge, it shall be argued that the law plays a pivotal role in the process of societal post-conflict resolution. It does so by providing for rules and for language that contain and capture otherwise dispersed understandings and value assessments as they once were expressed through a norm; provides, that is, a ruling or legal terminology. While law can only observe the dichotomy between *legal* and *illegal* (Luhmann, 2004), this reductionism is in fact able to capture the tensions that mark conflict communication in highly heterarchical societies. Post-conflict societies are of a dramatically fragile nature, and law assumes an organizing, memorializing, and guiding role in providing part of the communication structure of that society. As law is being put to an existential test in post-conflict situations, the very nature of law becomes open to question. It is in this light, then, that the inquiry into the law of post-conflict justice links ongoing searches of the role of law in society in different, yet comparable contexts. And it is here where the idea of transnational law begins to unfold.

The meaning of Transnational Law

The first usage of the term Transnational Law (TL) continues to be disputed. While scholarship focused on the origins of the term for a long time, it has since become apparent that the real challenge of TL lies in its scope and conceptual aspiration (Jessop, 1956;). Within an interdisciplinary research agenda concerning the transformation of globalized law, TL offers itself as a supplementing and challenging category. Famously conceptualized in a series of lectures by Philip Jessup at Yale Law School (1956), TL 'breaks the frames' (Teubner) of traditional thinking about interstate relationships by pointing to the myriad forms of border-crossing relations among state and *non*-state actors.

Jessup (1956, p. 2) writes that he 'shall use the term "transnational law" to include all law which regulates actions or events that transcend national frontiers. Both public and private international law are included, as are other rules which do not wholly fit into such standard categories'. When examining the inescapable

---

9   See also the intriguing novel by Vladimir Nabokov, *Bend Sinister* (1947), republished by Vintage, 1990. I am indebted to my friend, Achim Podak, who guided me to this book.

10   See the novel by Achmat Dangor, *Bitter Fruit* (2004), for a forceful illustration of the destructive impact of apartheid rule and human failings on humans even long after the fall of the oppressor regime.

'problem' of people worldwide whose lives are 'affected by rules', Jessup points to the striking contingency 'by which we attribute the label of "law" to rules, norms or customs that govern various situations'. It is the hallmark of TL to identify the hidden agendas and the blind spots of traditional regulatory law understandings. These latter are marked by the clear assignment of law-making authority to certain institutions on the one hand, and on the other, a clear view of which norms of societal guidance are to be recognized as *legal* rules. In contrast, TL suggests a widening of the law-making agenda and of our understanding of law as such. TL emerges from the increasingly interlocking spheres of societal norm production by public, official, and private, unofficial norm-setting agencies and actors.

Based on such an expanded understanding of law, TL has begun to reach deep into the heart of contemporary struggles over the role of law within dispersed and fragmented spaces and places of norm-production.[11] TL reminds us of the very fragility and *unattainedness* of law. At the beginning of the 21st Century, we are still at a loss to identify a theory of law that would be subtle enough not to stifle emerging identities in a post-colonial era (see, for example, Lyon, 2003), while providing *forms, fora and processes* (Wiethölter, 1986) for the collision of discourses that mark post-metaphysical, legal thinking (Habermas, 1996a; 1996b). TL is characterized by the emergence of norms that are no longer only generated by officially recognized sources of the law, but by a multitude of domestic, foreign and transnational norm-producers. This 'soft law' constitutes a radical challenge to the state-based concept of law-making that began to emerge in the 19th Century and that Max Weber, among others (Ehrlich, 1962), so powerfully captured as the rise of 'modern law' (Weber, 1914). In contrast to law originating in an official constitutional order, soft law encompasses norms that are not attributable to an official author of statutory norms, and which do not appear directly enforceable by recognized, traditional means for the execution and application of legal rules. Instead, the soft law that is now emerging in many fields of regulatory law[12] can be read as reactions to incapacities on the side of the state to proceed with adequate legislation. The proliferation of soft law thus offers examples of what anthropologists and legal sociologists have for a long time been describing as 'legal pluralism'.[13] It consists of expert standards, best practices, and recommendations as well as principles and standards that can be seen as fertilizing ongoing searches for 'better law' without due regard to political or geographical borders.

The relevance of TL to an understanding of contemporary regulatory challenges, however, is not restricted to the field of law as such. With regard to law, TL works

---

11   For the background of the distinction between spaces and places, see Sassen (1998).

12   See, for example, Linda Senden (2004); Blanpain and Colucci (2004); Kirton and Trebilcock (2004); Trubek and Trubek (2005, pp. 343–364); Zumbansen (2006, forthcoming).

13   Moore (1973, pp.719–746); Griffiths (1986, pp. 1–55); Arthurs (1988, pp. 50–88) describing the persistence of legal pluralism in light of the ever stronger tendencies to centralize law through statutory law and official courts. For further assessments of legal pluralism, see Teubner (1997, pp. 3–28), and Perez (2003, pp. 25–64).

itself like a drill through the few remaining security blankets hastily thrown over an impoverished and internally decaying conceptual body. But, beyond the study and practice of law, TL can serve to illuminate current searches in regulatory theory and societal self-regulation.

Transnational Law and Transitional Justice

In the context of and in concert with other complementing disciplines, TL is distinctly able to fertilize other conceptual searches while being informed by the transformations occurring within these disciplines. As much as TL has been shown to lay bare the raw and vulnerable foundations of law in all of its absurd contingency[14] and utopian aspiration, while being based in social practice administered with denominational authority (Moore, 1973; Bourdieu, 1987; Derrida, 1990)[15] law itself reaches out to disciplines such as history, cultural studies and anthropology to tell its own story. With legal history taking form as a transnational enterprise (Merry, 1992; Anghie, 2005)[16] it can build on and learn from the work being done by historians and cultural studies scholars. The emergence of *transnational history* gives overwhelming testimony to a border-crossing inquiry into the legality-legitimacy narratives of state and nation building. Formerly conceived and framed in discrete fashions, domestic or national historical narratives reveal and communicate common experiences and semantic appropriations in comparative, transnational and global perspective (Bright and Geyer, 1995; Bentley, 1996; Middell, 2000).[17]

The law of post-conflict justice shifts between the unattainable poles of retribution and reconciliation, between persecution and justice, between remembrance and forgetfulness (Adler and Zumbansen, 2002). It is destined and cursed to do so while its very foundations are exposed in their inadequacy at every turn. 'Law is caught between the past and the future, between backward-looking and forward-looking, between retrospective and prospective, between the individual and the collective' (Teitel, 2000, p. 6). Experiences with alternative routes to societal reconciliation in recent years have shown how very fragile and in many ways ill-suited the legal apparatus is in the context of post-conflict reconstruction. This moment exposes the co-existing poles of law, its *utopia*, *reconciliation* and *forgiving* on the one hand and *revolution* and *retribution* on the other. Law and the functions it serves do not exist outside of human imagination, but law is not merely the result of human action. Instead, it is through its function that we can begin to understand the unique quality of law. As developed by the German sociologist and legal theorist, Niklas Luhmann,

---

14   See the discussion of law in Jean Anouilh (2000).

15   See also the Special Issue of *German Law Journal*, Vol. 6, No. 1 (1 January 2005), available at: http://www.germanlawjournal.com/past_issues_archive.php.

16   See the contributions to Geschichte-transnational, http://geschichte-transnational. clio-online.net/transnat.asp?lang=en.

17   Geschichte-transnational, http://geschichte-transnational.clio-online.net/transnat. asp?lang=en.

law serves primarily to stabilize expectations. It does so by producing rules that preserve the identification of something as 'legal' over time and are therefore available for an assessment at a later point in time. The time-binding quality of law is thus the basis and the core of Luhmann's legal theory. By 'moving the problem to the temporal dimension [w]e can see the social meaning of law in the fact that there are social consequences if expectations can be secured as stable expectations over time' (Luhmann, 2004, p. 143).

The law of post-conflict justice can be observed to provide exactly that. It serves to establish a framework for the stabilization of societal expectations. Just which law is most adequate to guide this process remains a great challenge. The very connectedness of the assessment of past injustice with the normative architecture of a new legal order makes it evident that often, in the application of post-conflict justice, it is not merely a specific statute or practice on trial, but a whole system. Taking this into consideration, the realm of questions to be addressed is far greater than any piece-meal approach to remedying a wrong would ever entail (see Pogge, 2004).[18] Recent inquiries into the specific role of constitution-making and of constitutional law in the transitional process have begun to shed some light on the intricate dynamics of legal norms in post-conflict and other transitional contexts (Klug, 2000; Walker, 2002; Gross, 2004; Kumm 2005). But, while the creation of constitutional bodies bears the insignia of a fresh start, of new beginnings,[19] the big bang and bright lights of constitution making are only too likely to render us deaf and blind to the constant struggle for law's dominion in the everyday workings of established legal orders (Gross, 2004, p. 51). The particular attention paid to constitutional processes in periods of transition leads to an isolation of constitutional law and constitution making from the legal order in general. By that, the legal order becomes reified as something that functions smoothly and is in no further need of critical assessment. The exposition of constitutional moments in transition periods functions to cast a shadow on the persisting legitimacy challenges that are inherent to the legal order as such (see Koskenniemi, 2002; Orford, 1999, pp. 689–692). Constitutional beginnings, then, share a decisive characteristic with other narratives of new (legal) orders which we often find presented as creating a forum and framework for an untainted legitimacy of societal order through law.[20] Eventually, the pomp and glory of constitutional talk dissociates the fragile and constantly endangered emergence of a legal order from a long-standing critique of law. It is against this background that we ought to reflect on the role that law can play in transition periods: not isolated and put on a podium for the world's fleeting attention and excitement, but embedded in a continuing critique of the force and weakness of legal norms.

---

18   See Pogge (2004, p. 117) highlighting the way in which 'past injustice […] can affect present moral reasons for action'.

19   See the careful assessment by Dupré (2003); also Renata Uitz (2005).

20   For a critique, see Zumbansen (2002, pp. 400–432; 2004, pp. 197–211).

Remembrance and Utopia in law

The Reformation and its ensuing energies, as well as the subsequent bourgeois revolutions of early modernity, are characterized by the emergence of the individual subject as the centre of social and political activity. Henceforth, it has been against the individual that order and its legitimacy claims are measured. To the degree in which they are found to be foul and rotten, they are doomed and will be swept away: with the dawn of modernity, man begins to order his world in time. Human history became a search for direction in time, unfolding according to the lights of probability and prudence (Koselleck, 1979c; 1979a). Religious prophecy is replaced by supposedly rationalist forecast, although this forecast radiates a sense of stability similar to that which previously emanated from eschatologic trust in providence or the felt threat of demise. In the maturing interaction between the state and individual, the knowledge of the changeability of things is foundational in the state's creation of its own legitimacy grounds. Time's horizon is no longer as open as it used to be. Adopting the role of interpretor and direction-setter the state gives meaning to progression albeit into a now unknown, but also manageable future. This rupture, however, is not yet absolute. Eschatology remains persistently in the background and the consciousness of one's future is a strange but courageous mix of politics and prophecy (Koselleck, 1979a, p. 33). Within this rationalist philosophy of progress we can see the rationalism of future prognostics unfolding. These are in turn still dominated by an important incorporation of the past into the imagery of the future. The events that are expected within the political horizon of historical development are seen as reoccurring and reappearing events, repeating themselves instead of being grand beginnings or final ends. From this perspective, the future that is actually envisioned for the state is simultaneously present in the past, the realm of political action contemporaneously occupied as well as confined (Koselleck, 1979a, p. 33). Time is important, because with ever more rapid sequences of events – brought about by deliberate human action and understood as such – the 'realms of experience' (*Erfahrungsräume*) shrink and the experience of the present falls victim to an unforeseeability in a way that makes the present's experience of time uncertain vis-à-vis the future (Koselleck, 1979b). Presence can no longer experience itself as presence but is now forced to resort to its own historio-philosophical assumption (*selbstbezogene geschichtsphilosophische Einholung*). In parallel, the semantics used to describe these simultaneously opened and closed spheres of possibilities are changing as well: *Utopia* can no longer characterize the experience horizon of political thinking, only *Revolution*.[21] Yet, it is felt that revolution may put an absolute end to everything. In this respect revolution is always confronted with reaction (Koselleck, 1979c, pp. 34–35) and hence every future oriented action is of a political nature. While utopia and revolution are hence distinguishable by the absence (utopia) and presence (revolution) of deliberate human action and by the belief that change

---

21 Die Befürworter lernen, daß Revolution ein langfristiger Prozeß ist, die Gegner sehen Revolution als Folge falscher Ideen (Luhmann, 2000, p. 208).

can be brought about by abruptly ending traditional ways, usually under the *signum* of eventual responsibility, legal practitioners of post-conflict justice are operating somewhere in between the horizons of utopia and revolution.

The changing face of international law and the law of occupation

The transnational perspective can further illuminate the challenge to law and societal memory that we find in various post-conflict situations around the world. These situations can be seen as entering the legal imagination against the background of a dramatically enlarged and yet fragmented and incoherent human rights agenda. While the scandal of human rights violations drives legal efforts to address wrongdoings beyond jurisdictional boundaries,[22] we still seem far away from a comprehensive human rights regime. However, such a legal order might not even be desired in light of the different claims connected to the expansion of human rights. And yet it is from this ongoing search for a better law that the transnational law of post-conflict justice takes its cue. It develops in the light of a greater global awareness of the need for a human rights agenda and enters existing legal fields that are themselves undergoing dramatic changes (Bhuta, 2005).

Because it is dramatically intertwined with ongoing legal reforms in post-conflict situations, the law of occupation vividly reflects the changed legal agenda. Its recent past points to a much more encompassing agenda of reconstruction and nation-building,[23] in that the future-orientated perspective of the law of occupation has itself been subject to a transformation: from one applicable to post-military situations of (ideally) brief occupation focussed on peace and stability, to a more encompassing legal agenda aimed at administrative reconstruction and state-building. This transformation is nowhere more visible than in the current situation in Iraq. The present state of the law of occupation in Iraq finds a distinctive expression in the United Nations Security Council Resolutions 1483, 1546 and in the letter from the United States' and the United Kingdom's permanent representatives to the UN Security Council of 8 May 2003.[24] In this letter, both governments were explicitly outspoken with regard to the reconstructive efforts that the occupiers ought to undertake,[25] and it is this mandate that the Security Council Resolution adopted, almost *verbatim*, in UNSC Resolution 1483.

---

22 Scott (2001, pp. 45–63); Scott and Wai (2004, pp. 287–319); Zumbansen (2005) in ConWEB Paper 4/2005, available at: http://www.qub.ac.uk/schools/SchoolofPoliticsInternationalStudiesandPhilosophy/Research/PaperSeries/ConWEBPapers/.

23 See for example the remarkable, new introduction to Eyal Benvenisti (2004).

24 S/2003/538, available at http://www.globalpolicy.org/security/issues/iraq/document/2003/0608usukletter.htm .

25 *Ibid.*, 'The United States, the United Kingdom and Coalition partners are facilitating the establishment of representative institutions of government, and providing for the responsible administration of the Iraqi financial sector, for humanitarian relief, for economic reconstruction, for the transparent operation and repair of Iraq's infrastructure and

The transformation of the international law of occupation is closely linked to changes in public international law at large. While this in itself seems obvious, the actual impact is far less so (Williams, 2003). Few observers of the international legal scene today would be willing to testify to the state of its development. Instead, international law ranks among the most contested of legal areas at this time. Its present situation, characterized by a self-understanding still seeking the origins of its current disarray (Byers, 2003), bears witness to the seemingly eternal juxtaposition of international law and politics, of universalism and hegemony. Yet, at the same time, international law has become so much more reflexive that its period of untiring self-questioning and self-reassuring can now safely be declared to be past. Instead, international law's contemporary soul-searching calls for an extended exploration of the discipline's young, but troubled history, with its increased meeting-points and soulmateships with inquiries such as cultural studies, international regime studies, legal theory and transnational law, literary theory and transnational history.[26] At present, however, the noises of the 'real' (Zizek, 2002) are louder than the suggestions of the 'social' (Kennedy, 2003; Rittich, 2004). Current assessments of international law still struggle with old demons of inferiority and irrelevance in the ugly face of international politics, imperialism and hegemony, but they also reach out to encompass the particular nature of international law (Kirsch, 2005). The latter can only begin to be understood when reflecting on the very nature of the international order on the one hand, and of our understanding of law and legal regulation on the other.

Our assessment of the role of law in the dynamic and contested international order depends on our understanding of this order, but there is no simple causal relationship between the social reality and the legal order. Instead, our inquiries into the structure of the international order proceed in relative autonomy from the progress made in legal theory with regard to developing an international law for the global age (Luhmann, 2004, ch. 12). Where our understanding of law passes from first assessments of violence (Bodin, Hobbes) on to formalization (Kelsen) to realism (Llewellyn) or downfall (Schmitt), to reassessment (Kelsen, Hart, Fuller, Dworkin) on to fragmentation and dispersement (Teubner, Sousa Santos), the legal theory of international law has undergone dramatic changes, while international law itself has assumed a contested form that today differs greatly from earlier challenges of its weakness. At present, international law must remember and assess the combination of realism and utopia in its foundational myths only in the context of developments in other fields of regulatory law where changing modes of norm-creation have long been questioning dearly-held beliefs in public-private distinctions of political, legitimate rule-creation on the one hand and private, market-based profit seeking on the other (Zumbansen, 2004).

---

natural resources, and for the progressive transfer of administrative responsibilities to such representative institutions of government, as appropriate. Our goal is to transfer responsibility for administration to representative Iraqi authorities as early as possible.'

26   Koskenniemi (2005, pp. 113–124); for further references, see Zumbansen (2006, forthcoming).

The continuing, contested nature of international law illustrates particular challenges to the law in post-conflict situations. There is no well-contained, settled consensus on the scope and content of the international law of occupation, nor is there a ready-to-wear, normative outfit worn by the international law of post-conflict justice. Instead, the *transnational* dimension in which these bodies of law interact, collide and fuse with ongoing searches for better law and better norms of nation-building and societal reconciliation in different parts of the world, demonstrates the degree to which a transnational law of post-conflict justice is undercutting, accompanying and complementing the public international law of occupation in distinct ways. As the nation-state alone ceases to provide the context in which legal experiments unfold, norms are emerging in a de-territorialized sphere of world society. As narratives of post-conflict situations and the role of law and alternative ordering mechanisms continue to be developed and applied, we learn much about the approximation of once isolated and distant regulatory experiments.[27]

The recognition or execution of political will in the task of reconstructing a state after a massive and encompassing change brings to the fore every foundational myth that regularly appears in the context of nation-building. But so much more is produced by that process, as the law and politics of reconstruction collide with demands for societal reconciliation and a future-orientated, reconstructive agenda based on independent, self-governing terms. The law of post-conflict justice, for instance, collides head-on with the programs and ideologies of 'law and development' (Posner, 1998, pp. 1–11).[28] This conflict between shock programs and carefully, implemented, reconstructive and learning modes (Sen, 1999) seems to characterize the options available to international consultants and legal policy programmers. Which model of the state, of the market, of society will likely underlie and guide the reconstructive efforts that depend on the financial and infrastructural support offered by the international community?

In seeking a tentative answer to this question, we are caught between skepticsm and enthusiasm as to what conceptions of government, governance, democracy, social welfare and private autonomy will likely evolve from this inquiry. Realizing that path-dependent trajectories of capitalist markets and social welfare regimes reflect – to a certain degree – comparative institutional advantages, our perception can no longer remain blind to the intricate chains of causation between national reformist politics and the impacts of globalized markets. In light of the often repeated complaint of what globalization actually stands for and whether, for example, globalization has caused immense stress on welfare states or whether structural changes within these states instead promote and fuel certain globalization phenomena, we ought to take seriously the growing awareness within many international-orientated disciplines regarding the limits and constraints of their traditional analytical instruments. While legal analysis needs to embrace the sociological research that nourishes the phenomena of legal pluralism, experimental law making and public-private governance combinations

---

27 See, for a powerful illustration, Swanee Hunt (2004); Chesterman, (2004, pp. 180–182).

28 Posner (1998, pp. 1–11), on the one hand, and Rittich (2002), on the other.

(Arthurs, 1988), we see a similiar eye-opening within the discipline of political science as it moves from a state-orientated international relations approach towards increased research into ever more flexible forms of governance.

Likewise we see a sudden awakening within historical research to the phenomena of 'transnationalism' which to us, however, can be no less than disturbing. If, in law, we proceed in the firm belief that for the purposes of reassurance we can always turn back to law's history, to its tracks of development and even to its crossroads and turning points, it is nonetheless unsettling to have to realize that the historian herself will have had firstly to develop her own adequate analytical approach before being able to firmly guide us. We can recognize and should welcome this insecurity internal to private and public international law, embracing it in the context of questions that touch upon emerging forms of international governance that are quite intricately related to changes within national legal orders. For the participants on both ends of the debate, the *transnationalist* and the *traditionalist*, there is no simple home to be found yet, no ready-made bed to lie in any more. While the transnationalist will, sooner or later, be confronted with a struggle for legitimacy mirrored so pointedly in the history of our national legal and political orders, the traditionalist also can no longer draw the blinds in order to resort to old ways. The nation state and its legal order have undergone radical changes that prompt more questions than there are answers available. Radical changes in public administrative practice, the inescapable and ever-recurring necessity of speculative policy choices and the ensuing reflexive forms of law making in a dense public-private matrix, these features prompt closer inspection – but they do not resemble the quiet home to which some traditionalists want to return. From this it follows that both perspectives, the transnational and the traditional one, are valid and interdependent. In fact, in some sense, we can either be both or none at all.

Past and Future

> Ohne gemeinsame Begriffe gibt es keine Gesellschaft,vor allem keine politische Handlungseinheit. [29]

> Aus den Horizonten normativer und formativer Wertsetzungen kommen wir nicht heraus.[30]

At this point it becomes clear that any approach to 'working through the past'[31] creates linkages between the past and the future. 'We cannot ask the historians, as

---

29 'Without common terminology, there is not society, and above all no unity for political action' (Koselleck, 1979a, p. 108).

30 'We cannot escape the horizons of normative and formative value assessments' (J. Assmann, 1992, p. 129).

31 Adorno chose the term, *Aufarbeitung der Vergangenheit*, to address the problems raised by the term, *Vergangenheitsbewältigung*, which would be translated as 'coming to

Ranke did, to tell us '*wie es wirklich gewesen ist*'. Instead, history is a reflection on the past from the present, and we must be aware that the common identities that we forge and the narratives that we live with emerge from processes of remembering and forgetting' (Jorges, 2005, p. 250). Indeed, the deciphering of the differently shaded heritages and legacies of emerging polities – such as post-conflict, transitional societies as well as, for example, the European Union – unveils the inseparability of an assessment of the past from the design of the future (Zumbansen, 2005b, p. 331; Veitch, 2004). The law's role in this process of to and fro is crucial as it will aid in selecting (even on occasion completing[32]) and thereby illuminating, some aspects of the past, as well as silencing others. And here we apparently end back where we started. Law appears as a salvaging force that can guide us out of the dark by its very appeal to legitimacy. However, that the law has never been our own, is the tragic lesson learned by the man waiting before the gates of the law, as well as by all the others that wait for law's healing hand (Miller, 2002, pp. 201–211; 2005).

Bibliography

Adorno, Theodor W. (1998), 'The Meaning of Working Through the Past', in *Critical Models*, translated by Henry W. Pickford, New York: Columbia University Press.

Adler, L and Zumbansen, P (2002), 'The forgetfulness of noblesse: a critique of the German foundation law compensating slave and forced laborers of the Third Reich', *Harvard Journal on Legislation [also in: Zwangsarbeit im Dritten Reich: Erinnerung und Verantwortung / NS Forced Labor: Remembrance and Responsibility 333 (P. Zumbansen ed. 2002)]*, **39**, 1–61.

Agbakwa, S. (2005), 'Genocidal politics and racialization of intervention: from Rwanda to Darfur and beyond', *German Law Journal*, **6**, 513–531, at http://www.germanlawjournal.com/pdf/Vol06No02/PDF_Vol_06_No_02_513–531_Developments_Agbakwa.pdf.

Anderson, J L. (2004) *The Fall of Baghdad*, London: Penguin.

Anghie, A. (2005), *Imperialism, Sovereignty and the Making of International Law*, Cambridge: Cambridge University Press.

Anouilh, Jean (2000), *Antigone*, Ted Freeman (ed.), trans. Barbara Trans, London: Methuen.

Arnold, T. W. (1937) *The Folklore of Capitalism*, London, OUP.

Arthurs (1988), *Without the Law: Administrative Justice and Legal Pluralism in Nineteenth Century England*, Toronto: University of Toronto Press, 50–88.

Assmann, J. (1992), *Das kulturelle Gedächtnis*, second edition, Munich: Beck.

Baumgartner, S. (2002), 'Human rights and civil litigation in United States courts: the Holocaust-Era cases', *Washington University Law Quarterly*, **80**, 835–854.

terms with the past'. See, Adorno (1998, p. 89).

32 See the remarkable account of the impact of data protection and file archiving laws in Germany by Markovits (2001, pp. 513–563).

Bentley, J. (1996), 'Cross-cultural interaction and periodization in world history', *American Historical Review*, **101**, 749–770.

Benvenisti, Eyal (2004), *The International Law of Occupation*, Oxford and Princeton: Princeton University Press.

Bhuta, N. (2005), 'The antinomies of transformative occupation', *European Journal of International Law*, **16**, 721–740.

Blanpain, R. and Colucci, M. (2004), *The Globalization of Labour Standards. The Soft Law Track*, The Hague: Kluwer Law International.

Bourdieu, Pierre (1987), 'The force of law: toward a sociology of the juridical field', *Hastings Law Journal*, **38**, 805–813.

Bright, M. and Geyer, C. (1995), 'World history in a global age', *American Historical Review*, **100**, 1034–1060.

Byers, Michael (2003), 'Introduction: The Complexities of Foundational Change', in Byers and Nolte (eds), *United States Hegemony and the Foundations of International* Law, Cambridge: Cambridge University Press.

Chesterman, S. (2004), *You, The People. The United Nations, Transitional Administration, and State-Building*, Oxford and New York: Oxford University Press.

Christodoulidis, E. (2001), 'Law's Immemorial', in Christodoulidis and Veitch (eds) *Lethe's Law. Justice, Law and Ethics in Reconciliation*, Oxford and Portland: Hart Publishing, 207–227.

Conrad, S. and Osterhammel, J. (eds) (2004), *Das Kaiserreich transnational. Deutschland in der Welt 1871–1914*, Göttingen.

Dangor, Achtmat (2004), *Bitter Fruit*, New York: Grove Atlantic.

Derrida, J. (1990), 'Force of law', *Cardozo Law Review*, **11**, 919–1045.

Dupré, C. (2003), *Importing the Law in Post-communist Transitions, The Hungarian Constitutional Court and the Right to Human Dignity*, Oxford and Portland: Hart Publishing.

Ehrlich, E. (1962), *Fundamental Principles of the Sociology of Law*, translated by Walter Moll, New York: Russell and Russell Inc.

Eltringham, N. (2004), *Accounting for Horror: Post-Genocide Debates in Rwanda*, London: Pluto Press.

Frame, Nuri (2005), 'One Step Forward, Two Steps Back? The Failings of the Iraqi Special Tribunal', paper written for the *Globalisation and the Law* course at Osgoode Hall Law School, Toronto, April.

Fuller, L. (1958), 'Fidelity to law – a reply to Professor Hart', *Harvard Law Review*, **71**, 630–672.

Griffiths, J. (1986), 'What is legal pluralism?', *Journal of Legal Pluralism and Unofficial Law*, **24**, 1–55.

Gross, A. (2004), 'Reconciliation in South Africa', *Stanford Journal of International Law*, **40**, 40–107.

Habermas, J. (1996a), *Between Facts and Norms*, trans. William Rehg, Cambridge: MIT Press.

Habermas, J. (1996b), 'Paradigms of law', *Cardozo Law Review*, **17**, 771–784.

Hart, H. L. A. (1958), 'Positivism and the separation of law and morals', *Harvard Law Review*, **71**, 593–628.

Hay, D. (1992), 'Time, Inequality, and Law's Violence', in Sarat and Kearns (eds), *Law's Violence*, Ann Arbor, University of Michigan Press, 141–173.

Herbert, U. and Groehler, O (1992), *Zweierlei Bewältigung. Vier Beiträge über den Umgang mit der nationalsozialistischen Vergangenheit in den beiden deutschen Staaten*, Hamburg, Edition.

Hunt, S. (2004), *This Was Not Our War. Bosnian Women Reclaiming the Peace*, Durham and London: Duke University Press.

Jessup, Philip (1956), *Transnational Law*, New Haven: Yale University Press.

Joerges, Christian (2005), 'Introduction to the special issue: confronting memories: European 'Bitter Memories' and the constitutionalization process: constructing Europe in the shadow of its pasts', *German Law Journal*, **6**, 245–254.

Kennedy, D. (2003), 'Two globalizations of law and legal thought: 1850–1968', *Suffolk Law Review*, **36**, 631–679.

Krisch, N. (2005), 'International law in times of hegemony: unequal power and the shaping of the international legal order', *European Journal of International Law*, **16**, 369–408.

Kirton, J. and Trebilcock, M. (eds) (2004), *Hard Choices, Soft Law. Voluntary Standards in Global Trade, Environment and Social Governance*, Aldershot: Ashgate.

Klug, H. (2000), *Constituting Democracy: Law, Globalism, and South Africa's Political Reconstruction*, Cambridge, UK: Cambridge University Press.

Koselleck, R. (1979a), 'Begriffsgeschichte und Sozialgeschichte (1972)' in *Vergangene Zukunft*, Frankfurt: Suhrkamp, 107–129.

Koselleck, R. (1979b), ''Erfahrungsraum' und 'Erfahrungshorizont' – zwei historische Kategorien' in *Vergangene Zukunft*, Suhrkamp: Frankfurt, 349–375.

Koselleck, R. (1979c), 'Vergangene Zukunft der frühen Neuzeit (1968)' in *Vergangene Zukunft. Zur Semantik geschichtlicher Zeiten* (zuerst erschienen in Epirrhosis. Festgabe für Carl Schmitt, hrsg. v. Barion, Böckenförde, Forsthoff, Weber, Bd. 2, 549–566), 17–37.

Koskenniemi, M. (2002), '"The lady doth protest too much". Kosovo, and the turn to ethics in international law', *Modern Law Review*, **65**, 159–175. Koskenniemi (2005), 'International law in Europe: between tradition and renewal', *European Journal of International Law*, **16**, 113–124.

Kumm, M. (2005), 'The idea of constitutional patriotism and its implications for the role and structure of European legal history', *German Law Journal*, **6**, 319.

Lepsius, Oliver (2002), 'The relationship between security and civil liberties in the Federal Republic of Germany after September 11', in Paul Gewirtz and Jacob Katz Cogan (eds), *Global Constitutionalism: Privacy, Proportionality, Terrorism and Civil Liberties*, New Haven, Yale University Press.

Luhmann, N. (2000), *Die Politik der Gesellschaft*, Frankfurt: Suhrkamp.

Luhmann, N. (2004), *Law as a Social System*, F. Kastner and D. Schiff, R. Nobles, R. Ziegert (eds), trans. K. Ziegert, Oxford and New York: Oxford University Press.

Lyon, B. (2003), 'Discourse in development: a post-colonial theory 'agenda' for the UN committee on economic, social and cultural rights', *Journal of Gender, Social Policy & the Law*, **10**, http://ssrn.com/abstract=449301.

Margalit, A. (2002), *The Ethics of Memory*, Cambridge, MA and London, UK: Harvard University Press.

Markovits, I. (2001), 'Selective memory: how the law affects what we remember and forget from the past: the case of East Germany', *Law and Society Review*, **35**, 513–563.

Merry, S. (1992), 'Anthropology, law, and transnational processes', *Annual Review of Anthropology*, **21**, 357–379.

Mgbako, C (2005), 'Ingando solidarity camps: reconciliation and political indoctrination in post-genocide Rwanda', *Harvard Human Rights Journal*, **18**, 201–224.

Middell, M. (2000), 'Kulturtransfer und historische komparatistik – thesen zu ihrem verhältnis', **10**, *Comparativ*, 7–41.

Miller, R. (2005), 'Before the law: military investigations and evidence at the Iraqi special tribunal', *MSU–DCL Journal of International Law*, **13**.

Miller, Russell (2002), *Much Ado, But Nothing: California's New World War II Slave Labor Statute of Limitations and Its Place in the Increasingly Futile Effort to Obtain Compensation from American Courts*, in Peer Zumbansen (ed.), *NS-Forced Labor: Remembrance and* Responsibility, Baden-Baden: Nomos, 201–211.

Moore, S. F. (1973), 'Law and social change: the semi-autonomous field as an appropriate subject of study', *Law and Society Review*, **7**, 719–746.

Morgan, E. (2004), 'Slaughterhouse six: updating the law of war', *German Law Journal*, **5**, 525–544.

Nabokov, Vladimir (1947), *Bend Sinister*, republished by Vintage, 1990.

Neuborne, B. (2002), 'Preliminary reflections on aspects of Holocaust-era litigation in American courts', *Washington University Law Quarterly*, **80**, 795–834.

Orford, A. (1999), 'Muscular humanitarianism: reading the narratives of humanitarian intervention', *European Journal of International* Law, **10**, 679–711.

Perez, O. (2003), 'Normative Creativity and Global Legal Pluralism: Reflections on the Democratic Critique of Transnational Law', *Indiana Journal of Global Studies*, **10**, 25–64.

Pogge, Thomas W. (2004), *Historical Wrongs. The Two Other Domains, in Lukas Meyer ed., Justice in Time. Responding to Historical Injustice*, Baden-Baden: Nomos, 117–134.

Posner, R. (1998) 'Creating a legal framework for economic development', *The World Bank Research Observer*, **13**, 1–11.

Radbruch, Gustav (1946), 'Gesetzliches unrecht und übergesetzliches recht', in *Süddeutsche Juristenzeitung*.

Rittich, Kerry (2002), *Recharacterizing Restructuring. Law, Distribution and Gender in Market Reform*, The Hague: Kluwer Law International.

Rittich, Kerry (2004), 'The future of law and development: second generation reforms and the incorporation of the social', *Michigan Journal of International Law*, **26**, 199–243.

Sarkin, J. (2004), 'Reparation for past wrongs: using domestic courts around the world, especially the United States, to pursue human rights claims', *International Journal of Legal Information*, **32**, 426–460.

Sassen, S. (1998), *Globalization and its Discontents. Essays on the New Mobility of People and Money*, New York: The New Press.

Scheppele, K. (2004), 'Law in a time of emergency: states of exception and the temptations of 9/11', *University of Pennsylvania Journal of Constitutional Law*, **6**, 1001–1083.

Schmitt, C. (1986), *Political Theology: Four Chapters on the concept of sovereignty [1922]*, trans. George Schwab, Cambridge, MA: The MIT Press.

Scott, C. (2001), 'Translating torture into transnational tort: conceptual divides in the debate on corporate accountability for human rights harms', in Scott (ed.) *Torture as Tort*, Portland, OR and Oxford, Hart Publishing, 45–63.

Scott, C. and Wai, R. (2004), 'Transnational governance of corporate conduct through the migration of human rights norms: the potential of transnational "private" litigation', in Joerges, Sand and Teubner (eds) *Transnational Governance and Constitutionalism*, Portland, OR and Oxford: Hart Publishing, 287–319.

Sen, Amartya (1999), *Development as Freedom*, Oxford, OUP.

Senden, Linda (2004), *Soft Law in European Community Law*, Oxford, UK and Portland, OR: Hart Publishing.

Teitel, Ruti (2000), *Transitional Justice*, Oxford and New York: Oxford University Press.

Teubner, G. (1997), '"Global bukowina": legal pluralism in the world society', in Teubner (ed.), *Global Law Without A State*, Dartmouth: Aldershot, 3–28.

Timm, Uwe (2003), *Am Beispiel meines Bruders*, Frankfurt: Suhrkamp.

Trubek, D. and Trubek, L. (2005), 'Hard and soft law in the construction of social Europe: the role of the open method of coordination', *European Law Journal*, **11**, 343–364.

Uitz, Renata (2005) *Annual of German & European Law* Vol. 2, Miller and Zumbansen (eds), Oxford and New York: Berghahn Books.

Veitch, Scott (2004), 'Legal right and political amnesia', in Nuotio (ed.) *Europe in Search of 'Meaning and Purpose'*, Helsinki, Faculty of Law: University of Helsinki, 89–106.

Walker, N. (2002), 'The idea of constitutional pluralism', *Modern Law Review*, **65**, 317–359.

Weber, Max (1914), *Economy and Society: Part 2: Sociology of Law*, Berkeley: University of California Press. § 8: The formal qualities of modern law.

Wiethölter, D. (1986), 'Materialization and proceduralization in modern law', in Teubner (ed.), *Dilemmas of Law in the Welfare State*, Berlin and New York: Walter de Gruyter, 221–249.

Williams, Ian (2003), 'Will international law shape occupation, or the occupation shape international law?' *Global Policy Forum*, 14 May 2003, available at: http://www.globalpolicy.org/security/issues/iraq/attack/law/2003/0514shape.htm.

Zizek, S. (2002), *Welcome to the Desert of the Real: Five Essays on September 11 and Related Dates*, New York: Verso.

Zumbansen, P. (2002), 'Piercing the legal veil: commercial arbitration and transnational law', *European Law Journal*, **8**, 400–432.

Zumbansen, P. (2004), 'Sustaining paradox boundaries: perspectives on the internal affairs in domestic and international law', *European Journal of International Law*, **15**, 197–211.

Zumbansen, P. (2005, forthcoming), 'The parallel worlds of corporate governance and labor law', *Indiana Journal of Global Studies*, **13**.

Zumbansen, P. (2005a), 'Beyond territoriality: the case of transnational human rights litigation', in: ConWEB Paper 4/2005, available at: http://www.qub.ac.uk/schools/SchoolofPoliticsInternationalStudiesandPhilosophy/Research/PaperSeries/ConWEBPapers/.

Zumbansen, P. (2005b), 'Europe's darker legacies? notes on 'mirror reflections', the 'constitution as fetish' and other such linkages between the past and the future", *Osgoode Hall Law Journal*, **43**, 321–334.

Zumbansen, P. (2006, forthcoming), 'Transnational law', in Smits (ed.) *Encyclopedia of Comparative Law*, Edward Elgar.

'Remembrance, Responsibility and the Future', available at http://www.compensation–for–forced–labour.org/pdf/Foundation_law_consolidated_E.pdf

Special Issue of *German Law Journal*, **6** (1), 1 January 2005, available at: http://www.germanlawjournal.com/past_issues_archive.php.

Chapter 8

Sacrum, *Profanum* and Social Time: Quasi-theological Reflections on Time and Reconciliation

Adam Czarnota

For everything there is a season, and a time for every matter under heaven: a time to be born, and time to die; a time to plant, and a time to pluck up what is planted; a time to kill, and a time to heal; a time to break down, and a time to build up; a time to weep, and a time to laugh; a time to mourn, and a time to dance; a time to cast away stones, and a time to gather stones together; a time to embrace, and a time to refrain from embracing; a time to seek, and a time to lose; a time to keep, and a time to cast away; a time to tear, and a time to sew; a time to keep silence, and a time to speak; a time to love, and a time to hate; a time for war, and a time for peace.

What gain has the worker from this toil? I have seen the business that God has given to the children of man to be busy with. He has made everything beautiful in its time. Also, he has put eternity into man's heart, yet so that he cannot find out what God has done from the beginning to the end.
(Ecclesiastes) 3:1–11

Time present and time past
Are both perhaps present in time future,
And time future contained in time past
(T.S.Eliot)

Introduction

A few years ago I spent an entire day in the Aboriginal Tent Embassy, opposite Old Parliament House in Canberra, talking about reconciliation in Australia. The discussion was rather chaotic and arguments flew around in the thick air. I remember a very serious statement by one of the elders who told me, 'I am sick of this talk about reconciliation; we can talk about it when hostilities have stopped'. Strongly stated, and an interesting and important observation, it did not itself give me too much insight to the nature of reconciliation. Since that day, although I remained without knowledge of what reconciliation was, I have returned to the beginning, to the book of Genesis and subsequent books of the Bible because I knew that reconciliation was a theological concept and that helped me. Reconciliation is an old concept, one that has occupied theologians from the Eastern and Western Fathers of the Church to contemporary Christian theologians such as Karl Barth (see, for example, Barth, 2004). In the nineteenth century Hegel was preoccupied with a more secular project of how to reconcile man with himself and with history, and the idea is also present in Marx and his followers. And it is still present, in its secular forms, somewhere in the background of much contemporary political and legal philosophies.

Yet reconciliation has also become a secular concept, one that can sometimes seem overly prominent in contemporary social discourses. It has descended from the area of theology to psychology and now to politics and law: from *sacrum* to *profanum* we might say. The use, and abuse, of the concept of reconciliation in contemporary discourses is in itself worthy of detailed study. For the purpose of making a contribution to that study, one interpretation of the widespread employment of the concept is that it manifests – and not only in post-conflict societies – a change in the global situation of human societies. It encapsulates a sensibility that traditional politics has exhausted its potential in the new global world order.

The term, which in Christian theology is anti-conflict oriented, expresses the paradox and new needs of societies in the global situation. Even intuitively, even without the precise definition of the category of reconciliation, it is possible to note that the term, as it has come down from Christian theological discourse, is incompatible with the vision of the Western political tradition and of political life based on social conflicts and divisions. It is incompatible with the peculiar type of political thinking exemplified, for example, by Carl Schmitt and recently taken up and advocated by Chantal Mouffe (2005) – namely the concept of *the political*. This type of reasoning about political and social life accepts as its foundation conflict and struggle. Accordingly, the foundation of *politique politisante* is social division and political conflict, which translates into corresponding forms of institutional design in dealing with the conflict in the sphere of *politique politisée*. I do not want here to go to a deep analysis of the issue of the political and its usefulness in understanding of the contemporary processes. What I want to do instead is to delineate briefly the issue which this chapter will attempt to discuss: namely the problem of time and globalisation in the perspective of reconciliation.

The revival of the notion of reconciliation is partly a resurrection of, or going back to, some abandoned and forgotten traditions in the Western history of ideas, especially the political and legal ideas connected with medieval Christian philosophical, political and jurisprudential thought. The purpose of this chapter is, so to speak, to try to remove the dust from that thought and establish some connections to the use of the concept of reconciliation in order to shed light on the present state of global affairs.

In this chapter I am particularly concerned with what the problem of time has to do with reconciliation under the conditions of globalisation. From the point of view of approaching the problem in the intellectual tradition, which focuses on understanding the structure of society and social processes – a sort of *Verstandenssoziologie* – it is necessary to go more deeply into some archetypical paradigms foundational to our culture in order to understand the present. One such crucial category is time.

Globalisation, certainly in its present form, is an outcome of Western expansion. This includes the Western concept of time, specifically in its Enlightenment version, which means time understood as progress. What we are witnessing now was driven by a quasi-religious belief in the peculiar version of time and history understood as a rational process of progress through clearly defined stages, which other parts of the world could join or duplicate if they adopted the right worldview and the proper means. But this concept of time as 'progress' was also based on a belief in the superiority of western culture, and on its relation to another, often (from the dominant perspective at least) hidden and usually overlooked, dimension – namely violence.

Discourses on reconciliation presuppose that some elements of social communications are contradictory, and that violence as one means of 'communication' is renounced. If this is so, however, arguably the concept of reconciliation requires a more sophisticated concept of time than that of time as progress. Does such a paradigm of time exist in a Western culture whose basic paradigms are rooted in Christianity?

Concepts of time

In its common-sense understanding, the contemporary western concept of time is linear and mechanical. Time has lost its sacral dimension. Where some sections of society have preserved the distinction between *sacrum* and *profanum* in life, they tend to exist in the margins and not in the mainstream of social life.

Contemporary societies generally accept a linear concept of time. Time just flows from past through present to the future. However, this is no longer straightforwardly the Enlightenment or early modern concept of time so connected closely with the idea of progress. *That* idea of progress provided an eschatology to linear time and hence stamped time with a sacred dimension. Linear time, based on an idea of progress, thereby received meaning. Today, societies no longer share an idea of progress. The dominant social concept of time is still linear but it has lost its *eschatological* dimension. Consider an example of this: with the end of communism, and its eschatology, 1989 and the collapse of really existing socialism as part of the world system saw the end of that concept of time. It is not surprising therefore that a triumphant liberalism declared 'the end of history' in the writing of Francis Fukuyama. Such a concept of time emphatically possesses an appeal for the preservation of the status quo rather than for change. Therefore, time as linear still exists, but people live without the hope for any more profound eschatology. In such a situation, what the conservative Australian Prime Minister John Howard called 'practical reconciliation', is all that is possible.

If we move from ideological declaration to social theory, the end of history thesis is nothing more than a rhetorical catch-phrase without any heuristic power. But such a catch-phrase nonetheless has a masking power. It masks the structure of domination in the contemporary global state of affairs. The 'end of history' signals a fulfilment has been achieved: we have the best we can get, and there is no sense in searching for something else, for something new – an eschatology for consumers, perhaps, but not for everybody.

Another, relatively new problem faced by global society is the compression of time due to forces of globalisation. The concept of time, and the notion of historical time of the dominant societies, put pressure on other parts of the globe which had developed their own concepts of time and in which people understood their own historical times. Now, under the pressure of globalisation forces, in the situation euphemistically expressed by Anthony Giddens as 'compression of time and space', locally grown concepts of time and locally developed historical time are under threat. This is not an intellectual pressure but pressure imposed by the economically and politically more powerful over the weaker. Historically, similar (as it turned out, doomed) struggles were observable during the period of rapid industrialisation in the eighteenth and nineteenth centuries, where rural, archaic concepts of time lost out to the mechanical concept of time expressed by the factory sirens or whistles.

In the time of social constructivism, clashes between concepts of time and struggles between historical times embodied by different societies are forcing social scientists to change their approach to time and thus also to reconsider critically accepted concepts of social time (Staniszkis, 2003). But is a reconciliation between different concepts of time possible? This question's significance is underscored by the suggestion that it is perhaps precisely such a form of reconciliation which is a necessary precondition to political and social reconciliation in the contemporary complex world.

I will try to address, but it is not my intention to answer, the above question in this chapter. The analysis is rather an exercise in mapping the structure of the problem of relations between time and reconciliation. I do not think that it is possible at the moment to provide complete answers to the question, but it is possible to give directions as to how to approach the problem.

It is possible to identify two different problems in the general theme of 'time and reconciliation'. The first is the obvious question of which concept of time provides a better background or framework for social reconciliation. The second question is the problem of clashes between concepts of time which require change in approaches to time in order to reconcile them. Generally speaking, we can say that the first question is about reconciliation in time and the second about reconciliation of times.

The first problem – reconciliation in time – is based on characteristic thinking about time in Western culture and could be summarised as follows: things happen in time but time itself is neutral. Social processes are taking place in the river of time and time itself does not influence these processes. The second question – reconciliation of times – is based on the position that time is not neutral for social processes but instead time actively influences social processes. Time is not only an epistemological category but an ontological category as well. The first way of thinking, necessarily schematic, characterises the Western approach to time, the second characterises the South-East Asian and East Asian approach to time.

In what follows I will first try to describe different concepts of social time in Western culture remembering the reconciliation problem in the background. In the second part I will sketch the problem of compression of time and the need to accept a new approach to time which will treat time as an ontological category. In other words, I will tentatively try to map the territory for the possible reconciliation of times.

Morphology of social time: *sacrum* and *profanum*

On the level of intuition, reconciliation means special relations between two different persons or two different social groups. It is not enough to have a non-hostile relationship but rather reconciliation means a special relationship based on the recognition of two different identities: their specificities, particularities and, at the same time, recognition that these two elements are part of a bigger holistic unit. The stress is on a relationship based on *recognition* of differences, even contradictions, and positive relations between two units which enrich and fulfil each part of this relationship.

Such a relationship requires a very high level of self-consciousness of both units in the reconciliation process and also requires a positive, honest approach to one's partner: knowledge or insight and empathy into the nature of the partner and an inclination to action to fulfil the deepest needs of the partner. The quality of relations between the two elements changes the entire structure in which they operate.

From the social theory point of view, reconciliation is reduced to the creation of a situation in which the social system reproduces itself smoothly. In the contemporary complex social world it requires cooperation; that is, not merely indifference but communication in order to reproduce the social system.

But just as – for instance – not each type of music can accommodate different tones in one harmonious composition, so not all concepts of social time may accommodate such a concept of reconciliation. Below I try to describe a structure of time that accommodates this concept of reconciliation.

Different concepts of time depend on specific relations between culture and social systems, as well as on the different structures of culture and social systems themselves. That double subordination of social time to culture and social system is a consequence of the complicated genesis of social time. Social activity determined by social structure is expressed by myth, symbols, and beliefs – in other words, by means of symbolic culture. Elements of symbolic culture express visions of social time.

Belonging to two different orders, social and cultural systems require from social time a double functionality. That is, functionally time is subordinated to the social system and also to cultural order. From the cultural point of view the function of time is the realisation of the basic function of culture; namely that basic fear of human existence (as expressed by Martin Heidegger, 1992), overcoming the fear of death. Time in its cultural functionality dimension is an expression of eternity in a changing world; it expresses the desire for duration, overcoming change and temporal contingency of the world. The basic problem of human existence – of overcoming of change and temporality – has been addressed by all religions. Each religion attempts to neutralise the existential fear of death and entropy. The Polish philosopher Leszek Kolakowski wrote that religion means the 'paralysis of time' (Kolakowski and Eliade, 1993, p. 1). The Eastern Orthodox Church theologian David Bentley Hart put it in this way: 'History, as a strictly causal sequence, has no salvific power, reflects no universal or providential order, has no metaphysical yield. In a sense the eschatological liberates time from the burden of history, allows time a purely "aesthetic" character …' (Hart, 2003, p. 397). In a similar way Emmanuel Levinas wrote that, '[Eschatology] does not introduce a teleological system into the totality; it does not consist in teaching the orientation of history. Eschatology institutes a relation with being beyond the totality or beyond history, and not with being beyond the past and present' (Levinas, 1969, p. 22).[1]

From the point of view of culture then, time possesses a different dimension which functions, if not only to pacify our existential worries, then also to provide us with an other worldly dimension of our existence through neutralisation, one might say almost negation, of the historical time of change and entropy.

But time is also subordinated to the social system. In that role it has to coordinate human activities and regulate the rhythm of social life. It has to possess and express elements of change. Social groups need the concept of change for acting in a changing world, and to recognise that change is something natural. The concept of time therefore has to provide members of society with an understanding of and a meaning for social change.

The outcome of this double service or function expected from the concept of time expresses its complicated morphology incorporating both elements of *sacrum* and *profanum*. Social time has to be the time of infinite duration and change and entropy. Those two requirements look contradictory. Nevertheless, time through its double morphology, its double belonging, is thus able to fulfil its functions.

The crucial element which allows time to realise its double function – required on the one hand by the cultural and on the other by the social system – is the specific structure of time. All forms of social time are always a synthesis of two different rhythms: the rhythm of sacred time, and the rhythm of secular time. In this sense social time is measured by two different time clocks. One is the silent clock of eternal duration and the second the noisy clock of changing dynamics of social life. The closest illustration which comes to mind is the presence of two time dimensions in Anton Bruckner's symphony No.8 in C minor.[2] Different tones are harmoniously

---

1   A similar vision of the problem, but definitely from a very secular point of view, was expressed by Woody Allen who observed, 'Eternity is a very long time, particularly at the end' (Allen cited in Steiner, 2004). Eternity indeed means the annihilation of time. Steiner's article is the review of a book (Bouretz, 2003) worthy of attention as its subject also concerns time and forms of reconciliation.

2   The definitive 1890 version is edited by Haas.

connected in the structure of that long symphony. The listener can physically hear two different times, one secular and the other eternal. In the Finale the two times are reconciled in the serene music which, by including the two times, sounds like it embraces the whole world. The power of this musical illustration probably has something to do with Bruckner's deep Christian faith, and the innocence of the rural upbringing of that fascinating composer of the Vienna circle of the 20th century.

Thus, where the cultural function of time is realised by the eternal layer of the sacred in time's morphology, the social system function is fulfilled by its profane level focussed on change (see Flis, 2001, pp. 174–175). Interestingly, those different concepts of time also find expression in the two concepts of justice presented in ancient Greek mythology as two different goddesses: *Dike* and *Themis*, in Roman mythology known as *Nemesis* and *Justitia*. The first goddess represents the sacred dimension of justice. *Dike/Nemesis* dealt with the divine dimensions of justice, often referred to as providence or fate. Realisation of that dimension of justice was left in the hands of the gods. It appears that criteria for that type of justice were perceived as different from those applied and developed by human reason. Realisation of that type of justice was left to other times, usually outside human time. It was about the apocalyptic character of total justice. *Nemesis* was presented as the goddess of justice and revenge, a personification of that goddess's wraths and punishment (beautifully presented aesthetically in the intriguing engraving, *Nemesis,* by Albrecht Dürer).

Themis/Justitia was the goddess of the human dimension of justice. Her administration of justice was more understanding of, or softer to, human errors. She is usually presented as blind in the application of justice. That blindess shows on the one hand a commitment to principles of human justice and the impartial application of law, and on the other, the limitation of justice embodied in human legal systems. Those limitations of human legal systems are due to the limitations of human knowledge: how can we do justice when our knowledge about events and especially past events is always limited? Time imposes restrictions on knowledge and justice as well. That is why human legal systems contain so many principles which limit justice to the past, such as *nulla poena sine lege*, statutes of limitations, etc.

But this is only part of the picture. Another aspect, directly connected with the problem of reconciliation, is the apocalyptic character of the *Nemesis/Dike* type of justice. Until remarkably recently, there was no attempt to approach *legally* the great processes of political and social change. That was a matter of fate and divine justice. But the demand for *legal* redress in the wake of recent political transformations, such as for the communist past, is based on a refusal to accept blind fate and manifest change in the concept of time.

The two layers of social time therefore are separated but depend on each other. The combination of these two elements of social time is different in different cultures. While the two elements are put together differently in one integral concept of social time, social time nevertheless possess that universal double structure. The identification of the connection between the two dimensions of time, as *sacrum* and *profanum*, can be found in Emile Durkheim's sociology. *Sacrum* is, according to Durkheim, separated from *profanum* yet nevertheless interconnected: we can not have *sacrum* without *profanum*. According to him, things sacred are guarded by a system of forbidding norms and rules and the sphere of *profanum* or secular life is a sphere to which these norms and rules are addressed (Durkheim, 1995, p. 208). Hence, the two structural dimensions of time are also interdependent and the realisation of one in social praxis is based on the other.

Types of social time

Social time based on the integration of two elements was variously presented in pendulum, cyclical and linear conceptions. The first two – the pendulum and cyclical concepts of social time – are not suitable for accommodation of the concept of reconciliation. The pendulum conception of social time is based on such a combination of the sacral and secular elements that the latter is always in opposition to the former. Secular time is reduced to an unchangeable present and sacred time is expressed by a ritual of repetition of a mythical, sacral past. Time is a pendulum between a mythical past from time before time and an eternal present. In such a concept of time there is no room for reconciliation, since what exists in the present is only that which reminds us of something that existed in the past. The French historian from the *Annales* historical school, Jacques Le Goff, who devoted some of his work to the concepts of time, called it the 'structure of analogies' (Le Goff, 1970, p. 175; see also Le Goff, 1992). The ontological status of the present is dependent on a ritual recalling of a mythical, sacral past. The meaning and the very existence of the present is therefore dependent on the past. According to the logic of the 'structure of analogies' what happened in the past is happening in the present. It is impossible to change anything and so reconciliation as the expression of the free will to change is unthinkable. The activity of human beings is reduced to repetition in an eternal present where the mythical past is the source of creation.

The second, cyclical (or cosmic) time also does not accommodate reconciliation. That concept of social time accommodates social change but only as a closed process. On the social level, cyclical time explains historical change and on the cultural level undermines its independent ontological status and provides stability through embodiment of the concept of a closed cyclical process.

The old saying of Cicero that *historia magistra vitae est* is based on the cyclical concept of time. In the history of ideas there is near universal agreement that cyclical time was present in Ancient Greek thinking (although, as noted by Pierre Vidal-Naquet in his wonderful analysis of relation between gods and human time in Ancient Greece, that did not mean that they did not also use other concepts of time (Vidal-Naquet, 2003, pp. 62–85).)[3] Cyclical time was based on the thinking that movement and becoming – as the Ancient Greeks believed – represented lower degrees of reality in which identity can be expressed in the form of duration and continuity, through laws of repetition. In the cyclical concept of time true and full being meant

---

3   For concepts of time in Hinduism in comparative context see Umberto Eco *et al.* (1999, pp. 95–170).

being in itself eternal and unchangeable (see Detienne, 1999). That reconciliation in such a structure of thought was not possible is confirmed by the sophisticated research of Nicole Loraux on memory and forgetting in ancient Athens. There, it was Lêthê not Mnemosyne, which provided the guiding principle in terms of what to do about conflicts from the past. The Athenians who, in 403 BC, swore 'not to recall the misfortunes of the past' (Loraux, 2002, p. 15) epitomised this principle in action.

The cyclical concept of time also existed in the Ottoman Empire through a peculiar combination of Turkic nomadic pagan concepts with Islam. In popular belief, God Himself, as an arbiter of fate, made time irrelevant. The longevity of the royal line therefore appeared as an expression of eternity. Cycles started with each new sultan, and he acted as though his predecessors left him nothing, for instance where the new sultan ratified laws and treaties as if they were never ratified before. The elevation of the new sultan returned the Ottoman Empire to its cyclical pattern. Everything died with the old sultan and started anew with new sultan (see Goodwin, 1998, pp. 149–157). According to one interpretation, an attachment to the lunar calendar gave the Ottoman Empire the specific sense of transcendence and allowed the state to function in separation from the material world of agriculture and the peasantry. The moon, in comparison to the Sun, is changing and shows the illusory nature of time itself since the changes of the moon's appearance are themselves illusory as the substance of moon never changes. The specific symbol of the moon – the crescent – expresses that peculiar concept of social time. In the saying of the Prophet one might read that 'Every novelty is an innovation, every innovation is an error, every error leads to Hellfire' (Goodwin, 1998, p. 151).

We can also find traces of the cyclical concept of social time in the thought of Niccolo Machiavelli. His historiosophy, built around concepts of virtue and fate, is present in all his works including the famous *Prince*. The concept of time is based on the regeneration of history, which repeats itself again and again.

St. Augustine, leading thinker of Western Christianity criticised the cyclical concept of time because, as he famously stated '*semel mortuus est Christus pro nostris peccatis*' (Christ died once only for our sins) (Augustine, p. 14).[4] This saying of the theologian and philosopher who laid down the structures of thinking for nearly a millennium expresses the essence of the linear and historical concept of time along two vectors, one in the direction of creation and the other towards apocalypse.

Biblical *kairos* was radically distinguished from Greek *chronos*. The Judeo-Christian tradition of thought proudly claims that it was the first that fully defined the historicity of humanity. The concept of linear time was formulated by Judaism with its unrepeatable past and messianic orientation towards the future (Ricoeur, 1995, pp. 167–180). Here the relation between God and creation is not mythical but historical. The Covenant shows that God is acting in history. God is, on the one hand, transcendental and is far away, and on the other hand is very close. The

---

4   See also the interesting comments about the Christian concept of time and theology by French historian Jean Delumeau in (Eco *et al.*, 1999, pp. 45–94) but especially the chapter 'Jesus's Inauguration of the End of Time' pp. 64–69.

transcendental remoteness and close presence of God takes place simultaneously. Historical time is an emanation of God in the act of creation and is an element of God's eternity. History is part of eternity in God's plan for creation. In other words, in that conception of time, history is part of the 'paralysis of time'. The eschatological plan for creation was connected with the apocalyptical end.

A graphic presentation of this concept of time looks like this:

C – Creation
F – Fall
K – Kingdom of God

The linear concept of time is based on the consciousness that time has its beginning and end, and that the beginning is different from the end.

It is interesting to compare the concept of time in monotheistic Judaism with another version of linear time, that of the Iranian dualistic Mazdaism. According to Mazdean theology, Ohrmazd and Ahriman existed for eternity but at a moment in history Ahriman will cease to exist. Mircea Eliade wrote that 'according to Mazdean theology, time is not only indispensable for the Creation; it also makes possible the destruction of Ahriman and banishing of evil. In fact, Ohrmazd created the world in order to conquer and annihilate evil. The cosmology already presupposes an eschatology and a soteriology. This is why cosmic time is no longer circular but linear: it has a beginning and will have an end ... By creating linear and limited time as an interval in which the battle against evil takes place, Ohrmazd gave it both a meaning (an eschatology) and a dramatic structure ... This is as much as to say that he created limited time as *sacred history*. This is, in fact, the great originality of Mazdean thought that it interpreted the cosmogony, the anthropogony, and Zarathustra's preaching as moments constituting one and the same sacred history' (Eliade, 1982, p. 315). Significantly however, the Mazdean version of linear time and historicity does not incorporate the notion of reconciliation because of its strong moral dualism.

The western world's – and the nowadays globally dominant – concept of time, is based on the Christian concept which is a modification of Judaism's. In the Christian concept of linear time the birth of Jesus is a unique event in history. That event split historical time into two parts: before and after the birth of Jesus. Paul wrote 'when the fullness of time had come, God sent forth his Son'.[5] That fullness of time with the

---

5   Galatians 4:4.

coming of Jesus is represented in our time measurement as *Anno Domini*, the year of our Lord. This conception was, in fact, ironically enough a later invention by the monk Dinisisus Exiguus acting on the commission from Pope John I in 525 AD. He proposed to measure time from Jesus's birth, and since then we have documented time not according to the name of royalties, emperors or presidents, or from *ad urbi condita*, as was the case with ancient Rome. (That is why we now consider Rome's foundation as 753 BC.)

But the *sacral* element of Christian time is not only linear but also cyclical.[6] On the historiosophical level it means that in the end of time creation will return to the Creator. Moreover, the cyclical character of the liturgical year in the Eastern Orthodox and Roman Catholic churches shows elements of the cyclical character of time.

Linear time in Christian theology can be presented graphically as follows where:

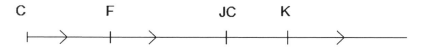

C – Creation
F – Fall
JC – Jesus Christ
K – Kingdom of God.

Reconciliation takes place at the meeting point between the sacred, eternal time outside time, and social, real, historical time. From the human point of view, the starting point of reconciliation is also the meeting of *sacrum* with *profanum*, in the sense that it is the effect of God's grace connecting with the effort of the human being (works, praying) accepting God. In Eastern Orthodox theology the concept which expresses this best is *theosis*, the 'deification of reconciled humans'. Reconciliation in time in Christian thought is not a negation of the essence of humanity and its replacement by the essence of deity, but fusion of the two elements. The beginning of reconciliation thus takes place in really existing historical time.

From the structural point of view, again as before, sacred time gives meaning to historical, social, changing time. It provides meaning for the organisation of time of the social system. The dominant role is played by the present, whilst simultaneously a causal or deterministic perception is stressed according to an eschatological vision.

The closeness of the two elements and the two functions performed by social time becomes even closer with the acceleration of social dynamics in heterogenic societies. Today, social time in Western secularised societies, has almost lost its

---

6   Oscar Cullamnn (1964) in his now classical *Christ and Time: The Primitive Christian Conception of Time and History* stresses only the linear character of Christian time.

element of *sacrum*, but it still performs the function of regulator of social life. The near annihilation of the sacred dimension of time and a shift of balance towards the regulatory, worldly function of time arguably signals that there is something wrong in these societies with the social generation of meaning. Those social institutions responsible for creating meaning which do not work at all or are pushed outside the mainstream of society are replaced by a systemic focus based on the reproduction of institutional rationalities only. The contemporary post-industrial secular, linear concept of time accordingly fulfils its main social functions subordinated to instrumental rationality. Thus, in the developed Western world since the collapse of communism, the triumphalism of an 'end of history' signifies an emptiness of time. In this reality time's only presence concerns a synchronisation function, supplemented only by the cyclical ritual time of political elections which symbolises merely a hollow renewal of social energies by ritualistic voting and leaves the spectacle of an almost grotesque liberal version as the fulfilment of time in some eschatological scheme

Yet people in Western liberal democracies, as well as people in other part of the world, have older cultural needs for *sacrum* which may soften existential fears and provide meaning for the present. And it is this element of *sacrum* that is necessary for social time, and also for reconciliation and *restititution*, which require in essence the recreation of sacral dimension of time.

Globalisation as compression of time

Globalisation is a phenomenon with indirect ontological status in a way similar to time; in other words we learn about globalisation and time in an indirect way, through results. Globalisation today is not only a very powerful process which is subjecting new areas to its influence. It is not only speeding up economic operations and it is not only extending the scope of those operations. From the point of view of the effect and consequences of the globalisation processes Anthony Giddens (1990, p. 63) coined the expression that globalisation is compression of space and time. The same presentation of compression of time-space in globalisation can be found in Boaventura de Sousa Santos's fascinating socio-legal work with its call for an epistemological paradigm shift and the creation of a new common sense. Santos tries to position law in that complex global structure, although it is true that his focus is largely on the spatial rather than the temporal dimension (Santos, 1995, pp. 111–122; 250–377). Whereas Giddens analyses globalisation in a neutral way, as if in the positivistic 'value free' social science tradition, Santos's arguments in favour of a radical, paradigmatic change in the description of reality and the perceptions of social reality in globalisation, suggest it is more surprising that he overlooked the problem with the concept of time itself. Perhaps it is in Michael Hardt and Antonio Negri's analysis of empire, one of the more prominent recent interpretations of the time – or sacred dimension – of globalisation, that we find a more suggestive presentation of globalisation as a global system of relations connecting spaces and historical times.

As they wrote, 'Empire is thus understood not so much as rule over universal space and time, but rather as a movement that gathers the spaces and temporalities through the powers of the social forces that seek to liberate themselves from the natural cyclical character of time and history' (Hardt and Negri, 2000, p. 37). I note only in passing that whether or not Empire – or rather their counter-Empire – can act as a redeemer of the age of globalisation, they nonetheless try to establish a new sacred dimension of time in globalisation.

Each interpretation however acknowledges that globalisation involves not only the compression of time but also the releasing of societies from their historical time generated by them in their evolution. This is perhaps the biggest visible consequence of globalisation. Globalisation processes are incorporating small social islands from particular countries into their own operational logics and thus their own time of *synchronisation*. Significantly, this process – the result of which may be the destruction of concepts of time generated by particular geographic communities – is not neutral. There is a conflict of rationalities in which the rationality of one historical time collides with the local rationality generated by different historical time. Since one function of time is to synchronize processes of the reproduction of social life – and to provide meaning for these processes – the clash of concepts of time based on different rationalities may engender a global confusion. That confusion, which is both cognitive and normative, lies in facing up to the complex problems created by the simultaneous coming together and deep fragmentations of concepts of time.

However, the trend in outcomes of this aspect of processes of globalisation is not the *reconciliation* of two different rationalities – the dominant Western and weak local – but their conflict in the implementation of structural violence through the asymmetry of rationalities. This structural violence is based on the dominant part of the globe imposing an institutional compatibility within the global system. Institutions and social changes which generate compatibility are artificial and not compatible with the historical time of local societies. In effect, the undermining of historical time and the asymmetry of rationalities usually creates a situation in which real *inclusion* into the global system is blocked due to the negation of the possibilities of a self-organisational and generative potential within the local society. The conclusive significance of this is that the operation of the local society suffers a fragmentation of rationalities and leads potentially to a normative anomie of the type described by Emile Durkheim.

Conclusion: A call for the reconciliation of concepts of time

It is possible to formulate the thesis that some concepts of time exclude reconciliation while others incorporate reconciliation. One of the necessary, but not sufficient, preconditions for incorporation of reconciliation in the concept of time is existence of its double function as *sacrum* and *profanum* in the synchronisation of social relations. In globalisation processes, the problem of the sacral character of time is however neglected and there are no institutions which are able to re-generate that character of time on the global scale. At the same time an instrumentally rational concept of time capable of fulfilling the needs of the global economy is further damaging the weak layers of institutions able to generate meaning or sacral character of time.

Yet perhaps some hope is provided by different concepts of time, alternative to the Western linear concept. The potential in alternative concepts of approach to time is connected with its possibility to reconcile different concepts of time. This means that in the global age the first need is to overcome the 'structural violence' of the implementation of instrumentally rational Western time. Genuine reconciliation of different times could then open further social spaces for social and also political reconciliations.

Crucial for that hope is a different approach or perception of time than in the Western world. Time in South-East Asian countries, for instance, is 'ontologised', that is, treated as a part of being. In contemporary Western culture being is in time but time is not part of being; it is only somewhere in the background of actions, for conventional measurement. Yet time is treated in South-East Asian societies as an element which is able to release from things their sleeping or frozen unknown potentials and characteristics. To achieve that it is necessary to harmonize the proper moment with action appropriate to this moment. Such an understanding of time, of the importance of time and proper time for doing something, is crucial for south-east Asian policies of institutionalisation through recognition of the necessary sequences in implementation of policies.

There are consequences of such thinking about time in its 'ontologised' version for reconciliation. Reconciliation does not merely happen in time but requires time for its happening. Two different units, elements, persons, societies have to re-establish contact at a moment proper for action to take place; a moment in which time allows two different units to realise their different particular potentials. Their different logics or rationalities became compatible. But in order to find the proper moment for contact initiating reconciliation, it is necessary to have in mind the sacred dimension of time. But how is this to be achieved in the context of a pluralism of rationalities and identities, and how are the catastrophic effects of asymmetries of rationality to be avoided? It seems to me from the foregoing analysis, that the answer lies in recognition of thinking through the problems of meta-time, importantly understood not as meta-narrative, but as the *ethical value of synchronisation*. Such meta-time will necessarily include the element of *sacrum*.

Bibliography

Augustine, Saint *De Civitate Dei*, XII.
Barth, Karl (2004) *The Doctrine of Reconciliation. Church Dogmatics*, London and New York: Continuum.
Bouretz, Pierre (2003), *Témoins du futur. Philosophie et messianisme*, Paris: Gallimard.

Cullamnn, Oscar (1964), *Christ and Time: The Primitive Christian Conception of Time and History*, Philadelphia: Westminster Press.

Detienne, Marcel (1999), *The Masters of Truth in Archaic Greece*, New York: Zone Books.

Durkheim, Emile (1995) *The Elementary Forms of Religious Life*, New York: The Free Press.

Eco, Umberto, Gould, Stephen Jay, Carrière, Jean-Claude and Delumeau, Jean (1999) *Conversation About the End of Time*, Cathereine David, Frédéric Lenoir and Jean-Philippe de Tonnac (eds), London: Penquin Books.

Eliade, Mircea (1982), *A History of Religious Ideas. From Gautama Buddha to the Triumph of Christianity*, vol.2, Chicago and London: The University of Chicago Press.

Flis, Andrzej (2001), *Chrześcijaństwo i Europa* (Christanity and Europe), Kraków: Zakład Wydawniczy Nomos.

Gibbs, Robert (1992), *Correlations in Rosenzweig and Levinas*, Princeton, New Jersey: Princeton University Press.

Giddens, Anthony (1990), *The Consequences of Modernity*, Stanford, California: Stanford University Press.

Goowin, Jason (1998) *Lords of the Horizons. A History of Ottoman Empire*, New York: Henry Holt and Company.

Hardt, Michael and Negri, Antonio (2000) *Empire*, Cambridge, Massachusetts: Harvard University Press.

Hart, David Bentley (2003), *The Beauty of the Infinite. The Aesthetic of Christian Truth*, Grand Rapids; Michigan, Cambridge; UK: William B. and Eerdmans Publishing Company.

Heidegger, Martin (1992) *The Concept of Time*, trans William McNeill, Oxford: Blackwell Publishers.

Kolakowski, L. and Eliade, Mircea (1993) 'Religia jako parali czasu', in Mircea Eliade, *Traktat o historii religii*, Lódz.

Le Goff, Jacques (1970), *Kultura średniowiecznej Europy*, Warszawa.

Le Goff, Jacques (1992), *History and Memory*, New York: Columbia University Press.

Levinas, E. (1969), *Totality and Infinity. An Essay on Exteriority*, Pittsburgh: Duquesne University Press.

Loraux, Nicole (2002), *The Divided City. On Memory and Forgetting in Ancient Athens*, New York: Zone Books.

Mouffe, Chantal (2005), *On the Political*, London and New York: Routledge.

Ricoeur, Paul (1995), *Figuring the Sacred. Religion, Narrative, and Imagination*, Minneapolis: Fortress Press.

Rosenzweig, Franz (1985) *The Star of Redemption*, Notre Dame: University of Notre Dame Press.

Santos, Boaventura de Sousa (1995), *Toward a New Common Sense. Law, Science and Politics in the Paradigmatic Transitions*, New York and London: Routledge.

Staniszkis, Jadwiga (2003), *Władza globalizacji*, (The power of globalisation), Warszawa: Wydawnictwo Naukowe Scholar.

Steiner, George (2004), 'Zion's shadows. The hidden thoughts of philosophers – including the guru of neo-conservatism', *The Times Literary Supplement*, February 27.

Vidal-Naquet, Pierre (2003), *Czarny Lowca. Formy myśli i formy życia społecznego w świecie greckim* (Polish translation of 'Le Chasseur Noir. Formes de pensée et formes de société dans le monde grec'), Warszawa: Prószyski i S-ka.

Chapter 9

Reconciliation as Therapy and Compensation: A Critical Analysis

Claire Moon

Therapeutic discourses on 'healing' the individual, social and political legacy of apartheid violence were intrinsic to South Africa's reconciliation process. In its public performance of reconciliation and throughout its final documentation and recommendations, the Truth and Reconciliation Commission (TRC) and many of those who came to speak before it, expressed reconciliation by recourse to psychotherapeutic metaphors, such as 'healing', and the technologies of the testimonial and the confessional. These shaped the assumptions central to reconciliation, namely, that the TRC was mandated to heal the individual and social body and to repair the national psyche, assumptions that were compounded by the co-presence of Christian discourses on forgiveness. These discourses framed the submissions of victims and perpetrators to the TRC and conditioned the social and political process of recasting the past, within which reconciliation was sought, and the material practices – granting amnesty to perpetrators and reparations to victims – by which reconciliation was thought to be instituted.

In 1995, when South Africa embarked upon its reconciliatory project, one might have predicted that the amnesty provision that both preceded and precipitated the TRC's work might eventually prove reconciliation's undoing. However, not amnesty for perpetrators but reparations for victims have come to represent a critical site of contestation of reconciliation since the TRC finished its investigations, with implications for other reconciliation processes world-wide. Reparations – symbolic and material – form the focus of this chapter because it is the tension between the way in which the TRC privileged symbolic (therapeutic) reparations and the very real material inequalities that have remained untouched by reconciliation, that lie behind the Khulumani campaign for financial reparations in South Africa, and provide the reconciliation process with a most serious challenge.

The first part of this chapter explores the ways in which the TRC made evident *symbolic* reparations. It looks at therapeutic discourse and practice and takes reparations to be homologous with 'repair', either with respect to repairing relationships between victims and perpetrators via the public testimonial and confessional, or by repairing and healing harm at the individual and national level. Reparations as therapy presents dilemmas, however, that are morally contentious and that are challenged by recent claims by victims to more substantial financial reparations, the promise of which was largely unfulfilled by the TRC.

Khulumani's campaign is now underway in the United States, and presents a powerful repudiation of the TRC's therapeutic reparations. This class action lawsuit against a number of multinational corporations who profited under apartheid seeks to secure financial compensation for those who suffered violations of human rights – both particular and systemic – as a result of the symbiotic relationship between business and the apartheid regime. It is this relationship that forms the subject of the second part of the chapter in which I investigate *material* reparations by looking at claims for compensation. The lawsuit prioritizes financial compensation over psychological repair and, in contrast to the therapeutic regime inaugurated and compelled by the TRC, draws attention to the structural context within which specific acts of violence were perpetrated, and looks beyond the boundaries of the state to address international agents who benefited from apartheid's exclusionary rule. It contests the ambit of symbolic practices upon which reconciliation in South Africa was negotiated, and does so by challenging the TRC's iniquitous reparations provision, reconstructing the subjects of reconciliation and challenging the national boundaries of reconciliation that the TRC sought to institute.

Repairing the soul: therapeutic interventions

The TRC was inaugurated by the *Promotion of National Unity and Reconciliation Act, no. 34 of 1995* and was mandated to investigate and document the nature, cause, patterns and extent of gross violations of human rights. The TRC was charged with granting amnesty to perpetrators in return for 'full disclosure' of the acts for which they sought amnesty, and with making recommendations regarding the reparation and rehabilitation of victims.[1] To this end, the Act established three committees, one of which dealt with amnesty applications, another with victim testimonials, and a third that made recommendations for reparations and rehabilitation measures for victims. Crucially, the TRC sought to 'restore the human and civil dignity of victims by granting them an opportunity to relate their own accounts of the violations of which they are the victims'.[2] The importance of narrating, of testifying to past violence, was connected by the TRC to the restoration of the human dignity of victims. Victim testimonials constituted the means by which official acknowledgment of experiences of past violence might be conferred, acknowledgement being pivotal to the restoration of dignity, and to healing the psychological legacy of past violence.

Throughout the public hearings at which victims and perpetrators testified, the many public declarations by officials of the TRC, and the narrative of the TRC Report, the metaphor of the wound and the language of healing were repeatedly iterated to evoke the legacy of apartheid violence. Justice Minister, Dullah Omar,

---

1   Gross violations of human rights were defined as torture, kidnapping, killing and severe ill-treatment.

2   Promotion of *National Unity and Reconciliation Act, no. 34 of 1995*, Section 3c.

spoke of 'ANC wounds' 'PAC wounds', and 'the wounds of our people'. He argued that 'people are in need of healing, and we need to heal our country if we are to build a nation which will guarantee peace and stability' (Omar). Archbishop Desmond Tutu, chairperson of the TRC, spoke of the need for 'national healing', eschewing the party political subjects central to Omar's appeal in favour of South Africa's new subject category of victim. He stated that 'victims and survivors who bore the brunt of the apartheid system need healing' (Tutu, 1996, p. 8). The TRC implored that 'the wounds of the past must not be allowed to fester'. They must 'be opened', they must be 'cleansed' and 'balm must be poured on them so they can heal' (Tutu, 1998, p. 27). Commentators on the TRC enforced and compelled these by reflecting popular therapeutic platitudes about denial and mental health: that recalling buried memories or truths about past trauma can help to alleviate anxiety and emotional suffering, and prevent the unsettling and disruptive 'return' of the past (Dowdall, 1996, p. 34, emphasis added):

> The Truth and Reconciliation Commission... can contribute to rehabilitation by breaking the culture of silence. *We all know* that concealing, suppressing or repressing painful memories commonly brings in its wake psychological symptoms: stress, anxiety, and depression. *We also know* that speaking about upsetting things in a supportive and affirming setting makes people feel better.

According to this view, testifying sets trauma to rest, closes the door on the past and allows a new orientation to the future.

Wounded victims became ciphers of the nation and particular individuals were key bearers of the nation's wounds such as Father Michael Lapsley and Constitutional Court Judge Albie Sachs, both former ANC activists. Lapsley, former ANC chaplain, lost both hands in a letter bomb attack in 1990 whilst living in exile in Zimbabwe. Where once his hands were, now are two metal hooks, which Lapsley describes as his '"entrée" into the Black community' (Scheper-Hughes, 1998, p. 127). Sachs (1990) lost an arm in a car bomb attack in 1998 whilst working as a civil rights lawyer in exile in Mozambique.[3] Scheper-Hughes writes that the narratives of their wounding contain 'in microcosm, the history of the anti-apartheid struggle, the courage of the comrades, their certainty in the moral goodness and rightness of their cause, their willingness to suffer the consequences of "putting one's body on the line"'. This was a narrative repeatedly iterated by the TRC in which accounts of individual suffering were conflated with national suffering, and individual healing with national healing, unity and reconciliation, such that individual healing became commensurate with national reconciliation. Therapeutic assumptions about individual processes of coming to terms with the past were transposed onto the nation. Each victim testimonial and every perpetrator confessional constituted a specific site of national healing where every wounded body, every story of suffering acted as a morality tale by which the national reconciliation process was guided and played out.

---

3   Sachs (1990) narrates his recovery from this event.

Two technologies governed the process by which the Commission produced the 'truth of suffering': the testimonial and the confessional. These techniques constructed and compelled the key subject positions of the TRC – victim and perpetrator. Victim testimonies were rendered in private statements and at public hearings where, as part of the healing mandate of the Commission, victims were encouraged to relate their experiences 'in their own words'. The TRC assumed that the act of testifying functioned as a talking cure, a cathartic process by which memories of past violence might be purged. It understood the testimonial to be integral to the recovery of victims, who, in return for their stories received 'official acknowledgement' of their experiences as reparation. The power, indeed veracity of testimonial truth was predicated on the spectacle of victim suffering at the public hearings at which were communicated not just the forensic details of a violation, but the personal pain emanating from the act, or perhaps the unrelenting anguish of not knowing, for example, whether a relative might be dead or alive, or where their remains might have been secretly buried.

By contrast, the power of a confessional truth lay in its potential to demonstrate the 'humanity' of a perpetrator, to which a public display of emotion, of remorse, or perhaps even an apology, was crucial. The public confessional attempted to lift the burden of responsibility insofar as the confession signified a statement of personal virtue and of repentance. Tutu argued, in a precarious conflation of victim and perpetrator, that 'perpetrators are victims too' and that they were 'victims of the apartheid system and they, too, need healing' (Tutu, 1996, p. 8). However, the confessional produced a contentious disparity between the symbolic order of the TRC, which created the expectation that confessions should be accompanied by remorse, and the specific legal requirements of the amnesty provision. Only 'full disclosure' of the facts concerning the acts for which perpetrators were seeking amnesty, and not displays of contrition and remorse, were required in order for an amnesty application to be successful. Yet there is evidence to suggest that those perpetrators who displayed remorse for their actions, such as Jeffrey Benzien, a police officer notorious for his interrogatory technique, the 'wet bag', were more successful in their amnesty applications than others who delivered an unembellished although full disclosure.[4]

The therapeutic culture that infused the post-apartheid political order was manifest, primarily, as a general ethos or orientation through which was constructed a particular understanding of the apartheid past. It provided a set of reference points and symbolic practices around which a new understanding of apartheid violence was negotiated, one which served to make victims symbolic of the new political order, and in which perpetrators were also to be understood as victims of the apartheid past. This, in turn, served to legitimise the early decision to grant amnesty to perpetrators, a decision that was crucial to the party-political negotiations that led to the TRC process.

---

4   For a discussion of this see Veitch (2001).

The therapeutic regime provided the language through which suffering was acknowledged and reparations administered. It demanded the public exposure of pain and open contrition for past wrongs. The therapeutic assumptions upon which the TRC was based reproduced some of the givens of popular psychology, and inscribed them as a system of moral understanding which ordered and made meaningful to the reconciliation process divergent victim and perpetrator experiences of past violence. The grammar of suffering and healing thus became the template upon which divergent testimonials at the public hearings, victim and perpetrator, were scripted, and through which was performed a suffering solidarity in which victim and perpetrator were identified by their respective wounds. The therapeutic ethos transformed the moral crisis about South Africa's apartheid past into an emotional or psychological one.

Features of the therapeutic ethos

Therapy as a moral frame of reference displays distinctive features that produce particular political effects, as Nolan (1998) argues, First, the therapeutic ethos, unlike traditional moral orders, is essentially self-referential and looks to the self rather than to natural law or divine reason in order to provide the moral boundaries of society and the tools for its navigation (Nolan, 1998, p. 3). The public belief in the confessional is predicated on a general conception of the self that bears an inclination to the good and is capable of reform and transformation. In this instance, the TRC required perpetrators to hold up their 'inner selves' for public scrutiny and judgement, and to express remorse as an outward sign of an inner regeneration.

Secondly, central to therapy culture is an 'emotivist ethic' that privileges open displays of emotion (Nolan, 1998, pp. 5–7). At the TRC, the public display of emotions was intimately linked to truth where truth was perceived to be accessible through an open expression of sentiment rather than through rational judgement and deliberation (Nolan, 1998, p. 6). Truth revelation as emotional performance is also related by the TRC to the process of healing, where catharsis and 'relief' were weighed in proportion to an open communication of feelings, and a failure to emote signified a failure to transform the wound inflicted by past violence. Conversely, an inability to emote was linked by the TRC to 'denial' and a refusal to come to terms with the past. Kaminer *et al.* argue in their study of the relationship of psychiatric health to forgiveness in survivors of human rights abuses that a lack of forgiveness in victims is related to 'poor psychiatric adjustment … where being unforgiving, although an understandable moral response to being violated, also carries an increased risk of psychiatric morbidity' (Kaminer *et al.*, 2001, p. 375). The study further states that a lack of forgiveness and understanding 'may be an important predictor of psychiatric risk in the population'. Such findings lend scientific credence to therapeutic assumptions that the psychological health of victims is jeopardized by a failure to forgive, and that displays of anger and calls for revenge only threaten to perpetuate the cycles of violence that reconciliation seeks to stem. In support of this assumption the TRC conflated retributive justice with revenge, arguing that feelings of revenge would militate against the possibility of reconciliation. It deployed therapy as a legitimising strategy in order to make palatable the political decision to grant amnesty to perpetrators, and in order to govern victim expectations of, and reactions to, a reconciliation process to which amnesty was central. Yet as Summerfield (2002, p. 1105) points out, 'one man's revenge is another's social justice', and feelings of revenge 'carry a moral interrogative that points to social and individual wounds and to shared ideas about justice, accountability, and punishment that hold a social fabric together'.

A third feature of the therapeutic perspective is that it pathologizes human actions, where particular forms of behaviour are represented as if they were diseases needing proper diagnosis and treatment. A pathological approach to human behaviour concentrates on causal factors, symptoms and development of a condition, and upon the necessary professional interventions required to ameliorate disease. Pathological approaches to wartime atrocities have a particular historical lineage, from the treatment of shell shock during the First World War to the invention of Post-Traumatic Stress Disorder (PTSD) in the wake of the Vietnam War, the key constitutive moment in psychiatric responses to war trauma.[5] The incorporation of PTSD into the lexicon of psychiatric diagnostic categories in 1980 brought with it a shift in interpretation of soldiers' agency in war since a diagnosis took into account the conditions under which war was fought rather than the 'intrinsic' psychological dispositions of individuals.[6] War trauma, or PTSD, came to be understood in terms of the structural and functional 'changes' produced by the experience of a 'psychologically traumatic event that is generally outside the range of usual human experience'. Characteristic symptoms of PTSD, according to the diagnostic criteria, include 'reexperiencing the traumatic event; numbing of responsiveness to, or reduced involvement with, the external world; and a variety of ... cognitive symptoms'.[7]

Pathological perspectives on and approaches to war trauma have particular implications for conceptions of accountability in war – criminal and otherwise – for atrocities perpetrated during war. Derek Summerfield notes that the invention of PTSD 'was a powerful and essentially political transformation: Vietnam veterans were to be seen not as perpetrators or offenders but as people traumatized by roles thrust on them by the US military' which 'legitimised their "victimhood" and gave them "moral exculpation"' (Summerfield, 2001). Medical professionals treating returning Vietnam soldiers were alert to these implications at the time, one of whom remarked upon the '"potentially explosive impact" of stress related diagnoses on "societal approaches to responsibility and accountability"' (Shalev, 1997 cited in Shepherd, 2000, p. XXII). Therapeutic perspectives feed into and legitimize self-

---

5   For a discussion of the historical development of psychiatric responses to war trauma see Shepherd (2000).

6   See American Psychiatric Association (1980), *Diagnostic and Statistical Manual of Mental Disorders*, Third Edition, Washington, D.C: APA, commonly referred to as 'DSM III'.

7   DSM III, p. 236.

understanding as victimisation to the extent that in South Africa, victims became the constitutive subject of the new political order, a subject category which was not, controversially, exclusive, but was one in which perpetrators were also included.

Political effects of the therapeutic ethos

Therapy constructs the moral boundaries of reconciliation in an attempt to organize and converge diverse experiences and testimonies about past violence. It replaces other moral codes that we might expect to play an important role in dealing with past atrocities. Specifically, in reconciliation processes that offer amnesty to perpetrators, it displaces the moral order represented by a retributive response to gross violations which emphasizes punishment as the 'correct' response to 'wrongs' committed. It operates *in place of* retribution, compelling 'self-reform' without punishment.

Therapeutic responses to the effects of atrocity were crucial to the work of the TRC because it was empowered to grant amnesty but not to prosecute. Therapy thus acted upon amnesty to legitimize it and to *discredit and disallow calls for retributive justice*, by grounding moral authority in self-reflection, remorse, repentance and internal change rather than in punishment. This, however, was problematic because therapy militates against popular understandings of right responses to violence that are predicated upon the notion of 'just deserts'. For example, as Wilson has documented, the TRC's restorative approach to justice was in conflict with popular interpretations and practices of 'local justice' in the townships which were thoroughly grounded in retributive responses to wrongdoing (Wilson, 2001, ch. 7).

Because the TRC was empowered to grant amnesty to individuals on the basis of claims about violations being perpetrated within a political rationale, the TRC acted upon the effects of transacted violence[8] rather than with the structures within which violence was made possible.[9] As such, therapy excluded a proper accounting of the structural effects of apartheid regime, of the race, education and pass laws, of which many thousands more people were victims. Because therapy emphasizes the psycho-social effects of conflict emerging out of individual acts of violence, it fails

---

8   The term 'transacted violence' is used by both Michael Humphrey (2003) and by Alan Feldman (1999). For both authors 'transacted violence' designates, within the TRC's logic, individual violent actions of state security and party political agents giving rise to 'gross violations of human rights' as defined by the TRC mandate. Transacted violence is counterposed by both authors to structural apartheid violence such as the pass and education laws. However, it would be to misconstrue the point if the two were seen to be distinct and separable, as the conditions within which transacted violence takes place were rendered by the particular history and structures of white power and privilege that gave rise to 'separate development' and the policies that implemented and enforced it.

9   The TRC did sketch out the structural conditions – the institutions and business interests – that kept apartheid alive. However, the TRC was not empowered to act upon any findings it made in this regard and these investigations were less fundamental to its public authority.

to acknowledge the material deprivations that were concomitant with past atrocity and, as a consequence, it works to *discredit claims for material compensation*. Therapy side-steps redress of the deep structural and economic inequalities within which gross violations of human rights are made possible, concentrating instead on changing people's behaviour through altering their self-perception. Simultaneously, therapy precludes an investigation into the *beneficiaries* of apartheid violence, as the subjects of reconciliation are 'victims and perpetrators' of party political violence alone. It does not address those who profited but did not, at least directly, perpetrate.

The more political implications of making victims central to the new post-apartheid order are astutely observed by Michael Humphreys who notes that the TRC staged the 'spectacle of victim pain and suffering in order to publicly project the power of the state' (Humphrey, 2003, p. 171). In other words, the TRC inverted the logic of apartheid power thus: where the power of the former regime was founded on the state's capacity for terror, the power and legitimacy of the new order is grounded in the public performance of the state's power to restore, heal and reconcile. However, it is arguable that the possibility of founding reconciliation on a therapeutic order is uncertain, since 'the therapeutic emphasis on the victimised and emotive concerns of the self are tendentiously anticommunal', presenting a fragile basis for reconciliation (Nolan, 1998, p. 301).

Overall, however, whilst therapy provided a compelling narrative through which to relate the harms of the past, the therapeutic performance of the TRC failed on several counts. It failed because the mandate of the TRC required victims to tell their stories 'in their own words', but the Commission decided quite early on in its work that allowing victims to record their full testimony was too time consuming and inefficient, taking around three hours in total for each testimony to be recorded. The TRC's information management system *Infocomm* required restrictive changes to the statement form upon which victim testimonies were recorded in order to be able to process the testimonies as 'forensic data' rather than as a free narrative. The TRC several times revised the form in order to make the victim statement concordant with the controlled vocabulary of data coding (see Wilson, 2001, pp. 38–41; Bozzoli, 1998). Each revision of the statement form contained a greater proportion of questions directed towards eliciting only the forensic details of the violation until the final version completely eliminated the 'free' section of the form in which victims could record the experiential dimension of the violation. Testimonials were eventually gathered through directed interviews, obviating the objective of testimonial healing. The work of the TRC attracted enormous research interest to the extent that victims expressed anger at the way in which their testimonies were reproduced, unacknowledged, by writers, researchers and commentators on the Commission's work, and complained that they ultimately lacked control over representation of their experiences (Ross, 2003, pp. 334–335).

The therapeutic culture was also at odds with the mechanisms by which the TRC granted amnesty. The TRC did not require remorse and apology as a condition of granting amnesty, but a public display of remorse came to be expected by some victims and audiences at the public hearings. All that was required of perpetrators, however, was a 'full disclosure' of the event in question. This created some confusion around what was required of perpetrators in order to be awarded amnesty and victims wanted to know how they could come to terms with a successful amnesty decision where no display of contrition had been made.

The therapeutic ethos seemed, symbolically, to place victims as the new constitutive pillar of society, but it is arguable, however, that perpetrators rather than victims were privileged by the process because amnesty was accorded with immediate effect, whereas victims had to wait for reparations to be decided. In addition, many victims placed a premium on financial compensation, a claim that was obscured by the TRC's broader therapeutic discourse that placed greater emphasis on symbolic reparations. These encompassed a range of practices, the significance of which lay to a large extent in their therapeutic intent of restoring the dignity of victims and survivors. For example, public truth telling and official acknowledgement of victim stories, many of which had met previously with various forms of official denial from, for example, state security operatives or the refusal of doctors to treat seriously the effects of torture, were indispensable to the TRC's attempt to produce a new historical record. Other gestures aimed to recognize and rehabilitate individuals – such as legal measures like granting death certificates in the case of disappearances, expunging criminal records for those individuals sentenced for politically related offences, accelerating outstanding legal matters, and rituals of exhumation, memorial and reburial – to gestures directed towards the reinscription of memories of apartheid violence – such as renaming streets and public facilities, erecting memorials and monuments, and declaring a national day of remembrance.[10] Community rehabilitation programmes were also set up to 'promote healing and recovery of individuals and communities affected by human rights violations'. These entailed interventions at both community and national levels including demilitarisation programmes, mental health and trauma counselling, and programmes aimed at rehabilitating and reintegrating perpetrators into 'normal community life'.[11]

Victims, however, did not receive all that they had been promised. The final settlement on TRC reparations was made over seven years after the TRC began its work and more than four years after the TRC submitted its initial reparations recommendations to the government. In April 2003, Thabo Mbeki announced that victims who had testified before the TRC would be eligible for a single payment of R30,000 ($4,500), and that a total of $85 million would be paid to just over 19,000 victims found by the TRC to be victims of one or more gross violations of human rights.[12] The total amount allocated was much less than that initially recommended

---

10   *Truth and Reconciliation Commission Report* (Cape Town: TRC, 2003), 6 (2), pp. 13–15.

11   *TRC Report*, 6 (2), p. 16.

12   The TRC recommended that reparations be granted on an individual basis. It received statements from 21,290 people of whom around 19,050 were found to be victims of gross

by the TRC which stated that the government should pay the equivalent of $474 million in reparations to all who testified to the TRC. Victimhood was arguably 'short-changed' by symbolic reparations (Humphrey, 2003, p. 184).

Taken as a whole, there was an important *disjuncture* between the *symbolic order* instituted by the therapy culture and the expectations it generated, and the *material processes* by which applications for reparations and amnesty were administered. The therapeutic script sought to forge unity around the experience of violence and suffering by privileging symbolic over financial reparations. But instead the TRC *displaced* the site of struggle and produced new conflicts around other issues, especially around the question of financial reparations to victims. In response, victim support groups in South Africa, dissatisfied with the reconciliation process, started the process of claiming financial compensation from multinationals for apartheid crimes.

'Unfinished business': compensating apartheid

In *Khulumani et al v. Barclays et al* filed in November 2002 in New York, Khulumani ('Speak Out'), representing some 33,000 South African victims brought the case for reparations against a number of US, UK, German, Swiss and Dutch multinationals from the oil, armament, banking, transportation and information technology industries – including British Petroleum, Shell Oil, Barclays, Credit Suisse, Deutsche Bank, Ford Motors, IBM and Rio Tinto – alleged to have profited from their business associations with South Africa.[13]

When the TRC started its work in 1995, Khulumani was established by survivors of political violence to provide support for victims testifying to the TRC. It helped victims to register their testimonies, fill out applications for reparations and

---

violations of human rights. More than 2,975 victims emerged from the amnesty hearings although in some cases these were not found to be victims of gross violations of human rights. Relatives and dependants of dead or disappeared individuals were considered by the TRC as victims and were also recommended for financial reparations.

13   *Khulumani et al v. Barclays et al*, United States District Court Eastern District of New York, Complaint, 12 November, 2002, full text available at www.cmht.com/pdfs/apartheid-cmpl.PDF. The case names from the oil sector, ExxonMobil Corp., Shell Oil Company, ChevronTexaco Corporation and Chevron Texaco Global Energy, Inc., British Petroleum P.L.C., Flour Corporation, Total-Fina-Elf; from the armaments sector, Armscor, Rheinmetall Group; from banking, Barclays National Bank Ltd., Citigroup Inc., Commerzbank, Credit Suisse Group, Deutsche Bank, Dresdner Bank, J.P. Morgan Chase, Union Bank of Switzerland AG; from transportation the Ford Motor Company, DaimlerChrysler AG, General Motors Corporation; from technology, Fujitsu Ltd, IBM; and from mining, Rio Tinto. The lawsuit is one of a number of other such cases launched, with varying degrees of success, since the TRC began its investigations,. In another example, British company Cape PLC agreed in March 2003 to a compensation settlement of £7.5 million to 7,500 South Africans affected by asbestos mining during the apartheid years.

appeals, and provided individual and group counselling throughout the process.[14] Khulumani also organized meetings with TRC officials and represented victim interests to the government, giving victims an active voice throughout the work of the TRC.

However, since 2001 Khulumani has concentrated on addressing the 'unfinished business' of the TRC, or financial reparations, arguing that the TRC had underestimated the importance of financial compensation to reconciliation. In addition, Khulumani argued that the majority of victims of apartheid were excluded by the TRC's mandate as they were not victims of party political violence but of the systemic effects of apartheid, such as the pass laws, labour practices and forced migration, in which a number of multinationals are alleged to be complicit. Nothing in the *Promotion of National Unity and Reconciliation Act of 1995* that established the TRC prevented individual business personnel from making disclosures about complicity with the apartheid regime, and yet not one foreign business agent approached the TRC on this basis to ask for amnesty.[15] Khulumani announced its intention to sue the government of South Africa in July 2002, for failing to consult victims on the reparations policy prior to submission of the TRC Report, and in November of the same year Khulumani filed the lawsuit against multinationals in New York.[16]

The lawsuit transforms therapeutic reparations into legal disputation and is notable for two reasons. First, it is a move that is consistent with increasing pursuits of financial reparations for past injustices that have become a conspicuous and contentious feature of contemporary human rights claims, and this case promises to be a paradigmatic moment in reinforcing such claims.[17] Secondly, it re-articulates therapeutic reparations as financial compensation, communicating differently the subjects, objects and practices central to reconciliation. In contrast to therapeutic

---

14   Khulumani gave referrals to those in need of additional psychological care and supported families of the disappeared by organising special counselling. When the TRC stopped taking victim testimonies in 1998, Khulumani extended its programs to providing direct medical assistance to victims and their families, equipment (such as wheelchairs) to injured victims, and educational assistance to children.

15   The TRC's institutional hearings received submissions from a number of South African companies. Khulumani argues that multinationals should also have made submissions to the TRC, with the implication that had they done so, they may not now be subject to petition.

16   Khulumani was working on these campaigns in collaboration with Jubilee South Africa, an organisation lobbying for the cancellation of Apartheid Debt. The case is based on common law principles of liability and on the Alien Tort Claims Act, 28 U.S.C. § 1350, which, under federal common law grants US courts jurisdiction over certain violations of international law regardless of where they occur as long as the accused have some presence in the US, as is the case with the corporations concerned. The venue of the case is eligible because the defendants have offices in the New York district.

17   High profile reparations awards have been made to Holocaust survivors, to those of Japanese descent imprisoned in North America during World War II, and there is a well-organized movement for slavery reparations for African-Americans.

reparations, it considers victims of *structural* violence and enquires into the *beneficiaries* of apartheid; it considers not only gross human rights violations but the 'everyday violence' of apartheid that shaped and constrained the lives of those who were subject to its regulations, and seeks *financial compensation* in furtherance of reconciliation from the corporations who benefited from apartheid.

The lawsuit makes compensation claims on an individual basis in relation to the experiences of racially structured violence, including specific acts of violence to which victims were subject in addition to their lived experience under apartheid, during which they were subject to the pass laws, forced removals, job and housing restrictions, poor living conditions and education provision and other direct forms of repression; with all of which the defendants are claimed to be complicit.

The case claims accountability for corporate violations under a host of international rulings on crimes against humanity, genocide, extra-judicial killings, torture, unlawful detention and cruel, inhuman and degrading treatment. It argues that apartheid is a *jus cogens* violation of international law equivalent to slavery, drawing upon Article I of the International Convention on the Suppression and Punishment of the Crime of Apartheid and the Rome Statute of the International Criminal Court. Both of these classify apartheid as a 'crime against humanity'.[18] In addition, the case invokes the third party liability precedent set by Nuremberg which ensured that the bankers that financed the Third Reich were held liable for crimes against humanity.

The case seeks to prove third party liability for 'aiding and abetting' the apartheid regime, and criminal enterprise liability imposed by customary international law and domestic law.[19] This deems that participation in a criminal enterprise can be found where a party participated in furthering the system within which a crime is committed, with knowledge of the nature of that system and intent to further it, and with a negligence of, deliberate indifference to, or a 'reckless disregard' for the welfare of others. The case alleges that 'during the relevant period, global industrialists and financiers knew or should have known of the danger to the black South African population' as the UN had 'put the world on notice' during the 1970s and an international boycott that included embargoes on arms, oil and technology was well under way by the 1980s. In spite of this, the defendants 'acted in conscious disregard of or with deliberate indifference to these dangers by providing substantial assistance or encouragement to the apartheid regime', with some corporations continuing to assist the regime throughout this period and, sometimes, concealing fraudulently their co-operation by establishing offshore trusts to obscure their transactions.[20] The plaintiffs argue that the defendants encouraged and furthered

---

18   International Convention on the Suppression and Punishment of the Crime of Apartheid (UN 1973/1976), Article I.

19   The case gives legal historical precedents and examples on third party liability as 'aiding and abetting' from US law, Nuremberg, the International Criminal Tribunal for the former-Yugoslavia (ICTY) and the International Criminal Tribunal for Rwanda (ICTR).

20   *Khulumani et al v. Barclays et al*, 165.

abuses that would not have happened in the same way without their participation, and claims that business interests were 'active participants and initiators in constructing a political and economic system which, in the end, was classified in international law as a crime against humanity' noting that 'the period of extreme repression, from 1960 onwards, was intended to save the system that protected privilege based on race, thereby continuing to guarantee business its exclusive place in the South African economy and society'.[21] The defendants are accused of acting as 'joint venturers' for which they are liable to plaintiffs for compensatory and punitive damages.

Numerous examples are cited of business aiding and abetting apartheid, including IBM and Fujitsu ICL both of which provided the computers that enabled South Africa to create the 'pass book system' which enabled control of the black population. Pass books made possible organized forced labour, and gross violations of human rights such as murder, torture and massacre. Car manufacturers provided armoured vehicles used to patrol the townships, oil companies and arms manufacturers violated embargoes on sales to South Africa, and banks funded the expansion of the police and security apparatus. Some of the companies are charged with defrauding (mainly) black employees who deposited money into pension, health, life, unemployment, and retirement funds but received nothing in return.

The lawsuit and the TRC

The lawsuit shifts the focus from individual perpetrators to a systemic analysis of violations and makes a strong case for charging the beneficiaries of the system with moral responsibility for apartheid. It draws heavily upon evidence produced by the TRC's own enquiry into the culpability of the business community in its support for and furtherance of the regime. The TRC had found that although some sectors bore more responsibility than others, business was culpable because it benefited from operating in a racially structured environment. In response to the findings, the TRC recommended that wealth taxes be imposed on business as appropriate restitution but it lacked any legal power to enforce these recommendations. The lawsuit draws upon statements from the TRC on the complicity of the business community and is in part legitimized by the TRC finding that:

> Business was central to the economy that sustained the South Africa state during the apartheid years. Certain businesses, especially the mining industry, were involved in helping to design and implement apartheid policies. Other businesses benefited from co-operating with the security structure of the former state. Most businesses benefited from operating in a racially structured context.[22]

The lawsuit plays into long standing debates in South Africa about the relationship between apartheid and capital, an argument that has a critical bearing on the question

21 *Khulumani et al v. Barclays et al*, 75 to 80.
22 *TRC Report 4* (2) 161.

of corporate accountability for apartheid violence.[23] This debate is usually pitched as one between 'liberals' and 'radicals', along with all the normative assumptions that those terms imply, and it shaped the business submissions to the TRC and responses to them.[24] In brief, 'liberal' arguments claim that apartheid was in conflict with free market capitalism since it entailed far-reaching state intervention into the labour market and other sectors of the economy and affected profit negatively by undermining productivity growth.[25] By contrast, the 'radical' argument claims that apartheid was a system of racial capitalism in which segregation minimized the cost of black labour in order to maximize white corporate profitability.[26] The radical position is the concordant basis for any claim to financial reparations since it recognizes the enduring effects of apartheid ideology on the economy, and upon the majority of the population subject to its deleterious material effects.

The liberal–radical debate was manifest in the various submissions to the TRC during its investigations into the business communities, in which it set out the relationship between business and the power of the regime, and articulated the continuing legacy of this alliance. The relationship between apartheid and business turned on the extent to which apartheid was considered to have facilitated or impeded business interests, and upon the responsibility of businesses for shaping apartheid legislation. Had business been involved in the commission of human rights violations, the TRC wanted to know. And did business benefit from apartheid or had it acted to hasten its demise?

In order to grasp the relationship between business and apartheid the TRC enquired into culpability, collaboration and involvement in apartheid of different sectors of the economy including white business, black business, employers' representatives and trades unions in which the mining, defence and banking sectors emerged as sectors central to the apartheid order. The TRC distinguished between first, second and third orders of business involvement with apartheid. A first order finding required direct collaboration in the design and implementation of apartheid policies, for which the mining industry was held directly accountable.[27] Mining capital played a major historical role from the early days of the Boer Republics in driving cheap labour policies and was instrumental in influencing legislation that forced black workers into a wage system in which pay was capped and the brutal

---

23   For a review of the historiographical dimensions of this debate see Christopher Saunders, *The Making of the South African Past: Major Historians on Race and Class* (Cape Town: David Phillip, 1988).

24   For an excellent account of the way in which the terms of the TRC investigation into business culpability is conditioned by this debate see Nicoli Nattrass, 'The Truth and Reconciliation Commission on Business and Apartheid: A Critical Evaluation', *African Affairs*, 98 (1999).

25   See Terence Moll, 'Did the Apartheid Economy Fail?', *Journal of Southern African Studies*, 117:2 (1991).

26   See for example Merle Lipton, *Capitalism and Apartheid* (Hounslow: Maurice Temple Smith, 1985).

27   *TRC Report*, 4 (2) 23.

repression of black workers and trade union action was endemic. The exploitation of black labour was key to the relationship between business and apartheid, and in its submission to the TRC, COSATU argued that the heart of apartheid was to be found in the racialized cheap labour system promoted and enforced by a mining industry that saw black wages in 1969 less than the wages paid in 1896. The mining industry was opposed to all industrial action directed towards raising the cost of black and white labour, although it accepted the enhanced position of white employees over time, whilst black worker power was progressively eroded by the mining industry. There were few admissions of accountability by the mining business community, and in fact the relationship between mining and apartheid was described by the TRC as 'complex and contradictory' since the protection of white labour, an effect of apartheid, was claimed by the corporations concerned to increase costs to business. Many submissions by the mining magnates to the TRC on the costs of white job reservation testify to what was perceived by mining business to be a 'major apartheid-related thorn in the side of the industry'.[28] Gross violations of human rights were perpetrated due to negligence of health and safety by covering up the dangers of asbestos, and the large numbers of accidents and deaths that were affiliated with working in the mines.

Second order involvement entailed the supply of goods and services for repressive purposes. The TRC maintained a distinction between those businesses that profited by direct engagement with state repression and those who could not have expected their business dealings to have contributed directly or subsequently to repression. Second order culpability required knowledge that products or services would be used for morally questionable purposes, an important example being the military-industrial complex in which the defence industry became 'willing collaborators in the creation of the apartheid war machine which was responsible for many deaths and violations of human rights' and out of which defence profited.[29] The imposition of an arms embargo against South Africa in the 1960s led to the development of a localized arms industry that provided the means for the maintenance and defence of the apartheid regime, and which profitably manufactured goods that it knew to be used in the perpetration of human rights violations both inside and outside South Africa. Armscor, the state-owned Armaments Development and Production Corporation, was largely responsible for the development of a local arms industry which provided the 'material means for the maintenance and defence of apartheid' and was declared by the TRC as 'guilty of directly and indirectly perpetuating the political conflict and associated human rights abuses'.[30] By the end of the 1970s, Armscor was central to a new military-industrial complex which contracted out much of its production and research to the private sector which included the majority of South Africa's private companies as well as some important multinationals such as Shell and IBM. As such, many private sector companies were made responsible

---

28 *TRC Report*, 4 (2) 69.
29 *TRC Report*, 4 (2) 73.
30 *TRC Report*, 4 (2) 74.

by the state for protecting essential state installations and for developing nuclear weapons. Armscor claimed to be doing 'normal work' in contributing to the defence of the state, a position questioned by the TRC which pointed to the domestic site of Armscor's security operations. Armscor could not have ignored the fact that the government was using military means for internal oppression.

Banks, particularly international creditors, were also found to play a second order role in supporting and sustaining apartheid. Swiss Banks in particular profited from sanctions, stepping in when other lenders, notably Chase Manhattan, reduced their services to the regime. According to the TRC, banks worked with government agencies, and were 'knowingly or unknowingly involved in providing services and lending to the government' including the use of covert credit cards for undercover intelligence operations.[31] The Anti-Apartheid Movement archives noted manufacturers' admissions that they were engaged actively with apartheid but that they raised the living standards of employees, but that this argument could not be applied to the banks as they lent directly to the government to 'repress South African citizens, wage war against liberation movements and invade its neighbours'.[32]

Third order involvement covered those who had benefited from the apartheid economy indirectly by virtue of operating within the racially structured context of apartheid, thus, argued the TRC, highlighting current inequalities in the distribution of wealth and income and challenging the liberal argument that business was harmed by apartheid.[33] Third order involvement, however, acts as a 'cover all' potentially making first and second order findings redundant: 'third order involvement is the most problematic of all the levels of involvement because it proceeds beyond the bounds of intention and implies guilt by association' (Nattrass, 1999, p. 388). It makes no distinction between the complicity of different sectors of business, and arguably conflates the culpability of corner shop owners with that of Armscor.

Overall, the TRC concluded that business was central to the economy that sustained apartheid whether it had been involved in designing and implementing apartheid policies, co-operating with state security structures, or profiting from the racially structured context of apartheid South Africa.[34]

Two clear views of the relationship between business and apartheid emerged out of the submissions, views that mirrored the liberal-radical debate. White business argued that apartheid raised the costs of doing business, eroded South Africa's skill base and undermined long-term productivity and growth.[35] It claimed that

---

31   *TRC Report*, 4 (2) 26.

32   *TRC Report*, 4 (2) 130.

33   Third order involvement was questioned by some participants in the investigation who wanted to know whether payment of taxes was tantamount to involvement.

34   *TRC Report*, 4 (2) 161.

35   These included business organisations such as the Steel and Engineering Industries Federation of South Africa (SEIFSA), the South African Chamber of Business (SACOB), the Afrikaner Handelsinstituut (AHI), the Council of South African Banks (COSAB) and the Textile Federation and the Johannesburg Chamber of Commerce and Industry; specific companies and corporations such as South African Breweries (SAB), the Anglo American

apartheid raised the costs of doing business as it engaged a set of politically inspired yet economically irrational policies that hindered rather than generated profit. By contrast, the ANC, COSATU and the SACP saw apartheid as a system of racial-capitalism that depressed black labour costs in order to maximize white profit. Their argument strenuously resisted the persistent liberal distinction between the economic and political spheres by emphasising the intrinsic relationship between apartheid ideology and capitalism on the one hand, and the concomitant relationship of the black trade union movement to the struggle for democracy on the other. The ANC submission argued that white business had played no role in opposing the regime, and instead, at key moments in the re-emergence of the democratic movement 'business' initial reaction was invariably one of opposition, victimisation of activist and union officials, and recourse to the regime's security forces' in which 'many violations of human rights occurred as a consequence'.[36]

Some businesses resisted the TRC's investigation on its own terms. Old Mutual, a large mutual insurance fund, argued that it was excluded from making a submission by the TRC's mandate because it investigated the commission of gross violations of human rights to which it was not party.[37] This complaint points to the limitations of a mandate that in fact circumscribed a full and proper enquiry into apartheid violence beyond the party political conflict at the heart of its investigations, a limitation which the lawsuit promises to address.

The TRC charged business with either direct or implicit collaboration, directly by arming and equipping the security apparatus, or implicitly by doing business with the state, paying taxes and promoting economic growth. It concluded that whilst business as a category was not homogeneous, and that there were varying degrees of complicity, economic power was in fact concentrated in the hands of a few conglomerations with enormous influence on state affairs that could have used their power instead to reform apartheid rather than strengthen and perpetuate it. It found that 'business was central to the economy that sustained the South African state during the apartheid years' and that many businesses were culpable either directly, or by omission, by failing to use their power to challenge apartheid policies and practice.[38]

For the TRC, the liberal-radical debate has a crucial bearing on the question of culpability because the different sides of the debate produce dramatically different interpretations of accountability. On a liberal account, business is cast as a victim of a regime that impeded profitability and growth, rather than as a beneficiary or

---

Corporation, Old Mutual and Tongaat-Hulett (South Africa's sugar producer); and corporate executives such as Mike Rosholt of Barlow Rand and Anton Rupert of Rembrandt International. See *TRC Final Report*, 4 (2) 15.

36   *TRC Report*, 4 (2) 19.

37   It might have added that commission with 'political intent' excluded the business community further. Yet other parties refused to make a submission including the Mineworker's Union and the South African Agricultural Union. Yet others did not respond to the invitation including the multinational oil corporations (largest foreign investors in South Africa), and the white labour organisations.

38   *TRC Final Report*, 4 (2) 161.

collaborator with apartheid. But on a radical account white business is inescapably culpable since it profited directly from the exploitation of black workers and the constraints placed on black entrepreneurial activity by apartheid.[39] Further, because the lawsuit draws heavily on the TRC findings in fleshing out its justification, the liberal-radical debate also infuses the terms of the claims contained in it, which are strongly oriented towards the radical interpretation of accountability of corporate interests. The radical claim represents a repudiation of the therapeutic regime projected by the TRC because structural violence escapes its individualistic, self-referential logic.

Challenging therapeutic reparations

It is arguable that without the TRC's investigations into business and labour under apartheid the Khulumani litigation would not have been possible. Whilst the TRC's therapeutic regime fleshed out the imaginative terrain upon which reconciliation was negotiated, it did not, could not, answer to the very real material needs of the majority of participants in the process. Indeed, the stated therapeutic aims of the Commission created expectations the TRC could not properly fulfil, thus prompting the lawsuit which promises to advance and consolidate human rights claims against multinational corporations.[40]

Crucially, Archbishop Desmond Tutu supports the lawsuit and stated in an affidavit to the court that 'the TRC always took the view that its mandate was to consider *reparations* rather than *compensation* for victims of apartheid', and that sums of money granted to victims by the TRC were only ever meant to be 'symbolic rather than substantial'. Tutu suggests that compensation could promote reconciliation by addressing the needs of those victims dissatisfied with the TRC monetary grant and added that whilst he would prefer victims to seek redress in South Africa he supports the right of victims to seek redress in any country where the courts have the necessary jurisdiction.[41] Tutu's affidavit was submitted in response to South African Justice Minister Dr Penuell Maduna's plea for the case to be thrown

39 However, this position argues that some sectors of white business profited more than others such as banks, mining and armaments industries.

40 This new mood, however, faces strong resistance. New cases for financial reparations struggle against the now hegemonic global reconciliatory regime which privileges truth telling and symbolic restitution over financial compensation to victims of gross violations of human rights. The World Jewish Congress (WJC) is a case in point. Charged with disbursing financial reparations to concentration camp survivors the WJC argues that whilst money is 'an important material expression of remorse and restitution' justice is, however, 'not about money'. It discredits claims for compensation by stating that those who chose to make reparations about money 'whether they were Jews or non-Jews, tried one more time to revise history and failed'. Justice, it notes, 'has many faces and it [is] indivisible [from] truth. The only way to struggle against injustice and anti-Semitism is to expose the truth. This has been the greatest struggle' (www.worldjewishcongress.org).

41 See Tutu's affidavit at www.woek.de/pdf/kasa_tutuaffidavit_dec_2003.pdf.

out of court because, he claimed, the case threatened the reconciliation process and would deter vital foreign investment.

The lawsuit was in fact thrown out of court on September 29th 2004 and at the time of writing is subject to appeal. Regardless of its success, the case is important because it answers to limitations of the TRC's therapeutic regime by transforming the subjects, objects, and practices of reconciliation. The TRC concentrated on the narrower categories of victims and perpetrators of gross violations of human rights perpetrated in a political context and with a political objective, and promoted symbolic reparations as the means by which the wounds of the past might be healed and past divisions transcended. This discourse represented all experiences of apartheid as victimisation, which included apartheid's 'beneficiaries' (Mamdani, 1998, p. 40):

> The TRC invited beneficiaries to join victims in a public outrage against perpetrators. If only we had known, it seemed to invite beneficiaries to say, we would have acted differently; our trust has been violated, betrayed, abused. So beneficiaries too were presented as victims.

Reconciliation as therapy over-individualizes the causes and effects of violence, privileging the effects of transacted violence over the effects of the structural imperatives of apartheid South Africa within which violence was an organising factor of everyday life, and in which business was not simply complicit, but out of which it actively profited. It undermines the importance of material redress of ongoing material inequality by prioritising symbolic reparations. In addition, the anthropomorphisation of the 'wounded nation/body politic' that the therapeutic regime engenders, reconstitutes the territorial boundary of the state as the physical, and hence moral, boundary of reconciliation such that international agents of apartheid violence are also excluded from scrutiny.

Relevant to the profound conflict between therapy and financial compensation, is what appears to be an intrinsic difference between the time of therapy and the time of compensation. This matters because it has a direct bearing upon the inauguration, indeed upon the possibility of reconciliation. That is to say, the difference helps us to understand when reconciliation might 'begin'. Therapy implies a teleological adjudication of trauma that necessarily engages inner psychological and emotional processes, professing to be destined, at some unknown point in the future, for wholeness or healing. By contrast, compensation, whilst it can never fully address the harms suffered under apartheid and their ongoing legacy, directly engages the subjects of compensation – past and present victims *and* beneficiaries – in a negotiation that entails an acknowledgement of past harm enacted at the very moment that compensation is awarded. This potential for acknowledgement and restitution is something that is made possible *retroactively* through recourse to legal categories activated in the present to address harms perpetrated in the past.[42] It is still important to remember, however, that financial compensation is not a universal panacea for the

---

42   I am very grateful to Scott Veitch here for his perceptive comments on the time of therapy and the time of compensation.

redress of past harms. Compensation has been rejected by victims in other contexts because it represents, to some, an attempt by the state to 'shut down' calls for justice. Families of the disappeared in Chile and Argentina refuse state compensation because for them it represents an attempt by the state to 'buy' their silence with the effect of deliberately 'deferring' reconciliation. To accept compensation would be to give up the right to see perpetrators brought to justice.[43]

Clearly, no single version of justice will satisfy multiple and divergent claims. But the fundamental value of the apartheid lawsuit resides, overall, in the way that it challenges the dominant, therapeutic, discourse of reconciliation by addressing the beneficiaries that profited from the racially structured social and political organisation of the apartheid state, and the intrinsic web of exploitation and violations that this structure produced. In addition, the claim for material compensation alters fundamentally the discursive image of claimants, transforming them from victims to creditors, such that they are no longer seen to be seeking concessions, but seeking what is *rightfully* due to them.[44] It subverts the reconciliatory story about healing the victims and perpetrators of party political violations by emphasising the social and economic circumstances within which violations were made possible, and against whom, thus shifting the emphasis towards the debt owed to black South Africans by corporate beneficiaries of apartheid. As a result, it demands a rethinking of what drove racial domination in apartheid South Africa. The claim for financial reparations reconfigures reconciliation as a racial justice that partly answers to profound and persistent economic inequality in post-reconciliation South Africa. It draws attention to the ways in which white supremacy was built on the pursuit of a wealth predicated on black exploitation, and it makes the relationship between racialized power and privilege and its enduring legacy central to reparations, in ways to which reconciliation as therapy seems blind.

Bibliography

Biondi, Martha (2003), 'The rise of the reparations movement', *Radical History Review*, **87**.
Bozzoli, B. (1998), 'Public ritual and private transition: the Truth Commission in Alexandria Township, South Africa, 1996', *African Studies*, **57** (2).
Dowdall, Terry (1996), 'Psychological Aspects of the Truth and Reconciliation Commission', in H. Russel Botman and Robin M. Petersen (eds), *To Remember and To Heal: Theological and Psychological Reflections on Truth and Reconciliation*, Cape Town: Human and Rousseau.

---

43 It is important to point out, however, that the material inequalities of South Africa are not the same in these contexts, and that compensation performs a more symbolic function – compensation as acknowledgement – the repudiation of which is an 'affordable' political gesture.
44 Martha Biondi (2003, p. 9) makes this argument in relation to the African American reparations movement.

Feldman, Alan (1999), 'Strange fruit: torture, commodification and the South African Truth and Reconciliation Commission', presented at the *TRC: Commissioning the Past* conference, University of Witwatersrand, 7–9 June.

Humphrey, Michael (2003), 'From victim to victimhood: truth commissions and trials as rituals of political transition and individual healing', *The Australian Journal of Anthropology,* **14** (2).

Kaminer, Debra; Stein, Dan; Mbanga, Irene and Zungu-Dirwayi, Nompumelelo (2001), 'The Truth and Reconciliation Commission in South Africa: relation to psychiatric status and forgiveness among survivors of human rights abuses', *British Journal of Psychology*, **178**.

Lipton, Merle (1985), *Capitalism and Apartheid*, Hounslow: Maurice Temple Smith.

Mamdani, Mahmood (1998), 'A diminished truth', *Siyaya*, **3**.

Moll, Terence (1991), 'Did the Apartheid economy fail?' *Journal of Southern African Studies,* **117** (2).

Nattrass, Nicoli (1999), 'The Truth and Reconciliation Commission on business and Apartheid: a critical evaluation', *African Affairs,* **98**.

Nolan, James L. (1998), *The Therapeutic State: Justifying Government at Century's End*, New York: New York University Press.

Omar, Dullah, 'Introduction to the Truth and Reconciliation Commission', Justice in Transition, http://www.truth.org.za/legal/justice.htm.

Ross, Fiona C. (2003) 'On having voice and being heard: some after-effects of testifying before the South African Truth and Reconciliation Commission', *Anthropological Theory*, **3** (3).

Sachs, Albie (1990), *The Soft Vengeance of a Freedom Fighter*, London: Grafton.

Saunders, Christopher (1998) *The Making of the South African Past: Major Historians on Race and Class*, Cape Town: David Phillip.

Scheper-Hughes, Nancy (1998), 'Undoing: Social Suffering and the Politics of Remorse in the New South Africa', *Social Justice*, **25** (4).

Shalev, Arieh Y. (1997), 'Discussion: Treatment of Prolonged Posttraumatic Stress Disorder: Learning from Experience', *Journal of Traumatic Stress*, **10** (3).

Shepherd, Ben (2000), *A War of Nerves*, London: Jonathan Cape.

Summerfield, Derek (2002), 'Effects of war: moral knowledge, revenge, reconciliation, and medicalised concepts of "recovery"', *British Medical Journal*, **325**.

Summerfield, Derek (2001), 'The invention of post-traumatic stress disorder and the social usefulness of a psychiatric category', *British Medical Journal*, **322**.

Tutu, Desmond (1996), 'Foreword' in H. Russel Botman and Robin M. Petersen (eds), *To Remember and To Heal: Theological and Psychological Reflections on Truth and Reconciliation*, Cape Town: Human and Rousseau.

Tutu, Desmond (1998), *Truth and Reconciliation Commission of South Africa Report*, Cape Town: Juta, Vol.1.

Veitch, Scott (2001), 'The Legal Politics of Amnesty' in Emilios Christodoulidis and Scott Veitch, *Lethe's Law: Justice, Law and Ethics in Reconciliation*, Oxford and Portland, Oregon: Hart Publishing.

Wilson, Richard A. (2001), *The Politics of Truth and Reconciliation in South Africa: Legitimizing the Post-Apartheid State*, Cambridge: Cambridge University Press.

Websites

www.woek.de/pdf/kasa_tutuaffidavit_dec_2003.pdf
www.worldjewishcongress.org

Cases

Khulumani et al v. Barclays et al, United States District Court Eastern District of New York, Complaint, 12 November, 2002, www.cmht.com/pdfs/apartheid-cmpl.

Other

American Psychiatric Association (1980), *Diagnostic and Statistical Manual of Mental Disorders*, Third Edition, Washington, DC: APA.

Chapter 10

Feminism and the Ethics of Reconciliation

H. Louise du Toit[1]

Introduction

> I give you my heaven as possibly the single element of consistency in my political life: my distrust of reconciliation. In this I proclaim a new life in South Africa, against those who proclaim a truce between old lives (...) I will not be an instrument for validating the politics of reconciliation. For me, reconciliation demands my annihilation.[2]

The question or issue of rape constitutes a blind spot, a particularly salient symptom, or even a paradigmatic or borderline[3] case of what was passed down as the dominant 'western symbolic order'.[4] This chapter forms part of an attempt to come to an understanding of the 'meaning' or significance of rape within this particular order, which I describe as patriarchal. The relevance of such an understanding within this limited context pans out in at least two ways: (1) I believe that we quite simply have a moral, ethical and political duty to form a sound understanding of rape as a phenomenon, not only to respond more adequately to victims[5] and perpetrators

---

of rape after the event, but also to think more clearly and strategically about rape prevention. The urgency that underlies or motivates my concern with rape can surely be traced back to my own situation in a country with a very high instance of rape[6] (estimated to be one of the highest in the world) but the problem does of course not only affect South Africans. (2) My analysis of rape is also meant to serve my broader project, namely to explore the question or issue of women's subjectivity or selfhood within the western philosophical symbolic order. I argue that 'the problem of rape' is intimately tied up with women's problematic selfhood within this same order.

This chapter looks in particular at South Africa's political transition and the discourses of 'reconciliation' and 'forgiveness' from the perspective of women and more specifically of women rape victims. In my reading of what was widely perceived as a simple or innocent exclusion of women victims from the processes of the Truth and Reconciliation Commission[7] (TRC) I show that the TRC's failure to do justice to victims of rape is not a simple oversight but is rather *constitutive* of the patriarchal political and symbolic order dominating our political landscape. Through its failure to create the vocabulary and space within which rape could be addressed as a political issue in its own right (amongst other things by modeling victimhood and political agency on masculine presumptions) the TRC set the tone for a 'new'

---

continued use of the term 'victim' is not meant to betray insensitivity towards the feelings of those who have survived rape, nor to further deny women's agency and subjectivity by emphasising our powerlessness in the face of rape. I believe we need to critically interrogate these feelings rather than simply affirm them. Rape victims much more than other victims (say of car crashes) resist the associations of powerlessness tied up with the term 'victim' because powerlessness lies at the heart of the humiliation and injury of rape. It is thus important to address the root of the problem (women's lack of political subjectivity and agency) rather than be satisfied with superficial linguistic changes. One does not become a survivor by denying the extent to which one has been a victim. In fact, such a stoic denial of victimhood with its emphasis on the victim's agency and resilience may well inadvertently prevent thorough investigations such as the one undertaken here into the ways in which wider societal beliefs endorse a rapist ethic.

6   In September 2004 the national police commissioner of South Africa, Jackie Selebi, reported that the police were achieving success in combating most crimes, but not rape. In 1994 there were 115.3 police rape cases per 100, 000 people and in 2003/4 there were 113.7 per 100, 000. In contrast with the Law Reform Commission's estimate that there are 1.7 million rapes a year, only about 54, 000 rape victims lay charges each year. According to Interpol, South Africa has the highest rate of rape in the world, as well as the highest incidence of HIV. In 2002, the Medical Research Council reported that 26 percent of doctors and nurses who treated rape cases did not think them a serious medical problem. And maybe the most horrifying statistic, in South Africa, 41 percent of those raped are under the age of 12. All of these statistics are from 'Rape has become a sickening way of life in our land', an article in *The Sunday Independent* of 26 September 2004, p. 5, by Charlene Smith.

7   The creation of this Commission was one of the results of extended negotiations among representatives of various political factions in South Africa during the early 1990s and the Commission was regarded from the start as an important tool for dealing with the moral, ethical and religious dimensions of political transition and power transfer.

or 'transformed' South Africa in which sexual difference could not and cannot be acknowledged. Moreover, it entrenched a single-sex model of politics, i.e. one in which masculine agency and victimhood, as well as masculine biased concerns and vocabularies still pose as the universal, thereby effectively silencing in political and public spaces the particularities and specificities of women's being and becoming. In South Africa, as in other societies that model themselves on the idea of a 'liberal democracy', there seems to be no space for a truly sexually differentiated politics and symbolic order.

It is not surprising, then, to find that rape rates have remained constant[8] rather than decreased since the transition to a 'democratic' South Africa. An important implication of my reading of the situation is that the locally dominant liberal models of feminist politics[9] based on universality, sameness and inclusion (often called 'gender mainstreaming'), seldom manage to reach the critical depth needed to do justice to women's (current or desired) position within politics, since women *qua* women are neither fully excluded nor fully included, which means that a political strategy of simplistic 'inclusion' is unhelpful. Our position[10] is rather that of delineating the political sphere. We as women occupy the position of border or horizon of the whole, and our uneasy position is constitutive of the political domain as such. The liberal paradigm of simple exclusion versus simple inclusion must therefore itself be opened up to critical scrutiny, since it uncritically assumes the border between 'inside' and 'outside' (politics) to be given and valid, to be incontestable and a-political. This is not the case. Women cannot, on my reading, be simply included within the political without a thorough (radical) disruption of the very structure of the political, of its 'borders' as well as its 'centre'.

---

8   National crime statistics from September 2005 show that all types of crime except hijackings, and violence against women and children, have decreased. With respect to the latter, there is a 4 percent increase since the previous year.

9   It might well be that liberal models of feminist politics are predominant to the extent that feminism is present in mainstream politics, also internationally. The likely reason for this is that liberal feminisms typically reinforce the legitimacy of the existing structures and logics by demanding that women be simply included in them. This is clearly a politically more conservative and far less threatening approach than the more radical critiques formulated by the various 'difference feminisms'.

10   I decided to use the first person form of the plural pronoun when I speak about women in this article, knowing full well that there are good reasons both for and against such usage. I have no clear solution to this dilemma, but decided to identify myself stylistically as a woman and to associate my speaking voice with the 'women…we / our' position, because the gist of my argument is precisely that we are always and thoroughly sexed (also in our thinking and writing) and that we all (women and men – maybe especially men) should become more self-consciously so.

The borderline 'feminine'

The concept of 'reconciliation' stands in a peculiar relation with what I shall call the 'feminine' of the symbolic order of 'western philosophical metaphysics'. Since the 'political fate of women' (understood in its broadest sense) is never to be fully separated or divorced from the fate of 'the feminine' within this symbolic order, although it might readily be distinguished from it, it would seem to follow that there is a sexual difference issue to take into account when one risks entering the discursive cross-fields of reconciliation, transition and forgiveness. But the theoretical gaze should also be inverted in the sense that women and 'the feminine' must not remain in the object-position only but should also take up a subject-position. This means that from the perspective of women, the issue of 'reconciliation' can also be fruitfully revisited and reformulated.

The argument is well taken from various feminist sources[11] that 'the feminine' and women occupy an uneasy, borderline type of position within traditional western metaphysics, of which currently dominant liberal political theories are an important off-shoot. This unease, this ambivalent and problematic positioning of women's subjectivity within the remaining politico-metaphysical and legal symbolic orders of the west[12] means that women / the feminine are simultaneously included in and excluded from these orders. Continental philosophers and others[13] have consequently arrived at the insight that a feminist politics cannot be satisfied with a mere demand for women's inclusion in existing philosophical and political frameworks, agendas and so on. This is the case because these frameworks and economies have always already 'included' women or the feminine in their ground structure, but in an ambivalent, ironic or exceptional way. Instead of trying to establish whether women are 'simply' included or excluded under a certain logic or paradigm, it makes more sense to view women's ambivalent position *vis-à-vis* any particular paradigm as *constitutive* of that paradigm itself. It remains a superficial gesture to ask whether women are included or excluded in any particular symbolic order when women and the 'feminine' serve to guarantee, uphold and symbolise, to *represent* the very borders, boundaries and logic of that universe. Women constitute the border as such – our bodies, places or subjectivities define the limits of the thinkable, the rational, of the political. In a memorable passage Jean-Francois Lyotard[14] visualises the same point thus:

---

11   Carole Pateman's 1988 *The Sexual Contract* and Luce Irigaray's 1985 *Speculum of the Other Woman* are examples of what I have in mind.

12   Although these have a western origin, the economic and military domination of the west has ensured that virtually no spot on earth remains fully outside the orbit of and thus untouched by the symbolic orders, 'meaningful universes' and master-narratives of western modernity.

13   See especially the essays collected in the volume edited by Carole Pateman and Elizabeth Grosz, *Feminist Challenges: Social and Political Theory* (1986) for evidence that a major contingent of Australian feminists have come to similar insights.

14   This is from his essay, 'One of the Things at Stake in Women's Struggles', from *The Lyotard Reader* (1989), ed. Andrew Benjamin, p. 111–121.

Everything is in place for the imperialism of men: an empty centre where the Voice is heard (God's, the People's – the difference is not important, just the Capital letters), the circle of homosexual[15] warriors in dialogue around the centre, the feminine (women, children, foreigners, slaves) banished outside the confines of the *corpus socians* and attributed only those properties that this *corpus* will have nothing to do with: savagery, sensitivity, matter and the kitchen, impulsion, hysteria, silence, maenadic dances, lying, diabolical beauty, ornamentation, lasciviousness, witchcraft and weakness.

For Lyotard, the 'masculine corpus attributes active principles to itself' and in fact 'cannot resist wanting to seize' the 'passive' object whose 'apparent humanity is always elusive', because 'the Voice at the Virile Centre speaks only of …the Empire's limits (which are women) and we [men, the dominant sex] have to struggle ceaselessly with their exteriority'. We meet here thus a strange reversal of roles at the heart of patriarchal logic: the marginal or silenced feminine can be seen at work in the very heart (centre) of the *corpus socians*. This leads Lyotard (1989) to ask:

If so, then is not such an object unconsciously endowed with what we call activity? And does not the power to scheme accorded this object betray the secret reversal of our role by theirs? (Is not there a desire on the part of western man to be sodomised by woman?) Is not the outside of the man's theatre the most important, even for men? Doesn't he discover his 'origin' there? And isn't it necessary that this origin be woman: isn't the mother the originary woman? That is, the way the exterior sex is represented in theory: as ground, itself ungrounded, in which meaning is generated? The senseless Being?

These paragraphs by Lyotard neatly pose the dilemma of 'women in politics' in the west: women are the ungrounded ground but must remain on the fringes of the Empire[16] from where we nevertheless play a key (instigating or inspiring, but always indirect, mediating) role. If the homosexual warriors form the visible and audible centre of western civilization – the *politeia* – and from there claim for themselves authority over society as a whole, then the women's circle or the circle of women's bodies forms its outskirts – our bodies are its outer limits, its frontiers, and as such we form part of the 'inside' as well as of the 'outside', the 'beyond', or even of the

---

15   I am not sure what Lyotard means by homosexual here. It might simply refer to the preference for homosexual over heterosexual love in ancient Greek philosophy and practice, for example in Plato's *Symposium*, but it also resonates strongly with Irigaray's (1985, p. 171) concept of the 'hom(m)osexual' political and symbolic order where masculine 'love of the self or love of the same' describes the logic of the economy.

16   In capitalism, women disappear by homologation, not exile: according to Lyotard (1989, p. 116), women 'disappear into the male cycle, integrated either as workers into the production of commodities, or as mothers into the reproduction of labour power, or again, as commodities; themselves (cover-girls, prostitutes of mass-media, hostesses of human relations), or even as administrators of capital (managerial functions)'. This implies that 'women can only be part of modern society if their differences are neutralised' and that the current 'erotic culture' is thoroughly capitalist: sexual differences become neutralised and 'come globally under the law of the interchangeable'.

'before' – we are the object that seems human but is not. We must thus still become, be transformed and civilised into 'the human' or universalised masculine. Defined by the order of homosexual warriors as its opposite, 'the feminine' is nevertheless *also* its central concern, insofar as the borders of its empire and therefore the conditions of its own possibility are central, even if often in silenced or repressed ways.[17]

I discern in Lyotard's description the notion of woman as border in at least two senses: (1) woman as man's origin, as ungrounded ground in which meaning is generated; and (2) woman as man's destiny – the outer limits of his existence, as that which calls him to (self-) transcendence, which draws him out of himself. So, while women as 'pre-humans' (in the sense of not-yet human) are surely associated with the *outside* borders or ultimate limits of sensible life, civilisation, politics and the law, as 'pre-humans' in a different sense (in the sense of those humans that always go before, or as originary humans, as mothers in other words) we are associated with the *inside* borders of sensible life. Put in more technical language, women constitute both a *transcendent* (abstract and idealised) and a *transcendental* (presupposed) border or horizon for the masculine symbolic order. Women('s bodies) are thus not only on the margins in that we are equivocally perched both on the very outside and on the peripheral inside of masculine orders; we are in fact also at the heart of these orders precisely *by virtue of* our absence from the Virile Centre.[18] Through our representation of masculine sheltering and transcendence – both men's (coming-into) being (or birth and sustenance) and men's becoming – women open up a space or a field of tension, a narrative frame, for masculine existence.[19]

On the impossibility of forgiving rape

Jacques Derrida's essay, 'On Forgiveness' (2002), neatly combines my concerns with women's subjectivity within contemporary philosophical discourse, rape and the South African politics of transition and forgiveness. The essay refers to the

---

17   In this vein, Luce Irigaray (1985) speaks of a symbolic matricide as founding gesture of the western philosophico-political and legal orders.

18   When the Socrates of the *Phaedrus*, for example, usurps and appropriates the maternal function, displacing physical birth with the birth of ideas and the midwife with the philosopher, he helps to erase the maternal and the material in favour of the paternal and the abstract.

19   An outstanding literary example of this feminine framing of the masculine journey of becoming is found in the relation between Odysseus and Penelope. Penelope, associated with man's timeless home, frames Odysseus' journey as he sets out from her in order to overcome her (or his own former self), and he expects to return to her as part of the logical fulfilment of his journey. Her loyal waiting provides him with a static and reliable backdrop and continuity throughout the shocks and surprises of his journey of becoming. Njabulo Ndebele in his novel *The Cry of Winnie Mandela* (2003) applies the image of Penelope to Winnie Mandela and cleverly exploits Winnie's apparent failure to wait faithfully on the triumphant return of her husband from prison to problematise commonplace assumptions of 'home' and of the role of women on the border of the political.

(non-) forgiveness[20] of a certain (unnamed) woman testifying before the Truth and Reconciliation Commission (TRC). Although her sex is not deemed relevant in the body of Derrida's main text, he adds to his description of her, translated as 'woman victim, wife of the victim', an interesting endnote in which he draws attention to sexual differences. He refers in this regard to Antjie Krog's[21] description of the situation of militant women who were raped during torture, 'and then accused of being not militants but whores' (Derrida, 2002, p. 60). 'They', says Derrida, 'could not testify about this before the commission, or even in their family, without baring themselves, without showing their scars or without exposing themselves one more time, by their very testimony, to another violence'. He goes on to say: '*The "question of forgiveness" cannot even be posed publicly to these women*, some of whom now occupy high positions in the State' (Derrida, 2002, p. 60; my emphasis). There are many things left unsaid and implied or assumed in this short but significant aside from Derrida. I find Derrida's engagement with sexual difference in 2001[22] encouraging, since he has often been interpreted as neutralising these issues in a manner similar to Lyotard and others;[23] nevertheless I find his relegation of the topic to an endnote ultimately regrettable, as well as irresponsible, in ways that I will delineate.

Derrida's text raises (but does not answer) many important questions. First, why could these women not testify about their rapes before the TRC (publicly) 'or even in their family' (thus privately)? Does Derrida simply refer here to the well-known fact that rape victims find it difficult to speak (openly) about the assault, feeling a sense of shame or stigmatisation? If it is just a question of talking about being raped, then why does he first say these women could not *talk* in public (or even in private) and then say the question of forgiveness cannot be *posed publicly* to these women, adding that many of them are now in positions of power? What has the public-private distinction to do here, if he immediately disrupts or overcomes the distinction by saying 'even in their family' these women cannot talk? In what does the impossibility lie? Is it impossible *because* they are public figures or *in spite of* them having political power? And what is the logic of this impossibility?

Note that he does not say that these women cannot forgive. That is implied, but his claim is far more radical: the question of forgiveness *cannot be posed to them* – publicly, but presumably also privately (in 'the family'). Does Derrida regard the public 'baring', the 'exposing' and the 'showing' of their 'scars' as integral to their testimony, and does he see this kind of exposing testimony as integral or indispensable

---

20   The particular woman was asked to, and consequently refused to, forgive on behalf of her husband, who was killed during the freedom struggle. She was thus only indirectly asked to forgive a harm done to herself, being the wife of the (actual) victim. This was the typical position the women who took part found themselves in during the TRC process – the position of being asked for their forgiveness on behalf of the actual, male victims, with whom they were closely associated. The woman referred to by Derrida in his main text is thus exemplary in this context in that she is not asked to forgive something done to herself.

21   The description comes from her text, *Country of My Skull* (1998, p. 177ff).

22   This is the year in which 'On Forgiveness' was published in the French.

23   Cf. as one example Rosi Braidotti (1994, p. 124).

to the question of forgiveness? And most importantly: why should such a testimony (about man on woman rape) *necessarily* translate into 'another violence' and a second (or continued) violation of the victim when all the other testimonies – even where men by their dozens testified about being 'sodomised'[24] – are seen *not* as a violation but rather as a kind of liberation and acknowledgement of the victim? If Derrida regards all testimonies as violations of those who testify, he doesn't say so.

Why is it impossible even to raise the very question of forgiveness with regard to these women but not with regard to all other victims of pre-1994 violence? And: does the situation of these women differ from those of all other rape victims in South Africa – those who were and continue to be raped allegedly 'outside' of 'political' concerns in a purely 'non-political', 'private' or 'criminal' sense? Does the political context of these militant women's rapes render the rapes more, or rather less, forgivable? It should be remembered that the TRC attempted to put some kind of closure on a violent and illegitimate past. One of the worse results of this attempted closure is that there is now a kind of vacuum concerning gross violations of human rights – now, when women and children are raped and battered, these are seen as purely 'private' matters. No harmful acts, it seems, can be politically motivated anymore, since we now ostensibly live in a 'just' political dispensation just as we used to live in a wholly unjust political dispensation before. During the political struggle, women's rape was justified in terms of the struggle, i.e. it was seen as a weapon of terror, an instrument of torture, or women's sexuality was simply used as a way of motivating or rewarding soldierly acts. This was, moreover, done by both 'sides' of the 'struggle' (see e.g. Krog, 1998, p. 181).

Rape thus served to exclude women from the struggle as a political space, and it also served as a way of symbolically marking off the 'homeland', the private sphere, the place of peace that used to exist and that will one day return. Women's bodies were associated with what essentially lies outside 'the real', outside politics and war, but which is then also crucially that which is being fought over: the land, the home, the womb, the humane existence. At the historical and political turning point (which I take to be the TRC's activities during the 1990s) rape was subsumed under or overshadowed by other (masculine biased) discourses of violation and oppression, even if rape did feature fleetingly as a political phenomenon and insofar as it could be understood as political. Unfortunately, however, the TRC and surrounding discourses served to obscure the political nature and relevance of rape in the time *after* the transition. This happened because of its black-white thinking about rape before and after democratisation, and also because the TRC failed clearly to expose rape as an

---

24 Antjie Krog (1998, p. 182) notes that during the TRC trials, men refused to use the word 'rape' when they testified. They would speak about 'being sodomised, or about iron rods being inserted into them'. Her comment on this: 'In so doing they make rape a women's issue. By denying their own sexual subjugation to male brutality, they form a brotherhood with rapists which conspires against their own wives, mothers and daughters...' According to Krog's interpretation, the term 'rape' is thus reserved exclusively for women's sexual subjugation, and thereby becomes *sexist in its meaning*.

action *definitive* of the political, as well as a way of inscribing the masculine power struggle on female bodies.

The inability or unwillingness to view rape as a political act of women's subjugation in the current dispensation signifies to me the extent to which the TRC failed to allow for or encourage a women's voice to develop within and in response to the national political processes of reconciliation. It moreover failed to conceive of the possibility of a need for a political reconciliation between the sexes or for a political transformation and transition on the level of sexual difference, sexual politics and sexual oppression. When the official version of those struggles was forged during the TRC hearings and consequent report writing, rape was eclipsed by other forms of oppression and violation where men were the vast majority of victims. Framing 'the' struggle in terms of men's struggles, leaving women on the road-sides of history, the TRC contributed to the disappearance of rape and women's particularities from the political and public consciousness and agendas after 1994 in ways that would ostensibly never have been possible with other forms of human rights abuses that mainly affect(ed) men, such as ('sex-neutral') torture. Thus, in spite of its enormous role in facilitating a remarkably peaceful and morally accountable transfer of political power, the TRC is also a clear instance of a contemporary refusal to politicise sexual difference, to allow sexual difference onto the political scene, and to allow women to appear and speak *as women* within politics.

It might thus well be that the answer about the impossibility of forgiveness that Derrida (rightly, I think) discerns here does not lie in any of the factors mentioned above, but rather in the way in which the torturous rapes seemed to have discredited the militant women *as militants*, in the way in which this act *symbolically transformed them from militants into whores*, and refused them a (sexually specific) place and identity within the political. Women's sexual identity was used to define the a-political, the beyond or before of politics, the horizon of the political. Rape was thus employed as a tool for symbolically defining and *demarcating the political as masculine-universal*, and for *unmaking* or undoing women's political and moral agency. As such, as an act of marking or tracing the boundary or horizon of the political and the moral, rape itself could not easily appear as a crime *within* the spheres of the political and the moral. The structural (necessary) symbolic invisibility of rape in the context of the liberation struggle feeds on and in turn reinforces the invisibility of women. It reinforces our pervasiveness in – through our (present) absence from – a system for which we act as guardians, gate-keepers and symbolic guarantees. It is thus crucial to ask in 2006, after the political transition and well on our way into a new political dispensation: if women (and children) continue to be raped at exceptionally high levels, what, in the deepest sense possible, is the political *meaning* or significance of this?

My reading of the struggle and transition is supported by texts such as Krog's (1998) and the report on the Special Women's Hearing before the TRC.[25] It is clear

---

25   These 'Special Women's Hearings' or the 'Gender Hearings' took place after the Centre for Applied Legal Studies (CALS) at the University of the Witwatersrand in 1996 made

from these texts, one of the commonest ways in which women militants were 'broken' in jail was through communicating to them that 'real women' are outside of politics and 'safely' at home, and are, moreover, 'responsibly' looking after their families – a sentiment ironically and ominously echoed by some inside the liberation movement.[26] Because good women are a-political, purely private creatures, a woman's involvement in the struggle had to be explained by 'reasons' such as 'you are not the right kind of woman – you are irresponsible, *you are a whore*, you are fat and ugly, or single and thirty and you are looking for a man' (quoted in Krog, 1998, p. 179; my emphasis). A responsible woman does not have an independent, mature or autonomous political identity, but only a private, sexual and supportive (secondary) one. The message was (and arguably still is) clear: you cannot both be a woman (sexually specific) and a political agent, and the only way in which your sexual specificity can obtain public or political form is through making your sexuality (in its most basic sense) available to the real political agents, namely men.

During, and as a vital part of the struggle, women's sexuality was activated[27] through rapist torture and consequently used to strip away their political identity, their dignity and their sense of self. There were deliberate attempts to tap into women's sense of responsibility for dependent others and to shame them sexually and morally – women's bond with their children or fetuses was exploited to expose their 'identity' as one of extreme vulnerability. Everything they stood for was reduced to unpaid prostitution, and this created the *license* for sexual abuse by the interrogators, the police, and the soldiers. Women were reduced to their sex and thus stripped of their full humanity. In ANC camps abroad women 'comrades' were raped (used as concubines) and their role in the movement thereby reduced to a sexual function. Maybe this is then the key to Derrida's 'impossibility of forgiveness' or of the posing of the question, irrespective of what the answer may be. Women were both at the heart of the struggle (on both sides they were often portrayed as the ultimate *reason* for the struggle) and fundamentally foreign to it – marginal, exceptional, excessive, exploitable and out of place, essentially displaced.

Little wonder that women experienced great difficulty during the transition accounting for their political role as well as for their sex-specific suffering in a language that would be understood within the context of the TRC and the 'new' political order. Women were expected to translate their sex-specific oppression into so-called 'neutral' (masculine-universal) vocabularies and logics. The terms and conditions that the TRC set for itself, the call for testimony it issued, were already

---

a submission to the Commission on their perceived 'lack of sensitivity to gender issues'.

26   Govan Mbeki, an ANC veteran, said 'women created problems for the liberation movement because they wanted to know [about politics, the movements of their husbands]'. *TRC of SA Report*, Vol. 4, p. 289.

27   Krog (1998, p. 182) quotes academic Sheila Meintjes who asserts that sexual torture of men and of women have opposite intentions. 'The sexual torture of men is to induce sexual passivity and to abolish political power and potency, while the torture of women is the activation of sexuality'. She adds significantly that '[t]here is a lot of anger about women – because women do not have the authority, but often they have a lot of power'.

strongly biased against the stories women had to tell about sex-specific oppression, already an effective silencing of the voices of women speaking as women, speaking out against the various ways in which they were silenced during the struggle.[28] It is thus no wonder that many women often chose to respond to this silencing gesture with a mere, mute staging of their silenced state: several women simply and profoundly testified that they could not testify (cf. Sanders, 2002, p. 209; Krog, 1998, pp. 178–179).

And just as Derrida's essay on forgiveness graphically and textually keeps women's issues on the margins by merely referring to it in an endnote and not allowing the issue of sexual difference to impact on the heart of Derrida's main argument about forgiveness, the TRC Report has also kept women's exclusion as a central, constitutive political issue in its own right on the margins of *its* text.[29] The failure by the TRC to deal with women's marginal position within political discourse and in reality, may have contributed to the unabated continuation after 1994 of rape as a 'private crime'. This would also account for the fact that the current local 'reconciliation' debate has not yet developed a view 'from women's side'. The failure of the TRC to struggle with and to forge a vocabulary in which to address women's fundamental, structural exclusion (in the sense of marginalisation) from politics expressed *inter alia* in our rape 'epidemic'[30] – whether it is struggle, transition

---

28   The *Promotion of National Unity and Reconciliation Act* (no. 34 of 1995) gave the South African Truth and Reconciliation Commission (TRC) the mandate to, amongst other things, 'get as complete a picture as possible of the nature, causes and extent of politically motivated gross human rights violations (i.e. acts of torture, killing, abduction and severe ill-treatment)'. Two aspects of this mandate can be criticized from women's point of view. (1) Historically and traditionally, women have been excluded within the South African context from definitions of 'the political' through highly patriarchal cultures and social institutions, so that the qualification of 'politically motivated' applied uncritically, may prejudice against the inclusion of women's suffering by e.g. the presupposition that women's lives belong per definition to the private rather than the political realm. And (2) the list of 'gross human rights violations' does not include rape whereas it does include torture, thereby implicitly linking the violations to sexually stereotypical masculine violations parading as universally 'human' rights violations.

29   What I mean by this is simply that women, along with children and military conscripts are treated in an appendix to the main report as 'special' cases, requiring 'special hearings'. Although it is of course better that there is some theoretical and actual focus on women rather than nothing, it would have been much better if the Commission had integrated some form of sexual differentiation or 'gender sensitivity' from the start of its process and throughout its report.

30   Talk about a rape 'epidemic' in 21st century South African cannot be divorced from consideration of that other epidemic, the HIV devastation, which rages here simultaneously. Because of HIV prevalence, rape is no longer a death sentence only in the metaphorical or spiritual sense, but often also in the physical sense. What is more, transmission of the virus from men to women during intercourse is eight times more likely than the inverse, and Unicef reports that six times more girls than boys in Africa are infected with HIV because women experience forced sex (Smith, 2004, p. 5).

or reconciliation politics – in fact ensured that it remained (structurally, logically, politically) impossible to publicly pose the question of forgiveness to women rape victims. This means that the marginalisation of women cannot be limited, 'closed off' or contained in an evil apartheid past. In contrast to some of the cruder forms of racism, it has survived the political transition remarkably well. The oppression of women is still a structural feature of the current South African nation and political landscape (as one can surely say of other 'feminised' categories of people such as the poor). This may be another and perhaps the crucial reason why the question of forgiveness cannot (in the present tense) be posed to these women. Their oppression has not yet passed, has in fact not been acknowledged. A public, shareable language has not yet been found in which to name 'it' (the large-scale sexual violation and rape of women and girls by men in this country) in a way that would *make sense* to women and men, rape victims and perpetrators, a language that would carry weight in a public-political, inter-subjective setting. It seems bizarre to ask someone to forgive even as the injustice transpires, in the very process of her being damaged and violated.

Forgiveness and reconciliation seem logically to come (if they come) only after the injustice has ended and the 'crime' or damage has been well defined and understood by both parties.[31] These terms only make sense after a lapse of some non-violent time and a redefinition of power relations.[32] There is a sense in which the parties to

---

31   For Derrida (2002, p. 48), 'a shared language' is needed for forgiveness: 'This sharing is not only that of a national language or an idiom, but that of an agreement on the meanings of words, their connotations, rhetoric, the aim of a reference, etc. It is here another form of the same aporia: when the victim and the guilty share no language, when nothing common and universal permits them to understand one another, forgiveness seems deprived of meaning; it is certainly a case of the absolutely unforgivable, that impossibility of forgiveness, of which we just said nevertheless that it was, paradoxically, the very element of all possible forgiveness'. The impossibility of forgiveness for rape has thus also to do with the absence of a language concerning rape that can be shared by the sexes.

32   Some theorists of forgiveness – including Derrida (2002), though in an extreme sense – emphasise that forgiveness is or may be intrinsically a one-sided affair, having more to do with the victim's continued state of mind than with any form of acknowledgement or repentance on the side of the offender. I can appreciate the value of one-sided forgiveness in general, especially for the victim, but my concern is with those instances of forgiveness where the crime or damage to be addressed through forgiveness is inherently, essentially and persistently *disputed in a clash between symbolic systems*, world views, and 'truths', as is the case in rape or child sexual abuse. If the clash is between two ideological forces of roughly equal power, then one can expect validation for one's world-view within at least one of the two groups, thus coming to feel sufficiently justified to forgive, sufficiently certain that there is something that stands in need of forgiveness, even one-sidedly if necessary. On the other hand, what makes forgiveness very problematic or virtually impossible in the scenario discussed here, is that the clashing symbolic systems or 'truths' are of such unequal ontological weight or caliber, that the victim has the greatest struggle just to convince herself (most importantly), her intimates and others (let alone the 'public') that there is something to forgive, and that what she has to address in her forgiveness is indeed something enormous, something close to

reconciliation and forgiveness have to be approximate equals and have to speak the same language, at least. There is thus a sense in which the damage, the wrong done to women *as women*, most clearly exemplified in rape but also in more 'everyday' experiences of sexual 'murder' or 'de-subjectification', cannot (yet) be expressed in the language of forgiveness. The nature of the violation in the case of rape is not and has not been obvious because symbolic orders dominated or heavily influenced by the history of western ideas have a blind-spot when it comes to acknowledging rape as a political act and as a sex-specific crime against women. Women can thus not be asked for forgiveness with regard to rape since there is no clear, public and political consensus that there is 'something' to forgive (as there nowadays clearly is in the case of apartheid and other forms of colonial oppression, for example). And amongst those who do believe that the rape of a woman requires a forgiveness of sorts, there is little clarity or agreement on precisely what needs to be forgiven, what exactly the harm is that had been sustained. Furthermore, this systematic 'misunderstanding' or misconception of rape is ideologically laden, not innocent. It is most intimately tied up with one of western modernity's most persistent dreams of self-deceit, viz. that the masculine-specific represents the universal. The inability to conceive of rape as something that cries out for forgiveness, as a historical and ongoing crime against women as women, and as something that men should ask forgiveness for publicly and in terms of political reconciliation, corresponds with, feeds on and reinforces the inability to allow systematic political expression of sexual difference and identity more generally.

Forgiveness is a woman[33]

In paragraph VII of 'On Forgiveness' Derrida links the history of sovereignty with forgiveness. The act of forgiveness, he says, is sometimes the affirmation of sovereignty. The 'I forgive you' is often 'addressed from the top down, it confirms its own freedom or assumes for itself the power of forgiving, be it as victim or in the name of the victim' (Derrida, 2002, p. 58). Although he finds this 'sovereign' forgiveness in typical style 'unbearable', 'odious', and 'obscene', he seems to assume nevertheless that at least some element of sovereignty is indispensable for forgiveness when he says 'it is also necessary to think about an absolute victimisation which deprives the victim of life, or the right to speak, or that freedom, that force

---

the unforgivable. Victims of sexual abuse are often relatively powerless in the wider social context, isolated in nuclear urban family systems and unlikely to be believed.

33   This heading of course echoes Friedrich Nietzsche's (1973, p. 12) question, 'Supposing truth to be a woman – what then?' which is also the central focus of Derrida's (1979) text, *Spurs: Nietzsche's Styles*. Antjie Krog (1998, p. 178) also uses the Nietzschean idea of 'Truth is a Woman' in her *Country of My Skull*, but, in contrast with Nietzsche, in order to suggest that 'truth has a gender' or is sexually differentiated. Not only does she suggest that women and men have importantly different stories to tell about the struggle, but she also emphasises that women were systematically sexualised in and through the struggle and disempowered through this sexualisation in ways that men were not.

and *that power which authorises, which permits the accession to the position of "I forgive"'* (Derrida, 2002, pp. 58–59; my emphasis). Here, the unforgivable consists in depriving 'the victim of this right to speech, of speech itself, of the possibility of all manifestation, of all testimony. The victim', he says, 'would then be a victim, in addition, to seeing himself [sic in translation] stripped of the minimal, elementary *possibility* of *virtually* considering forgiving the unforgivable.' And then he adds significantly, 'This absolute crime does not only occur in the form of murder' (Derrida, 2002, p. 59; emphasis in original).

Rape (whether it occurs in 'war' or not) is one such absolute crime, even if Derrida does not explicitly link rape and absolute victimisation. Rape is a form of absolute crime because it murders the subject-self of the person against whom the crime is committed. Rape is precisely a way of removing 'that freedom, that force and that power which authorises [and] which permits the accession to the position of the "I forgive"'. Victims of rape often cannot even access the position of the 'I accuse', let alone the position of the 'I forgive'. This, I would contend, is not the case due to any kind of innate nature of rape, but because of the way in which the function and significance of rape are constructed within a patriarchal, sexist, rape-prone society such as South Africa. The impossibility of forgiving rape must thus, maybe primarily, be sought in the systematically unequal power relations between women and men. This notion is supported by Derrida's argument to the effect that the 'unforgivable' may be defined or perceived as unforgivable not only by virtue of the degree of damage inflicted,[34] but also by virtue of the precise constellation of power relations that may render grave injustices systematically invisible[35] and unspeakable, forever unacknowledged and unappreciated. The question of power (the power to be asked for one's forgiveness, to forgive, to consider forgiving the unforgivable) belongs therefore to the heart of the question of forgiveness. It is finally only the relatively powerful who ever get into a position from where they might be entitled and empowered (symbolically, socially and otherwise) to consider forgiveness. Because humans are intrinsically social beings (socially and discursively constituted) it is virtually impossible to consider forgiving something that significant (private and/or public) others do not regard as standing in need of forgiveness because they cannot make sense of the alleged damage of the alleged crime. The language of forgiveness presupposes on some basic inter-subjective level a shared language of damage, a shared appreciation of the nature and degree of the violation.

Having stated that '[e]ach time forgiveness is effectively exercised, it seems to suppose some sovereign power', Derrida reiterates his 'dream', his 'madness', what he tries to think of 'as the "purity" of a forgiveness worthy of its name...*a forgiveness without power*: unconditional but without sovereignty' (Derrida, 2002, p. 59; my emphasis). We know that with this dream or madness of pure forgiveness

---

34   This would be the case in the examples of 'the unforgivable' that he gives, namely when a person's children had their throats cut, or a person's family was killed in a death oven (Derrida, 2002, p. 55).

35   Cf. Lyotard in *Le Différend* (1983) for an exposition of this idea.

('only the unforgivable *can be forgiven*' – my emphasis) Derrida wants to carve out a trans-political, trans-legal domain, an understanding of forgiveness which cannot be reduced to or contained in the political, but he nevertheless wants to make 'of this trans-political principle a political principle' in that 'it is necessary also in politics to respect the secret, that which exceeds the political or that which is no longer in the juridical domain' (Derrida, 2002, p. 55). This, I would say, constitutes the heart of his thesis on forgiveness. 'Pure' forgiveness, unconditional and without sovereignty, belongs to that which exceeds the political (the expedient, the calculated, the transparent, the reasonable) but which should nevertheless be respected by the political. This stance leaves him critical of the use of 'forgiveness' in the South African TRC process (for example) where he sees forgiveness as being reduced to pragmatic processes of reconciliation. The two poles he identifies, namely that of forgiveness understood in terms of 'non-negotiable, aneconomic, apolitical, non-strategic unconditionality' (or pure forgiveness) and forgiveness as political processes of reconciliation and reconstitution of the health or normality of the *corpus socians*, are simultaneously irreducible to one another and remain indissociable. This horizon of a 'hyperbolic' ethical vision of forgiveness is for Derrida indispensable for the possibility of progress of the law, and this 'field' between the empirical and the ideal is the 'space' he wants to open up and keep open for all ethical and political decision-making.

For Derrida (2002, p. 51), then, 'woman', in her latest guise as the form of pure forgiveness, also opens up a field for the (masculine) law's becoming. But as Derrida himself seems to acknowledge, if only in an aside, in spite of this positive evaluation of the 'figure of woman', or maybe partly because of it, 'woman' and 'women' remain caught in an in-between world where they are both inside and outside the legal, political and symbolic orders. The question of protest that I would like to pose to this tradition is (in line with Irigaray's thinking): how about women's *own* becoming, forgiveness and reconciliation? If women have this constitutive but borderline position *vis-à-vis* the 'real' and realistic processes of politics, reconciliation and forgiveness, keeping open through our non-inclusion and systematic violation a reminder of 'pure' forgiveness but paying the price amongst other things in that our forgiveness cannot even be asked, then should women resist or rather embrace this feminine, patriarchally apportioned, position as place-holders for the beyond?

This philosophical tradition, by feminising and at the same time idealising that which exceeds the political, the rational, the strategic, casts and recasts every time in a new format women's border status as that which draws, seduces and entices the masculine 'I' (or 'his' law, his morality) at the centre of the symbolic order towards self-transcendence, becoming, and growth. This means that woman's sexual difference from man is once again and always anew reduced to an enticement, a function in man's becoming. As the unconditional welcome (Levinas, 1975) and the unconditional, inexpressible and powerless forgiveness (Derrida, 2002), as the ungrounded ground or origin of man's becoming (Lyotard, 1989), woman's *border-line subject-position means that she lacks both a border and a ground of her own being and becoming*. She remains difference-from and difference-for the masculine universal. In these metaphysics, women's difference tends to remain always already appropriated for masculine being (belonging, home-coming) and masculine becoming (venturing forth), in both its transcendental and transcendent modes.

Metaphorically speaking, woman as boundary has never succeeded in coming to represent a border or boundary (a 'no') for masculine becoming, but always only an invitation, a beckoning from afar (a 'yes'), an aestheticised and domesticated difference. In the sense that every horizon[36] is always simultaneously an absolute boundary or negation – no one can see beyond their own horizon – *and* an open invitation, an indication of other worlds beyond one's own, the figure of woman as the horizon of masculine metaphysical orders has only ever been one-sidedly perceived or figured in her role as open *invitation* and not yet taken seriously in her role as *forbidding or limiting*. 'Until your "yes" is free, woman, your "no" has no conviction, and rape is implied in every manwoman relationship'[37] (Collen, 1993, p. 193). The inverse is also true, and not only on a symbolic level: as long as woman's difference is not recognised as posing a negative,[38] a limit and a 'no' to masculine action and transcendence, an absolute border beyond which man cannot pass, and a position he remains forever alien to, her 'yes', her desire, her invitation, her welcome and her forgiveness will also count for nothing, even as it is taken (grasped, seized) for granted. In Irigaray's terms,[39] this means that a relation between woman and man has not yet been established – woman is still caught up in man's mirroring of himself (even if it is an idealised self) to himself and he has not yet discovered that she represents to him an other, a radical alterity and an absolute limit beyond which he cannot pass and which his mind cannot contain. She has not yet established herself as an absolute, an undomesticated and ungraspable other to man.

Women lack a philosophical and political 'home'

In his reading of the story of general Sun-Tse who is commanded by the king to make soldiers out of the king's women, Lyotard[40] (1989, p. 112) shows how civility and order are associated with virility and death: 'there is chattering in the gynaeceum and silence among the troops; the aimless humour of women will succumb to the learned, socratic, teleological irony of men; and women are initiated into culture

---

36   Cf. in this regard Heidegger's contemplation of the 'horizon' in his 1949 essay 'Der Feldweg' published in 1959 as *Gelassenheit* (Heidegger, 1985, p. 36ff).

37   This quote comes from a novel called *The Rape of Sita* by Lindsay Collen, a South African-born author. The story of Sita takes place on Mauritius.

38   Irigaray (1996, p. 27) uses the term 'negative' to denote in sexual difference 'an acceptance of the limits of my gender and recognition of the irreducibility of the other'.

39   See for example the essay 'Sexual Difference' from *An Ethics of Sexual Difference* where Irigaray (1993) laments the nearly complete absence of a 'fecund encounter between the sexes'.

40   This reading comes from the same essay by Lyotard, 'One of the Things at Stake in Women's Struggle' quoted at length above.

through the fear of death and its overcoming', so that 'truly civilised women are dead women, or men'. But in general there seems to be a clear turn or conversion, at least within the continental tradition of philosophy, away from the battlefield and towards the gynaeceum, an attempt to relinquish horizonal projectiveness and a resolute and teleological living-unto-death[41] for the sake of entering a more passive, aimless and receptive,[42] *feminine* existence. Insofar as the history of the self-same and self-sufficient masculine philosophical subject of the west has reached its logical end during the 19th and early 20th centuries, to that extent there has been a positive revaluation from inside that tradition of the 'feminine' values of homecoming, the embrace, the touch, the welcome, the 'other', the body, the 'prior' and unconditional 'belonging'. 'Reconciliation' and 'forgiveness' can be read as concepts falling into this same category of concepts with feminine overtones, which are currently resurrected or revalued from within a masculine paradigm seeking to overcome itself.[43]

But where does this strategy of feminising the political or ontological, or of implicitly acknowledging the guardian role of the figure of 'woman' in politics and

---

41 'Horizonal projectiveness', 'resoluteness' and 'living-unto-death' are all Heideggerian phrases that he coined with very specific meanings in mind. Space does not allow me to discuss each of them in detail but the reader should keep in mind that they are embedded in an existentialist theory about human existence as worked out in the early Heidegger's 1927 *Sein und Zeit*. As such these concepts form part of Heidegger's understanding of 'Dasein's' mode of being-in-the-world as an intentional, self-concerned embeddedness characterised by the projection of one's abilities for acting in the world against the horizon of one's personal mortality. One could call this phenomenological description of 'human' existence masculine, even heroic. The point I make here is that in his later work Heidegger is paradigmatic of what I call the 'feminine turn' in philosophy, in that he abandons this heroic structure of the authentic self in favour of a stereotypically more 'feminine' understanding of the self's being-in-the-world.

42 Irigaray (1996, p. 38) suggests that woman's alleged passivity can be read as a kind of receptivity, which stretches beyond her relation to man to include the natural economy, and the cosmic one, 'with which her equilibrium and growth are more closely associated'. Her so-called passivity should thus not be understood as the opposite or absence of (virile) activity, but it would rather signify a different economy altogether, a different relation to nature and to the self that would amount to attentiveness and fidelity rather than passivity as traditionally understood within a paradigm that takes the masculine as normative. It is a relationship to others and to self that attends to growth without cutting itself off from the concrete life and place of the body and without mastering anything.

43 With regard to this turn to the feminine, Rosi Braidotti (1994, p. 124) refers to Nietzsche who had said that all decadent, diseased, and corrupted cultures acquired a taste for 'the feminine' or the effeminate. She concludes from this that the 'feminine' in this sense is 'nothing more than a very elaborate metaphor, or a symptom, of the profound discontent that lies at the heart of phallogocentric culture'. For her, '[i]t is a male disease, expressing the crisis of self-legitimation that…is the mark of postmodern societies'. As such, this male disease or feminine turn has little or nothing to do with women, whether philosophical women or not, and furthermore has little or nothing to contribute to women's quest for subject status.

philosophy as I have discerned them in Derrida for example, leave actual *women* within the political and specifically within processes of transformation such as 'reconciliation' and 'forgiveness'? It seems to me that the potentially disruptive borderline position of the feminine as a principle that transcends the masculine 'world' is rather thoroughly *domesticated* within the politico-ontological sphere of the western symbolic order. Even as her transcendence and outsider-status are needed for the perpetual self-renewal of the masculine paradigm, woman is excluded from the political and from the 'world'. This happens to the point that she poses no real threat to the masculine – only an invitation or challenge to him to transcend himself in the direction of the feminine, to feminise himself, to dress up in drag. In Heidegger, for example, feminised 'Gegnet' pre-exists, transcends and encompasses 'man'. In the final (political) instance, however, she remains 'for-man', she envelopes and envaginates, contains him but does not yet represent to him an absolute limit in which he finds radical alterity. She never becomes the concrete, female other with whom he needs to negotiate and enter into dialogue, from whom he needs to ask for forgiveness. She remains rather the feminine m/other who gives him his measure, his house. In Irigaray's terms, she remains 'other of the same' without gaining the aspect of (for the masculine) radically disruptive, fundamentally challenging 'other of the other' or another face which he has to face.

Against this background one could argue that a term like 'reconciliation' which implies a return to a lost 'home' or a severed 'belonging together' rests partly on a feminised and nostalgic notion of 'home' as the primordial and unconditional (almost senseless) Levinasian Ur-'welcome'(Levinas, 1975, p. 154ff), namely the mother or womb. This static and timeless 'home' has always been placed *outside the time of masculine becoming and used as a frame for that very journey*: the masculine subject both departs from and returns to the 'home', the home in relation to which he travels far and achieves heroic status (cf. also Cavarero, 1995). Everything significant takes place in men's time: the linear time of heroic action, growth, productivity, change and transcendence. 'Home' and 'the feminine' serve as the contrasting and static background against which masculine achievement and the passage of time can be measured.

The feminine represents something like an absolute, 'pure' and unconditional welcome – a logic or economy that can 'obviously' not function nor appear within the realities of the masculine journey, of (masculine, real and realistic) politics, but which nevertheless forms the silent inspiration for that journey itself. Translated into the terms of national political processes of reconciliation and forgiveness, one can argue that women will remain trapped in either one of two possible positions. (1) Woman may be trapped in the (original, transcendental woman or mother's) position of unconditional forgiveness, of the always-already sacrificed,[44] of the mother-home

---

44   Following Girard and Mauss, Van der Walt (2003, p. 641) explains sacrifice as a ritualistic action through which 'society maintains and/or endures its antinomies and ambiguities'. Sacrifice attempts to but cannot finally succeed in unraveling the antinomy and in reducing the ambiguous to the unequivocal. 'Sacrifice', therefore, 'concerns a cleansing

that ultimately sets no conditions or boundaries of her own and on whom we may count to forgive or accommodate all her 'lost' sons. Or (2) woman may remain trapped in the position of the (always eluding, idealised and distanced, transcendent) 'beloved', facilitating masculine becoming and overcoming towards the mysterious 'other', being herself thereby excluded or displaced from the opportunity for being and becoming. Woman's displacement from politics can lean towards either the transcendental (maternal) position or towards the transcendent (erotic) position, but both are clear forms of designating the political as masculine-universal and of refusing politics itself to become sexually differentiated. Women's boundaries and women's becoming thus become the casualties of uncritical (unreflective) theories about reconciliation and forgiveness: hence the structural impossibility of women accusing and women forgiving. Hence also the reduction of 'reconciliation' and 'forgiveness' to nothing more than a brotherly embrace in the mother's house, in the house that the mother has prepared (that she in a sense *is*) and that she is also supposed to maintain, but at the cost of the mother's own belonging (and becoming). *She is the necessary condition of the reconciliation from which she will remain erased.*

Despite their differences, Lacan and Irigaray seem to agree that a deep but repressed nostalgia, driven by guilt towards and longing for the mother, permeates masculine identity.[45] One can furthermore assume that this nostalgia would be heightened or deepened in times of (collective or individual) trauma, that the need to safely and unconditionally belong would become even more pronounced. Ironically, however, this deeply felt need to belong unproblematically and unconditionally would also seem to inform and fuel humanly inflicted traumas such as a genocide or apartheid. In other words, the same untheorised and unproblematised masculine nostalgia for the maternal would seem to inform both the infliction of trauma and the felt need for reconciliation. To the extent that genocide and reconciliation may well be implicitly based on the same (masculine) nostalgia for the mother/womb or a political (masculinised) version of the mother, both are obviously highly problematic. Put differently: the longing to belong, to be at home, may be equated with the longing to reside in the familiar, and this may easily translate into the desire to be where nothing is other or not-the-same, to remain forever in a virginal order of the pure, unshared and same, an order which is ruled by a basic intolerance towards the strange(r), other or non-similar.[46]

To summarise: man's nostalgia, understood as a flight from feelings and fears of loss, separation, birth and mortality, thus culminates in a constant search for a

---

that cannot rid itself of impurity'. In this context I see the sacrifice of the mother or womanly other as an unsuccessful attempt to deal with ('endure') sexual difference and ambiguity by reducing everything to the masculine-universal and its deviants.

45 Cf. Christine Battersby's reading of Lacan and Irigaray (Battersby, 1998, p. 112).

46 What was the Rwandan genocide other than an attempt to clear the home (country) of problematic, stressful relationships that have spanned centuries (Tadjo, 2002)? And what was apartheid South Africa other than an attempt to clear a space, a home, a country where white South Africans needed not to face, interact or compete with otherness in the form of blackness?

symbolic substitute for his lost home. He turns his wife's or beloved's body and labour into a substitute for his mother's womb[47] which is lost to him. Woman serves as material both on which to stand (as building place) and out of which to build (construction material) and woman likewise serves as primary object for reflecting himself – she is his mirror of self-affirming subjectivity. Woman supports and complements man's existence as both an origin of his creativity and the product in which he can see his self reflected. In women, Irigaray (1993, p. 101) claims, men look nostalgically to return to their own lost home and thus fail to face women as subjects with their own identities and needs for covering. Women are rendered raw materials, caretakers and goods to be traded, but do not emerge in men's world as the other subject or as subjects for ourselves. It is clear therefore that women occupy a very problematic position in relation to the patriarchal values attached to 'home' – a position that renders us both homeless and subject-less.

For Irigaray (1996, p. 4–5), women's homelessness and lack of subjectivity are mainly the result of a lack of *mediation* (distancing and objectification) of our desires and fears. Such mediation and objectification would allow women to do the 'labour of the negative' and thus to gain distance on our fears and desires. Its lack is due to women having no mirror for our own humanity and becoming. 'Immediacy is their [women's] traditional task', according to Irigaray, so that what women need most is not to have our immediate desires fulfilled, but rather to have them *mediated and represented in the symbolic order*. I understand mediation of our desires and fears here to mean that women need to have a way of expressing and symbolising our desires and fears objectively, that is to express them concretely and then gain some distance on them in order that we may also gain some psychological independence of them. Owing to the mono-sexual logic of western metaphysics and the one-sidedness of the dominant culture, it is men's desires and fears that are mainly and predominantly symbolised and expressed, leaving little space for women in which we may imagine our own sexual identities, apart from or beyond what the male gaze, masculine dominated media, economic relations and so on make of us. Autonomy, full-fledged agency and in particular public agency, are all dependent on the possibility of having one's fears and desires publicly and objectively mediated – in words, paintings, news reports, and so on.

A new maternal home?

The 'feminine turn' in modern western philosophy should be seen as an appreciation or celebration of the marginalised position of the feminine, from within a male-centred perspective, and in particular as an acknowledgement of and fascination with what that position offers the centred masculine subject in terms of self-transcendence, home-coming and the joys of passivity (Lyotard's masculine dream of 'being sodomised by woman') and touristic distraction. As such, the 'feminine

---

47   Cf. Irigaray's (1993) *Ethics of Sexual Difference* for elaboration of this point.

turn' assumes the accessibility and availability of the 'feminine' for men or masculine subjects. Insofar as she is associated with purity ('pure forgiveness', or 'pure justice' for example) she is seen as ultimately unattainable but she nevertheless stands for the dream or madness that inspires change and growth and self-transcendence in a paradigmatically masculine symbolic order. For Derrida in particular, a social institution such as the law becomes violent and tyrannical insofar as it cuts itself off or closes itself off from this 'feminine' ideal of the absolutely just – an ideal that lies necessarily outside of the domain of ordinary justice, although never completely outside. Even though the feminine position is thus idealised (and the ideal feminised) in modern western philosophy, and privileged with relation to truth and moral good, this idealisation does nothing to problematise or destabilise woman's traditional marginalised position with regard to the socio-symbolic and political domains, but it rather reinscribes and affirms it.

During the struggle, women were repeatedly sexualised and forced back into our role of private, caring creatures, and of sexual servants to men, and as such stripped of any public-political agency and identity. Rape during the struggle can thus also be seen as that which drew the line between the means and the end, the violent present and the utopian future, the reality of masculine struggle, heroism and pragmatic politics on the one hand, and the ideal of feminine passivity, justice and reconciliation on the other. Rape simultaneously divides the private and sexual from the public-political sphere by punishing and (re-) sexualising women who participate in the public-political, and it radically destabilises that same divide through the use of sexual violence as an instrument of war. Rape is neither private nor public, and it is both: it is used to draw the very distinction and to police the border.

For it to become possible for men to publicly ask women's forgiveness for rape, the private-public divide will have to be radically revised to the extent that women will have to appear as fully equal as well as fully sexually differentiated subjects within the public sphere. The unease reflected in Derrida's formulations about women testifying to their rape in public 'or in private' and his fear about their inevitable exposure to 'another violence' if they were to testify in public, should be understood against this background. Rape is the preferred method (at least in certain societies) of enforcing the divide between the two spheres, and moreover, of forcing women back into the private and out of the public-political through a violent sexualisation of our identity.

Clearly, then, women, acting generally as representatives of 'home' and belonging for and within men's politics, must have an extremely ambivalent relationship with 'home', as seen from our own perspective. Our association with 'home' is pervasively used to restrict or deny our public-political agency and identity. Moreover, insofar as our identity is used to create and sustain belonging for men, that is a private, sexual sphere for men's dominant public identities, as well as a masculine public-political dream of sameness and togetherness and reconciliation, it might be asked whether we as women can 'belong' or be 'at home' ourselves. Where do women's homes or at-home-ness reside, in distinction from the homes (including countries) that women create for men? If we, insofar as we women are associated with the 'feminine' who forms the transcendental and transcendent borders of masculine being and becoming, are the raw material out of which men fashion their homes, does this mean that we are essentially homeless, in exile, and derelict, within the patriarchal symbolic order? On a concrete, pragmatic level, women's intense involvement in the private, domestic sphere, and our sex-specific responsibilities for home-making and child-rearing severely limit our time, energy and capacity to play an active public or political role. On a more symbolic level, if a sense of belonging and acceptance and of having one's fears and desires symbolically mediated is a prerequisite for successful agency and subjectivity in the public domain, then it might be true that women are unlikely to form successful agency and subjectivity as women. Adapting Lyotard, one might say that public-political (similar to Lyotard's 'civilised') women are dead women, or men.

Against the background of women's very problematic relation with both the private and the public-political home, I find it important to consider alternative versions or understandings of home that may include a concept of home that does not render women homeless through the equation of women or the feminine with men's homes. Phrased more positively: I am interested in the idea of women's home or belonging, of being sheltered and affirmed in our full and sexually differentiated subjectivity. If women are to meet men as equal and sexually differentiated, 'sexually other' subjects in the public-political domain (so that the idea of forgiveness for rape becomes a real possibility) then it seems to me that the symbolic and physical sheltering or belonging of women as women is first needed as a kind of non-negotiable condition. Although 'sovereignty' is perhaps too strong a term to use (perhaps too masculine in its origins and orientation?) here, I do associate the idea of at-home-ness or belonging with a place to stand, a secure place and sense of self from which one may step in the direction of the other. For a politics of sexual difference to become a reality, women need to develop a strong sense of our (sexually differentiated and differentiating) subjectivity so that we may meet men in the public spaces in and through an affirmation of our different subjectivity rather than through the negation of what makes us different from them. In traditional western metaphysics, women's sexual difference was automatically associated with deviance, inferiority and imperfection, when measured against the male norm. Women's subject status was accordingly always regarded with great suspicion and consequently marginalised, placed on the ambiguous borders of 'civilisation', of politics, of the social. Defining the masculine norm through our abnormality and imperfection, we lacked both a border or horizon and a ground for our own being and becoming. This constitutes the heart of what I mean by women's dereliction under patriarchal conditions.

Iris Marion Young (1997) tackles this question when she looks for a notion of home that does not rely so much as the traditional notion on women's unacknowledged (physical, emotional and other kinds of) labour. For her the positive (critical and liberating) potential that can be extracted from the notion of home, in her phenomenological analysis of it, lies in the fact that home is ideally the materialisation of identity. Even as it does not fix or freeze identity, including sexual identity, it does *anchor identity* in physical being that creates continuity between past and present. Home as a visible space reflects in matter the events and values of one's life. Without such anchoring of ourselves in things, without such continuity in matter and in visible space, argues Young, we are literally lost. Home is thus not only (but importantly also) a physical space that extends our bodily habits and supports our daily routines. It is also the sedimented material of our personal narratives. This implies that homemaking activities (as distinguished from housework) give material support to the identities of those whose home it is, and this is always in process. Homemaking furthermore preserves histories that extend beyond the present occupants of the home to include the intergenerational; it can preserve the link with time and history, with family history, and can thus give one a sense of belonging to a particular history or ongoing narrative that transcends one's particular life. For Young, preservation of living spaces also entails the constant renewal of meaning in our lives such as preparing and staging commemorations and celebrations, the ritualisation of our times and 'stages on life's way'. In this way, homemaking also materialises and gives concrete form to the contours of individual lives. Story-telling, gift-giving and the teaching of children about the meanings of things also keep these things (values and histories) alive. Basically, then, home anchors identity in the concrete world by expressing personal and super-personal narratives, meanings and values.

For Young, 'home' therefore also carries (apart from its connotations with masculine and class privilege) 'a core positive meaning as the material anchor for a sense of agency and a shifting and fluid identity, describing conditions that *make the political possible*' (my emphasis). Because preservation of identity can also be reinterpretive,[48] it can serve as a source of resistance as well as of privilege. Drawing on the work of bell hooks, Young argues that 'the ability to resist dominant social structures requires a space beyond the full reach of those structures, where different, more humane social relations can be lived and imagined'. 'Homeplace' (hooks' term[49]) provides such safe, visionary space. Note the elements already refered to, namely belonging, being accepted and also the element of hope, the utopian element contained in home. Mutual caring and meaningful specificity provided by homeplace enables the development of a sense of self-worth and humanity. But then 'home' must constitute *a place-time for the being and becoming of each sex*, where we 'bring' ourselves and each other (especially the sexual other) home. Homeplace can be the site for a self-conscious constructed identity as a political project of criticism and transformation of unjust institutions and practices, but only if we take Young's point to heart, namely that 'home' should be understood as a verb, as an ongoing, creative and critical activity and labour.

---

48   Taking a more hermeneutical line of reasoning, one could argue that all interpretation is necessarily reinterpretation, that meaning can never be timeless in the sense that Hans-Georg Gadamer asserted in *Truth and Method* that 'one understands differently if one understands at all' (Grondin, 1994).

49   This comes from the bell hooks essay 'Homeplace: A Site of Resistance' in *Yearning: Race, Gender and Cultural Politics* (1990, p. 42).

Preservation and remembrance, commemoration as historical, collective activities, have potentially radical *political* implications.[50] Of particular interest here are the political implications for women (and men) if home, homecoming, homemaking and thus also reconciliation are not only scrutinised for their sexual difference assumptions and implications but if they are also consciously reformulated as verbs, activities and labours rather than as things, spaces or times that exist as given, as naturally as the womb and the home, when women's labours are systematically naturalised. In other words, looked at from women's (the traditional 'home-makers") perspective rather than from men's (those who traditionally simply 'come' home), home is transformed from a noun (suggesting a possibly 'natural' pre-existence and automaticity) into a verb (suggesting an infinite task, drawing attention to the labour that goes into making a home and making at home).

In Young's view then, and in contrast with its traditional image of safe haven or privileged, a-political isolation, or a place of entrenched gender hierarchies, home can be viewed as potentially one of the most transformative and politically challenging places within the dominant order. In this sense the borderline position of femininity and home is activated to disrupt rather than affirm the dominant order, including its insistence on a clear divide between the private, sexual sphere and the political. And because the dominant order in a sense 'knows' that homes create identity and the possibility of political and symbolic resistance, strategies to render the political enemy (women, within patriarchy) home*less* and root*less*, drifting and unsure of ourselves have always been in place. If all people need homes, roots, anchors and a material expression and preservation of their living and changing identities, without which they would be 'lost' in time and space in Young's terms, then one of the surest ways to deny a people their subjectivity is to deny them a home and a sense of belonging, to make of them displaced peoples,[51] politically and symbolically. To deny women a home or sense of belonging would, in Young's framework, also mean to deprive us of the opportunity to give physical expression to our existence,

---

50   In Toni Morrison's novel *Beloved* (1987, p. 88), the home of freedom on which the story centers contrasts sharply with 'Sweet Home', the farm from which the protagonists of the story have fled as slaves. In this 'new' or alternative home, identities are being formed and shaped that counter, deny and contest the selves formed and forged through slavery. In particular, this new home becomes under the leadership of Baby Suggs, the grandmother, a place of political resistance based on a new appreciation of their embodied selves. Baby Suggs tells them in her sermons that their hands, their faces, their black skins were not loved by their owners or within the symbolic universe of their white masters, but that their first act of resistance would be to start loving their own embodied selves.

51   The inhumanity of Apartheid South Africa possibly lies precisely in the extent to which it made use of diverse strategies aimed at destroying black South Africans' sense of belonging and at-home-ness in this country. These strategies included mass forced removal of people (whole communities) from places that they had occupied for generations, disruption of families through seasonal or extended periods of migration labour and night-time raids on the homes of political enemies of the apartheid state. See *A Bed Called Home* by struggle veteran and Black Consciousness representative Mamphela Ramphele (1993).

our sexual subjectivity and to our specific narratives, to preserve a memory and a history and a 'world' to which we belong. And without this preservation, this anchorage in the material world, people get lost – they have only their memories to rely on, they start to doubt their version of reality, ultimately their very existence, their ability to transcend the alienating self-definition forced onto them by an alien symbolic order. *They become those ideally placed to forgive the unforgivable.* In Young's view then, feminist politics should criticise those versions of home (also as a metaphor for the nation or state) that present it as 'feminine', and as permanent, existing or 'given' comfort, versions that deny its transformative potential as well as the constant creativity needed for its preservation and upkeep. The nostalgic picture of the home, which requires that women make men and children comfortable and protect them from 'outside' pressures, should be resisted, especially inasmuch as women's activities are portrayed as 'natural' rather than as a creative task of renewal, transcendence and reinterpretation.

Weaving together the different strands of this chapter, I think it is important to see that we need to confront openly and clearly the associations and connotations of reconciliation with the feminine. Insofar as reconciliation is associated with passivity, (self-)sacrifice, welcoming of the other, the *Gegnet*, the embrace, the return, the open-ended and beckoning horizon and the unconditional, it has several deep and enduring links with how the feminine was and is traditionally conceived within western metaphysics.[52] The problem identified in the conception of the feminine in the recent philosophical 'turn to the feminine' is that, although ethical priority is given to the feminine, and even though the feminine is held as an ethical model for the masculine, virile subject, the implications of these moves for women, and especially for women's own being, subjectivity, transcendence and becoming, are not thought through in the work of any of these philosophers. In my critical discussion of an oversimplified identification of woman with the home, I have tried to show that forgiveness and reconciliation should consistently and constantly be separated out from nostalgia for the mother, since nostalgia for the mother in the first place may exacerbate sexual violence against women (in an attempt to keep the private, sexual sphere pure and separate) and in the second place renders public forgiveness for rape an impossibility.

Reconciliation should instead come to hold for us the meaning of learning 'how to hang in space supported by nothing at all'. This formulation comes from 'Orion', a short story by Jeanette Winterson (1998). In the story, the god Orion rapes the goddess Artemis after she has managed to some extent to make herself at home in her hunting-grounds. Being a hunter, occupying a traditionally masculine role, is depicted in the story as a daring thing for a woman to do, even if she is a goddess: she has to twist her father's arm to get permission. Artemis tried to gain for herself something of men's 'long-legged freedom' to roam the earth by being a hunter. She quickly learns that the real challenge of freedom has more to do with spiritual strength

---

52 Levinas is central within this debate because he makes the implicit sexualisation of Heidegger's ontology explicit in his own work (cf. Chanter, 2001, p. 251).

(and learning to live with all one's various selves) than with physical ability. So she makes herself at home, she finds a make-shift home of sorts, living in a shack with her dogs and hunting, and learning to live with herself in all her guises (child, queen, hunter, and so on). She prefers this existence to deriving her identity from a man (father, husband or son) and creating a home for them. Her abode is then discovered by Orion who implicitly punishes her for leading a man's life and refusing to become his wife by destroying her home, killing her dogs, and finally raping her. Deprived by the rape of even this make-shift and temporary sense of security, precariously balanced between the world of women and the world of men, of this 'scant home', Artemis discovers that it is possible to 'hang in space supported by nothing at all'. The story leaves open multiple possible interpretations of this phrase. What I try to convey by it here is, first of all, a rejection of nostalgia for the perfect, timeless and maternal home, and, secondly, the idea or dream that one can 'hang in space' or 'hang on', without ultimately holding anyone or anything else responsible for one's own being or becoming.

It is thus also the dream of learning to carry one's own fears and losses rather than projecting them onto others who are then made to carry the burden of that projection. Through having her most basic sense of home or 'at-home-ness', her body, violated and her shack destroyed, Artemis learns to live largely without (metaphysical) supports. Rape so radically destroys all bases of a person's existence that it inevitably confronts her with the question of whether she can live, can occupy a space, can be someone, supported or grounded by nothing at all. Rape ultimately forces a woman to acknowledge that her existence is supported by nothing substantial – neither physical nor symbolic. The important question that this story raises is the question about women's belonging and subjectivity: is it possible to conceive of identity and subjectivity for women that are neither modeled on traditional (metaphysical) masculine identity and subjectivity, nor cease to *be* identity and subjectivity altogether? But this question cannot simply be reduced to the question about post-metaphysical identity or subjectivity in general, since such generality inevitably loses sight of anything sexually specific, and thus uncritically perpetuates the mono-sexual logic of western metaphysics. The story rather forces us to consider the possibilities for women to establish subjectivities that are neither metaphysical nor the nothingness metaphysics has traditionally attributed to women. This dream or madness (to borrow from Derrida's terminology) is captured by the phrase to 'hang in space supported by nothing at all', where both the occupation of space and thus the being of somebody, and the lack of final ground or support, are combined in a single notion.

To conclude: as long as reconciliation is framed or implicitly understood as a return to the all-forgiving, passive and nurturing mother whose acceptance should be unconditional and who sets no boundaries for herself, who never says no and who never fails to forgive,[53] such 'homecomings', whether understood in political

---

53   In this sense it is significant that Derrida chooses to include in his text on forgiveness the character of *a woman who refuses to forgive*. This female figure defies the role of the

or religious or any other terms, will always happen at the expense of women's own belonging and becoming and at the expense of justice to women as women. Reconciliation is nothing more nor less than the hard and seemingly never-ending, labouring *process* to *bring* people home, to help them (us) to heal and to allow growth and becoming into new beings who are no longer homeless in the universe, and this goes for women too – maybe especially for women. Home, belonging, having a sense of identity, is a prerequisite for participation (speaking and being heard) and for occupying a place in the public-political domain. Above all, coming and being (at) home implies that one recovers a sense of subjectivity and self, regains a voice that makes a difference, and accesses a time that accommodates a rhythm for one's becoming. In short, the condition for the possibility of forgiving rape is a definitive end to women's exile from the symbolic order. This moreover is only possible if the sexes can come to find in each other (in the irreducibly sexual other) their absolute limit and thus also their border, in a sense their home. The sexes must give birth and a voice to each other through a radical delimitation of each other, including political delimitation of the sexes and a sexualisation or sexual differentiation of the political. Nothing less than such a process is needed to heal the political rift between the sexes in South Africa – a rift that may prove to be more enduring, and more pernicious, than our admittedly atrocious racial divisions and violently racist past.

Bibliography

Battersby, Christine (1998), *The Phenomenal Woman: Feminist Metaphysics and the Patterns of Identity*, Cambridge: Polity Press.

Baudrillard, Jean (1990), *Seduction*, trans. Brian Singer, first published 1979, Macmillan.

Braidotti, Rosi (1994), *Nomadic Subjects: Embodiment and Sexual Difference in Contemporary Feminist Theory*, New York, Columbia University Press.

Caputo, John D (1985), *Radical Hermeneutics: Repetition, Deconstruction, and the Hermeneutic Project*, Bloomington and Indianapolis: Indiana University Press.

Cavarero, Adriana (1995), *In Spite of Plato*, Cambridge, Polity.

Chanter, Tina (2001), *Time, Death, and the Feminine: Levinas with Heidegger*, Stanford, California: Stanford University Press.

Collen, Lindsey (1993), *The Rape of Sita*, London: Bloomsbury.

Derrida, Jacques (1973), *Speech and Phenomena, and Other Essays on Husserl's Theory of Signs*, trans. David B. Allison, Evanston, Illinois: Northwestern University Press.

---

feminine-maternal that never refuses forgiveness mainly because it is never asked of her. In a (different, non-Derridean) sense this woman does the 'unforgivable' by refusing to forgive what she perceives to be unforgivable. It is furthermore significant that it is this anonymous unforgiving woman that Derrida chooses to textually mark with an endnote which draws our attention to problems and issues concerning sexual difference and forgiveness.

Derrida, Jacques (1979), *Spurs: Nietzsche's Styles / Eperons: Les styles de Nietzsche*, trans. Barbara Harlow, first published 1978, Chicago: Chicago University Press.

Derrida, Jacques (1988), 'The Politics of Friendship' in *Journal of Philosophy*, **75** (11), 632–645.

Derrida, Jacques (1996), 'Remarks on deconstruction and pragmatism' in Chantal Mouffe (ed.), *Deconstruction and Pragmatism*, New York: Routledge.

Derrida, Jacques (2002), *On Cosmopolitanism and Forgiveness*, London and New York: Routledge.

Govier, T (2002), *Forgiveness and Revenge*, London: Routledge.

Grondin, Jean (1994), *Introduction to Philosophical Hermeneutics*, trans. Joel Weinsheimer, New Haven and London: Yale University Press.

Hegel, G.W.F. (1977), *Phenomenology of Spirit*, trans. A.V. Miller, Oxford: Oxford University Press.

Heidegger, Martin (1966), *Discourse on Thinking*, trans. Hans Freund and John Anderson, New York: Harper and Row.

Heidegger, Martin (1985), *Gelassenheit*, first published in 1959, Tübingen: Neske.

Heidegger, Martin (1999), *Sein und Zeit. Zijn en Tijd*, trans. MarkWildschut, Nijmegen: SUN.

hooks, bell (1990), 'Homeplace: A Site of Resistance' in *Yearning: Race, Gender and Cultural Politics*, Boston: South End Press.

Irigaray, Luce (1985), *Speculum of the Other*, trans. Woman, Gillian C. Gill, Ithaca, New York: Cornell University Press.

Irigaray, Luce (1993), *An Ethics of Sexual Difference*, trans. Carolyn Burke and Gillian C. Gill, Ithaca, New York: Cornell University Press.

Irigaray, Luce (1996), *I Love to You: Sketch of a Possible Felicity in History*, trans. Alison Martin, New York and London: Routledge.

Jaspers (1954), *The Way to Wisdom*, trans. Ralph Manheim, New Haven: Yale University Press.

Kierkegaard (1988), *Stages on Life's Way*, Howard V. Hong and Edna H. Hong (eds and trans.), *Kierkegaard's Writings, vol. 11*, Princeton: Princeton University Press.

Krog, Antjie (1998), *Country of My Skull*, Johannesburg: Random House.

Levinas, E. (1975), *Totality and Infinity: An Essay on Exteriority*, trans. A. Lingis, The Hague: Martinus Nijhoff.

Lyotard, Jean-François (1989), *The Lyotard Reader*, Andrew Benjamin (ed.), Oxford and Cambridge: Basil Blackwell.

Lyotard, Jean-Francois (1983), *Le Différend*, Paris: Minuit.

Morrison, Toni (1987), *Beloved*, London and Basingstoke: Picador.

Ndebele, Njabulo S. (2003), *The Cry of Winnie Mandela*, David Philip: Claremont, South Africa.

Nietzsche, Friedrich W (1968), *Twilight of the Idols*, trans. R.J. Hollingdale, Baltimore: Penguin.

Pateman, Carole and Elizabeth Grosz (eds.) (1986), *Feminist Challenges: Social and Political Theory*, Boston: Northeastern University Press.

Pateman, Carole (1988), *The Sexual Contract*, Cambridge and Oxford: Polity.

Ramphele, Mamphela (1993), *A Bed Called Home: Life in the Migrant Labour Hostels of Cape Town*, Cape Town: David Philip; Athens: Ohio University Press; Edinburgh: Edinburgh University Press.

Sanders, Mark (2002), *Complicities: The Intellectual and Apartheid*, Pietermaritzburg: University of Natal Press.

Smith, Charlene (2001), *Proud of Me: Speaking Out against Sexual Violence and HIV*, London: Penguin Books.

Smith, Charlene (2004), 'Rape has become a sickening way of life in our land' in *The Sunday Independent* 26 September 2004.

Tadjo, Véronique (2002), *The Shadows of Imana: Travels in the Heart of Rwanda*, Oxford: Heinemann.

Truth and Reconciliation Commission of South Africa Report (1998), **4**, Susan de Villiers (ed.), Cape Town: Juta.

Van der Walt, Johan (2003), 'Psyche and sacrifice: an essay on the time and timing of reconciliation' in *Tydskrif vir die Suid-Afrikaanse Reg* (*Journal of South African Law*), **4**, 635–651.

Walker, Michelle Boulous (1998), *Philosophy and the Maternal Body: Reading Silence*, London and New York: Routledge.

Winterson, Jeanette (1998), *The World and Other Places*, London: Vintage.

Young, Iris Marion (1997) *Intersecting Voices: Dilemmas of Gender, Political Philosophy, and Policy*, Princeton, New Jersey: Princeton University Press.

Chapter 11

Constitution as Archive

Karin van Marle

And this has to do with the question of the future, the archive as being not simply a recording of the past, but also something that is shaped by a certain power, a selective power, and shaped by the future, by the future anterior. (Hamilton et al, 2000, p. 40)

That's what we are doing – just archive against the memory. (Hamilton et al, 2000, p. 54)

Introduction

In our reflections on the past ten years of law, politics and transformation in South Africa the notion of reconciliation occupies a central place. Reconciliation was – and probably still is – seen as the one ideal that *must* be fulfilled. Many other aspirations have been used in the same breath as reconciliation, some as *quid pro quo*s for reconciliation, others to reinforce the ideal of reconciliation. The obvious one to mention here is of course truth, as used in the mantra of the South African Truth and Reconciliation Commission (TRC), *No reconciliation without truth*. Memory, forgetting, mourning, past, future and justice are a few of the other notions used and abused in the reconciliation discourse. Despite the centrality of the notion of reconciliation in South Africa's legal and political transformation, both the discourse and the practice of reconciliation have often, from a variety of perspectives, been criticized. One strand of this critique has focused on the manner in which time is dealt with in reconciliation debates and practices.

The obvious institution to focus on and to chastise for the staleness of the discourse on reconciliation and for dubious practices of reconciliation is the TRC. The number of books, articles and dissertations that have been published since the commencement and eventually the closing of the workings of the TRC is proof of the amount of critical (and sometimes uncritical) attention that the TRC has received.[1]

In this chapter I would like to take a small step in participating in critical debates around reconciliation and focus on the role that constitutionalism plays within the reconciliation discourse. As a start, I want to repeat the point made several times before, that the creation of the TRC was an outcome of political and constitutional

---

1   See amongst others Asmal et al. (1996); Nuttal and Coetzee, (1998); Meiring (1999); Jeffery (1999); Dyzenhaus, (1998); Krog,(1998); James and Van der Vijver,(2000); Boraine, (2000); Tutu,(1999); Wilson, (2001); Sanders, (2002).

negotiations, which, albeit created by a post apartheid parliamentary legislative act, was ultimately provided for in the postamble of the interim constitution. I want to reiterate that one cannot and should not criticize the TRC without simultaneously challenging the political and legal framework and context within which it originated. It is no use criticizing the TRC while uncritically and firmly believing in the institutionalized and legalized politics of the constitutional endeavour. Although many commentators lament the legalized and institutionalized nature of the TRC and the connections it draws between truth, reconciliation and the law, they do not always explicitly critique the inherent problematic of a transformative politics based on constitutional aspirations and discourse. The constitution (and accordingly constitutionalism) shares the problematic of the TRC's dealing with time – the limitation, the reduction, the exclusion of many pasts, presents and futures.

Drawing on some Derridean-inspired insights on the archive, I attempt here a tentative 're-figuring' of the constitution as archive and argue that a similar problematic as that faced by the archive is faced by the constitution. Could a tentative refiguring of archive and constitution contribute to another kind of reconciliation, less limited and reductive?

The primary aim for now is to establish the following: a refiguring of constitution as archive; the distinction between monument and memorial; and the possible connection between monumental/memorial and the constitution and reconciliation. I do this with reference to Mahmood Mamdani's distinction between political and social reconciliation. I read Mamdani's use of political here as meaning strategic and instrumental politics. Social reconciliation for him would entail material redress but also a concern with democratic politics. I follow Mamdani's distinction and his call for social reconciliation with this meaning in mind. After setting this up I tentatively reflect on examples in constitutional discourse where a distinction between monument and memorial could be linked to Mamdani's distinction. I will focus on aspects of the equality jurisprudence that have developed over the past decade. My sense is that the tendency of the South African Constitutional Court to place dignity at the centre of the right to equality connects with the desire of the monumental (and what Mamdani calls political reconciliation) to erase the past, to close and fix it. Contrarily, I suggest, an approach to equality that focuses on material inequality, on social reconciliation and redress might be a better way to keep the memory of the past alive. In referring to an example where a monumental legal approach of closure can be contrasted to a memorial approach of opening a transformative politics – in the context of two historical sites, District Six and Prestwich Place in Cape Town – the reflection remains, for now, tentative and calls for further exploration in the future.

Reconciling the archive

In *Archive Fever,* Derrida (1995) sets out the complexity of meaning of the archive (Harris, B., 2002, p. 161). For him, the word 'archive' has at least three implications – it is the place where things 'commence' (in others words with reference to place (where) and also time (when)); it is the place from which order is given (in other words from where authority and/ or power comes); and it is the place that contains memory (van Zyl, 2002).[2] These three meanings of the archive are important for the refiguring of constitution as archive – like the archive the constitution lays claim to 'commencement' (or to the act of founding); as supreme law it gives and controls order, authority and power; and it aims to contain memory by being historically self-conscious.[3]

Traditional understandings of authority and truth are questioned in Derrida's writing on the archive. As Brent Harris notes, there is ambivalence in the idea of the archive as the place of commencement, because it can only contain 'traces of particular aspects of the past in the form of documents' (Harris, B., 2002, p. 161). These documents do not reflect reality or truth but are mere 'subjective constructions with their own histories of negotiations and contestations' (Harris, B., 2002, p. 161). However, the archive does present a claim of bringing an end to 'epistemological instability' – in other words an attempt to end instability and to fix meaning and knowledge. Harris explains the link between the archive and the production of history that was supported by an underlying belief that history was a science and that research could be done objectively and in a neutral manner. The archive was vested with 'the power to speak the truth' (Harris, B., 2002, p. 161) and thus became the place of commencement despite the fact that it held only selections of the past.

With reference to the archive's relation with memory, Derrida draws an important connection between memory and forgetting. The archive is not, as is traditionally understood, concerned primarily with preserving memory, but rather with forgetting – the archive itself produces forgetting (Harris, B., 2002, p. 165).[4] However, Derrida also observes that 'the archive is always open to … the future-to-come' (van Zyl, 2002, p. 47). Derrida emphasizes the fact that the archive is not simply a recording of the past, but that it constitutes the past. This constitution of the past is done with a future in mind, 'which retrospectively, or retroactively gives it so-called final

---

2   Van Zyl, (2002, p. 41) with reference to the word's Greek and Latin origins in the word archon, explains it also as a place from where authority came as well as a place where legal documents were safely kept. She highlights the temporal, juridical and material significance of the concept.

3   Van Zyl's emphasis on threads between authority and the word 'patriarch' is of importance for my tentative attempt below of reading the constitution as archive. She notes how 'the role of patriarch continues to reveal itself in the psyche of the archivist; obedience may be deferred but it is obedience nevertheless' (Van Zyl, 2002, p. 45).

4   Verne Harris (2002a) explains the conventional view of the archive in this respect as follows: 'To remember is to archive. To archive is to preserve memory. In this conceptual framework the archive is a beacon of light, a place – or idea, or psychic space, or societal space – of and for sight'. He responds to this view as follows: 'This notion of the archive, as Derrida has shown in Archive Fever … is bullshit. There is no remembering without forgetting. There is no remembering that cannot become forgetting. Forgetting can become a deferred remembering. Forgetting can be a way of remembering'.

truth' (Derrida, 2002, p. 42).[5] Coming to the heart of the matter, Derrida declares the archive as ultimately not being concerned with memory and remembering alone but also with forgetting. '[T]he trace is at the same time the memory, the archive, and the erasure, the repression, the forgetting of what it is supposed to keep safe' (van Zyl, 2002, p. 54). As a work of mourning, for example, the TRC is a work of memory and one of forgetting at the same time. Derrida explains this with reference to a safe: if one puts something in a safe, one does it in order to be able to forget about it. He refers to 'the unconfessed desire' of the TRC: 'That as soon as possible the future generation may have simply forgotten it ... Having kept everything in the archive, meaning the libraries, in the hands of remarkable archivists ... just let us forget it to go on, to survive. That's what we are doing – just archive against the memory' (van Zyl, 2002, p. 54).

Coming closer to the tentative refiguring of the constitution as archive, it is the question of the 'death drive' that stands central to the argument. Derrida explains archive fever with reference to the death drive, and he demonstrates that it works in two ways. The first is 'the drive to destroy the very memory, the very trace and the very testimony, of the violence, of the murder' (Harris, V., 2002a, pp. 66–67). The other works in a seemingly opposite way when memory is being put away in a safe, when the archive as such produces forgetting. Susan van Zyl refers in this regard to psychoanalysis as 'a science of memory, of unwanted remembering and active forgetting on the individual level' and explains Derrida's contemplation as a reminder that 'psychoanalysis is also a science of the death instinct, of that which dies and is destroyed as much as of that which defies it' (van Zyl, 2002, p. 51). She emphasizes Derrida's insight that without the death drive there will be no drive to archive. The death drive simultaneously seeks to maintain and store while seeking to 'destroy without remainder, to annihilate even beyond the point of ashes' (van Zyl, 2002, p. 59). As Verne Harris (2002a, p. 67) puts it, '[t]he archive ... always works against itself'.

---

5   See also Derrida, (1995). Verne Harris (2002a, p. 65) mentions four ways in which Derrida contributes to and widens conventional views on the archive:

'1. The event, the origin, the arkhé, in its uniqueness, is irrecoverable, unfindable.

2. The archiving trace, the archive, is not simply a recording, a reflection, an image of the event. It shapes the event.

3. The object does not speak for itself. In interrogating and interpreting the object, the archive, scholars inscribe their own interpretation into it. The interpretation has no meta-textual authority. There is no meta-archive. There is no closing of the archive.

4. Scholars are not, can never be, exterior to their objects'.

He continues by listing three reasons why Derrida's contemplations on the archive are of great significance. First, because he shows the need for archives, and secondly, that the need for archives should be 'embraced with passion' (Harris, V., 2002a, p. 69). Third, Derrida also shows that archival contextualization, contrary to the belief that it has something to do with 'revealing meaning, resolving mystery and closing the archive', exposes the 'multiple layers of construction in text' (Harris, V., 2002a, p. 71).

Derrida's *Archive Fever* is a successful attempt in, as Verne Harris (2002a, p. 81) phrases it, disturbing positivist notions of the archive. The task below is to continue the disturbance and take it further, to the constitution. Harris' remark that 'All forgetting of the past is also a forgetting of the future' bears heavily on constitutional construction and destruction. But before we come to the refiguring of the constitution, consider further a few explicit comments on the TRC via Derrida's *Archive Fever*.

Brent Harris recalls the objectives and tasks of the TRC as provided for in legislation: it had to uncover the past; provide a historic bridge between an undemocratic and divided past and a new democratic future; and it had to bring about nation-building through reconciliation. He explains that the past thus had to be shaped into an 'ideal configuration' to ensure the transition that those in power envisioned (Harris, B., 2002, p. 163). The creation of a united South African community was set out as an important aim for the TRC to achieve. As Derrida demonstrated, because the archive itself excludes memory, thereby silencing the voices of many and also because of multiple interpretations, the aim of unity was as problematic as it was impossible. Brent Harris discusses other problems such as the claim to authority, representation and a South African 'community of solidarity'(Harris, B., 2002, pp. 165–170). All these aspects are sometimes mirrored in constitutional discourse: the TRC's (false) claim to include the 'new nation' in the public sphere and public discourse is mirrored by, for example the constitution itself and more directly the new Constitutional Court building. Both of these are often problematically employed as symbols of unification representing the South African community, as well as their past, present and future.

Constitution as archive

Commentators have employed various metaphors to describe the constitution. The most obvious ones for my argument are those with reconciliatory, healing and uniting 'force'. The image of the constitution as bridge, as used in the postamble of the interim constitution and also further developed by for example the late Etienne Mureinik (1994) and the late Justice Mohamed (*AZAPO and others v President of the Republic of South Africa and others*) has been frequently recalled to stand in service of constitutional claims to reconciliation, healing and unity. Lourens du Plessis chooses three other images in his reflection on the constitution in the context of reconciliation, memory and justice, namely the constitution as promise, as monument and memorial. For Du Plessis, a constitution serves the dual function of narration as well as authorship of a nation's history. He relates what he calls, 'the potency with which [a constitution] can mould a politics of memory' to 'the authority with which it can shape the politics of the day' (Du Plessis, 2000, p. 63). However, he concedes that the constitution is but one of many participants in telling a nation's history and, accordingly, also one of many determinants of a nation's future. He explains that the possibility of the constitution's promise is dependent on how the constitution deals with memory, thereby drawing a connection between past and future, and, one could say, reasserting the point that future events should also influence constitutional memory. Du Plessis, like others (see, for example, Botha, 2000; Klare, 1998), focuses on the tensions within the constitution as a form of redemption. Following the work of Johan Snyman he describes the constitution as simultaneously monumental and memorial (Snyman, 1998). Although monuments and memorials share a concern with memory, they differ significantly in the way they remember. Monuments celebrate and memorials commemorate. For example, after a war has been won a monument will be created, celebrating the heroes and achievements of war. Memorials are created to commemorate the dead. In discussing the constitution as monument, Du Plessis (2000, p. 64) refers to the constitution as 'hardly a modest text'. Both interim and final constitutions make reference and lay claim to the achievement of a 'peaceful transition'; to a 'non-racial democracy'; to the recognition of the 'injustices of our past'; and the honouring of 'those who suffered for justice and freedom in our land'; to the need for healing the 'divisions of the past' and for building a 'united and democratic South Africa' (Du Plessis, 2000, p. 64). Du Plessis also refers to the entrenchment of the values of democracy, human dignity, equality and freedom as 'monumental flair' (Du Plessis, 2000, p. 64). As a final point of the constitution as monument he refers to some of the Constitutional Court's decisions, most notably *S v Makwanyane* in which capital punishment was declared unconstitutional. He describes the various decisions as 'imbued with value statements' that not only focused on constitutionalism nationally but also internationally. Du Plessis continues to argue that, although no one should be cynical about the 'monumental achievements' of the South African constitution, one should also embrace the 'restrained constitution'. According to Du Plessis the restrained constitution is the constitution as memorial: a written constitutional text cannot alone provide justice, but rather reminds us to strive for justice (Du Plessis, 2000, p.65).[6]

---

6   He uses the notion of subsidiarity (or constitutional restraint) as an example of how the constitution can operate as memorial. He further relies on 'the open community of interpreters' to partake in the fulfilment of the constitution as a promise that is as much reliant on the memorial constitution as on the monumental constitution. A notable example of South African writing treating not only the constitution, but also the Roman law tradition in a way that could resemble the notion of memorial rather than monument is that of André van der Walt. Van der Walt (2000) argues that Roman law should be approached with a concern to create a 'historical sensitivity, with reference to the crisis and the traumas of Roman law, rather than [to] concentrate on the golden thread of continuity [the monumental] in the life of Roman law' (Van der Walt, 2000, p. 162). He contends that Roman law's value lies in its experience of crisis, traumas, change and transformation and not in how it survived these, but in how it was changed and transformed by 'leaving the well-trodden paths and venturing into new and unknown territory' (Van der Walt, 2000, p. 163). In contrast to the traditional and monumental approach of teaching Roman law, in which its 'higher, more universal and more equitable values' are emphasized, Van der Walt (2000, p. 65) suggests a narrative approach that focuses on the 'breakdown point and discontinuities'. Similar to his reflection on Roman

Du Plessis's metaphorical description of the constitution is helpful in our tentative refiguring of the constitution as yet another image, constitution as archive. Going back to the meaning of archive as the place where things commence, the place from which order is given and the place that contains memory, an easy link can be made. As the archive traces only particular aspects of the past, the constitution similarly traces only particular aspects of the South African past and nation. Also, what is contained in the constitution are already interpretations of a past and a nation's aspirations. And just as the archive cannot contain memory, the constitution cannot. As the archive simultaneously urges to remember and to forget, the constitution does the same. The constitution as monument is the death drive of the constitution, the drive to destroy all traces without any reminder. Remembering Derrida's explanation of the death drive's dualism, the constitution as monument similarly wants to destroy memory while seemingly preserving it. Referring back to the 'promise' of the constitution my sense is that monumental constitutionalism negates this promise, but in a complex manner: memorial constitutionalism, notwithstanding it not fulfilling the promise, continuously strives to keep the promise alive.

Mahmood Mamdani's critique of the South African transition as an example of where 'reconciliation turned into a denial of justice' (Mamdani, 1998) relates to the monumentalism of the constitution (and the TRC) as well as Derrida's contemplations on the archive, reconciliation, justice and forgiveness. Mamdani recalls South Africa's conscious search for an alternative paradigm in its rejection of Nuremberg trials and its embrace of a 'negotiated revolution', which entailed an embrace of the Latin American ways of dealing with the past. However, he is concerned with what I understand as a move beyond the monumentalism of the South African process of reconciliation and constitutionalisation. His focus falls on something beyond the closure of these monumental acts, namely how to engage in material transformation, a transformation that reflects the *memorial* moments of the transition in keeping the past alive and possibilities of continuous change open (the promise of the constitution).

In order to substantiate this we need to follow Mamdani's argument closely. He criticizes the fact that during the process of reconciliation the difference between perpetrator and beneficiary has been obscured, and argues that a focus on the former would lead to a focus on criminal justice; the latter would lead to a focus on social justice. Taking this further he argues that the distinction between perpetrator and beneficiary encompasses another distinction, one between narrow, political reconciliation and broad social reconciliation. He contends that as social reconciliation is not possible without political reconciliation, political reconciliation will not prove durable without social reconciliation. Beneficiary and victim must be reconciled as the majority in order to deepen and broaden political reconciliation to include social reconciliation. He suggests that we should recognize the varied relations of reconciliation to justice: to view justice merely as criminal justice is

---

law is his approach to the constitution, in which he calls for tentativeness and sensitivity to the paradoxes of the new order and a resistance of orthodoxy (monumentalism).

limiting and not necessarily to the benefit of victims. He argues for a shift of focus that can be interpreted as a shift from a monumental to a memorial approach. As he puts it 'from agents and activists to that of winners and losers, from those whose victimhood was more anonymous and circumstantial, from gross human rights abuses – murder, torture, rape – to gross systemic outcomes like pass laws and forced removals, abuses which racialized both poverty and affluence' (Mamdani, 1998, p. 15).

To make reconciliation durable, Mamdani argues for a move from a narrow recognition of rights to a broad recognition that underlies the need to right historical wrongs (Mamdani, 1998, p. 16). Social justice and individual rights must be contextualized and revitalised (Mamdani, 1998, p.15). Recalling the distinction between the constitution as monument and as memorial, we can argue that political reconciliation would be reflective of the monumental, and social reconciliation of the memorial. As the monumental constitution shares the 'death drive' with the archive, political reconciliation does too. It aims to destroy traces of past inequalities by normalising these inequalities in the present, thereby negating possibilities of social justice in the future.

The South African constitution protects the right to equality in its section 9. The protection of equality is not merely formal – rather, a substantive notion of equality is embedded in the constitution. Such a substantive notion of equality should entail a concern with different contexts based on historical, present and future reasons. One might be tempted to read this notion of equality as one that would show concern with our country's past, remembering previous wrongs and, in line with the constitutional promise, an attempt in each and every case to take notice of broader political and social circumstances. Elsewhere I have criticized the Constitutional Court's approach in its formulation of a test to be followed when equality is to be considered as another example of the law turning to instrumentalisation and generalisation (Van Marle, unpublished). I have also voiced disagreement with a mere concern with material upliftment – argued for by some commentators – that negates other aspects of redress (Van Marle, 2002, 2003; see also De Vos, 2001 and Albertyn and Goldblath, 1998). I have reflected on the notion of an ethical interpretation of equality as an approach that would make politics central to each decision and that would realise the impossibility of ever fully recognizing difference and protecting equality. Now such a notion of ethical equality corresponds with the memorial constitution, an approach in contrast to the monumental that knows its limits, its failures and is thereby open for continuous transformation. The Constitutional Court's approach of formulating a test (an example of monumentalism) is an attempt to bring the difficulties of dealing with equality to an end, to make it easy, to reduce (see *Harksen v Lane NO*).

Earlier I referred to the Constitutional Court's tendency to place human dignity at the heart of its equality jurisprudence as another example of monumentalism, in contrast to a concern with material redress that would be closer to the memorial. Other commentators have criticized the Court's dignity approach for being too individualistic and for not sufficiently giving content to a materialist notion of equality (Botha, 2004).[7] The Court's pro-dignity argument holds that equality is an empty notion that is best filled with reference to dignity. The main problem with its reliance on dignity is that it follows, one can say, a classical liberal approach: for the Court it is the dignity of the autonomous individual that is at stake, the effect of which is that a universal neutral approach to equality is followed. This approach is monumental in the sense that it evades politics, thereby forgetting the memory of the past. More than that it closes and fixes present understandings of equality, preventing future refigurings. Yet, as we have seen with the archive, the tension from within will always prevent total closure, the success of the death drive. Commenting on the impossibility of closure of the archive Derrida explains that the archive will always be open to new readings, interpretations and contestations. In this way the archive's attempt to forget (its death drive) will be unsuccessful, because there is no final way in which to know or to measure if something has been forgotten – he refers to 'the coming back of the forgotten' in modern times. Just as the distinction between monument and memorial can not be total and final – in other words the tension between the two is inherent – one cannot do away with either dignity or material redress in the context of dignity. As Henk Botha has argued, the search should be for a more complex and multi-layered approach where a variety of values are taken into account (Botha, 2004, pp. 746–751). In fact social justice (reconciliation) should not be reduced to dignity or mere material redress. This reflects Mamdani's call for social reconciliation as one that follows a different approach to politics than a narrow, thin, instrumental or strategic notion as was found in the emphasis on political reconciliation. This would call for a much deeper concern with politics and democracy. The examples of District Six and Prestwich Place below echo this concern.

District Six occupies a central position in the South African historical consciousness. District Six was a vibrant multiracial and multicultural space in Cape Town and the apartheid government's act of forced removals of District Six residents to townships on the outskirts of Cape Town had implications far beyond its own racist and totalitarian shortsightedness. Julian Jonker notes that after these forced removals had been completed, District Six became a space for 'practices of memory as resistance' (Jonker, unpublished, a). It goes without saying that after the changes of 1994, former residents sought to move back and during 2004 this started to happen. For our purposes, the two programmes that came into play and the tension between them are significant. The one programme is concerned with the restitution of land and the other with memorialisation. The former, following a legal approach that is also in line with the government's land restitution programme, is again reflective of the closure (death drive) associated with monumentalism. The concerns here are along the following lines: 'Who is entitled to restitution?'; 'What does the right entail?'; 'Who is an ex-resident'. As Jonker (unpublished, a) notes, although this is a necessary process, it is a formal process that will exclude, in contrast to the approach

---

7   See also *National Coalition for Gay and Lesbian Equality v Minister of Justice* 1999 1 SA 6 (CC).

of memorialisation that would be more inclusive. In the process of memorialisation the concern would be with possibilities of constructing alternative histories and re-imagining other possibilities for citizenship and identities, rather than their reduction to legal entitlements and identities.

A similar dialectic came to the fore in the discovering of Prestwich Place, a slave burial ground dated to the eighteenth century. This area lies outside the walls of colonial Cape Town and is the place where slaves and the lower classes were buried after they had been denied access to the graveyards of the Dutch Reformed Church. As in the case of District Six and the process of restitution, the law, by way of the National Heritage Resources Act, restricts access and claims to Prestwich Place by insisting on 'direct descendancy' – only those who can show that they are 'direct descendants of those buried in the Place may participate in the process of deciding what to do with it' (Jonker, unpublished, b). An activist group was created to resist this formalised process. As Jonker notes, to prove direct descendancy is an impossible task in the absence of archival records of genealogies or other traces of direct descendancy. Additionally, they faced a lack of popular (public and political) recognition of the space as an important historical site, together with an inability to re-imagine new identities, citizenships and politics (unpublished, b). These events connect with the Constitutional Court's insistence on placing an individualist approach to dignity at the heart of its equality jurisprudence: instead of showing concern with a public and political recognition of past harms, the emphasis falls on individual and accordingly 'neutral' redress. Instead of using multiple events, processes and tools to resist the forgetting of the past and allowing possibilities for the re-imagining of new formations, the emphasis falls on grand closures.

The examples above illustrate (again) the gap between the law and justice, as well as the gap between formal instrumental approaches to reconciliation and justice. We can recall Derrida's view that strategic practices of reconciliation as nation-building and as compromise can occur without any justice being involved (Derrida, 2002). Derrida distinguishes 'authentic reconciliation' from reconciliation, as a way of thinking about reconciliation that could be closer to justice. Authentic reconciliation would entail a 'promise of perpetual peace' of 'indefinite friendship and peace' (Derrida, 2002, p. 50). Coming to forgiveness, Derrida emphasises that one can only forgive if one remembers. If forgiveness takes place in the context of forgetting, it is not real forgiveness; one cannot forgive without remembering what it is that one is giving forgiveness for. If reconciliation is purely about healing, about redressing wrongs from the past, (political and monumental) it is incompatible with forgiveness because the process of healing would be dependent on one's forgetfulness. Like social reconciliation and the memorial constitution true forgiveness would always entail a risk.

Reconciliation – a tentative refiguring

Verne Harris describes the potential of the archive as offering nothing more than 'a sliver of a window' (Harris, V., 2002b, p. 136). He rejects the common notion that archives reflect a glimpse on reality and argues that even if there was 'a reality' it is 'unknowable' – with reference to Derrida he explains that the event in its uniqueness is irrecoverable. Even that which could be recovered is fundamentally shaped by 'the act of recording' and thus always already interpreted. The reality reflected by archives is a complicit and deeply fractured and shifting reality (Harris, V., 2002b, p. 136). Harris focuses on what he sees as the connections between 'the archival sliver and social memory' (Harris, V., 2002b, p. 136). The archive, instead of closing down meanings, should strive for a releasing of meanings. The prevailing positivist paradigm would not allow a space for even 'the sliver of a window' (Harris, V., 2002b, p. 149). Four features of this positivist paradigm are: a pre-occupation with 'packaged information' excluding most if not all, competing narratives; a lack of understanding of the problematic of oral history; a belief that one true version of reality can be represented without any interpretation; and finally a neglect to expose the multiple layers of any texts (Harris, V. 2002b, pp. 150–151). These four features are also applicable to traditional approaches to the constitution. Legal formalism and positivism's main concern has always been with ready made, 'packaged' solutions. Traditional approaches to law share the insensitivity to oral history, thereby excluding many voices. The law can only acknowledge one version of reality/truth and accordingly neglects to see multiple layers of texts and contexts. According to Harris, viewing the archive as 'a sliver of a sliver of a sliver of a window' would help the archive to be recognized as an 'enchanted thing, defined not by its connections to "reality", but by its open-ended layerings of construction and reconstruction' (p. 151).

I started off by saying that I would like to address the South African reconciliation process in the context of the constitution and constitutionalism. On this view reconciliation cannot be seen separately from the choice for constitutional supremacy, human rights and ultimately the rule of law. Magobe Ramose's (1999) critique of this choice must be recalled. For Ramose, the South African constitution does not mirror the aspirations of the majority of South Africans and accordingly the constitution will always prevent real reconciliation and transformation. Because the foundation – what he calls the first order – of our transformation is not truly democratic, all subsequent – second order – actions will fail. He uses the example of a traditional South African hut, a 'rondawel', with rounded, circular walls: one cannot make the foundation of a hut rectangular and then afterwards attempt to build a circular hut – if the foundation is wrong the whole construction will seem wrong. This tension between the 'foundation' and design of the 'building' lies at the heart of present reconciliation and transformation. However, we always know that no foundation is that solid, foundations also can be disturbed and this exposes the tension of all present practices. South Africa has chosen the path of constitutionalism and human rights and with it came a lack of real democratic transformation, an absence of spaces for a politics of resistance to play out, a reconciliation that was aimed at doing business as usual. However, within these aspirations we find traces of the memorial, the 'sliver' that could be continuously explored.

I have tried to reflect on a possible refiguring of constitution as archive. The constitution shares the archive's paradox of remembering and forgetting, openness and closure. I have connected this paradox with the distinction between monument and memorial, celebration versus commemoration. The monumental aims to prevent future deliberations by way of closure and fixing, the memorial on the other hand is concerned with ongoing reflections, remembering and continuous refiguring of communities, identities and politics. With reference to Mahmood Mamdani these metaphors were connected to reconciliation in the South African context. The path of political reconciliation in Mamdani's use of the word connects with the monumental and with Derrida's explanation of reconciliation for strategic reasons. Social reconciliation, a concern with material redress through a constant remembering of the past, connects with the notion of the memorial. Derrida's argument that the archive will always resist its death drive, in other words the drive of total erasure of the past, total forgetting, can be applied to the constitution. Like the archive, the constitution (and Constitutional Court) will not succeed in its monumentalism, the drive of the memorial will always disrupt these grand gestures. This is the potential of the archive Harris described as 'the sliver of a window', and can again be linked to the potential of the memorial constitution. This sliver of a window can be kept open by an ongoing politics: in the context of equality, for instance, the attempts to neutralize must be challenged with an emphasis on not merely material reconstruction but material redress that keeps the past alive. Similarly the events around historical sites such as District Six and Prestwich Place must disturb and resist the law's negation of the past by its insistence, like in the Constitutional Court's dignity jurisprudence, on neutral notions of individualism. Will these attempts succeed? Perhaps not. However, they will not fail completely and between success and failure the sliver of a window, the memorial and potential for new refigurings and ongoing reconciliation, can appear.

Bibliography

Albertyn, C. and Goldblath, B. (1998), 'Facing the challenge of transformation: difficulties in the development of an indigenous jurisprudence of equality', **14**, *SAJHR*, 248.

Asmal, K., Asmal L. and Roberts S. (1996), *Reconciliation through Truth. A Reckoning of Apartheid's Criminal Governance*, Cape Town: David Philip.

Boraine, A. (2000), *A Country Unmasked. Inside South Africa's Truth and Reconciliation Commission*, Oxford: Oxford University Press.

Botha, H. (2000), 'Democracy and rights: constitutional interpretation in a postrealist world', *THRHR*, 563.

Botha, H. (2004), 'Equality, dignity and the politics of interpretation', *South African Public Law*, 724.

De Vos, P. (2001), 'Grootboom, the right to access to housing and substantive equality as constitutional fairness' *SAJHR*, 258.

Derrida, J. (1995), *Archive Fever. A Freudian impression*, Chicago: University of Chicago Press.

Derrida, J. (2001), *On Cosmopolitanism and Forgiveness*, London: Routledge.

Derrida, J. (2002), 'Archive Fever in South Africa' in C. Hamilton *et al* (eds).

Du Plessis, L.M. (2000) 'The South African constitution as memory and promise' in C. Villa-Vicencio (ed.) *Transcending a Century of Injustice*.

Dyzenhaus, D. (1998), *Truth, Reconciliation and the Apartheid Legal Order*, Cape Town: Juta.

Hamilton, C. *et al* (eds) (2002), *Re-figuring the Archive*, Cape Town: David Philip.

Harris, B. (2002), 'The archive, public history and the essential truth: the TRC reading the Past' in C. Hamilton *et al* (eds.) *Re-figuring the Archive.*

Harris, V. (2002a), 'A shaft of darkness: Derrida in the archive' in C. Hamilton et al (eds.) *Re-figuring the Archive.*

Harris, V. (2002b), 'The archival sliver: A perspective on the construction of social memory in archives and the transition from apartheid to democracy' in C. Hamilton et al (eds.) *Re-figuring the Archive.*

James, W. and Van der Vijver, L. (2000), *After the TRC: Reflections on Truth and Reconciliation in South Africa*, Cape Town: David Philip.

Jeffery, A. (1999), *The Truth about the Truth Commission*, Johannesburg: South African Institute of Race Relations.

Jonker, J. (Unpublished, a), 'A coloured place? Truth, reconciliation, and the archaeology of memory of Cape Town's emerging cultural landscape', unpublished manuscript.

Jonker, J. (Unpublished, b), 'Silence of the dead, Prestwich Place and the ethics of memory and recognition', unpublished manuscript.

Klare, K. (1998), 'Legal culture and transformative constitutionalism', **14**, *SAJHR*, 146.

Krog, A. (1998), *Country of My Skull*, Johannesburg: Random House.

Mamdani, M. (1998), 'When does reconciliation turn into a denial of justice?' in Molutshungu, S. (ed.) *Memorial Lectures.*

Meiring, P. (1999), *Chronicle of the Truth Commission. A Journey through the Past and Present – Into the Future of South Africa*, Vanderbijlpark: Carpe Diem Books.

Nuttal, S. and Coetzee, C. (1998), *Negotiating the Past: The Making of Memory in South Africa*, Cape Town, Oxford University Press.

Mureinik, E. (1994), 'A bridge to where? Introducing the interim bill of rights', **10**, *SAJHR*.

Ramose, M. (1999), *African Philosophy through ubuntu*, Harare: Mond.

Rose, G. (1992) *The Broken Middle*, Oxford: Blackwell.

Sanders, M. (2002), *Complicities. The Intellectual and Apartheid*, Durham, N.C.: Duke University Press.

Snyman, J. (1998), 'Interpretation and the politics of memory', *Acta Juridica*, 312

Tutu, D. (1999), *No future without forgiveness*, New York: Doubleday.

Van der Walt, A. (2000), 'Roman law, fundamental rights, and land reform in Southern Africa' in J.E. Spruit (ed.), *Roman Law at the Crossroads*.

Van Marle, K. (2002), '"No last word" – reflections on the imaginary domain, dignity and intrinsic worth', **13** (2), *Stellenbosch Law Review*, 299.

Van Marle, K. (2003), '"The capabilities approach", "the imaginary domain", and "asymmetrical reciprocity": feminist perspectives on equality and justice', *Feminist Legal Studies*, 255–278.

Van Marle, (unpublished), 'Towards an 'ethical' interpretation of equality', LLD thesis, University of Pretoria.

van Zyl, S. (2002), 'Psychoanalysis and the Archive: Derrida's *Archive Fever*' in C. Hamilton *et al* (eds) *Re-figuring the Archive*.

Wilson R. A. (2001), *The Politics of Truth and Reconciliation in South Africa. Legitimizing the Post-apartheid State*, Cambridge, Cambridge University Press.

Cases

AZAPO and others v President of the Republic of South Africa and others 1996 (8) BCLR 1015 (CC).

Harksen v Lane NO 1998 1 SA 300 (CC).

National Coalition for Gay and Lesbian Equality v Minister of Justice 1999 1 SA 6 (CC).

Chapter 12

The Time of Address

Carrol Clarkson[1]

In a striking passage from *Long Walk to Freedom*, Nelson Mandela gives his account of the initial hearing of the Rivonia Trial on 15 October, 1962 (Mandela, 1994a, pp. 311–312, my emphasis on '*embodiment*'):

> I entered the court that Monday morning wearing a traditional Xhosa leopard-skin *kaross* instead of a suit and tie. The crowd of supporters rose as one and with raised clenched fists shouted *'Amandla!'* and *'Ngawethu!'* The *kaross* electrified the spectators ... I had chosen traditional dress to emphasize the symbolism that I was a black African walking into a white man's court. I was literally carrying on my back the history, culture and heritage of my people. That day, I felt myself to be the *embodiment* of African nationalism, the inheritor of Africa's difficult but noble past and her uncertain future. The *kaross* was also a sign of contempt for the niceties of white justice. I well knew that the authorities would feel threatened by my *kaross* as so many whites feel threatened by the true culture of Africa.

The emphasis on performance here is unmistakable. The public becomes a 'crowd of supporters'; the 'spectators'. Mandela in full traditional regalia 'electrifies' the crowd: he is a spectacular 'sign', a 'symbol', an embodied cipher of more than could possibly be subsumed in a thematised, linear narrative. This is one way of understanding performance: that is to say, as theatre. But I would like to explore the implications of the 'performative' in language in its specifically linguistico-philosophical sense.[2] As a point of departure (but one that will have become more complicated by the end of this chapter) I refer to a handy distinction made by the linguist, Roman Jakobson – the distinction between what he calls the 'speech event' and the 'narrated event' (Jakobson, 1990, p. 390). The 'speech event' is the situation of address: the accent is on the speaker and auditors; the writer and the readers. It has to do with the sites of response to any discourse (spoken, written, imaged). The narrated event is the thematic content of the speech event – that which is spoken

1   The writing of this paper would not have been possible without conversations with Peter Fitzpatrick, Johan van der Walt and Stephen Clarkson. The paper was presented at the 'Time and Reconciliation' workshop held at the University of Cape Town, 16–17 December, 2004. Thank you also to Scott Veitch and Emilios Christodoulidis for insightful comments on earlier drafts.

2   Of course, the distinction between constative and performative uses of language was first made by J.L. Austin (1965).

about in the speech event. It is at the level of the narrated event that meaning is most commonly assumed to inhere, but in this chapter, I focus on the meaningful inflections of the speech event itself. With regard to the excerpts from Mandela's speeches, the question is therefore not exclusively, 'what is Mandela talking about?' – the question has to do with the antecedent fact *that* his speeches and writings talk to his addressees (in all that word's complex range). To approach the question in this way is to explore a fault-line between the event of the saying and what is said.

I return to the opening scene. At the level of communicated content, the binary oppositions could hardly be more clear-cut: Xhosa '*kaross*' versus western 'suit and tie'; 'black African' versus 'white man'; the 'true culture of Africa' versus the 'niceties of white justice'; 'African nationalism' versus a 'white man's court'; 'my people' versus 'the authorities'; the 'noble past' versus an 'uncertain future'. Mandela's opposition to the apartheid laws is unambiguously stated, to the extent that Mandela's forced presence in court is an expression of contempt. At this level of symbolic opposition, Mandela makes a plea for what Derrida might call a 'change of terrain' – a 'placing oneself outside … affirming an absolute break and difference' (Derrida, 1982, p. 135). In Derrida's terms, this would be one way of effecting a deconstruction – and with specific reference to Mandela here – a way of dismantling the apartheid regime.

But if Mandela's *kaross* is an emblematic protest, it is important to note that the protest is explictly (in Mandela's own words) against 'the *niceties of white* justice', and not against justice itself. This already begins to complicate any notion of an '*absolute* break' or change of terrain, and brings me to another crucial passage in *Long Walk to Freedom*, where, again, Mandela is as acutely sensitive to the *event* of his communication as he is to the communicated message itself. When he first appeared in court for the initial proceedings of the Rivonia trial, Mandela noticed the embarrassment of the magistrate and others whom he knew as colleagues. He makes the following observation (Mandela, 1994a, p. 304):

> … at that moment I had something of a revelation. These men were not only uncomfortable because I was a colleague brought low, but because I was an ordinary man being punished for his beliefs. In a way I had never quite comprehended before, I realized the role I could play in court and the possibilities before me as a defendant. I was the symbol of justice in the court of the oppressor, the representative of the great ideals of freedom, fairness and democracy in a society that dishonoured those virtues. I realized then and there that I could carry on the fight even within the fortress of the enemy.

It is here that one thinks of Derrida's description of another kind of deconstruction, a deconstruction that uses 'against the edifice the instruments or stones available in the house, that is, equally, *in language*' (Derrida, 1982, p. 135, my emphasis). A pattern is now beginning to emerge: Derrida speaks of two operative modes of deconstruction – on the one hand 'changing the terrain' and on the other, using 'the instruments or stones available in the house' – a reciprocal language. 'It also goes without saying', Derrida (1982, p. 135) continues, 'that the choice between these two forms of deconstruction cannot be simple and unique'. What he calls for is a 'new writing', one that 'must weave and interlace these two motifs of deconstruction' (p. 135). What I am beginning to suggest is that Mandela effects precisely such a 'new writing'. Clearly, the intention is not to trivialize Mandela's actions here, to read them as an allegory for an abstracted European philosophy that in itself has little, if anything, to do with political transformation in South Africa. Rather, to see Mandela as effecting this new kind of writing is to understand better the subtleties of a political strategy that, at once, operates both within and beyond the given order. But further still, Mandela's actions give point to Derrida's increasingly urgent appeal for philosophical *praxis*. It is not necessarily the 'professional philosophers' who are best able to effect 'transition towards political and international institutions to come', said Derrida in a late interview (Derrida, 2004, pp. 3–4):

> [t]he lawyer or the politician who takes charge of these questions will be the philosophers of tomorrow. Sometimes, politicians or lawyers are more able to philosophically think these questions through than professional academic philosophers. At any rate, philosophy today, or the duty of philosophy, is to think this in action, by doing something.

An extraordinary process of 'thinking in action' takes place at the scene of the Rivonia Trial. At the level of what is communicated or *said*, at the level of the 'narrated event', Mandela calls for a change of terrain, an end to the apartheid laws, but in the event of the *saying*, that is, at the level of the 'speech event' itself, Mandela uses the stones in the house, to stand as a symbol of justice. Differently put: *what* it is that Mandela represents, in the white man's court, is *opposition* to the apartheid laws, but *how* he does that, is to represent, to symbolise, to embody (these are Mandela's own terms) a justice which is ostensibly the cornerstone of the very house in which he stands.

Let me follow this through, with an emphasis on what is at stake in the conditions underwriting the symbolic. It is here, of course, that any notion of an *absolute* alterity or singularity has to be questioned. What Mandela symbolizes is opposition, but *that* he should be recognised as being symbolic of anything at all, demands, and in fact, instantiates a relation to that which he opposes. In the sense of Jean-Luc Nancy's *partage* (of both sharing and dividing), and taking the cue from Derrida (Derrida, 1992, p. 68):

> An absolute, absolutely pure singularity, if there were one, would not even show up, or at least would not be available for reading. To become readable, it has to be *divided*, to *participate* and *belong*. Then it is divided and takes *its part* in the genre, the type, the context, meaning, the conceptual generality of meaning.

The emphasis on readability and meaning is critical here.[3] To be readable, even as a symbol of opposition, presupposes a shared language; it instantiates a dialogic relation in its expectation and affirmation of a 'responsive range' (Fitzpatrick, forthcoming,

---

3   On the question of meaning and a 'shared language,' in relation to reconciliation and forgiveness, see Derrida's 'On Forgiveness' (Derrida, 2001, p. 36 and pp. 45–51).

p. 15). Further, the readable sign is never the *first* word;[4] 'The speaker is not Adam', as Bakhtin (1986, p. 94) points out, '[a]ny speaker is himself a respondent to a greater or lesser degree. He is not, after all, the first speaker, the one who disturbs the eternal silence of the universe' (Bakhtin, 1986, p. 69). The time of address is thus deeply imbricated in the past (Bakhtin, 1986, p. 69):

> Each utterance is filled with echoes and reverberations of other utterances to which it is related … Every utterance must be regarded primarily as a *response* to preceding utterances.

Yet if the utterance responds to that which precedes it, it is also a response to the future, in that it is oriented towards the audience it anticipates. Again following Bakhtin, (1986, p. 94) 'from the very beginning, the utterance is constructed while taking into account possible responsive reactions, for whose sake, in essence, it is actually created'.

The address is therefore never simply a statement in a present, to those present, but a dialogic response, which is readable thanks to a relation to the past (we recognise the language) and to the future, by virtue of its orientation towards potential responsive reactions. The time of address is more like that of a future anterior. I am reminded here of Derrida's reflection on the date in *Schibboleth*: 'La date est un futur antérieur, elle donne le temps qu'on assigne aux anniversaires à venir' ('The date is a future anterior. It gives the time one assigns to anniversaries to come') (Derrida, 1986, p. 48). An account of the time of address thus has to take cognisance of the implications of what is at stake in the instantiation of a 'responsive range'.

Mandela's statement from the dock is a response to the apartheid government that has occasioned his being in court in the first place, and it is also a response to the audiences it anticipates ('Which ones?' I hear you ask. We are coming to this). Any complacency about supposedly predetermined and static sites of response, however, is challenged – the 'authorities', for example, are unseated from a presumed position of control. Mandela makes this clear in his retrospective account of the hearings: 'I well knew the authorities would feel threatened by my *karos*' (Mandela, 1994a, p. 312). It is the audience, as active participant in the speech utterance, that generates what Mandela chooses to say and to symbolise: the auditors thus share the *responsibility* of what is said. Mandela's 'moment of revelation' about the role he could play in court is well-attuned to his performative moral force, a force that resists containment in *either* the content of what he himself says (an expression of opposition), or the event of his saying, because it presupposes a language *shared* with an audience that, as we shall see, infinitely exceeds the institutional confines of the courtroom. On the one hand, Mandela's role in court, as the defendant in a political trial, is rigidly defined: he is not there voluntarily; the speaking-positions and 'discussions' are determined in advance by rules of procedure that cannot be

---

4   I have benefited from Minesh Dass's Bakhtinian reading of Phaswane Mpe's novel, *Welcome To Our Hillbrow*.

negotiated; the passing of sentence is inevitable.[5] But Mandela's own reflections on the event point to the ways in which the supposedly clear-cut mechanisms of the court of law are unhinged. This shift in the settings according to which legal procedure is played out is made clear in another excerpt from *Long Walk to Freedom* (Mandela, 1994a, p. 304, my emphasis):

> By representing myself I would enhance the symbolism of my role. I would use my trial as a showcase for the ANC's moral opposition to racism. *I would not attempt to defend myself so much as put the state itself on trial.*

In Mandela's *response* to the voice of oppression, the roles within the courtroom are reversed, and the sites of responsibility destabilised and reconfigured, through language, in such a radical way that the question of holding only the *speaker* to account for what is said becomes problematic: that Mandela chooses to say *this* in his statement, that he chooses to 'put the state on trial', is the necessary consequence of his moral protest against the injustices of apartheid legislation. In that Mandela's statement is a response to the state, what he says cannot be accounted for without reference to that which has occasioned his response. Refracted through Mandela's dialogic discourse, it is an institutionalised racism that now becomes the object of judgement – and not only for the official judges. Mandela's speech makes an ethical demand that exploits, but at the same time redirects, the lines of judgement and defence that trace out the legal space.

Further still, and in turn, Mandela anticipates that his statement from the dock will be heard. The anticipation of an institutional hearing (in both a literal and a metaphoric, legal sense), and the ineluctable, institutional signal of being-heard by the state, is something that was not there before the first hearings of the Rivonia Trial. That the response (of passing sentence) is negative is, for the moment, of secondary consequence. In his distinction between reconciliation and forgiveness, Derrida makes this clear: 'Even if I say "I do not forgive you" to someone … whom I understand and who understands me, then a process of reconciliation has begun; the third has intervened' (Derrida, 2001, p. 49).[6] It is precisely the instantiation of

---

5   Thanks to Scott Veitch and Emilios Christodoulidis for their astute comments on these points.

6   Mandela's account of his first meeting with P.W. Botha in 1989 at Tuynhuys alerts us yet again to the value of the 'speech event' before the 'narrated event' in the process of being-heard. The meeting was very brief – less than half an hour long. Mandela describes the discussion as 'friendly and breezy' throughout. On the one serious question raised, namely, the unconditional release of all political prisoners, Botha was intransigent. But Mandela ends his account with the following comment: 'While the meeting was not a breakthrough in terms of negotiations, it was one in another sense. Mr Botha had long talked about the need to cross the Rubicon, but he never did it himself until that morning at Tuynhuys. Now, I felt, there was no turning back' (Mandela, 1994a, p. 540). Botha's Rubicon, as Mandela reads it, is to choose to reposition himself within a responsive range; the content of what is literally said or negotiated, or resolved, within this dialogic frame, is a different matter.

a response from 'the authorities' that Mandela's appearance in court effects. It is a response that he had not been able to bring into being before that day, and it draws a subtle distinction, namely, between the *ir*responsible and the *non*-responsible.

A striking instance of this is in the numerous references Mandela makes to letters he had written to the Prime Minister before the time of his imprisonment: the letters were never answered. Clearly, the government wished to position itself beyond Mandela's responsive range – to cast itself as 'not responsible' rather than as 'irresponsible'. To be irresponsible is to affirm a responsibility that has been breached. To be non-responsible is to deny that one falls within the ambit of a responsible field. In fact, it amounts to a denial that such a field exists at all. Now of course, the refusal to respond to the very same appeal can be read as 'not responding', or as 'irresponsible', depending on the respondent's relation to the appeal. Further, the reading can be affected by the perceived legitimacy of the appeal.

But now, in court, with all the official trappings of a *hearing*, it is impossible to deny that some appeal has been made. In Mandela's symbolic call for justice, it becomes increasingly difficult for the state to cast a refusal to respond to his statements as a simple non-response: an ethical demand has been made, irrevocably, and it has been given audience in court. At the very least, Mandela's appearance in a 'white man's court' situates the apartheid government within the boundaries of a responsible field. But the situatedness of Mandela's appeal 'in court' brings about a different, if infinitely nuanced, set of conditions of response – on all sides.

In order to discuss these conditions of response, it is necessary to address the question of what it means to voice a political protest 'in court'. In a subtle and carefully argued paper, Emilios Christodoulidis (2005, p. 180) makes the point that '[a]ctivist and judge inhabit different "universes" closed off to intertraffic meanings'. He goes on to argue that (Christodoulidis, 2005, p. 181, my emphasis):

> the objection that cannot be raised is not merely one that is sidelined in official discourse; rather … the very possibility of raising it, *in the courtroom*, is structurally removed.

Now seemingly this goes against my argument that Mandela's statement from the dock is *heard*, that it instantiates the apartheid government within responsive range. But what I want to suggest is that Mandela's statement is not made entirely 'in court', and that it is precisely the inability, on the part of the government, to suppress 'intertraffic meanings' (between law and politics, between what is inside and what is beyond the courtroom, between the present time of address and its chiasmatic relation to the past and the future), that does indeed constitute a responsive field.

What is Mandela's 'responsive range' in the Rivonia Trial? In order to address this question, I want to jump forward in time to the speech Mandela delivered on 11 February 1990, after serving sentence for twenty-seven years. In his address to the gathered crowds in Cape Town, Mandela cites (let us say reiterates) part of the statement he had made in the Rivonia trial. The way in which he frames the citation already alerts us to Mandela's own awareness that his statement does not speak to only *one* time or space (Mandela, 1994b, p. 217, my emphasis):

In conclusion I wish to quote my own words during my trial in 1964. *They are true today as they were then:*

'I have fought against white domination and I have fought against black domination. I have cherished the ideal of a democratic and free society in which all persons live together in harmony and with equal opportunities. It is an ideal which I hope to live for and to achieve. But if needs be, it is an ideal for which I am prepared to die.'

The time and the site of the text of the address are not restricted to once-off co-ordinates of the calendar or the map – of which Mandela himself is acutely aware. Just before the end of the Rivonia Trial, in full knowledge that he would be found guilty, and that sentence would be passed, in the here and now, Mandela concluded his statement with the following observation: 'I have no doubt that *posterity* will pronounce that I was innocent and that the criminals that should have been brought before this court are the members of the government' (Mandela, 1994a, p. 319, my emphasis). The time of address cannot be arrested in history: it is ever open to rereading, to countersignature. In Scott Veitch's (2001, p. 36) deft formulation of the workings of amnesty, each utterance can be rewritten: '*that is what happened then and that is what happened then now*'. Certainly, this is an instance of Mandela's anticipation of a *future* 'what happened then now', of a 'justice to come' which would be recognised thanks to the iterability of the address in contexts never to be repeated in exactly the same way.

To add another layer of complexity: the symbol of the *kaross* certainly speaks to those physically present in the room, but let us consider the language in which it speaks. Mandela, wearing his *kaross* during the trial, raises questions about the *justice* of the apartheid laws. He is the 'embodiment of African nationalism' (Mandela, 1994a, p. 312), the very 'symbol of justice in the court of the oppressor' (Mandela, 1994a, p. 304). The symbol thus speaks on political and ethical levels not quite contained within the parameters of legal discourse and procedure. It is in this sense that Mandela's statement is not made 'in court'. It is as if the symbolism of the *kaross* reconfigures the legal setting. The judge is an 'oppressor', and Mandela himself is not reducible to the speaking-position of defendant in a trial. In addition to his being a symbol of justice, and an embodiment of African nationalism, he is 'an ordinary man being punished for his beliefs' (1994a, p. 304). With regard to his addressees, many of the people in the courtroom were Mandela's 'friends and family, some of whom had come all the way from the Transkei' (Mandela, 1994a, p. 311). Thus, it is not simply a question of speaking to those in legal office from an absolutely legally prescribed site and in an absolutely determinate role. Mandela's statement from the dock is not simply a case of 'us[ing] the law to oppose the law' (Dyzenhaus, 2001, p. 77)[7] – as embodied symbol, Mandela speaks in the present, *but not only here, or now*, 'in court'. His appeal is to a justice that falls beyond the compass of apartheid law. His audience is wider than

---

7   David Dyzenhaus offers a philosophically rigorous and thought-provoking account of Bram Fischer's dilemma in relation to the law: the choice between going underground, or using the law to challenge it (see especially, Dyzenhaus, 2001, pp. 69–78).

the one subscribing to these laws, and of course, the South African government was painfully aware of this. In a desperate and vain attempt to curtail Mandela's responsive range, the authorities would not allow him to wear his *kaross* on his way to and from court, 'for fear that it would "incite" other prisoners' (Mandela, 1994a, p. 312). In more complex and subtle ways, the appeal to the administrators of the law within the courtroom, if this appeal is to be *heard*, is one which bypasses the racist legislation that prescribes each individual's official role and interlocutory position. The appeal is heard by fellow human beings with a higher sense of justice than the apartheid laws they are legally bound to administer.

Mandela's address upon his release from prison is a striking, performative instantiation of himself *insofar* as he stands in relation to his people: this is a moment in the 'posterity' to which he refers in the Rivonia Trial. This is the audience Mandela anticipated in 1962; the one that would pronounce him innocent. Mandela's speech of 11 February 1990 pays elaborate attention to the inauguration of himself as speaking subject in intricately sophisticated relation to his addressees. Much of the speech comprises an extended greeting to a 'you' variously inflected by the immediate past, and in specific relation to the 'I' instantiated by the discourse itself (Mandela, 1994b, p. 214):

> Friends, comrades and fellow South Africans, I greet you all in the name of peace, democracy and freedom for all:
>
> I stand before you not as a prophet but as a humble servant of you, the people ... Your tireless and heroic sacrifices have made it possible for me to be here today. I therefore place the remaining years of my life in your hands ... .

The rhetoric of performative address becomes more insistent as the speech gathers momentum, as the following (edited) quotation demonstrates (Mandela, 1994b, pp. 214–216):

> I send special greetings to the people of Cape Town ... I salute the African National Congress ... I salute our President, Comrade Oliver Tambo ... I salute the rank and file members of the ANC ... I extend greetings to the working class of our country ... I greet the traditional leaders of our country ... I pay tribute to the endless heroism of youth, you, the young lions. You, the young lions, have energised our entire struggle.
>
> I pay tribute to the mothers and wives and sisters of our nation. You are the rock-hard foundation of our struggle. Apartheid has inflicted more pain on you than on anyone else ... .

Each specification of 'you' extends the addressive range that radiates out from the 'I' – an 'I' in turn rendered more complex in each stated relation to an incremental and ever more nuanced 'you'. In his *Problems in General Linguistics*, Benveniste makes the following observation about the subject positions 'I' and 'you'. 'I' and 'you' (unlike the grammatical position of the third person) always have reference to the present *utterance*, and not to a stable referent outside of the context of the present situation of address. Thus, '*I* is "the individual who utters the present instance of discourse containing the linguistic instance *I*'" and similarly, "'*you* [is] the individual spoken to in the present instance of discourse containing the linguistic instance *you*'" (Benveniste, 1971, p. 218). Further, the pronominal forms 'I' and 'you' do not 'refer to "reality" or to objective positions in space or time but to the utterance, unique each time, that contains them' (Benveniste, 1971, p. 219). The lyric 'I' of Mandela's address to the Cape Town rally is offered and refracted, through the utterance, in relation to a multi-faceted 'you' present at the time of the address, but identified in terms of the echoes of history.

Now if the I-you logic of address is present to the utterance, each time, in Benveniste's terms, it is a present that can be understood only insofar as it destabilises linear or historical notions of time. Utterances themselves (and the you and I they necessarily comport) can be infinitely cited, grafted, disseminated, which is to say, uprooted, from a particular moment in time and space, in ways that always leave open the possibility of speaking – and being heard – beyond the here and now. Thus, even though the I-you logic refers to the present moment of each speech event, in order to have any addressive purchase at all (in other words, in order for a you *to be called*), the speech event depends upon its capacity for temporal and spatial iterability. In Mandela's address, the simultaneous harking back and reaching forward, the evocation of an elsewhere through the present site of address, the instantiation of a multivalent and trans-historical 'you' – all of this aporetically constitutes the here and now as a moment of *interruption* in the present. This brings me back to Mandela's reflections on his symbolic role 'in court' at the time of the Rivonia trial: 'I felt myself to be … the inheritor of Africa's noble but difficult past *and* her uncertain future' (Mandela, 1994a, p. 312, my emphasis).

I would like to consider further the question of the time of address by referring to Paul Celan's prose writings on poetry.[8] The 'poem is not timeless', writes Celan, 'True, it lays a claim to the infinite and tries to grasp through time – but *through* it, not above it' (Celan, 1986, p. 34). It is in this sense that the 'you' of Mandela's Cape Town address is singular in *each* relation to the 'I': each 'you' is situated within a political and historical trajectory, but instantiated *as such* in the singular event of the address itself.

Celan speaks of the poem as a movement through time: he uses the expressions 'Bewegung', 'Unterwegssein', 'en route'. Further, in this reaching through time, '[t]he poem speaks. It is mindful of its dates, but it speaks' (Celan, 1986, p. 48). What the poem – or for my purposes here, the address – evinces, is an implacable tension between historically-bound instances of address on the one hand, and the infinite capacity for future readings on the other. In 'The Meridian', Celan (1986, p. 49) puts it this way:

---

8   Derrida's *Schibboleth: Pour Paul Celan* and Christopher Fynsk's *Language and Relation … that there is language* both offer brilliant accounts of Celan's prose writings. Derrida's text constitutes a meditation on the concept of the date in Celan; Fynsk, taking the cue from Celan, discusses the temporally inflected relation to the other instantiated through language. My chapter is indebted to both these works.

The poem holds its ground on its own margin. In order to endure, it constantly calls and pulls itself back from an 'already-no-more' into a 'still-here.'

This 'still here' can only mean speaking. Not just language as such, but responding and – not just verbally – 'corresponding' to something.

In other words: language actualized, set free under the sign of a radical individuation which, however, remains as aware of the limits drawn by language as of the possibilities it opens.

In its iterability, the text enacts what Christopher Fynsk calls '*a movement* of self-situation' (Fynsk, 1996, p. 141), a self-situation that is effected in the approach, the relation opened to the time of the other. That is to say, the lyric 'I' is reconstituted – differently – each time it is read by the 'you' that the discourse engages. In the Cape Town Rally speech, in the speech event itself, *and* in the communicated message, Mandela gives himself over to the time of the 'you' he addresses, in a gesture that is 'simultaneously a recollection and a reaching forward' (Fynsk, 1996, p. 149).

Let us recall Benveniste's insights about 'I' and 'you': namely, that these pronominal forms 'do not refer to "reality" or to objective positions in space or time but to the utterance, unique each time, that contains them' (Benveniste, 1971, p. 219). The addressee, the anticipated 'you' that comes into being in each 'reading' of the text across time and space, cannot possibly be contained within the intentional grasp of the 'I'. 'You' are always incipient in, and coincide with, the site and the time of the address, and it is you who recall to yourself an 'I' uprooted from the time and the place of writing. But in order for you and I to be instantiated, to effect the relation in language which shares the time of the other, we need to recognise that the text is an address in the first place. This, in turn, presupposes a shared language. At the very least, it is this shared language that is asserted in the anticipation of a response. It was the context of the Rivonia Trial that first insisted that Mandela's words could call the apartheid government to account, even in the teeth of the opposing legal proceedings still taking place. The 'language shared' in this instance, I am suggesting, was not contained by the apartheid laws, and could not be suppressed by those laws, even *in court*.

Each event of address is an instantiation of and a giving of an 'I' to a 'you' who hears. In that the text of the address is infinitely iterable, the 'I' can reach through time and space to an elsewhere that interrupts the presence of the utterance. Mandela's statement from the dock during the Rivonia Trial is one striking example of this interruption, where the rule of apartheid law is already seen to have been short-lived – paradoxically in the very instant of staging its institutional force. 'In court' Mandela symbolically addresses and appeals to a 'you' beyond the range of an apartheid hearing. In this symbolic interruption of the presence of the law, the 'you' of Mandela's statement makes an appeal that is greater than one that could be addressed to those *in office* in the courtroom in Rivonia, South Africa, in 1962. Mandela's gesture of a giving over of an 'I' to a 'you' as co-participants in the interlocutionary event brings with it an altered and more subtle sense of the sites of legal, political and ethical responsibilities.

Ten years after the first democratic elections, on the 14th of April 2004, Mandela yet again draws our attention to the intricate dynamics of responsibility subtending the I-you logic of the speech event: when Mandela cast his vote, he was asked, in a live television broadcast, who he had voted for, and he replied, "*I voted for you.*" 'For you' – in all its multivalency, which is to say, on your behalf, in your best interests, in your stead – and importantly, *for you*, in the sense that you are the one to whom I entrust legal and political responsibilities to come.

Bibliography

Austin, J.L. (1965) *How To Do Things With Words*, Oxford: Clarendon.

Bakhtin, M. (1986) *Speech Genres and Other Late Essays*, C. Emerson and M. Holquist (eds), trans. V.W. McGee, Austin: University of Texas Press.

Benveniste, E. (1971) *Problems in General Linguistics*, trans. Mary Elizabeth Meek, Coral Gables, Florida: University of Miami Press.

Celan, P. (1986) *Collected Prose*, trans. Rosemarie Waldrop, Manchester: Carcanet.

Christodoulidis, E. (2005), 'The Objection that Cannot be Heard: Communication and Legitimacy in the Courtroom', in Duff *et al.* (eds) *The Trial on Trial*, Oxford: Hart.

Dass, M. (2004) 'Response and responsible community in Phaswane Mpe's *Welcome To Our Hillbrow*' Unpublished Honours Dissertation, RAU, November.

Derrida, J. (1982) 'The Ends of Man', in *Margins of Philosophy*, trans. Alan Bass Chicago: Chicago University Press.

Derrida, J. (1986) *Schibboleth pour Paul Celan*, Paris: Galilée.

Derrida, J. (1992) 'This Strange Institution Called Literature', in D. Attridge (ed.), *Acts of Literature*, trans. Geoffrey Bennington and Rachel Bowlby, New York and London: Routledge, pp. 33–75.

Derrida, J. (2001) 'On Forgiveness', in *On Cosmopolitanism and Forgiveness*, trans. Michael Hughes, London and New York: Routledge, pp. 25–60.

Derrida, J. (2004) 'For a justice to come', Online interview with Lieven Cauter. http://www.brusselstribunal.org/pdf/Derrida_EN.htm, accessed 25 October 2004.

Dyzenhaus, D. (2001) '"With the Benefit of Hindsight": Dilemmas of Legality in the Face of Injustice', in E. Christodoulidis and S. Veitch (eds), *Lethe's Law: Justice, Law and Ethics in Reconciliation*, Oxford and Portland, Oregon: Hart Publishing, pp. 65–89.

Fitzpatrick, P. (forthcoming), 'Juris–fiction: Literature and the Law of the Law', *A Review of International English Literature*.

Fynsk, C. (1996) *Language and Relation ... that there is Language*, Stanford: Stanford University Press.

Jakobson, R. (1990) *On Language*, L. Waugh and M. Monville-Burston (eds), Cambridge, Massachusetts and London: Harvard University Press.

Mandela, N. (1994a) *Long Walk to Freedom: The Autobiography of Nelson Mandela*, Randburg: Macdonald Purnell.

Mandela, N. (1994b) *Nelson Mandela: The Struggle is My Life. His Speeches and Writings 1944–1990*, Cape Town and Johannesburg: Mayibuye Books in association with David Philip.

Mandela, N. (2004c) Live Television News Broadcast: SABC, 14 April.

Mpe, P. (2001) *Welcome To Our Hillbrow*, Pietermaritzburg: University of Natal Press.

Veitch, S. (2001) 'The Legal Politics of Amnesty', in E. Christodoulidis and S. Veitch (eds) *Lethe's Law: Justice, Law and Ethics in Reconciliation*, Oxford and Portland, Oregon: Hart Publishing, pp. 33–45.

Index